PROPERTY, POWER, AND —PUBLIC CHOICE—

AN INQUIRY INTO LAW AND ECONOMICS

SECOND EDITION

A. ALLAN SCHMID

PRAEGER

New York
Westport, Connecticut
London

Library of Congress Cataloging-in-Publication Data

Schmid, A. Allan (Alfred Allan), 1935–
    Property, power, and public choice : an inquiry into law and
economics / A. Allan Schmid. — 2nd ed.
    p. cm.
    Bibliography: p.
    Includes indexes.
    ISBN 0-275-92797-0 (alk. paper)
    ISBN 0-275-92828-4 (pbk. : alk. paper)
    1. Economics. 2. Property. 3. Social choice. 4. Welfare
economics. I. Title.
HB73.S35 1987   87-22893
330.1—dc19   CIP

Library of Congress Catalog Card Number: 87-22893
ISBN: 0-275-92797-0 (hb)
ISBN: 0-275-92828-4 (pb)

First published in 1987

Praeger Publishers, One Madison Avenue, New York, NY 10010
A division of Greenwood Press, Inc.

Printed in the United States of America

The paper used in this book complies with the
Permanent Paper Standard issued by the National
Information Standards Organization (Z39.48-1984).

10 9 8 7 6 5 4 3 2 1

Contents

Part V. Testing the Paradigm

List of Figures and Tables

Acknowledgments

I want to thank all of my "teachers." Some commented on this manuscript and some contributed to its formative period many years ago: Carl Bögholt, Kenneth Boulding, Dan Bromley, André Brun, Marion Clawson, Frank Convery, Gianluigi Galeotti, Kenneth Parsons, Raymond Penn, David Reisman, Warren Samuels, Alfred and Florence Schmid, Alice Todd Schmid, James Shaffer, Robert Solo, Leanna Steifel, and J.F.A. Taylor. Figures were drawn by John Schmid.

Introduction

Little can happen in economic life that does not have distributional impact. Whose interests then count in the economy and in politics? This book addresses that question and explores the determining factors and forces. We are interested here in what governs institutional and systemic performance and how we may, objectively and nonpresumptively, analyze and understand the variables governing performance. The underlying motivation is twofold: first, to enable us to better know what is going on in the economy and the polity; and second, to enable us to better choose and effectuate meaningful and consequential institutional changes. The focus is on human interdependence and how alternative property rights affect its outcome.

The western painter Charles Russell has portrayed a dramatic interaction between cowboy and Indian during a mid-1800s trail drive through Indian territory (see frontispiece). The cowboys are bringing cattle from the western ranches to the rail heads for shipment to the population centers of the East. The Indian is seen signaling to the trail boss as other Indians are cutting from the herd a cow that will be taken back to the tribe for food. But what is going on in the minds of the participants? Is it theft? A prize of battle? Or is it a gift or act of charity? Does the cow represent the payment of a tax to a sovereign with the Indian as tax collector? Or has a trade been consummated where the Indian has agreed to allow passage and use of his land in return for a negotiated rental payment?

The physical movement alone tells nothing about the intangible relationships between the parties or their thoughts. Yet these relationships and perceptions have tangible consequences. They may affect the production of beef, grazing practices, and of course the relative distribution of wealth.

The relationship between agreements on property rights, as formalized in institutions, and the performance of the economy is the subject of this book. This is an inquiry into law and economics. What are the legal foundations of any economy? What determines whether a consequence of action is considered in a private or governmental choice to produce or consume, invest or save? Where interests conflict, what determines who has power over whom? If these questions can be answered, we shall understand how law (formal and informal) influences the production and distribution of wealth.

How then will a change in rules affect behavior with respect to today's problems, such as dirty air, inflation, poverty, unemployment, or noisy neighbors? A range of institutional alternatives comes to mind. If markets are present in the problem area being considered, we could ask why they have failed to get the desired results. Can we change the rules and get more competition? Would more competition make a difference? Can we do something to lower the cost of obtaining information and finding interested buyers (or sellers)? Are people perhaps confused over who owns the resource in question? Should we redistribute ownership among different individuals?

Maybe there is no way to alter the market to yield the performance desired. Consider a nonmarket decision system, where group choices are explicitly made rather than being a composite of individual choices. What are the voting rules for group choice? What are the political boundaries and levels of government involved? If the good or service is provided by a government agency, what is its jurisdiction and does more than one agency operate in a given field (that is, is there competition)? How will the good be financed and the cost shared among taxpayers? Maybe regulation is the solution. Can we use the threat of punishment to deter undesirable behavior? These are just a few of the wide range of institutional alternatives available to shape the performance of an economy.

Can we predict the results of any of these rule changes? Are there some desired results for which no institutional solutions exist? It is ironical that we seem to go in cycles on many issues of public policy. If we do not like the results in a given area and markets are being used, it is common to hear a recommendation that we turn to government enterprises or regulation. If government is already directly involved, reformers will suggest that markets be tried. If we do not like the performance of our government officials and they have been appointed, someone will suggest that the positions be filled by civil service professionals. And, if they are already civil servants but seem unresponsive to change, we say power is too dispersed and more managers should be selected by elected officials. If we note that the garbage does not get picked up and bus lines are poor, we may advocate that all of the individual political subdivisions be consolidated into a single metropolitan government; if we already have a large centralized government, we may advocate forming neighborhood school boards, giving more power to precinct police captains, and creating mini-city halls to bring government closer to the people.

With respect to institutional choice, we seem to be acting in ignorance. We go through cycles of reform with great promise of results only to find failure and some new round of reformers advocating return to where we started. This situation could be the result of a change in the balance of power. Different groups who benefit from different rules may come to power and change the rules to their benefit, and when they are defeated, the rules are changed back. But even those who control choice cannot always find the institution that really serves their interests. They can choose any rule they want, but they are not sure what the result will be. How many times have we watched a group spend their political capital, obtain a new rule, and then receive no change in performance?

Economics and the other social sciences have historically played only a minor role in predicting consequences of institutional change. Trial and error have played a large role. Economic theory has served to reinforce current ideologies more than to advance predictive capacity (Gerschenkron 1969).

This book presents a theory to guide empirical study of the link between the rules of the game and the performance of the economy—amount, kind, and distribution of welfare. The emphasis is not primarily on explaining the present or predicting the future but on defining instrumental variables that are capable of being manipulated to produce a given impact.[1] In other words, what institutions will yield what results? What rules will enable the cowboys of our Russell painting to get more beef to market? Conversely, what rule or institution would put more beef in the Indian cooking pots? Who decides and how?

Is it a zero-sum game, where the cowboys' loss is the Indians' gain and vice versa, or is there a way for both to gain? The purpose is not to argue for the interests of either cowboy or Indian. It is to inform their choices by predicting the substantive consequences of institutional alternatives. The book is not a resounding prediction of universal beneficence if only the supply of money were reduced (expanded), or the antitrust laws could be enforced (business controls relaxed), or welfare payments could be increased (decreased), or taxes and government spending could be increased (decreased), or the revolution of the proletariat could be achieved. The reader wanting new support for these traditional remedies will not find it here.

It will be suggested that performance is in part a function of many cumulative rights governing a host of varieties of human interdependence. If situations of interdependence have many sources, the power of a person or group to participate in resource-use decisions and the ability to achieve control of (or, better, harmony with) nature are influenced by many different kinds of rights. Such a suggestion will not appeal to politicians. Ideas for reform must be condensed into a slogan to fit a headline. It will not be news to lobbyists for special-interest groups who are on hand when the detailed rules relating to their areas are being decided with little public scrutiny or understanding. There is an uneven contest between the interests of small groups, whose welfare is largely determined by the details of a few key rules, and those of larger groups such as consumers, whose welfare is a function of a wide variety of rules, no one of which makes a lot of difference by itself.

If this suggestion of performance (especially income distribution) as a function of the aggregation and interaction of many different kinds of rights is supported by further research, it is a problem for reformers and a source of relief for supporters of the status quo. Transaction (especially information) costs mitigate against change of enough different rights to make much difference to our lives. Change is even harder if the value judgments of conventional theory remain hidden from public debate or if we look in the wrong place and limit policy debate to the rights highlighted by the models of pure competition of Keynes, say, or of Marx for that matter. This is not to say that policy variables suggested by these models are to be ignored. The theme suggested is one of supplementation. Those who seek significant change in performance must escape the simplistic institutional dichotomies of the past.

OVERVIEW

Chapter 1 outlines the components of a model, or paradigm, relating alternative institutions to performance. It integrates concepts from welfare economics, institutional economics, political economy, industrial organization, law, and public-choice theory, among others. Characteristics of goods are viewed as central to predicting institutional impact on who gets what, rather than the usual welfare-economics categories of barriers to maximization. Rights and opportunity sets are seen as reciprocal, where one person's freedom to act is another's limitation. Major attention is given to power and fundamental distributions that underlie subsequent calculations of efficiency.

Chapter 2, which explores property in a social context, is a diversion from the primary concern with impact analysis. It is included to remind analysts that without some sense of community, there is no willing participation and no public to make public choices.

Part II, containing Chapters 3 through 7, identifies the key goods characteristics of incompatibility, exclusion cost, economies of scale, joint impact, transaction costs, and surpluses. Hypotheses are formed relating the impact of institutional alternatives interacting with these goods characteristics in a variety of policy applications including natural resources and the environment, consumer protection, cities, farm, public utilities, industrial policy, developing countries, public services, constitutions and civil rights, business organization, and education and voluntary organizations, to name a few.

The chapters, however, are organized by functional goods characteristics and not by application or type of institution. Readers who specialize in only one applied area are nevertheless urged to study the various chapters to see if the problem interdependencies have more than one source. The theory also reminds applied specialists that they can learn from the experience of rights alternatives implemented with goods functionally similar to the one of interest.

For example, the reader interested in natural resources may have little institutional variation to observe and can only improve prediction of yet untried rights by using theory to observe outcomes in functionally similar areas.

The basic theory is elaborated, further applied, and restated in Part III. Chapter 8 uses the theory to explore some fundamental issues in capitalism, firm and government boundaries, and politics. Some scholars limit the term *public choice* to denote issues of constitutions and voting rules. These issues are explored in this chapter, but the term is used more broadly throughout the book to refer to not only the rules for making rules but also to the impact of the rights chosen by government. In the light of the previous analysis and application, the paradigm is restated in Chapter 9.

Chapter 10 focuses on psychology as it affects the impact of alternative property rights. In common with conventional economics, the theory has been developed primarily as a theory of advantage rather than a theory of behavior. However, it does not insist on simplistic behavioral assumptions of narrow rationality and maximization but recognizes information bounds to rationality, interdependent utilities, and opportunism.

Part IV and Chapter 11 represent a diversion from the book's emphasis on the non-value-presumptive impact of institutions. It explores the possibilities of a normative analysis and constitutes a critique of modern welfare economics. Welfare economics tries to avoid arguing for the interests of one person over another but nevertheless does so implicitly.

Finally, Part V and Chapter 12 test the institutional theory of the book by a review of empirical studies. Most of the studies did not explicitly use the theory as herein formulated, but the theory is used in interpreting empirical experience, suggesting other variables that should have been controlled and formulating alternative hypotheses.

The following discussion will develop theory to help search for institutions that can serve widely shared interests but will not assume that all is harmonious. Where interests do conflict, intelligent choice requires an understanding of how the rules affect the question of whose interests count.

NOTE

1. Institutional economics can be divided into institutional-change theories and institutional-impact theories (Pryor 1973, p. 28). This book focuses on impact theories. In a theory of change, the situation, including technology and preferences, evolves to modify the character of conflict, and interdependence and perception of opportunity can change performance in the long run. Impact theory focuses on given legal change in the structure of opportunities.

I

A Theory for the
Study of
Institutional
Performance

One

A General Paradigm of
Institutions and Performance

COMPONENTS OF THE PARADIGM

Empirical investigation of the impact of alternative institutions and property rights requires a conceptualization of potentially observable and measurable variables and testable hypotheses. The components of a paradigm for relating institutional alternatives to performance will first be stated briefly and then developed in the sections to follow.

Vilfredo Pareto aggregated the dimensions of policy into three major categories—knowledge, psychology, and power (Samuels 1974b). The model of the role of institutional structure developed here emphasizes the variables of power that give form and direction to costs and benefits. Choice of emphasis does not mean that other dimensions are not important. The rationale for this choice is partially related to remedying the balance of variables emphasized in the literature of economics as well as a pragmatic judgment of where practical levers of change lie in the span of a lifetime. Neoclassical economics has been very selective in the variables it considers. It emphasizes knowledge of the production function and largely takes it as exogenously determined. This narrow emphasis has drawn criticism from Thorstein Veblen and scholars in that tradition such as Clarence Ayres (1962), who gave much attention to technological change as a driving force for changed performance.

Neoclassical theory has focused narrowly on that part of psychology that can be captured in its concepts of utility and preferences as reflected in effective, revealed demand. How these preferences came to be what they are and how they might be related to the prevailing mode of production and institutions remains the province of Marxist scholars, Veblen, and a few economists who have some background in the behavioral sciences (Shaffer 1969 and Solo 1967). Preferences, including that of interdependent utilities, are surely learned and in time could be changed. Psychology is important for some institutional analysis as it affects perceptions of institutional structure and opportunities, but it will not be a major focus of this book.

Orthodox economics misses many issues of power (Perroux 1969; Rothschild 1971). K. William Kapp (1968, p. 17) notes that a common theme in institutionalist thought is concern "with such unorthodox issues as the role of conflict, coercion, and power in economic life." Don Kanel (1974, p. 832) suggests that orthodox economics focuses on "consumers and asks whether the economic system delivers efficiently what consumers want, given available resources, technology and consumer wants." The only power variable that arises from this is controlled by budget constraints and competitive markets. It will be argued that resource ownership and competition address only a portion of human interdependence and thus only a portion of the sources of power that affects the question of whose interests count, both as consumers and producers. The ability to participate in an economy depends on much more than competitive markets, ownership of factors of production, and money income as conventionally defined.

Welfare economics provides a number of useful concepts applicable to a broad political economy and policy analysis. However, it is most commonly devoted to specifying changes that can improve welfare in a restricted domain (Mishan 1981). It explores change that is consistent with individualism and real or potential Pareto-improvements. The Marshall-Pigou approach also accepted diminishing marginal returns and its implied justification for movement toward equality. But modern welfare theorists make no explicit argument for the interests of person A over B. It avoids the question of power by accepting some distribution of factor ownership and then testing subsequent allocative changes for welfare improvement. It can get significant assent on its explicit ethics of individualism and Pareto-improvement by raising no questions about fundamental distribution. This book does not employ this escape route and in fact narrows it. Welfare economists have identified a number of product characteristics that create problems in identifying efficient welfare-improving allocative changes. These will be utilized and added to, but not for the purpose of defining barriers to optimization. Rather than asking what causes the market to fail to reach *the* optimum, institutional economics asks how rights interact with these characteristics to determine whose preferences will count when the components of the optimum are selected out of many possible optima. It is public resolution of power conflicts that determine what is efficient. Welfare economics explores possible gains from trade, but the institutional economics of this book explores who has what to trade.

To summarize, institutional economics must include knowledge, psychology, and power variables. It is the judgment here that emphasis on further development of the power variable is most useful at this juncture in the evolution of neoclassical and neoinstitutional economics and that it is the most amenable to modification in the short run as a public-policy variable.[1] The emphasis is always one of degree, and the interaction of all three variables must be kept in mind. (This remains a tentative position, as the author is mindful that any change in institutions requires a willingness to change power variables, and this willingness is heavily circumscribed by current knowledge and psychology.)

The system of analysis used here begins with the facts of human interdependence. It is the public choice of property rights (institutions) that control and direct this interdependence and shape the opportunity sets of the interacting parties. The relative opportunities of people can be further described in terms of costs, externalities, and power. There are several ways to classify rights alternatives, but initially this will be done in terms of the type of transaction created. These elements are then combined to describe the structure of human relationships, and this can be used to hypothesize expected performance. Finally, the possible measures of performance are discussed.

HUMAN INTERDEPENDENCE AND PROPERTY RIGHTS

Scarcity is a learned social phenomenon and can be observed as people try to occupy incompatible positions. People manage to get in each other's hair. One person's striving to meet perceived needs gets in the way of someone else trying to do the same thing—for example, both may be trying to occupy the same land, or one person's use of one aspect of land affects use by others.

Interdependence is the occasion for both cooperation and conflict. The relationships of physics and biology may suggest a production possibility. For example, a beam can only be raised by the joint action of two people. The physical advantage of cooperation, however, does not mean that joint effort will be forthcoming. Often a dispute over the division of the fruits of joint effort keeps the beam from being raised at all. Technology and knowledge affect the character of the output of interdependent effort, but the images of rights that people carry in their heads affect what is realized.

Property rights describe the relationship of one person to another with respect to a resource or any line of action.[2] This person-to-person focus differs from some definitions that describe person-to-thing relationships. Rights are the instrumentality by which society controls and orders human interdependence and resolves the question of who gets what. Alternative rights are of interest because of their effect on economic performance and outcomes. The conventional study of rights emphasizes their role in motivating production effort. A person will not plant if it is expected that someone else will take the harvest. This is important, but as will be outlined below, it is only one variety of human interdependence.

The term *property right* includes both real and personal property. It includes both tort and contract law, common and statutory (public) law, civil and criminal law, vested and nonvested rights, judicial procedure, and civil rights. It includes informal practices and traditions embedded in the culture as well as formal legal institutions. These things shape the content of people's opportunities. Perhaps a better term would be *property rights and rights equivalencies* or simply *rights*.

The terms *institutions, rights,* and *rules of the game* are used here more or less interchangeably, though there are slight differences in the degree of aggregation and abstractness implied. The term *institution* can really only be adequately described by the subject matter of the book as a whole, but if a simple definition is necessary, institutions are sets of ordered relationships among people that define their rights, their exposure to the rights of others, their privileges, and their responsibilities. Or, as John R. Commons (1950, p. 21) said, "An institution is collective action in control, liberation, and expansion of individual action." In the words of Kenneth Parsons (1942), "Property is a set of social relationships which ties the future to the present through expectations of stabilized behavior regarding other persons and things."

The term *institution* implies a broad aggregation of particular rights that are often grouped in sets. A *market institution* refers to a set of rights and rules of a particular variety (which can vary somewhat and still be regarded as a market). Rights and rules are essentially synonymous. When we speak in the abstract, the term *rights* is used, while a *rule* is a specific statement (written or informal) that notes what A may do or expect B to do; for example, the rules of tenure give a faculty member the opportunity to be free of arbitrary dismissal and to obtain a hearing and so on. Rules can also be expressed as power, for example, the power to force a hearing even if the employer does not want it. A rule describes the extent of potential effective participation in decision making. In other words, rights and rules govern access to and use of power.

OPPORTUNITY SETS

In an interdependent world, the opportunities of one person are shaped by the opportunities of others (Samuels 1972). Rights define potential opportunities. An *opportunity set* is defined as the available lines of action open to an individual. The individual's choice of these lines of action is conditioned by the expected and actual choices of others from within their opportunity sets.

At any given time, a person has certain lines of action open—that is, not prohibited by criminal law or violating the private or communal rights of others—so that he or she may act without seeking the formal consent of anyone. Actual execution is affected by personal taste, skill, knowledge, and so on. To own some option for acting is to be able to act without the formal consent of others and without others getting in the way to the extent defined by the right. Ownership cannot be defined without at least implied reference to all parties affected by and affecting an action. Ownership means the owner has the opportunity to create costs for others who are affected by the owner's acts and to create benefits for the owner through use or exchange.

While a property right implies that A does not need the formal consent of others to act, others are not powerless if they do not like the action. They may possess legal countermoves that could discourage the act. This constitutes mutual coercion. For example, A may have the right to raise hogs. Neighbor B is not in a position to go to court and claim theft when offended by A's hogs, but B may exercise certain options within his or her own opportunity set—for example, to threaten not only to raise hogs also (on B's land) but also to play loud music at 3:00 A.M. or B may offer to pay A to cease. When B acts to create cost for A (as opposed to making a market bid), A's opportunity set is reduced. A's opportunity set at any moment is a nominal one that depends on the actual future choices of others acting within their own opportunity sets. Person A often benefits from the forbearance (perhaps love) of B, or B's lack of skill, knowledge, and so on. Opportunity sets can never be described in a static sense or in individual isolation.

When trade is allowed, B can escape from some effects of A's resource use by offering payment to A. This power of A to deny access to B unless payment is agreed upon is limited by the number of alternative places where B may secure the wanted product—that is, the degree of competition. In this case, the size of B's bid depends on the availability of materials to screen out the smell, sight, and noise of hogs as well as any rights to create costs for A.

An individual's opportunity set is composed of physical and emotional capacities plus legal or customary understandings of potential options that are conditioned by the actual choice of others. Power is a function of rights and personal characteristics as well as the choices of others. Thus the opportunity set of an individual is composed of alternative lines of action that are open because of the relative structure of rights as well as the relative capacity of the person to make use of the rights. For example, the slaves freed after the U.S. Civil War did not have the means to make use of their freedom and thus the distribution of welfare did not change for some time. Also, the value of a right is limited by available knowledge and technology. Interacting opportunity sets (which can also be described in terms of property rights) are what is meant by the institutional structure and can be distinguished from nature, technology, knowledge, tastes, and other aspects of personality. The opportunity sets of individuals interact and condition the outcome of human transactions. The components of institutional structure are one of the points of leverage in changing outcomes.

COST, EXTERNALITY, AND POWER

The model of human interaction outlined above emphasizes interdependence. This interdependence can be further described in terms of cost, externality, and power. One person's right to act really means that others are limited in avoiding the consequences of that act. John R. Commons suggested that the rights, liberties, immunity, or freedom of A can be seen as the lack of freedom or exposure of B to A's acts. This interacting conceptualization was developed from W. N. Hohfeld (1913). The right of A is a duty in B to allow what A claims under that right. One person's freedom is another's limitation if interests conflict in the face of scarcity. Scarcity is a function of nature and human tastes, while property rights constitute the disaggregation of that scarcity into individual terms.

What do we mean when we say something is scarce? Something must be given up to obtain it and some people must do without. The fundamental choice behind this allocation can be masked by emphasizing natural phenomena (much water and few diamonds). This is relevant, but its impact is conditioned by social choices of who has rights that become inputs and costs to the production of a product and who has enough rights to sell so that income is available to buy a given product. These rights decisions range from trivial to tragic choices, because they fundamentally decide who counts, who is fat or hungry, and so forth. These choices ultimately rest on moral judgments about the shares and entitlements of different people and the meaning and degree of equality (Calabresi and Bobbitt, 1978). Scarcity is partly a matter of physical constraints (resources and technology), but it is also a matter of fundamental public choice.

The institutional meaning of cost as seen by a given actor is quite different from effects forgone. It is the difference between human purpose and physics. Institutionalized cost is a chosen structure. Those physical opportunities (effects) that a decision maker can or must consider are a matter of specified property rights. Cost is a matter of shares obtained by others.

When is an opportunity that is foreclosed by a resource use also a cost as seen by the user?[3] The maximizing owner will consider some effects that are seen as costs and ignore others. The owner will consider alternative use values. For example, if forest land is used for corn, the opportunity lost (cost) is the forgone utility of lumber and firewood. Second, in an exchange economy, the owner will consider the bids of others. A neighbor may wish to preserve a sylvan view but may lose this opportunity if the landowner chooses to grow corn. This effect will be a cost to the landowner to the extent that the neighbor can make an effective bid. The bid is a cost to be considered along with the owner's own alternative use values. If the bid is rejected, the neighbor's lost view or hunger need not be further considered. The neighbor's participation in the land-use decision can be increased by giving the neighbor more rights in other things so that the bid can be enlarged or by making the neighbor a "part-owner" so that permission to alter resource use must be directly obtained. If the latter is done, the new part-owner may have to be bought out if the the other owner wants to cut the trees. Rights determine who has to make a bid to whom (and even if bids are allowed at all).

It is confusing to regard some inputs as "bads" rather than goods. Any input you have to buy is a bad in the sense that it is a cost and this cost is externally set by its owner's reservation price and not your own internal opportunity cost in use. Calling something a bad prejudges ownership.

The number of people who would like to participate in a resource-use decision is often great. Generally, the more people who have the right to participate, the more the costs to any person who wants to act. At some point, it becomes too costly for A to act to meet his or her objectives and tastes. The obverse is that some other interests fulfill their objectives. To have a right is to have the potential power to be represented in resource-use decisions and to create costs for other would-be decision makers. (The cost takes the form of either a bid from B that A can consider or the necessity for A to obtain B's permission for a certain action. The latter may require A to make a bid to B.) Power can be described (measured) in terms of the ability or degree of participation in decisions. One person's right is another's cost. One person's property right is the ability to coerce another by withholding what the other wants. There can be consent to the current distribution of the opportunity sets. Then within these sets, the parties may mutually coerce and finally consent to a transaction. The non-owner then only has the option of trying to pay off the right's holder to avoid the greater injury. This coercion is limited by the rights of others in a process of mutual coercion (Samuels 1972). To own is to have the right to coerce. It is not just government regulations that coerce.

A poor person is one who has no or few rights and cannot create costs for others, one who therefore has no personal income. No persons need get his or her consent for anything they want to do. In the economics of national income accounting, we learn that one person's income is another person's cost, and therefore we are warned not to count both expenditure and income in the sum of national wealth. In the economics of institutions, we are concerned with the disaggregation of this national income or expenditures and ask, Why it is that some people never seem to be a cost for anyone else and therefore have little income? To understand income distribution then, rights institutions must be understood.

Some have said, "I seek no power, I only want to be left alone." If tastes differ, however, this statement is not possible to implement. Power is inevitable if interests conflict. If everyone cannot have what they want simultaneously, the choice is not power or no power, but who has the power. Power is the ability to implement one's interests when they conflict with those of others. With respect to a single issue or resource, equal power is impossible. Over a variety of issues, it is possible for A to win some and B others and thus to speak of equality.

The above approach can be contrasted with conventional theory, which has been very selective and value presumptive in its classification of the varieties of human interdependence. Out of all of the ways that the acts of A impinge on B, Mishan (1981, chap. 52) labels some as being "externalities," which are incidential and unintended effects caused by A but external to A's accounting.

It is an easy step to say that some effects on B are properly accounted for or may be ignored while others are improper, and it is implied that public policy should correct them. This is the thrust of many distinctions between so-called social and private cost. The very term *social cost* already suggests that the effect so named has to be altered. This has set up a struggle between conservative and reform economists. The latter see the cause of externality as a technical failure of the market and a justification for collective, governmental action. The common illustration of an externality is that of pollution. The reformists say there are many other such external effects not properly accounted for by the market, and the conservatives and classical liberals say that there are few and that even the commonly cited examples could often be corrected by market improvements and extensions (Coase, 1974b; Rowley and Peacock, 1975).

The position taken here is that externalities are not only many but ubiquitous if defined without any presumptive value judgments. If interests conflict, one or more of the interests are inevitably external and must go unmet. This is just as true when two people want to eat the corn from the same acre of land as it is when the use of land affects a neighbor's view or sense of smell. The one is no more or less intentional than the other. Various sources of human interdependence can be distinguished, and these will be discussed in Part II. Some of the confusion in the literature with respect to the term *externalities* will be clarified in Chapter 11. Here it is sufficient to only note that externalities are the substance of the exercise of rights—that is, the interplay of mutual coercion.

One reason a person seeks a right is to create an external effect and have his or her taste, rather than a conflicting one, count. Property rights determine which effects of A's actions on B must be considered by A and which can be ignored. Rights determine which effects are costs and which are external to the decision maker in question. If one party has expanded opportunities, that party has fewer costs and more ability to affect others (create costs for others). One party's opportunities create external effects (or simply costs) for others. To reduce the external effects on B of A's acts is to increase the external effects on A of B's acts. So there is no suggestion here that externalities must be eliminated or internalized. It will be argued that public choice of rights directs externalities and influences who gets to make a choice when it means a forgone opportunity for another. Mutual interaction can also produce external benefits, and alternative rights affect their realization and distribution.

TYPES OF TRANSACTIONS

If the impact of alternative rights on peoples' relative opportunities is to be systematically studied, a taxonomy of rights is needed. Care must be taken with any classification that attempts to be all-inclusive and to make sharp distinctions between classes. Nevertheless, some groupings are analytically useful to specify a type of institutional structure (set of rules) to achieve a given performance. They are also useful in specifying the institutional variables in empirical tests, such as is done in Chapter 12. The outline of the model developed so far suggests that an important issue is the definition of opportunity sets. How shall people be related in making decisions on the production of a good or service? For example, how do people get blood for transfusions? The persons with need can bargain and offer to pay a supplier. Or the needy person can assert a claim on some other person's blood and if the request is not honored, the person can turn to an administrator who orders the transferral. Or the person's need is met by others without a bid, request, or order simply because of the status of the parties (such as in a charitable grant). Each of these implies a different sort of right and will be distinguished as relationships of bargaining, administration, and status-grant transactions. Some general hypotheses contrasting the performance that might be expected from each type of transaction will be noted here, and more-specific hypotheses in the context of different situations of interdependence will be developed later.

Various writers on institutional economics have developed a taxonomy of organizational alternatives. While there are differences in emphasis and purpose, there are striking similarities. For example, John R. Commons (1950, chap. 3) distinguishes bargaining, managerial, and rationing transactions. Robert A. Solo (1967, chap. 19) distinguishes four types of economies: entrepreneurial, political, household, and institutional (not-for-profit). Robert L. Heilbroner (1962, chap. 1) distinguishes institutional approaches of tradition, command, and market. Karl Polanyi (1957, p. 250) distinguishes three forms of economic integration: reciprocity, redistribution, and exchange. Dahl and Lindblom (1953) discuss market, democracy, hierarchy, and bargaining; and Bruno Frey (1978) speaks of exchange, love, and threat as alternative decision-making procedures.

The parties to a transaction may be individuals or groups of individuals. One's opportunity to participate in a transaction is a matter of rights held individually (can act without the permission of others) or mutually. The right itself can create interdependence by requiring group action according to some decision rules.

Bargained Transactions

In a bargained exchange system, rights are transferable upon mutual consent of the parties. The parties involved are considered legal equals with respect to the given transactions. Each party is acknowledged to have certain rights that are antecedent to the transaction and that imply a degree of mutual consent. Each party has an opportunity set with some content (not necessarily equal), and each is free within that limit to join or abstain from further transactions. Each party may deny access to another party who may have need but does not own the resource in question—that is, there is mutual coercion. Through a process of negotiation, the parties agree to transfer something they own in exchange for what the other owns. Thus, a bargained transaction implicitly involves both coercion and consent.

The bargained transaction implicitly involves four parties, the actual buyer and seller and alternatives thereto. If one has no alternatives, the buyer and seller are not legal equals, and one party really has no choice. This rule is relative, and differences in the alternatives facing each party affects their relative bargaining power. This rule is the basis of the economists' traditional interest in competition.

The outcome of a bargaining transaction is an agreement to transfer rights, and this agreement can be described in terms of price, which is the ratio of income to outgo for each of the parties. The result is a function of many things, but all are structured by the content of the interacting opportunity sets.

Bargaining may involve the offer of both goods and bads. The good is the right to act with reference to something valuable. In addition, the opportunity set may contain the right to create certain injuries to others, which may involve things not directly related to the items under consideration for transfer. For example, a threat to compete and enter into production of X may help get the agreement of the other party to accept a favorable price for Y.

Bargained transactions may involve exit or voice (Hirschman 1970). On the one hand, parties may never actually speak to each other. The decision is to buy or not. The price is marked, and the buyer either takes the product or exists to seek another elsewhere. This is often the situation in pure competition, where buyers are "price takers." The exiting buyer may have no further concern with that seller. Yet, if numerous buyers exit, the seller will get a message that price or quality needs changing (Adam Smith's famous "unseen hand"). The ability to exit means no one person can affect price and also serves to maintain performance. On the other hand, in small-number situations the parties may communicate specifically by voice. Offers and counter-offers are made in person. Other market forms include cost-plus contracts, auctions, sealed bids, spot, and futures. Bargaining is usually associated with the market, but public agencies can also be related to each other by bargaining.

Knowledge of the nominal opportunity sets of the parties is not sufficient to predict the content of a particular trade, which is influenced by the perceptions of the parties, past history, the degrees of benevolence and malevolence, and so on; yet in many cases the analyst can estimate these perceptions by empathy or formal investigation (see Chapter 10).

Administrative Transactions

The parties to administrative transactions are not legal equals but are related as superior to inferior. The party in the superior position issues a voiced command to be carried out by the inferior. Administrative transactions involve a position of authority whose occupant has some range of discretion as determined by the opportunity sets of the parties. The position of authority can be that of legislator, police officers, public or private administrator, or simply private owner. Administration seems the stuff of politics but is also the base of private action and the material of bargained transactions, including contracts.

For example, a legislature may make a law enforced by police; a person is ordered to cease using the pesticide DDT. This is clearly an administrative transaction, but the same effect might be implemented by private rights. A private person (or group) who owns the right to be free of the effects of DDT has the authority to order people to stop using the chemical. If the chemical continues to be used, the owner of the chemical-free environment can claim theft and turn to the courts for enforcement. An owner is an administrator as surely as any governmental bureaucrat. Owner-administrators may or may not have the further right to transfer their options. Frequently, in the case of public administration, the affected party is prohibited from subsequent bargaining. For example, bids to receive government permission to use DDT are prohibited and regarded as a bribe. Such a situation could also arise with private owners who have a use right but no right of exchange. Where exchange is permitted, it is the right to administer that is the material of bargained transactions. The right to relinquish command over the use of a resource is the ability to obtain income from its sale.

The options to command may be owned by an individual or shared by many. In the case of joint ownership (as with corporate stockholders and citizens of a state), there are rules for the aggregation of individual preferences, which may or may not involve bargaining. Where representatives of owners, such as corporate managers or political representatives, are involved, the owners are often faced with costs in effectively combining their commands—a situation exemplifying the issues of separation of ownership and control in private corporations and of accountability of politicians to voters. The representatives may administer with little control by the owners who are nominally at the top of the hierarchy.

The category of administrative transactions is potentially confusing because it can change rights but is itself subject to rights (rules for making new rights—that is, civil and political rights). Its root may be in previous private contract or some public agreement reflected in constitutions and laws. At first glance, the administrative transaction appears to be based wholly on force, but it is a transfer of rights rather than implicit warfare because, while new control is created without unanimous consent, this new control is in turn limited by other rights rather than simply superior physical force. Thus, administration is regarded as a transfer of rights and not as just a goods movement of war, though this distinction is a matter of degree.

While the administrative transaction involves two parties (an administrator and the inferior), the order (or command) is often for the benefit of some third party. Care must be taken so that the transaction between administrator and inferior does not obscure the transaction between inferior and the beneficiary of the administrative action.

Empirically, it is often hard to distinguish an order from a persuasion. An administrator may not have the formal authority to order a given action, but his suggestion may carry a lot of weight if the administrator has other discretionary choices affecting the subordinate's pay and working conditions; or the administrator's prestige may simply set an attractive example to follow.

The individual administrative transaction involves a limited one-way movement of rights. The inferior delivers a right and receives nothing in return. At the moment, the delivery may be quite involuntary. The avoidance of the harm that the administrator may be able to inflict (possible imprisonment) is not the same as a two-way flow of rights in a negotiated bargain. It may appear to be a contradiction in terms to speak of transfer of ownership in response to an order. If ownership is subject to forced transfer, then was it really ownership in the first place? The fact is that so-called private ownership is always a residual. To be subject to an administrative act is not to own fully. Some authors speak of "rights attenuation" when an owner does not have exclusive control and the right of exchange. But, in the sense noted here, all rights are attenuated. One seldom owns fully and wholly independently of others' actions. This applies to all transactions, since opportunity sets interact whether related by bargaining or administration. Nevertheless, one holds part of the bundle of rights until it is ordered to be delivered up under specified conditions and limits. A right that can be exercised until it is overridden by an administrative action can be seen as part of the traditional concept of a bundle of rights. The inferior loses some utility formerly enjoyed but that was always subject to withdrawal. The former utility was the result of administrative forebearance.

The source of positions of authority may be private contract or some political process. An earlier bargain may create the right to execute future orders. The labor bargain and private contract may precede the right of the manager to give specific orders to employees once they occupy the manager's premises. If each of these specific orders had to be negotiated in the market, transaction costs would be high. When a firm buys out a supplier or subsequent processor of its product (vertical integration), it is substituting a future administrative transaction for a formerly bargained one, that is, hierarchy for market (Williamson 1975).

The political process often substitutes administration for former market relationships to change the former balance of mutual coercion. Administration is the method for making nonunanimous changes in opportunity sets, including those upon which bargained transactions take place. The rules of political representation and process set limits on how far government can go in changing access to economic goods and the rules for private bargaining transactions. Changes are limited by constitutional rights. In private organizations, there are also positions of authority that allocate opportunities within the organization without unanimous consent of the members. The establishment of a budget by a corporate board of directors is an example. These orders are limited by the charter and perhaps ultimately by the ability of members to exit the organization. In other words, there is always an element of bargaining attached to an administrative transaction. While the administrator may have the power to imprison a citizen or fire an employee, there are usually some costs associated with such action that the inferior can affect. The person in the inferior position thus has some bargaining power when dealing with an administrative superior.

The distribution of administrative rights can be dispersed or concentrated. It may be lodged in national or local government. It may be centralized in the executive or decentralized into executive, legislative, and judicial branches. These dimensions of centralization apply to both government and private firms (Pryor 1973, pp. 279–88). Various splits are possible, such as along functional, product, or geographical lines. To conclude, while bargaining and administration represent alternative systems of rights, there are important structural differences within as well as between each that might be expected to affect performance.

Status and Grant Transactions

In these two types of transaction, there is neither bid nor command. It involves a one-way movement of rights rooted in the learned habits or benevolence of the giver. In a status transaction, transfers are governed primarily through the prescribed roles associated with a person's social position. The amount and kind of good is prescribed and fixed by custom. The transfer is necessary to discharge a social obligation. There is little calculation of advantage in the fact of changing relative scarcities. One does what one is expected to do. The behavior is learned and internalized into one's personality, little thought is given to alternatives, and there is no bargaining. There may be a two-way flows of goods, but the exchange rates are customary rather than negotiated, or the return flow is nonspecified and left open. There may or may not be direct, voiced communication between the parties, though direct personal contact is most common.

Anthropologists have described a number of societies that transfer goods via a complex set of interconnected but indirect transactions. Person A may have an obligation to provide a good or service for B (often related by kinship), B in turn has an obligation to C, and perhaps C then gives something back to A, thus closing the circle. People's needs as defined in the learned custom of the group are thus cared for. Anthropologists call such a system *reciprocity* though it is not the direct quid pro quo that economists usually have in mind (Polanyi 1957).

The internal transfer of goods and services of most families is carried out by this method. The practice of mutual aid among farmers who might be injured during the critical harvest period is another example. The transfers at the moment are one-way and predictable as a result of learned habits, so that people in the role of neighbor know what is expected relative to the role of incapacitated farmer. If a person never occupies the status of need in the future, he is owed nothing by those aided in the past.

If access to goods is by status, objective skills may be less important than position or whom you know. For example, a rich and a poor person may have equal management skills and ideas for new production, but the former can obtain bank credit and the latter cannot. The same distinction often applies with respect to government favors.

A closely related transaction is the grant. Kenneth Boulding (1973) uses the term *grant* much more inclusively than it is used here. For Boulding, everything that is not a two-way transfer of commodities is a grant: all government orders including taxation; all habitual, learned social obligations such as those involved in the family; and all acts of charity. Therefore his grants economy includes all of what here is subdivided into administration and status-grant transactions. He also distinguishes an explicit grant such as charity, from an implicit grant such as a political change in property rights (see also Pfaff 1976). The grant is also a one-way transfer of rights but is distinguished from status in that the grant is less systematized and reflects more individual discretion and calculation. A good example of a grant is an act of charity. (For a review of the literature, see Macaulay and Berkowitz [1970] and Phelps [1975].) Charity is not something necessarily attached as an obligation of a certain identifiable position running to another socially defined position. The butcher may feel kindly toward a poor baker as a result of a quite private reasoning and set of experiences. This relationship can be contrasted with the rather fixed set of expectations that tie a husband to his wife's uncle—expectations that are embedded perhaps in ritual and shared by all in the community. A donor of charity does not incur the displeasure of the community if he changes a gift from one person to another, but a father does if his gift is changed from his son to someone outside the family.

The essence of a grant is that the grantor receives no right in return, which is a matter of degree and selective perception. An example of a pure grant is the transfer of wealth between present and unborn generations; the latter cannot do anything in return, not even give the donor honor while he lives. However, the living can give honor to the giver for his act, and the giver may gain self-respect even if not acknowledged by others.

The existence of a two-way movement is a matter of perception, and it changes over time. One person may make a gift and expect nothing in return, while another may give and expect deference. Whether this latter is regarded as grant or bargain is a matter of perception. The certainty of getting a return good when the initial transfer is made is also a matter of degree. The recipient of a grant makes no specific agreement with the grantor and in fact could be ignorant of the gift's source. If any good is returned in the future, the amount and kind are matters again of status and not of present or future negotiation.

A one-way, status-grant transfer involves a degree of bond between the donor and recipient that is not usually present in the bargained or administrative transaction. Somehow the utility of A is interdependent with that of B, and A feels better knowing that B's welfare is enhanced, even if A has fewer goods as a result. This topic is important in understanding the social foundation for any system of rights to exist (Taylor 1966).

Since the substance of the status-grant transaction is relatively more internalized in the minds of people and is learned over a lifetime, it is not subject to quick change. If A has been bringing two coconuts to his wife's uncle everyday for ten years, this habit is hard to change even if technology makes cassava roots relatively much easier to acquire or even if the uncle develops a new taste for cassava. To repudiate the gift would be to repudiate the person. Simple exit by the consumer is frowned on. Change would require common learning of new expectations.

Some grantors may be reluctant to initiate or continue a grant, and some grantees may be reluctant to see a grant cease when the grantor's sense of bond declines. Where the grant is supported by community expectations, it has the character of a right held by the grantee. If not, the right is ultimately held by the grantor subject to individual preference. This is the difference between a status system and private charity. Status rights are nontransferable (Montias 1976, p.118).

What are the reinforcers available to restore deviant status transactions to some prior level of performance? One of the common reinforcers is that of voiced social disapproval and the utility of conformism (Jones 1984). The person expecting the transfer (or third parties in the community) may voice disapproval to the obligated party. Disapproval could be as subtle as a frown or as forceful as social ostracism or, ultimately, removal from the community. To prevent theft, rights subject to exchange have jail sanctions, but status rights are maintained by social pressure. The fact that all transactions have sanctions doesn't make all types of transactions the same. Social disapproval can accompany violation of bargained and administrative transactions as well. Its effectiveness as a sanction depends upon the degree to which the actor has learned to be sensitive to it.

When one has no administrative or bargaining power, then the voice of disapproval is the only recourse. One hopes that an expression of disapproval carries enough mental pain for the receiver to modify his or her behavior. For example, a consumer who writes a letter to a seller of a faulty product may not be in a position to command or bargain. Even a threat to stop buying the product would have little effect as an individual event. The writer hopes that the seller will respond to avoid the voice of social disapproval. Where there is no internalized sense of community, disapproval is ineffective. This is considered further in Chapter 2.

Alternative Transactions Structures Summarized

To summarize, bargaining involves a two-way rights transfer, while both administration and status-grant transactions are one-way. Bargaining involves mutual coercion, administration involves one-way coercion, and status-grant transactions involve no overt coercion to initiate the goods flow. Administrative and status-grant transactions generally involve more voiced, direct communication than do bargained transactions.

One aspect of contrasting alternative transactions is the character of goods movements. But these goods movements also exist in nature (mutualism, parasitism, and commensalism). What makes biology or physics different from social transactions is the mental imaging; that is, grant and administrative transactions both involve a one-way, physical goods movement but differ in attitude and resultant utility.

While many aspects of performance can be related to the type of transaction, there is no necessary connection between the type of transaction used and the distribution of wealth and power. The partners to bargained transactions may differ greatly in their assets. The bargaining may be between individuals or involve concentrated wealth in corporate groups. Administrative transactions can be used to disperse wealth widely or narrowly. The power represented by the administrator may be based on contract, democratic election, or military domination. The administration can be highly centralized or widely dispersed in many agencies and levels of government. Status-grant transactions are similar and can disperse or concentrate wealth.

Further, there is no necessary connection between the type of transaction used and the existence of a rationalized plan to achieve certain objectives. A bargained transaction proceeds from an initial distribution and definition of rights. These rights do not specify specific acts that must transpire, but they do influence the direction of what happens. It is true that those who choose from within their opportunity sets may discover that the aggregate result of their choosing was unanticipated. In this sense, market results are unplanned. But it is unlikely that no one was aware of how private rights and rules of contract would influence market results. In this sense, no market economy is unplanned.

It is an important issue for public choice to decide whether human interdependence with reference to a given resource shall be organized via rights of a bargained, administrative, or status-grant character. However, useful as this trichotomy may be for suggesting connections among institutional structure and performance, other categories of rights will be developed later. The above discussion makes clear that there are as many important differences in rights alternatives within each of the three as among them.

SUPPLEMENTING THE COMPETITIVE MODEL AND
NEOCLASSICAL WELFARE ECONOMICS

If a model of the economy is to be useful for public policy, it must contain a full conceptualization of how one person can affect the welfare of another. In a self-sufficient, nonmarket economy, this interdependence was unidimensional. One person affected another by physical intrusion. Thus the law of trespass was created. The remedy for unlawful intrusion was to sue in a court of law, claiming theft of the use of your property or to have the state act for you in criminal proceedings. One person's opportunity set was framed by the limits that the law placed on the ability of others to remove or destroy physical commodities.

As market exchange developed, the law of physical trespass no longer spoke to all of the ways one party could affect another and incorporeal, intangible property became important. Value in exchange could be affected without any physical intrusion. Attention shifted to the distribution of market power by which one party could affect price. A critical ingredient in bargaining power is the existence of alternatives. The ability of one party to drive a hard bargain is limited by alternative sellers (or buyers as the case may be). Accordingly the concept of the purely competitive market was formulated. In a competitive market no one person could affect price because the other party always had the option of exit. Power was limited by rights in competition.

From this perspective, many economists argued that all government needed to do was to define factor ownership, and thus the law of trespass and theft, and to enforce pure competition by such means as antitrust laws.[4] The individual who does not like what is happening has two options: court action or exit. This is essentially the position taken by Milton Friedman, who states, "If a consumer finds he's being sold rotten meat at the grocery store, he has the very best protection agency available: the market. He simply stops trading at that store and moves to another. Eventually, the first seller gets the message and offers good meat or he goes out of business." As to faulty, harmful products, "You sue" (Friedman 1975, p. 10).

This view leads easily to the ideological position that the only appropriate role of government is to maintain competition. If no one person could affect price, it appears to follow that people are rich or poor according to their preferences, genes, and human capital. In a word, the poor are lazy. This is a bit of an oversimplification, since it has always been clear that some people start with ownership of more factors than others. An old topic in political debate is the law of inheritance. Inheritance taxes reduce the inequality of resource ownership as a result of intergenerational transfer. But the theory of competition does not pay much attention to differences in income distribution. As long as there are many buyers and sellers, it makes no difference whether you are rich or poor; no one can influence price. But income distribution does make a difference for whether you eat or not. The conventional theory also tends to ignore how new resources get to be owned. There is often an implicit assumption that all valuable things were owned by someone or another since year one and that any currently contested ownership can be deduced from prior rights. The most limited version of this ideology has it that legislatures should not make new property rights and courts should not make law but merely deduce and clarify existing law (Buchanan 1972). To do otherwise is theft. However, it is the ability to get access to newly valuable aspects of resources and knowledge that constitutes a major explanation of differences in the distribution of wealth.

Are there ways that one person can affect another that are not controlled by the laws of trespass and enforcement of competition? Is there more to the structure of rights than is addressed in antitrust laws enforcing competition? To understand the character of the paradigm of this book, it is necessary to review briefly the history of economic thought.

There have been several challenges to exclusive focus on market competition as the ultimate public policy. One was the Marxist challenge, which predicted the demise of capitalism and noted that it produced an alienated personality whether the person was rich or poor. While the demise has not happened yet, the problems of mental health and cyclical unemployment are very real. Since the Keynesian revolution, mainstream economics has accepted some stabilization, or offset function, by government. However, there are those such as Friedman who would have the money supply grow by a predetermined annual rate and deny any role for periodic government change in monetary policy. In any case, the Keynesian perspective saved the competitive market as the primary institutional focus.

Schumpeter (1942) argued that achievement of competitive equilibria was less important for economic growth than the disequilibria created by innovative technologies and products in a process of creative destruction. These two types of competition require different institutions and are often incompatible. (Langlois 1986, p. 11).

Veblen challenged the pecuniary mind set of market participants and advocated the abolition of ceremonial institutions to let the natural and assertedly superior order of the instinct of workmanship and engineering values to emerge. Both Veblen and Marx emphasized class conflict of owners versus producers and developed themes defining exploitation. The Veblenians, the Marxists, and the neoclassic mainstream all have a welfare economics founded in a natural order that a putatively rational person would use to choose the best institutions. All will be critiqued here.

Another challenge came out of the understanding of the role of the inelastic supply of some commodities, particularly land. The lucky owners of these resources were in a position to extract large rents and skew income distribution in their favor. This situation led to suggestions for government ownership or taxation from such reformers as John Stuart Mill and Henry George. While the importance of land in the distribution of income has declined, some people still seem to take advantage of short-term supply inelasticities, and natural resources are the source of many large fortunes.

Still another challenge, from such writers as Pigou and Samuelson, has led to what is now called the basis for "market failure." Certain characteristics of goods prevent market bids from being organized even where it can be imagined that people with income want the product (exclusion-cost and free-rider features). Other characteristics, such as marginal cost being zero or less than average cost, were thought to lead to inefficient pricing practices if the goods were provided by competitive, private market firms. Public utilities have always been thought to need special treatment by government, but the Pigou-Samuelson thrust extended the definition of public utilities considerably. This thrust has been resisted by conservatives. James Buchanan and Gordon Tullock have argued that government cannot get any closer to the optimum in the context of market failure because of government failure. Bureaucrats pursue their own self-interests and not the public interest or efficiency. The point will be argued here that the basic problem is that there are many publics and many optima and there can be no presumption of what constitutes failure.

An empirical question is raised about how competitive the economy is. "How much competition is enough?" Theoretical work from J. M. Clark to William Baumol has led some to the idea of effective competition, which says that even where there are not large numbers of competitors, there may still be enough (potentially) so that no one has undue bargaining power. Economists are divided on this empirical question as well as the meaning of *undue*.

Another challenge comes from the economic planners. Galbraith, for example, argues that the character of industrial technology and production is such that a situation of many alternative suppliers is not desirable because of scale economies. The perfectly competitive market assumes perfect information. The efficient use of modern technology requires a predictability of the future, which cannot be secured by contract among many market participants. This predictability requires some type of planning. Such planning could and is being done by private corporations, but some type of public participation and overview seems necessary for accountability. Simple right of exit is not enough.

Various subdisciplinary fields in economics reflect the classical focus on competitive markets as well as the challenges thereto. The inheritors of the conventional focus are in the field of international trade, with its traditional emphasis on free trade, and in the field of industrial organization, with its emphasis on antitrust policy. The challengers are in monetary policy and public finance with planning, development, and public-utility economics in the wings. This book does not fit neatly into any one of these fields but encompasses them all and perhaps adds a few concepts that have not yet been made the focus of a subdiscipline. In doing so it makes no general argument for or against government, market, Keynesian policies, rent collection, competitive practices, planning, or whatever. It does argue that all of these involve fundamental distributive questions requiring public choice of rights not dictated by technical economics. And, more important, it provides a theory to better relate policy instruments of all kinds to specific measures of who gets what (rather than whether abstract optima are nearer or further away).

Part II contains a conceptualization of a wide range of human interdependencies that will subsequently be referred to as the "situation." It includes those where the degree of competition and the right of exit are relevant plus many where competition is irrelevant and noncontrolling. The categories of situational interdependence are grouped under incompatible uses and users, exclusion costs, economies of scale, joint-impact goods, transaction costs (contractual and information), and consumer and producer surplus (including inelastic supply and rents). In some of these instances of interdependence, it is difficult to establish an effective right of exit, and in other cases, even if established, the right is not decisive. In some cases, there are interests that depend on rights other than those of exit and protection from trespass. There are interests not served no matter how finely tuned an economy is with reference to the Keynesian variables. Some of the gaps in the traditional fields of economics need to be filled.

The paradigm to be developed is important for two reasons. One is for empirical prediction, and the other is for raising the level of public debate over ethical choices and competing ideologies. If we are going to predict performance under alternative institutions and property rights, we need to know much more than the degree of competition and the nominal opportunity for exit and suit for fraud and theft. Also when testing the effects of the degree of competition, we must be aware of what other institutional factors need to be controlled if we are to interpret our findings.

The conventional focus on competition also has ideological consequences. Some interests are not served whether or not there is competition. Those who gain from policies and rights unrelated to the degree of competition are benefited when public discourse ignores the wide-ranging sources of their differential wealth and focuses on such questions as whether or not to enforce antitrust laws or even whether a particular product should be provided by public or private firm, whether it should be regulated or unregulated, or whether welfare subsidies should be changed.

The reader will note that the title of this section refers to supplementing the competitive model, not replacing it. Many heterodox writers concentrate on finding real-world exceptions to the assumptions of pure competition that vitiate its efficiency conclusions. Here the purpose of detailing the several categories of interdependence is rather that they represent situations and interests that are not affected, directed, and controlled by the degree of competition and the exit option. Therefore, if the analyst would prescribe something to help one interest vis-à-vis another, some structural variables in addition to the degree of competition must be sought. For example, it is not sufficient to argue over the degree to which perfect information assumptions are met, but rather

the analyst must investigate how the rules alternatives shape the size and distribution of information cost.

MEASURES OF PERFORMANCE

After an initial conceptualization of alternative institutional structures, there
remains the choice of performance variables in empirical studies. Institutional
performance will be measured here in terms of who gets what and whose costs
get considered. Specific groups of people will be identified as to their level of
living, security, quality of environment, and general quality of life. While the
distribution of money income is an important measure, we will see that it is
inadequate as a description of the full range of relative opportunities of people.
A better performance measure might be the distribution of wealth and opportunities.

The approach to be used here contrasts with that of many studies that utilize
freedom, growth, and efficiency in a global or societal sense to describe institutional performance. Theory can be used to specify certain institutional structures that by definition produce efficiency and optimum resource allocation in
the abstract without any reference to who is a gourmand and who is hungry.
Some studies can label the institutions of one country as being more efficient
than those of another without ever comparing actual GNP or other measures
of level of living. The categories of efficiency, freedom, and growth are often
vague and value presumptive. They are discussed in Chapter 11. By contrast,
the focus here is on how a particular institution or set of rights affects whose
freedom and whose view of efficiency and output will dominate when interests
conflict. This is what is meant by substantive performance.

NOTES

1. The placement of emphasis differs among institutional economists. Some emphasize the institutional fine tuning in the context of private negotiation after the primary
ownership conflicts have been settled by public choice of legislatures and courts. Oliver
Williamson (1985, p. 17) says, "The inordinate weight that I assign to transaction cost
economizing is a device by which to redress a condition of previous neglect and under-
valuation." The emphasis here on the consequences of alternative distributions of power
does not deny the role of economizing within structured power and the essential two-
way interdependence of the two levels.

2. Richard T. Ely says, "The essence of property is in the relations among men
arising out of their relations to things" (1914, p, 96). "Property is the right, and not
the object over which the right extends" (p. 108).

3. Orthodox economics contrasts economic market determinants of prices and costs
with political determinants. But, as Charles Bettelheim (1975, pp. 16–17) points out,
this is an illusion "because the market does not determine anything. It is simply the

imaginary place where the exigencies of . . . the material and social conditions of production are imposed."

4. The Chicago School goes one step further and argues that competition is a natural state of affairs that occurs if government does not interfere. Thus, antitrust law is seldom needed.

Two

Property in a Social Context

Chapter 1 outlined the study agenda. Before proceeding to analyze the effects of alternative property rights on economic performance, we must inquire into the foundations for any set of rights to exist. The study of institutions involves several levels of analysis.

PROPERTY IS A SOCIAL FACT

Modern Western economics has tried hard to make love superfluous to the working of the economy. The competitive market is thought to be a system where welfare is maximized without anyone caring for anyone else. Selfishness is guided by Adam Smith's "unseen hand" and produces Pangloss's "best of all possible worlds." It will be argued below that this idea is a delusion. The market rests on ethical choices, as does any variety of transaction system. The unseen hand is not a spontaneous gift of nature but a publicly chosen set of property rights resting on some minimum of self-restraint. The focus of this book is on the consequence of alternative rights, but this analysis takes place in a social context.

A popular notion of the foundations of property rights is that of John Locke, who regarded property as a natural and technological fact (Hamilton 1932). He begins with a virgin forest with nuts falling to the ground. If a person stoops to pick them up and incorporates labor into the nuts, they become that person's property. *Property* is defined as incorporated labor. There is no doubt that our ideas on the legitimacy of property have something to do with an acknowledgment of human effort. But, as we have already seen, the labor that is regarded as imparting a right is always a socially selective thing. Otherwise it is impossible to distinguish the labor of the Indian in cutting out a cow from that of the cowboy in the Russell trail-drive painting. If labor is all that counts, we are back to thievery or warfare, which is certainly laborious. The labor of gathering the nuts from the forest floor and the labor of the thief who subsequently removed the nuts could not then be distinguished.

Theft is a social concept applied to certain specified goods movements that lie outside a limit commonly agreed upon by both parties. Without some agreement on these bounds, it is not possible to define theft. In the Russell painting, the Indian's taking of a cow could not be distinguished from his killing of a buffalo or picking a wild berry or catching a drop of rain in his mouth.

Property is not simply a derivative of a physical fact; it also reflects a group choice about what kinds of effort are to count in creating an image in people's minds that acknowledges a person's rights. The fleet-footed thief is not admired like the professional athlete. The result of labor that is afforded the status of property is always selected from a wide variety of possible exertions.

But what is meant by *selected*? Who does the selecting? How many have to agree? The difference between a threat system of warfare and the exchange system of bargaining, administration, and status grant is one of self-limitation and willingness to treat others as subjects rather than objects. In all-out war, others are treated as objects, and the extent of the treatment is limited only by countervailing force (Umbeck 1981).

To make war is to regard the other person as an object to be manipulated and overcome. To make an exchange is to regard the other person as a subject to be respected. War is a relation of things, while exchange is relations of persons with respect to things. The distinction is related to Kant's categorical imperative, "Act so that you treat humanity, whether in your own person or in that of another, always as an end, and never as a means only" (Kant 1959, sec. 2, p. 47).[1]

In peaceful situations, people treat each other, at least in part, as subjects. A subject is regarded as having some set of opportunities that the other person accepts as limiting on his or her own action—for example, will drive a hard bargain but not steal (however defined). This self-limitation will be referred to here as a bond or covenant implying a degree of benevolence. A bond is not the same as a property right. It is the background condition for any right, indeed for any peaceful discussion or argument over rights. The true test for the existence of a covenant is whether the behavior associated with a right continues when the swordsman sleeps—even when no cost can be generated by an external party. (It literally does not have to be a swordsman, but anyone who can create cost, even for example, the frown of social pressure.) If A's use and other opportunities are guaranteed only as long as B believes A holds superior force, then when that force is absent, B will move in. But if B acts from habit or has some feeling of volunteered self-limitation, A's relationship is one of right and not begrudged submission waiting for a reversal when A sleeps or when the technology of war changes. John F. A. Taylor says, "A man's property in the market depends not upon performances which he requires of others, but upon forbearances which others require of themselves" (1966, p. 110). Forbearance is part of ethical choice.

The policeman is effective only at the margin. When a substantial number of people will not limit themselves, the police are often unable to do anything about it. If the nominal holders of property rights are not willing to go to all-out war (armies instead of police), a certain degree of self-imposed limitation, or "willing participation," is necessary.

Self-imposed limitation suggests some degree of interdependence of utility functions. It goes beyond selfishness toward benevolence. It involves some degree of integration between people, an ethical bond, covenant, or understanding. It is an answer to the question, Who is my brother? The degree of limitation may be slight, but there is a fundamental difference between war and exchange. You cannot trade or grant something that other persons already regard as theirs. There can be argument over the rate of exchange (price), but this is civilized by some self-imposed limit of what one person will do to the other.

Behavior is learned, and its source is often lost in the mists of time. People can be involved in exchange and be unaware of any bond or benevolence that makes trade of any particular set of rights possible. Much behavior is habit, perhaps even based on some ancient, forgotten submission, which, whether they are aware of it or not, limits people's struggles and competition. Occasionally exchange is interrupted and people are forced to rethink their involvement. They either reaffirm their bonds of self-limitation, learn new ones, or turn to force. Thus there is created the anomaly that, while the present existence of bounded exchange does not prove that all or even most of the parties are benevolent, these exchanges reflect moral judgments and cannot continue, if challenged, unless shared judgments can be learned or rediscovered.

THE MARKET IS AN ETHICAL SYSTEM

It is popularly argued by reformers that the market must be tempered by social values; people in the market are urged to have a social conscience and to refrain from acts that are possible under a particular set of market rules. Or, it is urged that government regulation and subsidies should modify market results to obtain a particular social purpose. The point of this chapter, however, is not to indicate the role of self restraint in the face of market imperfections or as a substitute for administration. Rather it is to inquire into the antecedent conditions for any rights to exist at all. There is no market, perfect or otherwise, without some widely shared underlying value judgment and publicly chosen rules. A particular ethical choice may not embody the values preferred by the given reformer, but it involves some self-limits. Any set of market prices reflects some minimal agreement to an ethical covenant. Changes in the prevailing ethic will tend to create changes in the price structure. Social value is not something in addition to market value, though additional restraints can be volunteered beyond those of market rules. There are no market values without underlying ethical judgments even if this delusion is what John F. A. Taylor calls one of the "masks of society." The absence of ethical values is not a bad exchange but no exchange—for example, the physical removal of goods in war. (The distinction between exchange and a mere movement of goods from one hand to another is from Polanyi [1957].)

Person B is a subject of rights and not merely an object for use or abuse to the extent that A has the self-limit not to act in certain ways without the consent of B. For example, A's values may not allow him to eat a certain cow without the consent of the cowboy, and further A will not do certain things in obtaining that consent. For example, A agrees that the use of his superior physical strength will not be relevant to the interaction. He may agree further not to discriminate in his attempts to secure meat on the basis of race or sex. Within these bounds, the two parties will use whatever resources and skills are at their disposal (except as they choose forbearance in the specific instance). These understandings (images) are antecedent to the particular interaction.

These understandings and acknowledgments (property rights) are not themselves the subject of a particular economic transaction, though over time the particular transaction and these limits interact and affect each other. In a manner of speaking, then, these limits have no price and are withheld from the present interaction. They are antecedent, and their source lies outside of any particular present transaction that utilizes and reflects them.

What is true of the market with its bargained transaction is also true of other transactions. An administrative system may employ the sanction of imprisonment, but if a society is not to be an armed police state, there must be some background ethical judgments made or learned by most individuals that make the rights of the administrator legitimate to some degree.

A status-grant transaction also reflects some self-restrictive ethical behavior. A beneficiary of an obligatory act of another depends on the self-limitations of the obliged person as much as any social pressure. Whether a person enjoys a set of opportunities as a result of being a private property owner with bargaining power to obtain other resources or is the beneficiary of the expected delivery of goods from someone in a status transaction, he or she is in part served by the self-limitations of the other party to the transaction. A self-limitation usually is rationalized in terms of some ethical judgment. In that sense, all types of transactions rest on an ethical base.

PROPERTY IS A PUBLIC FACT

Property as we have seen above is never a unilateral act but always involves some degree of shared understanding. Another way of expressing it is to say that "property is a public fact, or it is no fact at all" (Taylor 1966, p. 109).

But how public must it be to be regarded as a right? What about disputes at the margin? Persons may share a basic covenant of self-limitation but differ over some specific interpretation of it. Also not all persons will agree to everything at a given moment, and then the immediate parties to dispute turn to their fellows for resolution (or they turn to war). Again there is some basic covenant or no one would agree to be bound by statements of rights created by others. At the disputed margin, property becomes what third parties (often reflected in the state) say it is. For example, A and B may sign a contract when B buys A's house that it will not be resold to blacks. If B later changes her mind, A will get no help from U.S. courts in enforcing the contract. Property ultimately is what the government says it is (Unger 1986). But this is not to say that government can decree anything to be property if there is no minimum degree of shared covenant among people. If there is no community, there is no property, but only the victors and the vanquished. Two persons can have rights between themselves, apart from government, to the extent that they mutually honor them. Locke was mistaken when he argued that "the great and chief end . . . of men's uniting into commonwealths, and putting themselves under government, is the preservation of their property" (Locke 1690, chap. 9, sec. 124). If there were no minimal community of agreement prior to instituting formal government, there would be no property.

PROPERTY, DISTRIBUTIVE JUSTICE, AND THE SENSE OF COMMUNITY

Can the study of public choice and group action assume the existence of the group? Where do bonds of community come from? Kenneth Boulding (1970) notes that "the theory of public goods cannot simply assume that there is a public. Why the publics are what they are is part of the problem, not part of the assumptions." One relevant hypothesis is that a community is usually defined either by a common problem or by the mutual advantage of joint action. For example, people located on a certain piece of geography may be subject to the attacks of mosquitoes. Will they band together to act to be rid of the common enemy? There are many examples of gains from joint action, such as combining the specialization of labor into a large firm. A closely related hypothesis assumes that property emerges (and changes) whenever it is profitable in the aggregate (Demsetz 1967; Schotter 1981; Schultz 1968). In this view, rights formation is subject to a type of benefit-cost analysis involving potential Pareto-improvement. When the value of certain goods increases, rights emerge. For example, as the value of human capital increases, there is a demand for new rights of workmen's accident compensation and the shifting of a worker's exposure to dangerous machines to the liability of the employer. This is examined further in Chapter 11.

Contractarian theories of constitution and rights formation postulate an equilibrium based on production functions for goods, theft, and policing

(Buchanan 1975; also see Rawls 1971). The neoinstitutional theory adds love, caring, forebearance, and concepts of distributive justice. As already noted, what constitutes theft is not a given, but a matter for social choice. A person cannot by his or her own assertion claim that another's action is theft when the other person claims it is rightful. Property can't be the outcome of efficient trades when it defines what it is that one has to trade. One gets something to trade not alone by one's own choices among production, protection, and theft but also by the forbearance of others. And that forbearance rests fundamentally on moral choices of divisional justice. The gains from trade are illusory if they violate the sense of fairness that makes any system of rights acceptable (Baumol 1982).

There is no doubt that geographic factors, technology, human propinquity, mutual advantage, and changing prices are factors in the formation of property rights. But, there are many examples of unfulfilled possibilities for mutual advantage (Heckathorn and Maser 1987). Of course, it is possible to say that when groups do not form and new rights do not emerge, it is because the gains did not exceed costs. This is a reason that can be applied after the fact, but it explains little. Why are the benefits and costs perceived as they are? Malevolence and concern for relative distributive shares plays a part in preventing group organization where everyone gains materially but where some feel worse if their neighbor gains absolutely or relatively. Empirical research indicates that people do act in accord with principles of distributional outcomes (Alves and Rossi 1978). Kenneth Boulding suggests that "a public requires some sort of organization, an organization implies community, a community implies some kind of clustering of the benevolence function . . . which denies the assumption of independent utilities" (1970).

It is beyond the scope of this book to explore fully the hypothesis that long-term maintenance of systems of peaceful bargaining, administrative, and status-grant transactions require a widespread, but not universal, antecedent bond or covenant, benevolence, and even love. Some level of a shared concept of distributive justice is required. Such transactions are not alone a product of interdependence, propinquity, potential for mutual benefit, or fear. Some brief examples are suggestive. Edward Banfield (1958) studied a village of southern Italy, and two facts were striking: the village was very poor, and it was almost totally lacking in any kind of local group action. There were practically no local associations of people. There was no chamber of commerce, no parent-teachers association, no farmers groups; even the church seemed unable to organize elementary charitable functions to care for orphans. Why? This is certainly a complex phenomenon, and simple answers are suspect. But there certainly would seem to have been no shortage of possibilities for mutual advantage. For example, the farmers were exposed to disastrous floods, but no common works of water control were attempted. Farmers were subject to the vagaries of ill health during the harvest season, but no mutual aid from neighbors was forthcoming. The people were peaceful and did not constantly steal from each other, but neither did they seem to acknowledge sufficient rights in each other to form expectations of mutual aid even in times of disaster.

Banfield found that the most common behavior seemed to be based on the following rule: "Maximize the material, short-run advantage of the nuclear family; assume that all others will do likewise" (p. 85). He conducted extensive interviews and psychological tests and found that people had little trust in or loyalty to anyone outside the immediate family. In the economist's language, there was little interdependence in utility functions. In fact, these people seemed models of the much-maligned and touted "economic man." All action was carefully calculated in terms of individual advantage. To act for another was not part of their thinking, and those who claimed to do so were regarded as suspect. Banfield compared the preferences, attitudes, and behavior patterns of these people to people in other areas who were capable of group action, and he noted significant differences.

Another example is from Alice Dewey's (1962) study of peasant marketing in Java. Trade was dominated by people of Chinese descent who were bound together by complex webs of extended families. The security of promises necessary for long-term and distant trade was not present in the customs and attitudes of the native population, and whatever commercial law existed was not effective. In this environment, the bonds of the Chinese made them the dominant merchant class. This is additional evidence of Kenneth Arrow's hypothesis that the efficacy of alternative modes of contracting depend on trust and integrity (1970, 1974).

A theory of ethical and ideological development is beyond the scope of this book. Banfield suggests that the independent utilities of the people he studied were related to a high death rate, certain land-tenure conditions, and the absence of the institution of the extended family. The experiences that affect human personality development are immensely complex. Economic development and human personality are both independent and dependent variables. Bargained, administrative, and grant transactions are reflective of existing human integration and also contribute to its creation and reinforcement. There are many sources from which we form and change our ideas of the legitimate rights of others and self-limits on ourselves. Boulding (1968) suggests the following: positive payoffs, negative payoffs, age, mystery, ritual, and alliances with other legitimacies. He also emphasizes the role of the grant as part of the process of building human integration.

It takes us too far afield to explore these sources, but the role of positive and negative payoffs needs comment. The basis for treating the other person as subject, rather than object to be manipulated in any possible manner, is one that is learned over a long time and in many diverse experiences inside and outside the marketplace. Persons who are consistently on the short end of what they consider to be unfair bargains or demeaning grants may eventually wonder why it is that they afford others the position of rightful owner. Combined with other factors, this continued bad experience may destroy the bond necessary for peaceful trade and lead to revolution or the hatred of submission to police and an unwilling participation in the economy. Such a person may have the outward appearance of belonging to the community, but such is not the state of his or her mind. Any employer who has dealt with a constantly surly employee knows that unwilling participation has its costs.

In sum, participation in the market is not itself a legitimation of the bonds that are necessary for its long-run sustenance. A person can trade without agreeing to the validity of the balance of rights brought to the trade. But, if this disequilibrium becomes widespread, peaceful transactions disappear.

It has been popular to believe that the wealth of nations could be built on greed; with a few simple rules, people would be productive without any care for their fellows. However, the unseen hand turns out to be some system of property rights that people carry around in their minds, and this system of rights is ultimately founded on some degree of benevolence and interdependent utilities. Greed, mutual advantage, and common problems are not enough, though their importance cannot be denied. An awareness of benevolence is not necessary in each transaction. But what is not seen in the marketplaces and parliaments of the world, or in paintings thereof, should not lead us to ignore intangible bonds.

It is not the purpose of this short chapter to be dogmatic about the role of the human personality and social integration in economic affairs. The evidence does seem strong enough to suggest those matters as subjects for serious study of joint interest among many disciplines. The economist has no particular comparative advantage, but the material here should suggest some of the bridges between the sciences. The economic domain seems both a derivative of and a causal factor in the human personality. Thus there is more involved than simply taking tastes as given in constructing a demand curve. Economists must be mindful that the policies in their domain potentially affect the very fabric upon which peaceful economic transactions take place. A sense of community, bonds, rights, and performance interact. If some of these interconnections are not tended, we may discover we have no domain left to study. We cannot study alternatives in the institutions of public choice if we have no publics.

CONTINUITY AND CHANGE

The purpose here is not to argue for any particular or existing expression of human bonds. To say that some degree of bond is necessary for peace is not to say that an existing set of rights is to be respected. When bonds collapse, it may be necessary to change rights to recreate a minimum degree of bond. None of the above should be interpreted as support for a conservative or revolutionary stance toward existing rights.

There is a deep philosophical and practical issue involved in the choice between continuity and change with respect to rights. Some stable set of expectations is necessary for good mental health and for any long-term investments. There is a definite practical case to be made for continuity. Continuity is in fact built into the U.S. system of law, in which precedent weighs heavily in all court decisions. (At least the appearance of precedent is maintained.) At the same time, a degree of change and variety also seems necessary to prevent boredom and stagnation. The world changes and people learn, and the two interact. In the face of these changes, existing rights are going to be challenged. It is indeed a civilized accomplishment of the highest order for a society to change rights and maintain willing participation.

THE NECESSITY OF PUBLIC CHOICE

From all of the competing and conflicting interests for resources, some choice has to be made. Some decision has to be made on who gets the resources and what is to be the character of the interdependent opportunity sets and subsequent transactions. The choice is not between government or no government, not between an understanding in people's minds or no understanding, and not between planning and no planning. Even no action is to choose the distribution and kind of rights.

Consider the court case of *Miller* v. *Schoene* (Samuels 1971; Schmid 1960). It was discovered in Virginia that an organism that depended on ornamental red cedar trees caused the death of apple trees. The respective "owners" of the two types of trees discovered an interdependence that neither was formerly aware of. Should they have fought to determine which trees perished? Evidently the bond (or possibly fear) was sufficient for the parties to respect the processes of the government of Virginia and the United States Supreme Court. The legislature passed a law that in effect gave the apple owners the right to a disease-free environment. In practice this meant the cedar trees had to be cut. This was executed by the actions of an administrator required to make certain findings. If the legislature had failed to act, the effective property right would have been that cedar trees may be grown without the apple growers' consent, whose only option then would have been to try to buy out the cedar owners' rights. It is not that the market would not have allocated resources but that the outcome would have been different. Without going into any detailed analysis, it seems a reasonable hypothesis that this decision had something to do with the supply of apples and their price as well as the distribution of income between the parties (and some third parties as well).

The property-right decision represents a planned increase in apple production as surely as any target set in a socialist country's five-year plan. Some writers regard this choice of rights by the legislature, backed by the courts, as a forceful intrusion of government when a voluntary option of trade was possible (Buchanan 1972; Buchanan and Samuels 1975). But regardless of ownership, trade is possible. The issue is who has to buy out whom. There is a market option in any case. Cedar owners can always offer a bid to apple owners to entice them to accept the disease. Who had the original right? It is not obvious that the vesting of this right in cedar or apple owners can be deduced from the Constitution or Magna Carta, though this fiction is often cultivated by courts. The issue never came up before, since the character of the ento-mological interdependence was not understood until recently. The court had to make a choice between conflicting interests. After that choice, voluntary market trade could proceed. Trade, however, is not an alternative to deciding who has rights, since trade presumes rights.

The individual cedar or apple owner is probably most aware of the state entomologist (administrator) who may issue a nonnegotiable order. But the process of rights allocation and definition may have itself been arrived at within a process of bargaining or one-way administration or perhaps a grant from some recognized sovereign. The legislature is subject to rules and property rights that control who has access to it and what is available to get the consent of its members. In other words, there are political rules for making economic rules. Thus we come to the constitutional level, which in a country like the United States or Italy is the most basic formal statement of property rights and rules for their change. People interact with each other for the purpose of setting rights governing control of goods and services. This interaction may involve bargaining within the rights and rules of access to government. Those who are always on the short end of the stick may feel that they have little bargaining power and are only the object of one-way negative transfers by others.

In this book, only passing reference will be made to this process of making rules, which is the focus of political science. Since the rights-making process also involves bargaining, administrative, and status-grant transactions, there are certain informative spillovers from one type of study to another. Still, for want of space and experience, this book will concentrate on how rights to goods and services affect the performance of the economy, rather than on how civil rights affect what economic rights get chosen. In passing, however, note must be made of the interdependence of civil and economic rights. Once again, we must not be distracted or deluded by arguments over whether to have plan-ning or not or whether there should be government action or not. The only issue is whose objectives will public choice implement.

INTERDEPENDENCE OF LAW AND ECONOMICS (GOVERNMENT AND MARKET)

If one has the power to get one's tastes taken into account and to participate in market decisions, one's power in the political process to get new rights allocations and definitions may be enhanced, and vice versa. In the case dis-cussed above, the income of the apple growers probably had something to do with an effective lobbying effort with the legislature and in helping elect fa-vorable judges. Market and political power are seldom equal, however. A par-ticular person may have more power via his or her vote than via his or her dollars, but the point to watch for is how one type of power enhances the other. Economic resources help shape the flow of information available to government decision makers and also provides campaign money to elected officials (Bartlett 1973).

The interdependence of economic and political power is noted only briefly here as background for impact models. In a book concerned with long-run institutional developmental theories explaining the emergence and pattern of particular property relations, this interdependence would be a central ingredient (see Frey 1978; Galbraith 1967; Hirschman 1984; Myrdal 1974; Perroux 1969). Also important would be the role of ideology in shaping what rights alternatives are considered (Solo 1967).

IMPLICATIONS FOR RIGHTS-IMPACT ANALYSIS

In general, the social perspective on property rights is more useful for developmental theories than for impact theories. However, it is one purpose of this chapter to develop further the dimensions of the three broad types of transaction systems conceptualized in Chapter 1. It is argued here that while all types of transactions reflect a degree of self-limitation and ethical judgment, they differ in degree. Modern market economics is a theory of advantage. To be sure, it involves a calculation of advantage always bounded to some degree by self-limitation and external limitation. But this theory does not illuminate status transaction where advantage is not calculated. Chapter 3 contains a discussion of some situations of interdependence where it would be very costly to apply any external sanctions. Therefore, if people are opportunistic and calculate advantage, it will be difficult to provide goods when external sanctions are costly to apply whether in market or administrative form. In this case, status transaction could have a special role. Empirical study of the impact of different decision-making systems (transactions) may sometimes require careful specification of the structural variables as to their social context.

NOTE

1. Institutions can be evaluated as instruments furthering commodity production or valued as instruments furthering human dignity. Mashaw (1985) suggests that legal due process is valued in part to recognize people as subjects rather than commodities to produce commodities.

II

Concepts for Property-Rights
Analysis: Varieties and
Degree of Interdependence

Three

Incompatible Use and Exclusion Costs

IMPACT THEORY COMPONENTS

Systematic research that can develop and test hypotheses relating alternative institutions to performance requires a theory. This theory or paradigm should suggest a logical connection between alternative property rights and the performance results of who gets what. The paradigm to be developed here has three major components: situation, structure, and performance (SSP). Situation includes attributes of individuals, the community, and goods. Relevant attributes of individuals include preferences, values, and ends in view; knowledge of the rules and production functions; and information processing and decision strategies. Community attributes include the number of decision makers and the degree to which individual characteristics are shared. These individual and community attributes are included below as needed in an ad hoc fashion and then brought together in Chapter 10 on psychology. The major situational classification used here is not individual attributes but, rather, goods attributes. It is these goods characteristics that determine how one person's actions can potentially affect the welfare of another person. Different inherent characteristics create different contexts of human interdependence and thus the same institution or right can result in a different performance when applied to goods having different characteristics.

Economic theory has given some attention to the characteristics of goods, but for the most part it has regarded goods as homogeneous. Graphics and equations describing production relationships are largely for some abstract good whose character is not deemed important. The shape of the production or cost function differs from product to product, but the theory is general and in fact is often illustrated for some make-believe good (such as a widget) or some equally abstract notion. All of the goods characteristics to be described in the following chapters will be familiar to economists, but they have not been systematically integrated into an institutional-impact theory. The characteristics include incompatible use, economies of scale, joint impacts, transactions costs, surpluses, and fluctuating supply and demand. It should be emphasized that these situational features are a matter of physics and biology and inherent in the good. While they may be variable with long-run technological change, this is a given in impact analysis.

The second part of the theory is referred to as the structure and is composed of institutional or rights alternatives. In contrast to inherent situational variables, the rights structure is a matter of human choice. Structure can be classified in various ways. Reference has already been made in Chapter 1 to three varieties of transactions. This is a useful typology for initial inquiry into the impact of institutional alternatives, but further specification will be suggested below and remains an underdeveloped component of the theory. Structural variables include the type of right and which party holds it. Kiser and Ostrom (1982, pp. 193–94) suggest the following typology: (1) boundary—the entry and exit conditions for participation; (2) scope—allowable actions and allowable outcomes from interaction; (3) the distribution of authority among positions; (4) the aggregation of joint decisions; (5) procedural rules linking decisions together; (6) information rules; and (7) sanctions and payoff rules. It is essential in applying the paradigm that the structural rights being analyzed are not used to define the character of the good. Remember that for the period of the analysis, situation is inherent while structure is chosen.

The third component of the theory developed here is performance. The specific measures chosen depend on the expressed interests of the competing groups. A measure that is emphasized here is that of income distribution. Choice of rights is the instrument of changed performance. So in a sense, performance is a function of alternative rights given the situation. The particular and intermediate performance variable induced by the incentive structure of rights may in time be an input into final consumer products and results. These subsequent results may be influenced by other variables, some of which are those of standard microeconomic theory. For example, an inquiry might be made into the performance outcome of a boycott under a certain set of rights. The performance variable for the institutional analysis might be the number of people who participate in the boycott or the changed sales of the boycotted firm. Further noninstitutional analysis using microtheory might inquire how the change in demand for the firm's product affects profits. Still further analysis might inquire whether the loss in profits will cause a change in the behavior of the firm that was objected to by the boycott participants.

The three components of the theory then are situation, structure, and performance, which may be referred to as SSP institutional-impact theory. Since the emphasis in this book is on demonstrating the importance of different goods characteristics and situations to institutional performance, the chapter titles of Part II refer to the different situations. When the basic situations are exposited in Part II and some applications demonstrated in the first chapter of Part III, Chapter 8 will contain a further elaboration and restatement of the paradigm.

The approach developed here is sufficiently novel that further introductory statements will be useful. Another way to express the theme of the book is to note that people can get in each other's hair. There are many ways for one person to affect another, and, even when interests are shared, people may fail to act to obtain mutual advantage. The chapters of Part II contain a discussion of a number of classes of interdependence in the production and consumption of goods and services; these classes will be used to analyze the relation of alternative property-rights definitions and structures to performance of the economy or subsets thereof. The role of property rights is to order the opportunities for one person to affect another and vice versa by influencing what both parties take into account in their decisions. Property rights disaggregate scarcity and apportion opportunities among conflicting parties. Rights influence who participates in resource-use decisions and thus who has power. If we are to predict the consequences of alternative opportunity sets and property rights, we must understand the specific variety of human interdependence raised by a particular good or service, that is, the situation.

The concepts of Part II will be familiar to economists, but their use for property-rights analysis is not conventional. When most people think of property rights, they think of ownership of resources (factors of production). They think of yearly income flows; bank accounts; and stock, bond, and real estate titles. The distribution of these are what economists have in mind in their partial-equilibrium analyses when they speak of holding income distribution constant in ceteris paribus as they explore the effect on price of a change in demand or supply. It will be demonstrated in Part II that the above specification of rights in income distribution is inadequate to control all of the ways in which people can affect each other. It is inadequate because the sources of interdependence are much more complex than those that are influenced by ownership of resources whose use by one person precludes use by another. The opportunities for one person to affect another are not completely contained in nominal ownership of the factors of production and the conditions of a competitive market.

Various physical and technological characteristics of goods affect interdependence. The same is true for some characteristics of people and the groups they comprise. Goods are frequently multidimensional, and it is often difficult to speak of the quantity of a named good.[1] For example, a given activity such as sheep raising produces more than one good—meat and wool. Further, a good has multiple attributes and the physical consumption of a good may be the source of several distinct satisfactions, possibly to different people (Lancaster 1966). For example, wool may keep A warm and also stylish and attractive. In addition to A's satisfaction, B may also derive satisfaction or dissatisfaction from observing A's coat. The word consumption can be misleading since goods seldom just disappear. Person A derives a service from a certain physical object, and the object is transformed and then possibly affects B. Another example is the pollution case. There is also a possible confusion over whether we are counting users, uses, or units of some physical object. We may describe the number of people that can hear a certain kind and size of loudspeaker, the number who enjoy it, the number who are offended by it, the utility as affected by distance from the speakers, the kind of material it carries, and the number of such speakers. Each product dimension may have different implications for human interdependence.

A common assumption in theories of public expenditure is that spending is for final goods and services (Burkhead and Miner 1971, p. 33). This assumption avoids problems of imputing the values of intermediate goods. But this avoidance has its problems, since one person's intermediate good can be another's final good.[2] For example, some people feel satisfaction only if they know the crime rate has dropped in their neighborhood (final good), while others are satisfied to see merely more policemen, which is an input or intermediate good. The conflict here is also clear if we acknowledge the interests of input suppliers. In this book, the goods chain may be cut into at any point of interest. The approach is eclectic, though hopefully precise, in the definition of the unit of a product or resource used to describe the situation or specify performance.

Some writers make a distinction between a literal physical consumption and a psychic consumption. A person derives satisfaction from eating an apple, talking with a friend, or simple observance of another's being comfortable in a warm coat or abstaining from alcohol. There are differences along this continuum, but all are rooted in the human psyche. There is the childhood saying, "Sticks and stones can break my bones, but names will never hurt me." Yet it seems that for some just the reverse is true; for some, names or some words can indeed hurt and even destroy a mind. Some persons have a greater tolerance for hunger (and indeed may choose to die) than for a painful social relationship. The misnomer *victimless crimes* is often applied to behavior that has no physical effect on another person, a conceptualization that ignores psychological interdependence. This book includes a wide range of human interdependence where the link between persons is physical (technological), psychological, pecuniary (market-price effect), or political.

The topic includes public choice of regulatory activity as well as the government budget. For example, government is used to prohibit the sale of certain drugs as well as to spend for public education. We need to see how property rights affect whose interests count when they conflict regardless of the source or the conflict. We also need to see how rights affect the realization of shared interests.

Applied analysis using this paradigm begins by asking what kind of good is at issue, that is, what is the inherent situational character of the good that causes people to be interdependent so that one person's actions affect another person. (The next several chapters provide a checklist of situational features.) The next step is to characterize the possible alternative rights structures available for public choice. Then a hypothesis is formed relating situation and structure to predict performance. Finally, the hypothesis can be tested by observing performance involving the same good but different structures across time and space. There can be variation within a situational category (for example, a range from low to high information cost) and this can affect the performance of a chosen structure.

Frequently the alternative rule for which we wish to predict performance impact has never been tried on the good being analyzed. The theory then helps select other experience to observe where the proposed rule (right) has been used on another good where the situation is functionally similar. This allows us to extend our previous institutional experience to warrant predictions in new cases. Note that the amount and distribution of the good named in the situation may be a performance variable. So we may begin by asking what kind of interdependence is created by a good such as land and then measure performance in terms of who uses and derives income from land. The major question of interest is, What performance is achieved by choosing a particular rights structure in a given situation?

In Part II, we will look for how different kinds and distributions of property rights affect substantive performance. We shall not be concerned until Chapter 11 with whether or not a particular rights set and performance may be termed optimal. In the classification to follow, terms such as *private goods* or *public goods* will be avoided so as not to bias the question of institutional choice from the beginning. Such language will only be used to cross-reference these classes to those common in the literature. It should be kept in mind that any given good may be characterized by one or several of the following features.

The best-known source of human interdependence is the distribution of ownership in incompatible-use goods described below. Yet, as this section will demonstrate, there are many more sources. Failure to appreciate all of the sources means that policies affecting income distribution will be imperfectly understood.

INCOMPATIBLE USES OR USERS

The most common way in which people can affect each other is when one person's use is the denial of use by another. If A eats a bushel of corn, it cannot be eaten by B. A good that has two or more physical uses and users that are incompatible is termed an *incompatible-use good*. It is in this sense that it was said in Chapter 1 that externalities are ubiquitous and not rare and freakish. B's hunger is an external effect and opportunity cost of A's consumption. Scarcity means conflict over control of resources, and recognition of ownership is sought after for that reason (though it is not the only reason). To have a right to an aspect or a resource is to be able to deny its use to another or possibly to extract a payment in exchange for your consent. A person who does not have the right to participate in resource-use decisions cannot create costs for others and consequently is without income or sustenance (except as a recipient of grants). The ownership of an incompatible-use good influences who can create costs for whom and thus the distribution of income. Ownership influences whose interests are realized and whose are forgone. It is the distribution of rights in incompatible-use goods that most people have in mind when they speak of a given distribution of income or property rights. At the end of this chapter, it will be clear that this definition of income distribution is much too narrow.

What is here defined as an incompatible-use good is often referred to in the literature as a private good. E. J. Mishan (1969, p. 330) says, "Each unit of a private good enters into some particular individual's utility function but not into those of any others." The conventional wisdom regards private goods as the antithesis of goods with externalities or interdependence. If more than one person wants an incompatible-use good, they are unavoidably interdependent. But this interdependence has been held to be a matter of political choice of income distribution and beyond economic science. The incompatible-use good is conventionally seen as being owned and priced in the market, and if a person could not pay the price and went hungry, this was not a matter for economics but for politics and morality.

The rights that allocate basic physical incompatibility are often taken for granted. Can we say that the consumption of a private good like corn creates no externalities while the production of steel, which pollutes the air or water, creates externalities?[3] At base, these both amount to incompatible uses when the common unit of the resource is identified. Both result in lost opportunities for others. In one set of words, we speak of two goods—steel and a by-product, smoke, which causes lung cancer. But, if we look at the resource air, it is simply not possible to use air for disposal of particulate matter and for healthful breathing at the same time. The same kind of problem occurs when two people cannot eat the same bushel of corn. Use by A simply means that use by B is forgone. There is no more reason to presume that the denial of B's hunger is a functionally different kind of interdependence than that involved in creation of B's cancer. One is no more or less an externality, side-effect, or spillover than the other. This is not to say that the preferred direction of the opportunity and exposure is the same for all people. (Readers familiar with the conventional literature should note that no separate major category of externalities is included in this chapter. In the conventional literature, externalities are treated as a rare case where the market fails. Here they are regarded as the common substance of most transactions including markets.) There is no logical presumption that one is more or less deserving of alteration by government than the other. Neither is there any presumption that economic analysis can prescribe policy for one or the other in terms of who owns or whether bargained or administrative transactions are necessary. Thus, the term *private good* is not used here, since it tends to suggest that certain goods should be exchanged in private markets.

While the issue of ownership of incompatible-use goods by A or B is a zero-sum game, there are aspects that are positive-sum games. The incentives involved in capturing the fruits of one's efforts and excluding others have something to do with the amount and direction of effort. Some of the empirical evidence is examined in Chapter 9. Failure to clarify ownership may mean a natural resource is destroyed or goes unused (though this latter result may appear to be a benefit to a naturalist). People often have a common interest in activity that enhances total wealth in whatever way they may agree to define it. For example, institutional economists have emphasized property rights as they affect the rate of technological development and application. A fundamental preoccupation in economics is with resource allocation (choice of product and input combination). People must have some incentive to do X rather than Y. This can be given by command and physical penalties, monetary gains and losses offered to and by resource owners, or custom.

The role of private property in allocating resources is subject to two qualifications. First, the private-property market approach can confuse common wealth with an individual's assets. A person can increase his or her own assets by enhancing their scarcity value via restrictive practices that create bargaining power. This effort increases a person's ratio of income to outgo at the expense of others. The more common interest is related to the ratio of output per man-hour, which enlarges supply by increasing human power over nature (Commons 1934, chap. 8; Thurow 1985, p. 161). Economists' traditional interest in competitive rules is an attempt to control bargaining power and channel effort to enhancement of output, but this is not enough.

Second, while people can be taught to respond to private-property incentives, such behavior is not the only way to organize productive effort. People can learn to work to the full extent of their abilities with no material rewards beyond what the average person receives or with the fear of being excluded from sustenance (Hostetler 1975; Kanovsky 1966). In a status system such as true communism, each person would be entitled to receive a share of goods according to some defined need and would learn to contribute according to some defined abilities.

EFFECTS OF ALTERNATIVE RIGHTS

The issue of use rights in incompatible-use goods is common to all types of transactions—bargaining, administrative, or status grant. All require a continuing fundamental public choice about whether A or B has access to an incompatible-use good when interests conflict. The general discussion of alternative types of transactions in Chapter 1 applies here. There is the further issue of exchange value in the case of bargained transactions. When describing rights in this case, the rules that determine the degree of competition are critical. These include antitrust legislation and tariffs that control interdependence with respect to bargaining power and the ability of an individual to affect price.

Ownership of land is a classic example of incompatible-use rights. In an agrarian economy, the effect on income distribution of having 75 percent of the land owned by 25 percent of the people is obvious. There are similar implications with stock and bond ownership and access to jobs, housing, and education. These rights are not further explored here, not because they lack importance but because they are relatively well understood and have been discussed extensively elsewhere.

One area that is an extension of classical monopoly, however, deserves comment: not monopolies by a single firm or brand, but a monopolization of the right to provide a basic good or service by a class of people (often a profession and often involving a mass-produced industrial tool). To distinguish this from the conventional type, Ivan Illich (1973, p. 55) refers to these as "radical monopolies." An example is provided by modern medicine. Only highly trained physicians are allowed to prescribe treatment and drugs. However, it is clear that lesser-trained nurses are capable of recognizing the symptoms of many common and curable health problems and prescribing the necessary drugs. The barefoot doctor system of the People's Republic of China is illegal in the United States. Entry of competitors is denied under the argument that service by a physician is superior. But, if there are not sufficient resources for all to have the so-called superior service on a round-the-clock basis, a lower level of care is better than nothing. Similar examples can be seen in education, home building, and burial of the dead. Not only do exclusionary practices create high prices but they prevent widespread self-help, mutual aid, and mass participation for people to determine their own needs rather than having them defined by select professionals.

In summary, the interdependence created by simple incompatible-use goods is largely controlled by public choice of factor ownership (both by private parties and ownership implicit in governmental regulation and administration) and, in the case of bargaining transactions, by rules affecting the degree of competition. This is not the case, however, when transaction costs are significant and there are substantial scale economies, as will be demonstrated below. These factors create additional varieties of interdependence that nominal factor ownership and competition do not address.

EXCLUSION COSTS

Exclusion cost refers to the cost of excluding unauthorized users of a good. A high-exclusion-cost (HEC) good is one where if the good exists for one user it is costly to exclude others. High exclusion cost means that use of an existing good cannot be limited to those who have contributed to its cost of production. Just because a person has the nominal right to exclude others from a resource or occupation unless they secure permission does not mean that that exclusion can be made effective.

Exclusion costs arise from two different sources. First, if the good is supplied (available) for A to use, it is inadvertently available for B, even if detection of B's use is cheap. Person B's claim that the good has no value cannot be tested by withdrawing supply from B independently from the supply available to A. Detection of use may be cheap, but detection of demand is costly. Examples are breathing air and national security. Second, if the good is supplied to A, it is available to B because of detection (policing) costs. Examples are ocean fishery and broadcast television. These detection costs are a type of information cost, and other aspects are discussed below in Chapter 6. In case one, if any of the good is supplied, B cannot be prohibited from using even if detected. In case two, if it were not for detection costs, A could be supplied independently of B.[4] Exclusion cost may exceed the value of the product.[5]

If the good is an incompatible-use good, high exclusion cost greatly expands the ability of one party to affect another. In the case of a natural resource, failure to exclude may lead to resource destruction. If there were a strong bond between people, A would limit himself with respect to B's interests whether or not B or the police are asleep or ineffective. Our attitudes toward rights are in part affected by the ease and symbolism of exclusion. A person who would never open the door of a neighbor's house to steal even if fear of police were absent may not feel it is theft to hunt on a farm or dig clams along a beach.

It is not simply material goods that have high exclusion costs. For example, a market price is available to all buyers and sellers. This is one of the free-entry characteristics of pure competition.

Free Rider

The character of interdependence created by high exclusion costs depends on whether one party is made aware of the effect action has on supply. With low exclusion costs, A knows she cannot get a good belonging to B without B's consent, which may require A to trade something to B. Or if A already owns and is considering investment to augment the future flow of services of the good (or remove a bad), the relationship between individual investment and future supply is clear and does not depend on the action of others (except of course not to interfere with A's use of the incompatible-use good). With exclusion, the acts of others are predictable. The connection between individual effort (bid or cost bearing) and obtaining the good is clearer in the case of a low-exclusion-cost good. This connection is not clear with high-exclusion-cost goods, where a person can use a good without contributing to its production or maintenance. The noncontributing user of a high-exclusion-cost good is called a *free rider*.

The individual finds herself in one of two positions depending on the size of the affected group. (For further discussion of group size, see Chapter 8.) If the size is large, the individual may reason that whatever she does cannot affect future supply. Knowledge of a common problem or advantages of joint action will not necessarily lead to the desired objective. An individual acting alone cannot be assured of having any effect. In the case of an ocean fishery, it is possible to imagine that although each fisherman would prefer to have the fishery maintained, all might act in such a way as to destroy it. This preference may be impossible to determine empirically, but its conception is important nevertheless. It warns us to be suspicious of an assertion, based on observation of individual behavior such as that leading to the destruction of a fishery, that no one wanted it otherwise.

If there are few individuals involved, they may engage in strategic bargaining. When there are few, the actions of one person are more obvious in their effect on others. It is clear that what one does can make a difference. If communication is possible, someone may suggest that each limit his fish catch to an equal amount of the self-sustaining yield. But it may occur to A to pretend that he has no interest in the future fishery, knowing that if others limit themselves, he cannot be excluded from the benefit. There may be strategic bargaining over their relative shares. If someone overdoes it and asks too much in terms of the limitation of others, no agreement will be reached. In effect, some people may be tempted to be a gambling free rider, willing to give up the possibility of sharing in a future fishery for the possibility of getting a lion's share. This can be distinguished from the unwitting free rider of the large-group situation. The former is consciously opportunistic; the latter is not. (From observation of noncontribution alone, the psychological frame of mind of the gambling free rider, the unwitting rider, and the person who does not intend to ride at all cannot be distinguished.)

One can imagine that face-to-face strategic bargaining may create the possibility of malevolence. If one is perceived as violating the spirit of fair play, there may occur a response of hatred rather than mere selfishness. A group with a common problem is unlikely to settle on a solution that would be perceived as superior to the existing situation by all if they are hateful and distrustful of one another.

Where exclusion costs are relatively high, A knows that his use is limited only by the total supply regardless of nominal ownership. The obverse of this is that the fruits of investment to the individual are limited by the acts of others. In the case of an ocean fishery, the resource has limited sustained yield, exclusion cost is high, and fishing enterprises are many. An individual party cannot affect future supply by acting alone to limit his catch. Future supply can only be assured if others also limit their catches. One person's welfare is a function of the acts of others. The individual who calculates his advantage will use the resource to the point where additional use adds more to cost than benefit. Others will do likewise. The aggregate result is that several of the fisheries of the world are near exhaustion, to the detriment of all fishermen. Where learned behavior in common is absent, those affected sometimes turn to government. In negotiations between maritime nations, there is a small-group situation. It is clear that the actions of one nation in limiting its fishermen does affect future supply. But strategic bargaining and mistrust make agreement difficult. Each nation may agree that a sustained fishery is better than none, but they may not agree on their relative shares of the total. The result may be the destruction that no one wants. Such are the dilemmas of interdependence created by high exclusion costs.

If the good in question is not a natural resource, the problem is essentially the same, though a bit more complex. If the good requires investment to bring it into being, we can again imagine that even where members of a group may be willing to share equally in its cost (in the sense that their utility is greater than their share of the cost) they may nevertheless fail to organize. A popular example in the literature is mosquito control (Tullock 1970, chap. 1). When a producer offers to produce the commodity, people in large groups may fail to volunteer their payment, reasoning that their contribution will make no difference anyway. Even people in small groups may get so involved in strategic bargaining hoping that others will pay and give them a free ride that no good will be produced.

This leads some to turn to governmental or administrative transactions. After some political decision process, government formulates a budget, purchases the good with compulsory taxes, and free riders are eliminated. Issues of relative benefit and tax incidence remain with different degrees of unwilling riders. Unwilling riders also occur with tax expenditures, whereby purchase of specified goods (such as donations to church and charity) is tax deductible. An *unwilling rider* is defined as someone who, in the situation of high exclusion cost and the structure of administration, must pay for something they do not want (willingness to pay is less than the price). The term should not be used as a general term for the losing party regardless of the source of interdependence.

There is more at stake than the question of who owns the factors of production and income. People are interdependent also because they care how their share compares with that of others. Some may not volunteer to buy goods they prefer because they think that they might get the good for nothing by hiding their demand or because they perceive that someone else's share of the cost is unfairly small or large; or they may refuse to participate because past transactions were regarded as unfair. In a sense, we are dealing with rights to the gains and advantages of cooperation as well as rights to factors and regular incomes. If A does not have the right to expect some self-limit by B, her action is different than when she does possess this right. In situations where these rights are rooted in learned, internalized custom, it does not occur to individuals to try to be free riders. If A does not impose a self-limit, it is unlikely that she will enjoy the benefit of a self-limit of others, and fisheries will be destroyed and floods uncontrolled. (There are important thresholds in the proportion of free riders. Such behavior is seldom stable. Free riders are soon seen for what they are, and those volunteering payment may come to regard themselves as "suckers.")

In the literature that addresses the "market-failure" conception, the existence of relatively high exclusion costs is listed as a cause of market failure.[6] Consumers may not reveal their preferences to producers. But, as we have just seen, the consequence is not an inevitable corollary of a physical feature but depends on the character of property rights. Where the images of property rights allow A to expect that B will limit his use and vice versa, we can expect A to limit his catch of the fishery to obtain a future flow or to contribute to the production of a new good even where exclusion is difficult. People in the United States give money to support a public television station even when they know they could not be excluded as long as the service exists. In the market-failure literature, this behavior is considered irrational. But it is not irrational if there is a community that shares a common expectation that each will give as he or she can or give some semblance of what each would bid if the good were exclusive. Whether the voluntary revelation of preferences through bids in a market is present or not depends not only on relative size of exclusion cost but also on the type of property rights present in people's minds. A market cannot reflect a right that is not present. This is not the fault of the form of the bargaining transaction but of the specific rights represented. A particular opportunity set may fail to reflect a given interest while giving weight to other interests. Changed performance may only require a redistribution of rights and not replacement of market with administrative transactions.

While market-like bids from individual members of large groups in the face of high exclusion costs are not unknown, they seem more common in small groups. Mancur Olson (1965, p. 24) suggests that this is so because the ratio of the benefit received by the individual relative to the total cost is greater in small groups. Olson's focus on individual benefit to total cost ratios misses the more general source of large groups' failures to achieve their purposes. The producer of the good could aggregate the fractional bids (reflecting individual benefits) to cover total cost if it were not for high exclusion cost. The problem that large groups have is not alone that each person's share of the benefits is small, but that markets may fail to aggregate the bids.

Broadcast television signals have a large total cost and conceivably a large total value to all possible recipients. But any one or a few recipients' benefit is likely to be small relative to the total benefit or, more important, to the total cost. In this situation, an individual is unlikely to go ahead and provide any of the good. And, because of high exclusion cost, the seller can not aggregate individual bids. Where the benefit to the individual is greater than the cost, however, an individual may provide some of the good rather than do without, even though others benefit at no cost to themselves. This can happen as long as this individual does not feel malevolence toward the free riders. A malevolent person would begrudge others any satisfaction, even when doing so would also hurt him- or herself, since the benefits to be gained exceed the total cost of the good. Again, the fact that the free riders can be identified in small groups makes an emotional response to others' behavior more likely. An unpleasant experience in the past may affect all future transactions. Historical knowledge may be necessary to predict performance.

The phenomena that Olson describes often lead to what might be termed the "exploitation" of the strong or rich by the weak or poor—for example, in such organizations as the United Nations or NATO, where the rich nations may pay much more than their share proportionate to population since they have more to lose if the organization fails. Where a few have benefits that exceed the total cost, they may provide the good even if others get a free ride. The rich sometimes pay for a good that others in the area cannot be excluded from rather than do without the good. The same is sometimes true when large central cities pay a disproportionate cost of regional projects or when the largest firms in an industry pay a disproportionate cost of a trade organization. But, if utilities are interdependent, a person whose individual benefits exceed production cost of at least some quantity of the good may not buy any because they are angry and want to teach the free riders a lesson.

The products of international cooperation are high-exclusion goods. Stability has often been provided by hegemonic leadership of powerful states. Robert Keohane (1984) argues that institutional regimes of rules and procedures can still maintain cooperation even in the absence of hegemony. He cites the examples of multilateralism, free capital flows, and payments unions.

Note that sampling and fear of being caught ameliorate intrinsic HEC with administrative transactions. The police and other monitors do not necessarily have to detect every possible free ride. The question becomes a behavioral one involving probability of being caught times the fine and the effect of risk aversion. The analyst may need specific behavioral data to estimate reaction to different combinations of probability and fines to deter free riders. This applies to things like enforcement of use rights protected by hunting or fishing licenses or prohibitions against additives in livestock feed or human food, against air and water pollution, or against income-tax evasion or speeding on highways.

Alternative Rights: Bargaining related to Decision-Unit Size

The existence of relatively high exclusion costs means that bargained transactions, where every person calculates individual advantages, may cause individual demand not to be revealed and aggregated. Certain market and political relationships, however, accommodate to exclusion costs. Such accommodation involves attempts to change the size or boundaries of private firms and governmental units. If the public spending projects of a central city inadvertently create external benefits to neighboring suburbs, the city may try to annex the surrounding territory. (Alternatively, if external costs are created, the state may force the city to annex, and thus the costs are internalized to the extent that the annexed citizens have a voice in the enlarged unit.) Rules for firm amalgamation or political annexation become important.

A private developer of new land for homes may note that she makes surrounding land more valuable for shopping and other commercial use but that there is no way to exclude surrounding land from this value. This situation may cause the developer to develop on a larger scale and to include all types of land use in an integrated project. An example is to contrast the original Disneyland in California, which includes only the amusement area, with the newer Disney World in Florida, which includes associated hotels for visitors. Another example is development of large, new, independent towns and cities by one private company as has happened in the United States or by public action as in other countries. Within the area of value influence, it is impossible to exclude individual owners unless, of course, there is only one owner. However, as a new town developer tries to assemble a large parcel of land, the original owners may try to bargain for some of the gains from the total development. The rules controlling the growth of firm size affect the realization of this type of attempt to accommodate to high exclusion cost.

Alternative Rights: From Private Associations to Government

An individual who wishes to acquire a good that has high costs of exclusion has several alternatives other than expanding firm size. One possibility discussed previously is to create new rights in mutual expectations. Where such action is not possible, people may try to organize private associations of various sorts. For example, every producer of an undifferentiated product in a competitive market knows that if prices rise as a result of advertising or supply restriction, each producer will share in the benefit whether he or she contributed to the cost of the rise or not. In the case of supply restriction, where a person or subgroup has no right to expect contributions from others, it does not pay to restrict supply in order to raise net profits. If supply is reduced enough to affect price, the others will benefit more because they produce the same quantity as before but enjoy the higher price. The history of supply-restriction efforts in agriculture is a good example. In the United States, the National Farmers Organization has urged its members to withhold supply. Even if the members have enough integration and bond to do this, it would benefit nonmembers even more. In this instance, consumers are the beneficiaries of the relatively high exclusion costs that prevent cartels and other supply-restricting organizations from forming. The lack of community and rights among farmers is part of the opportunity set of consumers. One group's collective failure is another group's success. Some groups are successful in developing conventions or a code of ethics that serve to control free riders and avoid prisoners' dilemma (Benham and Benham 1975; Runge 1984; Ullman-Margalit 1977).

Where private groups fail, farmers turn to government, which institutes marketing orders restricting sales of all farmers upon a majority vote (or requires that a percentage of sales be collected for advertising and promotion). Is the success of labor unions in raising wages an exception to the problems of exclusion? Labor is like agriculture in that if all its members withheld supply, the price would increase for all. But a laborer who cannot be sure of collective behavior may not agree to join a strike or pay union dues in the hope of being a free rider or reasoning that his dues will not make any difference anyway. The name of the national headquarters of one of the large U.S. unions is not Solidarity House by chance. Unions try to create a sense of community and a group consciousness so that in effect all (or a sufficient number) of workers will acknowledge each other's rights and contribute to the common cause even if the benefits are not exclusive to members. (The most successful early unions were organized on a craft basis, where the sense of solidarity and common interest and identity were the strongest.)

Where community is insufficient, union leaders may turn to government to establish administrative transactions. One possibility is legislation (property rights) that allows a majority vote of labor in a certain factory to create a union and bargain for a union shop. With this latter feature, after being hired a laborer must join the union. Where such rules are prohibited, the union may bargain for an agency shop where a new employee must pay an equivalent of the dues. Thus the free rider is eliminated. A certain degree of community is necessary to acquire the legislation (and the majority vote) but not the extent required to restrict supply without government help. The use of strong-arm tactics and violence was common in the early union movement to discourage free riders, who were regarded as "scabs" (really thieves) by the community of like-minded workers. Violence was also used by employers to prevent workers from voluntarily joining unions.

The rights of labor to organize and to bargain for the privilege of collecting dues from all workers in the plant (agency shop) are important property rights vis-à-vis employers and consumers.[7] The workers' collective freedom is the employers' exposure to increased bargaining power (and vice versa). It also constitutes an exposure of individual workers whose tastes differ from the ones dominant in the union but who must join or pay dues. The union shop can be seen as a laborer-employer rights relationship, but it is also the right of one laborer to avoid theft from another free-rider laborer. Theft is a value-laden word, and of course the free or reluctant rider would use a different term. Indeed, an equally emotional term, *right to work*, is used to describe the right of the free rider to stay free at the expense of others. Union shops are illegal in a number of states. As was noted in Chapter 1, freedom for A is a limit or restriction for B if interests conflict. Agency shops are not found in Italy, but union membership is nevertheless high.

Many well-funded organizations lobby the government for favorable subsidies and legislation. In many instances, any producer (or consumer) can benefit from governmental favor and none can be excluded. How do these groups succeed in the face of exclusion costs? Denton Morrison points out that many large groups are made up of small groups. For example, some national lobbying organizations are composed of local cells and chapters, where face-to-face contact and social pressure for participation are possible. Social pressure can create unwilling riders just as do taxes. There are many free riders, but the large national group does exist even though it produces only goods with high exclusion costs.

Another method is for the organization to produce multiple products—some with low and some with high exclusion costs. For example, the American Farm Bureau provides many services where farmers must pay or be excluded (such as feeds and insurance). However, to be eligible to do business with the organization and receive discounts and patronage dividends, farmers must pay dues to the organization, which can be used (along with profits) for lobbying, the benefits of which cannot be exclusive.

A similar illustration is the American Medical Association, which produces a medical journal that advertisers must pay to be included in. These revenues finance a large-scale lobbying effort whose benefits to physicians are nonexclusive. The right of a lobbying group also to run a market-oriented business is critical to accommodate the free-rider problem.

As noted above, a broadcast television signal is a high-exclusion-cost good. Such a product creates a large group of potential free riders. In many countries of the world, television is provided by government and paid for by general taxes, or taxes on television set sales, or annual fees related to the number of sets owned. Such systems reduce free riders. It is relatively easy to detect existence of television sets and to collect a fee. Failure to pay the fee voluntarily is defined as theft. In the Federal Republic of Germany, a fee is collected for every set, and the fee is used to finance programming. Inspectors effectively enforce the fee, and those who are discovered to have a set but have not paid their fee can be fined. While it is cheap to detect sets, it would be costly to detect which among several stations were being watched, and thus voluntary fees paid to different individual owners of broadcast signals are impractical. Most countries of Europe charge an annual fee for public television (*European Broadcasting Union Review* 1976).

In the United States, broadcast television is privately provided. While the signal is a high-exclusion-cost good, it is possible to finance the cost of program production by selling advertising, which is a low-exclusion-cost good. Viewers nominally ride free, but advertisers do not. The cost of producing television is included in the price of advertised products. A person who watches no television still pays for it when purchasing advertised products. Is this person any more or less an unwilling rider than the person in a country where public television is financed by general taxes but who watches no television (or only commercial television where available)? Abolition of free riders appears to be at the expense of unwilling riders.

In certain cases, advertising has high-exclusion-cost characteristics. Reference has already been made to the advertising designed to increase demand for an undifferentiated good like milk or beef. Potential free riders prevent farmers from contributing to advertising, which has led to support for government-enforced collections for industrywide promotion. More generally, the advertising of a good with complements creates high-exclusion-cost benefits for producers of the complementary goods. For example, the makers of peanut butter create demand for bread and jelly whenever they advertise. The manufacturers of a product create demand for the retail good whenever the brand is advertised. Thus a manufacturer retains the names of retailers in its advertising or offers the retailer an allowance whenever the brand name is mentioned in the retailer's advertising. It is in the manufacturer's interest to do so even if the retailer cannot be excluded and does not help pay. Sometimes the owners of the complementary products will contract for a joint effort (perhaps facilitated by an advertising agency), and sometimes transaction costs may prevent such cooperation. The previous distinction between large and small groups and the role of benevolence and sense of community apply here also.

Further institutional and situational variables affecting the provision of high-exclusion-cost goods are explored empirically in Chapter 12.

Common Property

The preceding discussion has been of exclusion costs that arise from certain inherent characteristics of goods. Occasionally, through political choice, low-exclusion-cost goods are treated as if exclusion were not possible among community members, though outsiders may be excluded. It is critical for application of the SSP paradigm that during the period of analysis the situation is inherent and given and not a function of the particular structure being analyzed. A policy of nonexclusion does not itself make a high-exclusion-cost good.

The term *common property* lacks precision but generally refers to a distribution of rights in resources in which members of the defined community are legal equals in their rights to use the resource. It implies unanimity in any change. People have use rights, but usually no exchange rights. Individual shares cannot be capitalized. Rights are not lost by nonuse nor can they benefit the holder if he leaves the community. Common property does not necessarily imply that all rights holders are equal with respect to quantity of resource use. The individual may use a certain proportion of the resource but not a particular physical unit (particularly relevant when the resource is physically indivisible).

Ownership in common of certain natural resources, such as land, has an ancient history (Ciriacy-Wantrup and Bishop 1975). Common lands were a feature of communal hunting societies and of medieval Europe for centuries, and some still survive (1.5 million acres in England and Wales). It is clear that with relatively minor cost, agricultural land can be fenced and people excluded. If we choose not to do so, we must anticipate some of the same kinds of interdependence associated with high-exclusion-cost goods. History reveals a number of results. In some instances, while exclusion was formally and nominally prohibited, there were nevertheless learned habits of limited use, preservation, and even investment (Hoskins and Stamp 1963, pp. 36–37, 50; Lee and DeVore 1968). These habits constituted rights for those who wished to have the land's productivity maintained. These were often as effective in preventing theft and destruction of the land as are individual private-property rights in land.

Hypothesis: The structure of common property without learned use limits is destructive of flow resources with critical maintenance thresholds.

If a good has a cost of production or maintenance (marginal cost not zero), a policy of no exclusion may result in excess demand and exhaustion of the resource. If the situation is mistakenly assumed to be high exclusion cost because of a policy of no exclusion, the analyst may not see that private property could prevent resource destruction. There was a period in the United States when some western grazing lands were in effect common property. Each rancher could take what he could get without limit. There was no sense of community, and each expected that if he did not take all the grass possible, the neighbor would, and there would be no tomorrow in any case. The only way to exclude others was to consume the resource. Severe erosion and loss of the resource resulted, as well as armed conflict (Webb 1931). However, the record is mixed. What is sometimes called "the tragedy of the commons" is not inevitable.

Hypothesis: Common property with high cost of dissolution can create incentives resulting in resolution of conflict rather than exit.

In U.S. property law, the concept of common ownership is somewhat less expansive than that discussed above. The common law "permits any party to a tenancy in common or joint tenancy to obtain a partition of the property into separate, individually owned parcels (Posner 1972b, p. 32). It thus seems to be a public policy not to encourage common owners to work things out among themselves to maintain the common enterprise. A father may have a strong preference that his two sons farm his land together after his death. Yet the law can make it cheap to dissolve the relationship. In some cases, it can be imagined that joint operation is more or less productive of marketable output than individual effort. But, in addition, one can imagine a society that would prefer the type of social relationships that are possible in joint rather than individual ownership.

A lazy joint tenant cannot be excluded from the benefits of the partner's work. Thus, some oppose property in common. In a market system, reliance is heavily placed on the fear of loss of income to maintain productive effort. In a partnership, threat of exit by one of the joint owners is an incentive for the other partners to perform. But, in a status system, effort is maintained by voice and social sanction rather than simply the fear of hunger. Where common property is preferred because of the human relationship involved, it is possible to exclude slackers from social approval even if policy does not allow or wish them to be excluded from material output.

Where the habits of a status system are not learned or have atrophied, there may be no way to achieve joint operation even when it could be materially productive. For example, some types of land reforms, such as in Mexico, have resulted in extremely small individual holdings called *minifundia*. These are too small to utilize much modern technology, and there may be no tradition whereby plowing could be done in common. Various countries of the world are experimenting with institutional arrangements to make small-holding agriculture productive. These include improved markets for custom hire, cooperatives, and communal and state farms (Dorner 1971; Raup 1975b). (These are explored empirically in Chapter 12.)

U.S. policy toward the common enterprise reflected in marriage differs from that with respect to joint tenancy, say, of land. In marriage, the tradition has been that unilateral action or even mutual consent could not dissolve it. The court had to find a serious breach of contract. There seemed to be a presumption that the partnership should be maintained and high cost for dissolution might cause the parties to try harder to work out their differences. Where exit is costly, voiced communications and persuasions are more likely. The law may have been influenced by public concern for third-party interdependencies, namely, the children. In practice, dissolution barriers were frequently lessened and unenforceable, and even nominal policy is changing toward making marriage dissolvable like any other joint tenancy. The performance consequences of the change are subject to debate and further research (Glass, Tiso, and Maguire 1970).

Opportunity and Coercion in Incompatible and High-Exclusion-Cost Goods

We are so used to thinking only of factor ownership when speaking of property rights that it may seem strange to view rights in high-exclusion-cost goods in the same light. There is a tendency to see factor ownership by private parties as the height of freedom, while the opportunity sets of individuals relative to high-exclusion-cost goods are seen as expressions of coercion. The interdependence created by incompatible use and high exclusion cost is controlled by rights. Both involve coercion of one party if the other is to have opportunity.

Labor seeking higher wages through unions or people who want mosquito control need government to help them exclude noncontributors from benefits. The custom of giving a union-negotiated wage to all employees is not a natural attribute of the situation, but for purposes of impact analysis, it is a given and not a result of the structural rule (union shop) being analyzed. Thus, application of the paradigm treats higher wages for all as having inherently high exclusion cost, in the same manner as mosquito control, which has by nature high exclusion cost. Since it is costly to exclude non-contributors if the good exists at all, one structural alternative is to make everyone a contributor and prevent free riders in that manner. Government allows unions to bargain for contracts that require workers who are nonmembers to pay union dues whether their tastes then go unmet or not. The same is true for thick-skinned mosquito tolerants who do not want to be taxed for mosquito control. This coercion is no less present for a holder of property rights in goods with relatively low exclusion costs, though the form is different. Just because a person can build a fence around a cornfield, we should be under no illusion that this fence alone creates property. Public choice creates property.

In the case of exclusive goods, B seeks A's permission for use and offers income to A, not because of the fence but because of the right. In the case of nonexcludable goods, B pays for the labor union or mosquito control even when she would like to get it for nothing or even does not want its effects, obviously not because of the ease of exclusion (no fence is possible) but because of A's right. Both involve coercion if interests differ. The cost of exclusion changes the character of human interdependence. Thus, for a given taste to count, the right that makes it effective takes a somewhat different form than when exclusion is cheap. The basic property rights issue in determining performance (who gets what) is the same for both cases. Whether A's interests are met or not is a function of A's rights relative to B. We are used to thinking that B must pay A if B wants to enjoy the product. But this is the same as saying that A's income derives from a right to prevent B's consumption without A's consent. If A is to have income, B cannot be a thief. The same is true for nonexcludable goods. If A is to enjoy them, B cannot be a thief and free rider and fail to contribute to the good's production costs. In both cases, A's welfare depends on rights that cause B to pay. And, in both cases, B would be better off if the rights were differently distributed.

Summary

A number of situations of relatively high exclusion cost have now been explored, from the ocean fishery, television signals, higher prices for farm products and labor, and air-pollution control to multinational security.

The interdependence created by high exclusion cost can be summarized as follows: Inherent HEC means there is an opportunity for free riders. The free-rider conception needs to distinguish the small- and large-group situation and the intentional, gambling free rider from the unconscious, unwitting free rider. People may ride free in either case, but the link between exclusion cost and behavior is affected by group size. In the large group, people may be aware that they are free riders, but they do not see how to avoid it because they cannot see how their action can be assured to affect supply when they cannot be sure others will act in concert. In the small group, they are intentional free riders. They know their action affects future supply and are trying to take advantage of the situation to get something for nothing. The uncertainty of the acts of others, however, creates a game-theoretic situation, and no one in the group may get anything.

Hypothesis: Where large groups of people are involved, high-exclusion-cost goods are maintained and produced only under certain conditions that can unhorse the free rider.

First, there is some bond or covenant among people that creates a convention or habitual expectation in people's minds so that each can count on the other to limit his activity or make monetary bids (contributions) reflecting his preferences even where exclusion is difficult (Collard 1981). Consumers do not bargain for individual gain but are related to each other in a variety of status transactions. Individuals reveal their demand because they have learned that it is expected behavior and individual advantage is not calculated. The federation of small groups is a device for achieving large-group action and obtaining the social reinforcement possible in small groups. Second, there exists some administrative transaction (or selective incentive) where would-be free riders are forced to make a contribution to the provision of the good. One alternative is the mixed-product case where a firm produces both exclusive and nonexclusive goods. If the firm is able to offer products at less cost to members than can competition, it can use membership fees or profit to support the production of nonexclusive goods. All members may not agree that surpluses should be used in this fashion. Another approach is to expand the size of the firm so that all components are related by administration. Still another approach is to obtain government help in requiring all those affected to contribute and become members of a collective. Or government can make a regulation or provide the good itself via taxation. Most of these rights, other than status transactions, that eliminate the free rider also create the unwilling rider. Anything other than a status transaction that gets rid of the free rider is likely to create an unwilling rider regardless of whether the transaction is public or private.

These involve a degree of coercion. This is just as true of so-called private organizations, such as labor unions, or governmentally enforced farm-marketing orders that control outputs as it is of direct governmental purchase of goods with taxes. Mancur Olson states, "Collective bargaining, war, and the basic governmental services are alike in that the 'benefits' of all three go to everyone in the relevant group, whether or not he has supported the union, served in the military, or paid the taxes. Compulsion is involved in all three, and has to be" (1965, p. 90).

Learned covenant and administrative transactions turn out to be functionally the same in terms of resulting property rights. In terms of the opportunity set of an individual who favors maintenance of the fishery, clean air, unions, and so on, the implications of the two conditions are that he or she possesses a property right that defines certain acts of others as theft when they affect his or her use or exchange values. There is either a learned definition built into the habits of people or some political process for creating new definitions that are made a matter of property right. People who do not contribute to producing the good are regarded as stealing the welfare of the rights holders, since they deny the existence of the good (or reduce its quantity) by being free riders as surely as taking someone's car is regarded as theft. Private property rights of the common sort define which incompatible user is owner and which thief. Another type of right defines whether people who want high-exclusion-cost goods are owners and free riders are thieves or whether unwilling riders who do not want the goods are protected from forced payment, which they might regard as thievery. The factor of exclusion costs creates a unique source of interdependence and thus the type of controlling right, but not the inescapable fact that when interests conflict, rights affect performance, including income distribution. When preferences differ, rights determine whether the interests of the voluntary contributor, free rider, or unwilling rider are to count.

Ownership of factors, such as land, controls interdependence arising from incompatible use but not interdependence arising from high exclusion cost. The latter is controlled by rights in such things as government taxation and spending, marketing orders to restrict supply, union shops, consolidating or expanding firm boundaries, education that increases group solidarity and integration, and selling low-exclusion-cost goods for profits to provide high-exclusion-cost goods. To understand income distribution, we need to know more than factor ownership and degree of competition.

NOTES

1. Economic theory is concerned with services that yield a flow of utilities. Frank Knight (1966) reminds us that the basic unit of economic analysis is "service not good." Yet service and utility are difficult to make concrete, and we often use diagrams and equations that refer to observable physical units of goods. James Buchanan (1968, p. 54) suggests that "the theory of public goods can be meaningfully discussed only when the units are defined as 'those which are jointly supplied' and when 'equal availability' and, less correctly, 'equal consumption' refer only to jointly-supplied production units or inputs, which may and normally will embody widely divergent final consumption units, measured by ordinary quality and quantity standards."

2. Albert Breton (1974, p. 17) defines "a policy objective as a variable which enters the utility function of the individual members of a government's jurisdiction, while a policy instrument is one which does not. Such a definition is useful but mostly in pointing out that members of society will often disagree on what is an objective and what is an instrument."

3. Mishan (1969) calls steel a private good with external effects or collective disservices. He distinguishes externalities from ordinary incompatibilities by whether the

effect is intentional. But he fails to convince that when A eats and B goes hungry it is any more or less intentional than when A makes smoke and B gets cancer. Mishan says an external effect "is always an unintentional product of some otherwise legitimate employment." But the assertion of legitimacy begs the question. Person A may have the right to use the air as he pleases, but B's cancer is legitimate just as her hunger is legitimate. We certainly need to distinguish the reduction in B's opportunity set by a thief as opposed to the reduction by A's lawful exercise of rights, but interdependence is a fact regardless of intent.

4. A builds a dam. It is cheap to exclude B from the electricity produced and more expensive to exclude B from boating on the surface of the reservoir. But if the "owner" does not build a dam and instead keeps the land wild for his own enjoyment, it will be costly to exclude a neighbor from the inadvertent view or use by a surreptitious hiker who may degrade it. Precise product definition is critical for empirical investigation.

5. The role of exclusion costs is always in relation to other costs and benefits. The issue is not the absolute size of these costs but their relative size, and this distinction is implied in all subsequent discussions even where not made explicit.

6. The market-failure convention can be turned on its head and regarded as "collective failure." Some group fails to achieve its objective (as against other groups) because it cannot prevent entry to the group's benefits, and thus ultimately the group is destroyed. Since one group's failure is another's success, this label is avoided in the text since the language of failure suggests that something must be done to correct it. To call something a failure is to express a value judgment. The fact that conventional wisdom regards exclusion costs as leading to market failure rather than collective failure (or competing-group success) says something about the role of ideology and selective perception in scientific analysis.

7. Mancur Olson (1965, p. 77) observes that the first major lasting increase in unionism on a national scale occurred between 1897 and 1904 and was correlated with successful bargaining for compulsory membership. Selig Perlman (1928), however, argues that the motivation was job security rather than a solution to the free-rider problem.

Four

Economies of Scale

The character of the cost functions of some goods can be a unique source of human interdependence. Many goods exhibit economies of scale where unit or average cost falls as more units are produced. Several sources of increasing returns must be noted. One is the fact of indivisibilities where a certain physical resource must be present if one is to produce at all. As that resource is spread over more units of output, cost falls. Second, there are certain facts of physics as illustrated by a pipeline of unit length. The maximum volume of material moved in the line per unit of time increase with the square of the diameter, while the cost of production is a linear function. Many sizes of pipe are possible (divisable), but there is a nonlinear relationship between costs and capacity. Third, there are dynamic economies of scale where people learn by doing. Not all advances in technology are a matter of lab science; some come from the experience of repeating a given operation. This is what business means when it speaks of getting out a new product and getting a jump on competition in movement along the "learning curve."

Two sources of scale economies need to be distinguished. The first is related to the long-run average cost curve as plant size is changed. For some products, the character of the technology changes with the size of the plant, which can produce at lower unit costs the larger the design capacity. The second source refers to conditions of a given-sized plant or indivisible input. Some goods require a large fixed investment whether one or many units are produced by the plant. This is a type of indivisibility. And, even when plant capacity can be adjusted in the long run, an existing plant may have economies of scale up to its design capacity.

As output increases, if average cost rises again before one firm equals the industry, a situation of ordinary economies of scale exists and produces the familiar convex U-shaped average cost curve for each firm. Each of the firms in the industry will grow to the point where average cost is at a minimum and new firms enter until demand and supply are equilibrated. But,this is not the case with superordinary economies of scale, which create further interdependence.

INTERDEPENDENT BUYERS

How do decreasing costs affect human interdependence? One implication is that the cost (price) to consumer A is a function of how many Bs share the same taste. (Interdependence among producers in the context of investment coordination is discussed in Chapter 6). This situation is affected by the distribution of tastes and the distribution of income among people with different tastes (Bator 1962, p. 119).

In the case of some products, economies of scale are relatively easily realized. But, in the case of others, there may not be enough people who want the good to take full advantage of economies of scale. It is to A's advantage if all of her neighbors buy the good, because unit costs fall as the number of users increase. A will want the right to try to influence B's tastes. But if B treasures his divergent and unique tastes, there is conflict.

Producers are aware of economies of scale and try through advertising to create a large number of people with common tastes. In the United States, private advertisers have the right to change people's tastes if they can.[1] The result is that advertising intrudes everywhere—on the roadsides, airwaves, and so on. People who object to visual pollution of billboards can claim either that they own that particular use of the roadside land or that they have the right to form their tastes independently of organized advertising. In the United States, there are severe limits on advertising for governmental goods and services, but not for market goods.

This case can be contrasted to educational behavior, where there are no scale economies. If the good exists, it is in A's interest for B to have no desire for the good. Wilderness hikers would be well advised not to tell their sit-at-home brethren how much fun it is in the great out-of-doors. The character of interdependence related to cost as a function of the number of physical units produced (or the number of people using it) has a lot to do with advertising and other educational efforts.

To conclude, one person's real income is influenced by the effective preferences of others, which affect where the producer is on the cost curve and thus product price. A's income is affected by rights that influence both the tastes and income of others.

With economies of scale, there is a motivation to create large national markets. The implications can be illustrated by a bit of history. Europe has been marked by variations in food, clothing, and housing products from one locality or river valley to another. In the time of small-scale craftsmen, this variation did not affect costs. With the type of production associated with the industrial revolution, economies of scale were such that production of many variations in a basic product became very expensive compared to large-scale production of a homogeneous product. Producers wished to expand their scale and sought access to wider markets. Thus large public investments in roads were required. Widely divergent tastes had to go. Mass production requires consumers with homogeneous tastes. Some regard this as progress and others as loss of human individuality (Illich 1973, p. 41; Lancaster 1979).

There are contrasts between Europe and the United States regarding the homogeneity of food products and tastes. There are large-scale national and international manufacturers in Europe, but there are still significant regional variations in basic food ingredients and thus more small-scale producers and sometimes higher unit costs. In the United States, almost everyone consumes Gallo wine and Kraft cheese whether they live in the North or in the South. The food may cost less per unit than some produced by smaller-scale European producers, but interregional travel in search of food variety is far less interesting in the United States than in Europe. In the face of economies of scale, variety has its costs. It is quite a different matter to have unique taste in a world where others also have unique tastes and quite different still to have the same tastes as the majority and be able to enjoy the lowest possible unit costs. The fulfillment of tastes is affected by who shares your taste.

In order to achieve large markets, barriers to trade must be limited. One of the most basic property rights in U.S. business is the evolutionary interpretation of the commerce clause of the Constitution (Commons 1924; Swisher 1954). Early tests of this clause made possible the extension of national markets at the expense of local interests. In the early years of the United States, it was common for the states to regulate commerce within their borders. A grant of monopolies within the state encouraged a certain type of development. One such example was the grant of a 20-year monopoly to navigate the waters of New York State if a steamboat could be invented. Robert Fulton took advantage of this in 1807, but the statute was later voided by the United States Supreme Court (*Ogden* v. *Saunders*). A national market with large-scale factories cannot be developed if states can grant monopolies in their area.

Another important case involved the right of a state to franchise and regulate a ferry crossing between New York and New Jersey (*Gibbons* v.*Ogden,* 22 U.S. 1, 1824). Interstate barriers to trade were probably also sought by the local cheese manufacturer, who feared loss of market and livelihood. Perhaps the person who enjoyed local cheese did not want a national brand taking consumers away and, because of economies of scale, raising the price of the local cheese while the price of the national cheese declined. The determination of property rights at this juncture had a lot to do with the future character of the U.S. economy. (The United States may not have had a five-year economic plan as is common today in many socialist countries, but its choice of property rights did constitute a choice of the major paths of development, investment, and resource allocations. The courts constituted an economic planning function.) The courts found in favor of the national merchants and manufacturers. The local businessmen were exposed to the competition of outsiders, and the person who prized variety and had unique tastes lost his local cheese. But the person who was not fussy got a lower price per unit. This conflict is settled in different ways in different countries. Centrally planned economies may choose to have less product variety in exchange for lower per-unit cost.

The first half of the nineteenth century in the United States is often characterized as one of government inactivity, but in fact there was direct federal involvement in canal building (Goodrich 1968) and there were other measures undertaken to secure a national market in spite of local opposition. The courts, in striking down barriers to interstate commerce, gave some firms income as surely as if the government had given them a tax subsidy or a tariff benefit (which in some cases it also did). It is not enough to own the factors of production if you do not have access to the market. So the issue is much more than who owns the acre of land or the bushel of corn. The issue is who can enter a market, who is exposed to competition, who is exposed to having his or her tastes modified, who is exposed to having consumer prices rise as others shift consumption to goods with economies of scale. The value of factors of production and the price per unit of any output as well as product variety are at stake.

The realization of economies of scale is much more than the negative removal of barriers to trade. It involves facilitating institutions. Large-scale firms required aggregation of capital from many sources and their corporation laws providing limited liability are essential (Hurst 1956). Even small firms can capture economies of scale by such things as joint buying, as in the case of federated grocery stores, each independently owned but sharing a common brand with economies of scale. The same principle applies to agricultural production where small farmers belong to a machinery cooperative. Small cities can buy services from a large city or private supplies to achieve scale economies (Warren 1966).

As firms grow to take advantage of economies of scale, human relationships change. A community of farmers who are owner-operators is socially different from one made up of a few large owners and tenants or hired labor (McWilliams 1945). A community of individual proprietors and shopkeepers is different from one of absentee owners, large department stores, and firms with many employees. Large-scale production is associated with depersonalization and alienation. In U.S. agriculture, these factors have led some states to pass laws banning corporate farms (Cook 1976; Raup 1975a).

The points made here about interdependent buyers can also be applied to interdependent producers. When one farmer adopts new technology suitable for large scale, others must adopt or go bankrupt as prices decline.

To summarize thus far, economies of scale create interdependencies where A's options are affected by B's choices. With economies of scale, unit cost is affected by the number who share a given taste. A persons's tastes are well served if they are shared by millions. This interdependence can be termed a variety of mob rule (Scitovsky 1976, pp. 9–11). The right to exit, the right not to use a product, may create higher costs for those consumers who remain. Contrary to conventional wisdom, markets involve a type of compulsion. Many buyers and sellers do not alone protect a consumer against the pressures of conformity, an unwanted change in unit price and product variety, or changed social arrangements accompanying large-scale firms. Rights in addition to those implicit in factor ownership and competition control whose interests count in the face of interdependencies created by economies of scale.

CUMULATIVE CAUSATION AND ECONOMIC DEVELOPMENT

In the context of economies of scale, there is no equilibrium of price and outputs (Kaldor 1972). As output increases there is a reorganization of production activities and there is an opportunity for further change that would not have otherwise existed. It will be more important to achieve economies of scale than to allocate resources optimally for a given level of output. There can be no sharp distinction between resource creation and allocation. The extent of the market depends on the division of labor, which in turn depends on the extent of the market. The capital-to-labor ratio is a function of the extent of market and not just of relative factor prices.

When industry increases supply and costs fall, it induces increased demand, and this increase in demand induces further cost-reducing increases in supply. As Kaldor (1972, p. 1247) puts it, "The pre-condition of cumulative change is that the rise in production of any one commodity a, should be associated with an increase in demand for all other commodities." One of the links is that an increase in supply of one output increases the value of stocks of inputs. The realization of economies of scale then becomes a key ingredient to economic development and is central to what Gunnar Mydral (1957) called the "principle of circular and cumulative causation."

EFFECTS OF PRICING RULES

The right of a seller to choose a pricing scheme is an important determinant of performance and income distribution. The value of one's nominal income depends on the prices one faces. Specialization to achieve economies of scale means that consumers are exposed to potential market power of large firms.

Antitrust laws and the maintenance of competition are important structural rights emphasized in microeconomic theory. Consumers differ in their willingness to pay for a given good. Some would pay more than they actually pay in the market for a good, and this difference is called consumer surplus. The producer of the given good would like to capture some of this surplus if possible and charge different classes of customers different prices. This is only feasible when the classes can be cheaply differentiated and arbitrage prevented. But, even where this is possible, it is prevented by the rules of pure competition. If one producer tried to charge a higher-than-customary price to a group that highly prized a commodity, the group would quickly turn to a competitor, and if price were lowered, losses would ensue if marginal cost is constant or increasing. The right to be free of price discrimination is obtained by competition.

Firms with reserve resources may try to lower prices in one market to increase their market share and drive out competitors. Losses are recouped in another market or in the future when monopoly pricing can be used. Firms harmed by this practice have sought remedial legislation, such as the 1914 Clayton Act. If price differences affect competition, these differences could only be related to the cost of supplying different customers. A big buyer could be charged a lower price only if the costs of supply were less to that buyer (that is, economies of scale).

In the above cases, firms would like to capture consumer surplus by selectively raising the going price or would try to increase their market share by selectively lowering prices to drive out competitors. Such strategies are prevented by enforcing competitive rules. But, in another case to be described below, a firm may selectively lower prices to entice purchases by the formerly extramarginal customer or to increase its market share. Competitors will follow the innovator. (The extramarginal customer is the person who formerly did not purchase, but does so when the price changes by a small increment). Competition here does not prevent price discrimination but rather increases its widespread practice. In fact it can lead to destructive price wars. Rules other than pure competition affect the resolution of conflicts over pricing practices in this case.

Any firm with a certain capacity and high fixed costs will have an incentive to differentiate its market and charge different prices to different groups of consumers in order to expand use up to capacity. For example, the total cost of operating an airplane of a given seating capacity is not greatly affected by the number of seats actually filled. Most of the cost is fixed and does not vary with occupancy. Marginal costs are less than average costs up to capacity. After selling all the seats possible at the regular price, this cost relationship causes airlines to search for ways to fill their planes. One device used in the United States was the stand-by youth fare at a reduced rate. (The French nationally owned trains offer a special family vacation rate. The hovercraft between Calais, France and Ramsgate, United Kingdom in 1975 offered reduced rates to people less than 18 years old and students up to 26 years old.) A person under 18 could fly for less than the regular fare if willing to accept a seat if available at the last minute before take-off. It is in the interest of the airline to differentiate in such a way as not to reduce the number of tickets sold at the regular price. Such differentiation is never totally possible, and some rich youths have flown for less than they would have been willing to pay. It is also possible, of course, that a rich youth benefits while a poor adult who needs to see a dying relative pays the full fare.

The possibilities for discrimination are many when capacity is limited and not everyone who wants to buy at the lower marginal cost can be accommodated. Why just youth? Why not old people? The right to differentiate is an important producer of income to the airline. It is an exposure to those who do not qualify. It is not enough to say that a marginal cost-pricing rule leads to efficient utilization of idle capacity. The next issue is who qualifies as the marginal user. The Clayton Act expressly forbids price discrimination, but only if such discrimination serves to lessen competition or create monopoly. Thus, as long as other competitors do it, discrimination on its face is acceptable, and theaters, airlines, and hotels are free to discriminate among groups of people. Our obsession with the form of competition rather than the substance of performance is nowhere better demonstrated. The law does not ensure equal treatment of consumers.

The right to be treated equally always has to be defined in terms of the characteristics of the class to be treated equally. This definition is not likely to agree with everyone's notion of fairness. The right for equal treatment conflicts with the right of producers to maximize revenues and the right of certain consumers who are benefited in the process by being declared the marginal consumer. There is hardly any good that is equally treasured by all consumers. Any producer stands to gain if he can charge a different price to high demanders than he does to low demanders. He gains regardless of the cost function, but the practice is especially tempting if costs are falling, when it can be practical even in competitive industries. No producer can afford to lower the price to intramarginal customers, but all firms striving for profit will seek extra customers by lowering the price to extramarginal buyers. Competition prevents one firm from raising price, but it ensures others will follow if price is lowered to one group.

Where marginal costs are falling, every consumer wants to be the last one on the plane or into the theater or hotel and to pay only the marginal cost while the intramarginal consumers pay the fixed costs among themselves. But it is the system of property rights that determines who is the lucky marginal consumer. From a profit standpoint, the producer may be indifferent toward young and old, black and white, and will choose among them on the basis of administrative convenience. But if the producer accommodates another of his tastes (we often call them prejudices), the situation is ripe for discrimination.

The same questions arise whether we are speaking of private or socialist firms. Where fees are charged by government-owned firms there exists the opportunity for price differentiation. For example, a city-owned bus line may have reduced fares for senior citizens (that is, it charges only the marginal costs). Such reductions are valuable property rights to some and constitute obligations to the other consumers who pay the fixed costs. The same question might be investigated with respect to pricing by private and public electric utilities.

It may appear to be a dog-in-the-manger attitude for the intramarginal consumer to begrudge not the free ride but the reduced-cost ride of the marginal consumer. The reduced-cost rider is no skin off the intramarginal consumer's nose. The latter does not pay any more when the plane goes off full or half full, so why not allow the marginal reduced-cost rider to benefit as long as he is willing to cover the marginal cost? But, in the reality of human relationships, people cannot escape their notions of what constitutes fair play and interdependent utility functions (Zajac 1978).

It is hard for some to feel sympathy for the professor or minister who gets reduced weekend rates at major U.S. hotel chains. It is hard to feel sympathy for the rich senior citizen who rides cheaply on the bus while a poor, young adult pays full fare. The private airline or public bus agency may agree that the discrimination ought to be on the actual basis of income rather than age, but this gets us back to an aspect of exclusion cost. It is costly to check income tax records when a passenger boards, but it is easy to estimate age roughly. And, of course, all may not agree on the basis for the discrimination even if it is cheap to administer. People are not indifferent to who is declared the marginal consumer and at that point asked only to pay for the extra resources necessary for their ride. The existence of economies of scale raises new ways that the choices of A can affect the opportunity set of B, and some of these ways are not controlled by rights in competition. Most people would make the moral judgement that no one should forceably be required to buy a product with economies of scale just so other buyers could have lower prices. But, it is a tougher issue to decide how to share fixed costs among those whose willingness to pay (marginal utility) is greater than marginal cost.

SUPERORDINARY ECONOMIES OF SCALE AND REGULATORY PRICING

Whatever the source of the scale economy, if the output of the plant with the lowest cost per unit output is equal to the size of the industry, the plant will be said to have superordinary economies of scale. Examples of this sort are found in the supply of water, natural gas, and electricity systems (for background discussion see Bator 1962, pp. 91–97). Electrical generation is, however, becoming increasing cost to scale.

Whereas we find many farms each producing at minimal average cost, we usually find only one electric utility supplying a given piece of geography. (Only a few cities in the United States offer customers a choice between two totally independent utilities. One example is Bessemer, Michigan.) These goods often have relatively low exclusion costs. People have to make market bids if they want the good. Thus, a demand schedule emerges, but costs keep falling beyond the point where average cost equals average revenue. These relationships are shown in Figure 1. The cost curve may eventually become U-shaped, but over the relevant range, it declines. Such a good is characterized as having technical nonconvexities, or increasing returns.

If average cost is still falling when the entire market is served, the viability of competition as a regulator of bargaining power is questionable.[2] To insist on many firms would mean that each would produce at a higher cost than the single plant and delivery system. But a single firm would be in a position to extract monopoly profits, as shown in Figure 1, at output X_1. If consumers want to achieve the benefits of supereconomies of scale without monopoly prices, some administrative system of regulation is necessary.[3] The right of consumers to prices related to designated costs of production cannot be implemented by the rules of pure competition but rather requires an administrative transaction.

The administrative transaction need not be price setting. It is possible to

Figure 1
Decreasing Cost to Scale

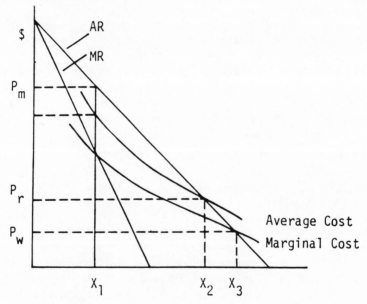

Physical Units of Output

have competition for the field rather than competition within the field. A public authority can specify the amount and quality of product and accept bids from firms competing for the right to supply the product. The contract is awarded to the firm that offers the product to the consumer for the lowest price. Franchise bidding was used in Paris for natural gas in the 1850s (Crain and Ekelund 1976). For a critique of this alternative, see Trebing (1976.) If there is uncertainty and immobile assets, franchise bidding may not avoid the necessity for an administrative agency (Williamson 1985, chap. 13).

An example of a decreasing cost service is garbage collection. Some cities have accepted bids contracted with a private hauler while others have their own employees. An empirical study (Savas 1977) found that when cities contract with private firms competing for the field, costs per unit hauled are lower than when its own agency does the work. Those cities that provide no service and let individuals arrange for their own have the highest costs, since several private firms serve the same area and lose economies of scale.

The interdependence created by superordinary economies of scale is not easily settled. The choice of institutions is not just a matter of minimizing transaction costs but of giving effect to the preferences of different people who have differential power to affect outcomes under public provision, regulated private monopoly, or franchise bidding. Most consumers would agree they do not want monopoly pricing, but will they be able to agree on another type of pricing? With ordinary convex (U-shaped) cost curves, an output can be found where the firm is operating at the lowest point on its average cost curve and price is equal to marginal cost. The firm earns normal returns, and average costs equal average revenues. The marginal consumer pays just what it costs to produce an additional unit of output. Each intramarginal consumer pays the same. This equality is an important property right to some people. However, with nonconvex (falling) cost curves, these relationships are altered.

The reputed objective of state public-utility regulatory commissions is to expand production to the point where average cost equals average revenue and monopoly profits are earned (output X_2 on Figure 1). But, at this point, it would be possible to increase output such that the additional customer would still be willing to pay the marginal cost of an additional unit of output. This situation would persist up to output X_3, where price equals marginal cost. In welfare theory, this is regarded as the optimum output that maximizes welfare (for the logic of this concept see any text on economic principles). This output is such, however, that average cost exceeds average revenues, and the firm would exit unless a subsidy were provided. (If a subsidy is provided, consumers are encouraged to substitute services produced under decreasing cost for services produced under increasing cost even when the former has higher total cost.) If these additional consumers are to have the right to increased output as long as they are willing to pay marginal cost, then someone else is going to be exposed to a higher price (or tax) to get the system paid for. Depending on transactions costs, it may be feasible to charge different prices to different consumers,[4] a practice sometimes referred to as a two-part tariff. Some may be charged a higher price so that others can pay a price equal to marginal cost. This procedure is not likely to be warmly embraced by all.

Continuing from Figure 1, it would be possible to achieve output X_3 and price P_w by charging a tax on some consumers and using this to subsidize production. This tax would not be neutral in its effect on consumption. The effective price facing some consumers would be more than the marginal cost, which will cause them to shift to other products. The resulting loss in consumer surplus is referred to in the literature as an *excess burden* or *deadweight loss*—terms that are hardly value neutral. A lump-sum or head tax does not directly affect relative product prices and quantity demanded, but it does indirectly if the tax affects real incomes and the products differ in their income elasticity of demand. In addition, such a tax may affect the income-versus-leisure decision. Whatever is done affects the distribution of income and welfare.

The discussion has gone far enough to indicate that pricing under economies of scale is fraught with interpersonal conflicts whether a single monopoly price, a single regulated price, taxes, or differential prices are used.[5] There is a conflict between the right of the marginal consumer to obtain the product if he or she is willing to pay marginal cost and the right of other consumers to all pay the same price for the good. This conflict is not addressed by property rights and income distribution measured in dollars or ownership of factors of production, since the welfare significance of a unit of money depends on prices.

The effects of economies of scale on human interdependence can now be summarized as follows:

1. The cost facing one buyer depends on the number of people with similar tastes. The right of one consumer to alter his or her purchases affects the welfare of other consumers. Rights affecting the ability to shape the tastes of others and the ability to form large national and international markets affect a given person's real income. Variety is costly. Some are willing to pay for it and others are not.

2. Competitive firms with economies of scale in a fixed plant will attempt to differentiate their market and to charge one price to regular customers and a lower price to attract new customers. Price differentiation affects relative welfare of different groups as surely as any tax or subsidy. Here, enforcement of competition does not settle the price-differentiation conflict.

3. Since there is no competitive equilibrium with economies of scale (Baumol 1979; Bittlingmayer 1982), some collective action is necessary to avoid instability and suicidal price wars. This can range from horizontal mergers and trade-association practices dividing markets geographically to government regulations. Stability of private orderings depends on whether firms can agree on equitable shares among themselves, and public approval depends in part on whether consumers agree to an equitable price structure among classes of consumers.

4. Where economies of scale are not reached until there is only one firm in the

industry (or service area), governmental regulation can be used to prevent monopoly pricing. The choice-of-pricing rule under regulation affects income distribution. Just putting an activity in the public sector or subject to public regulation does not solve conflicts within the public.

5. The discussion has been largely in terms of the classical examples of superordinary economies of scale, such as natural gas, water, and electric utilities. However, there is no neat boundary to the continuum of decreasing-cost activities. For example, what can be said about the existence of four gas stations on a corner with apparent unused capacity? It is not possible for the analyst to draw a line and say that there is a social benefit to a single supplier or several. It all depends on whose interests are to count. Some people may derive benefits from a capacity that is regarded by others as wasteful duplication (DeVany 1975). Some are not willing to make the trade-off between avoidance of monopoly prices (or high service costs) and what they view as the evils of regulation and consolidation.

6. Large scale requires capital contributions from many otherwise unrelated people. Corporations with limited liability and credit laws are important in this context.

7. Economies of scale depend on the rules defining relevant input and output. Large-scale firms often use resources (impact the environment and cause human alienation) not used by the small. Whether they then are more efficient depends on whether these effects are considered costs.

Economies of scale create a human interdependence that is not controlled simply by ownership of factors of production. To advocate competition is not simply to favor consumers over would-be monopolists but to favor the interests of one group of consumers (or producers) over another. And, of course, public regulation does the same thing.

NOTES

1. The effect of advertising on preference change is more a matter of institutional-change analysis than impact analysis.

2. This situation is sometimes called a "natural monopoly" (Sharkey 1982). This term is avoided here because of its value-laden connotations. Competition as a regulator of product quality is also absent. In the case of utilities like electricity, the achievement of economies of scale means that the consumer is stuck with only one firm's notion of product quality and service. This situation may not be serious for a good like electricity, which does not come in very many varieties, but it can still be a source of conflict of tastes with respect to utility service practices. Whose tastes count is determined by the regulatory agency (Caves and Roberts 1975).

3. Some of the experience with regulation is reviewed in Chapter 12. Some commentators are not willing to make the trade-off between avoidance of monopoly prices and what they view as the evils of regulation. "In my opinion, the best of a bad lot is unregulated private monopoly" (Friedman 1975, p.15). Also see Stigler (1975).

4. The exposure of consumers with high elasticities of demand to differentiated pricing depends on the transaction costs of obtaining information as to individual or group demand schedules and the costs of policing against arbitrage (reselling by one buyer to

another). A firm faced with a situation of high policing costs may seek to integrate vertically with firms providing the arbitrage function. Thus those who would be free of price differentiation could seek laws directly prohibiting it or prohibiting vertical integration and other attempts by firms to lower transaction costs.

5. The matter was and remains a subject for debate in the profession. For background see Coase (1946) and Lerner (1944, pp. 179–80).

Five

Joint-Impact Goods

Another source of interdependence arises from a situation that will be termed *joint-impact goods* (JIG). Some goods can enter two or more persons' utility irreducibly.[1] The term *irreducible* emphasizes that the good is described in physical terms. These goods are used but not consumed. Thus, A can utilize the good without subtracting from the quantity of the good available for B. In terms of the cost function, this relationship can be stated as follows: The marginal cost of another user is zero over some range (MC = 0).[2] This is the polar extreme of economies of scale, where marginal cost declines and is less than average cost but not zero. Note that the cost function is expressed in number of users and not units of the good. The relationship must exist for two or more people, but it need not apply to an infinite number of people. Interdependence arises over pricing policy. Who pays fixed cost and who pays only marginal cost?

The MC = 0 characteristic may be combined with several other characteristics of goods and people that create different varieties of interdependence. These other characteristics are cost of avoidance, preemption exclusion cost, and degree of jointness. These will be briefly introduced below and given separate consideration later.

The classic example of a joint-impact good is national defense. Whatever level and kind of national defense is present in the United States is available to all residents. One person may feel more secure if the army has no nuclear weapons, while another person prefers a nuclear army. But, if they live in the same nation, they cannot simultaneously obtain their preference. Whatever exists is costly to avoid. While the same physical good can enter two or more persons' utilities, the satisfaction derived may differ greatly. If tastes differ, there is conflict, and property rights determine whose taste counts. If two persons have different tastes for some nonoptional joint-impact good, they can negotiate to adjust the commonly available quantity and quality and the price each pays. But they must deal with each other rather than independently buying different amounts from producers. Consumers of non-joint-impact goods may, independently of other consumers, adjust the quantity taken to the price offered by the producer, but such adjustment is impossible with nonoptional joint-impact goods. If A has the initial right to choose, such right is a potential source of income to A if B tries to avoid that particular level of joint impact by bargaining.

Further, if the good is desired by B but exclusion is not too expensive, A's ownership may generate income for A even when A's own use value exceeds the cost of supply—for example, A could drive his car to the office and take B along without cost but charge B for the ride. How much of the fixed cost can be charged to B given B's willingness to pay?

If the military force of the United States increases the feeling of security (or insecurity) of neighboring countries, this illustrates that jointness is a matter of degree. For many people of the same taste in the United States, each one can enjoy equally without subtracting from the good available to others. But the strength of a neighbor does not give the same kind of security as one's own military. Therefore the goods are not perfect substitutes, and people in the country that has a strong neighbor may apply a discount to the physical good that enters their utility function. Jointness is usually a matter of degree and sometimes leads to a mixture of public and private financing.

If whatever total supply of military force exists is available for all (even if in differing degrees), the marginal cost for another user is zero. (Note that this is not the same as saying that the marginal cost of another physical-output unit, such as number of soldiers or amount of deterrence, is zero). The issue then is whether the marginal user is allowed to pay zero. Who is regarded as the marginal user is a matter for public choice.

The capacity for joint impact is found in many goods. For example, whatever ambient air quality is available for A to breathe, B can breathe it too at no extra cost. The fact that B can avoid it by carrying her own bottled supply does not alter the potential jointness. B may be a smoker and unable to perceive changes in air quality that are quite troublesome to a nonsmoker. Each cannot simultaneously and independently have just the ambient air characteristic that she wishes, except at a cost of avoidance. You can have corn to eat and I wheat and all we must pay is their individual costs of production. But, if you like classical and I like rock music, I not only need to buy my own records but also must pay the cost of insulating my ears from the sound of your nearby speaker.

Whatever variety of goods is available for purchase on the market is available to all. If selection is narrow, it is narrow for all. Variety often raises per-unit costs, as was seen in the case of economies of scale. One person may prefer fewer goods at lower unit cost while another prefers a larger variety at higher costs. But there is no way for both to exist simultaneously for a national economy (although coexistence can be achieved on a limited scale in local markets and differences in stores). Another example of this type is the availability of television program channels. If A can choose among three channels, the same range of choice can be made available to all, even if some are satisfied with one or two at an appropriate saving in prices of advertised products, taxes, or cable fees.

Many visual experiences have joint impacts. A's house exterior and lawn give her more pleasure than is engendered by B's viewing them, but there is also jointness. If B would prefer a different view from her window than is afforded by A's taste in house and landscaping, there is no way to please both simultaneously if they deal independently with producers of housing and turf.

If A is innoculated for polio, this good decreases the probability of B contracting the disease, since its incidence in the population is decreased. The good is probably discounted by B and is not as valuable as being vaccinated himself, but there is a degree of jointness. Education is similar in that the human capital of the educated person can benefit that person plus others who are better off for living in a community of educated people. Also note that the classroom and laboratory space are not joint-impact goods, and their marginal cost is not zero.

In the section to follow, several dimensions of joint-impact goods will be analyzed. The source of interdependence and thus the kind of controlling right will be seen to vary with the degree of jointness, cost of avoidance, and preemption.

DEGREE OF JOINTNESS

A joint-impact good enters two or more persons' utility, but the physical products may differ somewhat, raising questions of relative cost share. The substitutability of a unit of the good created by another person for a unit initiated by yourself can vary. Examples noted above include military protection, education, and immunization.

Albert Breton defines a *nonprivate good* as one that "though not available equally to all, has the property that the amount available to one individual does not reduce that available to others by an equal amount" (1965, pp. 175–87). This definition suggests that jointness is a matter of degree. There is a debate in the literature over whether the most-useful distinction is between incompatible-use goods (sometimes called private) and joint-impact goods (called public) as polar cases, with most actual goods falling somewhere in between, or whether the incompatible-use good is a knife edge, with most goods having some degree of jointness. The former is argued by Richard Musgrave and the latter by Paul Samuelson. Samuelson believes that most goods have some degree of jointness in use, or what he calls "consumption externality." His examples include cinemas, electric lines, and roads. Samuelson believes that the private good can be defined cleanly. The remainder of goods form a continuum of jointness within the category of joint-impact goods.

The argument is significant for welfare theorists because it affects the scope for application of global welfare-maximization propositions (to be examined in Chapter 11). The implications for forming hypotheses linking property-rights alternatives to substantive performance are less clear. The analytic consequences of applying a different value (discount or premium) to the same physical good versus specifying the difference as two separate goods need further study. The author's preference is for the latter, because physical differences can be observed, but it is hard to distinguish whether values attached to a given good are owing to differences in accessibility or in preference. It is clear that empirical analysts must be very careful in specifying the good they are studying. For theoretical work it may be all right to draw a diagram whose horizontal axis is labeled "joint-impact good" (such as education), but this gross specification will not do for empirical work.

COST OF AVOIDANCE AND PREEMPTION

There are two other characteristics of JIG that affect human interdependence—cost of avoidance and the degree to which the availability to person A limits the choice of quality or quantity available to B. The interdependence issue focuses not only on cost sharing but also on who gets to choose the quantity and quality of the JIG.

Output and cost relationships are studied by varying quantity of the good. But, quantity is far from a simple concept. This chapter has shown the need for distinguishing another physical unit of a good from another user of a given physical unit. Further distinctions are necessary to understand sources of interdependence. The literature speaks of joint supply and joint consumption. While a given physical unit is potentially available without added cost to another user, it may or not be actually utilized or its level of use can be varied. The cost of this variation is defined as avoidance cost.[3] A nonoptional or *high-avoidance-cost joint-impact good* is one whose frequency or level of use can't be varied by an individual but is given by the available physical unit. The avoidance dimension of quantity is measured in such things as frequency and time of use in reference to people.

Quantity is always with reference to a set of quality characteristics that define the good. One variety of interdependence depends on whether people can simultaneously utilize different qualities. A preemptive good is defined as one where qualities used can't be varied by an individual independent of the use of others. The preemptive dimension of quantity is measured in physical characteristics of the good, such as size, weight, speed, and so forth.

The interaction of consequences of avoidance cost and preemptions are summarized in Table 1. Consider first a joint-impact good that is unavoidable (nonoptional) and whose existence is preemptive of some other physical qualities and quantities (Table 1, line 1). For any given quality and quantity, two or more people who place positive value on the good will conflict over cost sharing. Each would prefer to be the marginal user and pay zero. But, the preemptive character creates additional interdependence. If tastes differ, the individuals will not each be able to optimally adjust the physical quantity utilized to the given price, which is the same for all. The physical quantity (or quality) is not optimal because someone's choice is preempted by another's.

Ambient air quality and national defense are examples. Whatever is the air quality for one breather is unavoidably utilized by other breathers and there will be an argument over production cost sharing. The good is omnipresent and frequency of use can't vary by individuals. Further, one ambient quality level is preemptive over others, since two qualities simultaneously are impossible. So there is conflict over the right to choose the quality. Regulation versus deregulation is meaningless here. Different quality levels are incompatible, and if A is free to choose his or her optimal level, B is constrained and

Table 1
Interdependence Created by Interaction of Avoidance Cost and Degree of Preemption

	UNAVOIDABLE	PRE-EMPTION	INTERDEPENDENCE	EXAMPLE
1.	B-postive utility	High	Who chooses and cost share	Air
2.	B-positive utility	Low	Empty set	--
3.	B-negative utility	High	Incompatible use	Outdoor music
	(OPTIONAL) AVOIDABLE			
4.	B-positive utility	High	Who chooses and cost share. B can adjust frequency	Road
5.	B-positive utility	Low	Only cost share (and cost per person and variety trade-off)	Cinema
6.	B-negative utility	High or Low	No problem	

Note: The B in column one refers to the utility of person B, who is affected by A's actions.

vice versa. Income distribution is not determined solely by factor ownership or income, but by rights in collective choice.

The positively valued, unavoidable, and low-preemption-good category may be an empty set. Intuitively, it would seem that if B has to utilize a good available to A, it would be impossible for B to utilize another level of the good. The characteristics that makes it unavoidable make it impossible to utilize more of it than does another person. For example, if a dam or dike is built along a stream, it gives a certain level of protection to everyone in the flood-plain. If a person who wants a higher level of protection builds a dike just around their own property, it is not additive but rather makes the commonly available supply worthless to that person. Put another way, there is an avoidance cost to escape the common supply and supply your own higher level.

The negative valued, unavoidable, preemptive good is similar to an incompatible-use good and is controlled by factor ownership (Table 1, line 3). For example, if person A plays loud music in his or her back yard, the sound is costly to avoid and another type of music or level would be interfering. Person B, who finds the nonoptional JIG to have negative utility, wants to be paid if the good exists at all, but the bid will run the other way if the neighbor owns the preemptive choice.

Turning now to avoidable (optional) goods whose existence is preemptive of other physical quantities and qualities, the interdependence among those with positive utility is both a matter of cost share and who chooses (Table 1, line 4). The interdependence is less severe here because one individual can adjust utilization in some dimension such as time (avoidance) but not in other dimensions such as size or speed. Consider a road between two points. What are its dimensions of utilization? It is optional in the sense that a person can avoid use altogether or can make any number of trips independent of others. In the quality-quantity dimension, the road may be one or more lanes, and so on. There are more alternatives here than in the unavoidable, preemptive case, but people are still interdependent with respect to who chooses and preempts the other. Each added lane is nonmarginal and quite costly. If tastes related to speed and congestion differ, the right to choose the physical quantity (or quality) of the good at a given price is critical to performance even if it can be avoided altogether and even if marginal cost of another user of the given physical quantity is zero. Other examples include various goods involving lines such as electric lines or cable TV. People do not have a complete inventory of their wealth unless it includes their right to influence public and private agencies that decide such things as quality of roads, cable TV systems, and telephone, electric, and gas utility lines.

Nonpreemptive and avoidable goods only create cost-share conflicts among those with positive utility (Table 1, line 5). For example, a cinema is MC = 0 up to capacity, but it is self-contained, avoidable, and nonpreemptive. One person can go to one cinema once a week while another can go every night or to another cinema. Each person can adjust their frequency of utilization and quality independently. There is conflict over how to share the fixed cost if they go to the same theater. And if one person prefers a different picture, it does affect the per-person cost of each. This is the interdependence trade-off between per-person cost and variety explored in the previous chapter on economies of scale. Another parallel example is letter and package delivery, although here MC is declining and not zero.

Finally, there is the avoidable JIG with high or low preemption but where some people have negative utility. Since avoidance of this and similar goods is cheap, there is no interdependence, and one person's choices do not affect abstainers (except as full economies of scale may not be realized).

To summarize, with JIG the issue of cost share (price) cannot be separated from choice of output level. If physical quantity is preemptive and cannot be adjusted to price, any given price to all will not be acceptable to people with different preferences (even if the good is avoidable and frequency of use can be adjusted).

In contrast to standard welfare economics, the point here is not that unavoidable and preemptive goods prevent global optimal resource combinations but that unless the relevant property rights are previously determined, optimality has no meaning. The conflict over who chooses when utilization is inherently interdependent is a fundamental distributive question, as is factor ownership of incompatible-use goods.

RELATION OF JOINT IMPACT AND EXCLUSION COST

There is another reason to emphasize the potential availability for joint impact: where exclusion is relatively cheap, a user may be denied access even if his or her use adds nothing to resource cost. Some goods with joint impact can be private property and allow the exclusion of others. An example is broadcast television signals. A signal, once it exists, can be used by all who have receivers at no extra cost. But, with some expenditure, a scrambler can exclude users who do not pay the producer. The so-called social-welfare and efficiency considerations of allowing ownership and exclusion when marginal costs are zero will be explored in Chapter 11. Here we will just note the implications for how one party can affect another.

The previous discussion of marginal cost being less than average cost can be discussed in Chapter 4 with economies of scale.[4] People do care how total cost is shared even when marginal cost is zero. The right to exclude in either case is an important factor in income distribution.

Consider, for example, the right to exclude people from making copies of scholarly journals. Once a journal is produced, the cost of making a copy for an additional user is minimal. If the original subscribers pay enough to support the journal, photocopies do not directly affect them. Yet it is in the interest of the publishers to control photocopying. And, if the publisher's profits could be controlled, the regular subscribers would appreciate the photocopier's helping to reduce their subscription costs. A U.S. court case declared that the publisher did not have the right to exclude a library from making extra photocopies of a journal that it subscribed to (Weinberg 1975). The same issue arises with copying musical and video recordings when producers are forced to accept marginal cost pricing (often zero). This is "fair use," although the term is value presumptive (see Schmid 1985a).[5] The value of the right to exclude is, however, limited by policing costs.

A television program once recorded on videotape may be used by any broadcast station or cable system at marginal-cost-equals-zero to the producer. The right of program suppliers to sell exclusive rights to programs raises their income, but at the same time a station and its viewers are denied a good that costs no more resources to create. The sale of exclusive rights to show a certain program in a broadcast viewing area was common in the U.S. When cable television was developed, it threatened the value (advertising revenue) of these local exclusive rights if the programs were imported from a distant station. New technology requires new public decisions on property rights. In the United States, the Federal Communications Commission limited the importation of these signals and protected the value of the exclusive right in 1972 (Besen 1974).

Copyright questions also arise with respect to cable television. A television signal once beamed from a station's broadcasting antenna can be picked up by a cable television firm for delivery to its subscribers. This use adds nothing to the cost of producing the original signal. Yet the courts in the United States seem to be leaning to the granting of copyright to the originating station if it is a "distant station."[6] This enhances the station's income at cable subscribers' expense. Those who think price is a matter of demand and supply with the latter being technologically determined should take note. Price is related to proprietary scarcity, and thus so is income distribution.

A related example is the right to sell radio and television rights to sporting events. Sports teams and facilities cost no more to create if seen only by spectators that are present or enjoyed by distant television viewers and radio listeners. A source of great private fortunes in the United States is the right to exclude broadcasters and thus their consumers from this joint-impact good, where the addition of the electronic use adds no additional cost to creating the event. Some professional sports teams were profitable before television was invented, and the new value created by use of new technology made multimillionaires out of a lucky few. Such is the stuff that the rich are made of. This is the type of rights that separates the very rich from the middle class, who basically only own their labor power and a bit of accumulated savings.

Any group that feels its income is unjustly low may wish to try to have itself declared the owner of some joint-impact good with zero or minimal marginal costs for additional users, but where exclusion is not too expensive. Why should the publisher make extra profit because of new copying technology? Why should the owner of a sports team make extra profit when television is invented? Why not the poor? Or why should the users have to pay anything more than the marginal costs? To users, price above marginal cost would be the same as if the government were to put an equivalent tax on all photocopies, televised sporting events, and cable television transmissions. If the profits were used to stimulate still newer inventions, the distributional impact would differ. Thus, the rights question is not only who pays cost of production, but who gets rents after total cost is recovered.

To summarize, the situation of marginal-cost-equals-zero indicates that rights in pricing policy give an opportunity to affect income distribution. The income from the right to charge for a marginal use that has no cost of production can be allocated without necessarily affecting the firm's breakeven point or the goods physical supply. Depending upon society's moral judgment, this added use can be given to the consumer free of charge (as in the case of the video cassette recorder), to the owner who controls the decision on the fixed costs (as in the case of sports teams), or to any member of the public. With JIG, society has the luxury of pricing added uses over some range without affecting physical supply.

A common policy is to tie price to cost. If another use or user causes extra cost, the person causing the extra cost must pay. But, with JIG, there is no extra cost. What then should the extra user pay? The producer would like to shift the focus from cost to demand and just ask what can be collected, thus maximizing producer net revenues. This raises the moral question of why the producer is any more deserving of the extra revenue than any one else, be it the consumer or welfare mother. The concept $MC = 0$ breaks the necessary connection between bearing costs and receiving benefits. Who is the marginal user, eligible to pay only marginal cost, is a matter requiring public choice of rights. A subsidy cannot be defined independently of rights.

With increasing cost goods, enforcement of competition takes care of the price-differentiation question. But, with decreasing cost or $MC = 0$ goods, many firms and heavy competition may not be desirable even where possible, and this necessitates a public choice of price differentiation rights whether the good is privately or publicly produced. Several dimensions of joint-impact goods have now been discussed. For quick reference, the interaction of avoidance and exclusions cost is summarized in Table 2.

RELATION TO OTHER DEFINITIONS IN THE LITERATURE

Readers familiar with the literature in public finance and welfare economics will realize that what is here called joint-impact goods goes by many other names. It will perhaps make the implications of these goods clearer if some of the similarities with as well as the reasons for rejection of these other terms are made explicit. The most common term applied to these goods is that of

Table 2

Interaction of Avoidance and Exclusion Costs with Respect to Joint-Impact Goods

	Avoidance Optional	Avoidance Non-optional
Low exclusion cost	1. Cable television system 2. Access to existing electric, gas, and telephone lines up to capacity 3. Cinema seats up to theater capacity	Empty set*
High exclusion cost	1. Broadcast television 2. Outdoor fireworks 3. Local roads	1. Defense 2. Ambient air for breathing 3. Flood control 4. Use of air waves for audible sound

*Is it possible for A to exclude B, but if A decides to make it available, B cannot avoid it? If B cannot avoid it, can A utilize it and exclude B? No, for if B cannot exclude herself, neither can A exclude B.

public goods. This term is rejected here because it already suggests the policy conclusion before analysis of consequences can be made. Samuelson (1969, p. 108) says, "For the $(n+1)$th time, let me repeat the warning that a public good should not necessarily be run by public rather than private enterprise." That this warning has to be repeated indicates it was an unfortunate choice of terms. Samuelson's definition is essentially the one used here. He uses the synonym *consumption externality* as well, but it is also misleading, because an essential feature is that the goods are enjoyed but not consumed. This is why the above discussion avoids the term *consumed* and refers to enjoyment and utilization (or disutility).

Musgrave (1969, p. 126) uses the term *non-rivalness in consumption*. His definition is, "Social goods are defined as goods, the benefits from which are such that A's partaking therein does not interfere with the benefits derived by B." Except for the value-laden term *social goods*, this is similar to the definition used here. Musgrave refers to a good's substitutability and the discount that is applied to what he calls "outside consumption." While A's partaking does not interfere with some degree of partaking by B, the utility may differ greatly, as Musgrave notes. In one place, Musgrave defined them as goods that "must be consumed in equal amounts to all." Equal amounts refers to equal physical units.

Buchanan's categorization of "public goods" emphasizes the degree of divisibility and the number of persons involved. He illustrates his definitions by saying, "The death of one mosquito benefits each man simultaneously, and is thus equally available to each man" (1968, p. 11). He suggests that "the theory of public goods can be meaningfully discussed only when the units are defined as 'those which are jointly supplied' and when 'equal availability' and, less correctly, 'equal consumption' refer only to jointly supplied production units or inputs, which may and normally will embody widely divergent final consumption units, measured by ordinary quality and quantity standards" (p. 54). He emphasizes that because of the indivisible (preemptive) character of the goods, it is impossible for each individual to equate marginal valuations to tax charges (or market prices), and thus for any given tax, some individuals would want more and others fewer governmentally provided goods. These points are consistent with the above discussion.

Goods in "joint supply" are not the same as joint-impact goods. The theory of joint supply was well developed by Marshall in the classic case of the activity of sheep raising producing both meat and wool, which is quite a different situation than that discussed here, since joint supply products, when produced by large numbers of suppliers, can be independently purchased and consumed, with each person adjusting quantity to the price. Many public investments produce goods in joint supply—for example, a dam and reservoir produce irrigation water, hydropower, flood control, and recreation. Individuals can adjust their own consumption to price, although the MC of water use for hydropower is zero if the water is already produced for irrigation uses. There is an issue of allocation of the overhead or joint cost.

Another distinction is necessary. A joint-impact good is not the same as what is usually meant by the term *interdependent utilities*. Earlier the fact that people can derive satisfaction from knowledge of the consumption of others was discussed. In that respect all goods conceivably could enter the utility of more than one person. It is not the good that enters, but rather knowledge of the good's use by others. The consequences of this type of interdependence must not be confused with those of joint-impact goods. Samuelson (1969, p. 109) notes that "little is left of the 'true property' of private goods in U, if people through altruism or envy have in their u_1 the bread consumption of other people, namely x_2 in u_2." In the negative sense, all conspicuous consumption goods are subject to possible Veblen effects, where A feels worse after seeing B's ostentation.

There are differences of opinion on the relationship between jointness and externality. The discussion here differs from the general concept of spillover or externality, such as where the activity of steel production produces both steel and pollution. (Mishan [1969] calls this case "private goods with external effects.") This general concept is in fact a misconception of the ordinary case of incompatible uses of a resource such as the air for either waste disposal or breathing. Of course, from the point of view of a buyer of rights to clean air (perhaps from a factory that owns the air), this clean air once created is here considered as a joint-impact good that can be utilized by more than one person. If the unit of product is not carefully defined, the same nominal good will be found used to illustrate contradictory points.

In summary, the relationship between incompatible-use and joint-impact goods can be made more explicit, as shown in Table 3. An example of item 1 is when A eats corn, B cannot eat the same unit. The users are incompatible. Another example is when A consumes clean air as an input in the production of steel and B cannot consume clean air because it has smoke in it. Uses are incompatible. This fact sometimes is conceptualized confusingly as an exceptional externality where A engages in an activity that produces steel and also smoke, but it is simply an incompatible-use controllable by factor ownership.

An example of item 2 is when A consumes national defense and B must consume it also, but B places a negative value on it. National defense is in this case a nonoptional joint-impact good. Use is compatible, but utility of use is not (some would call this a negative externality). The issue in all of the above cases is who gets to own and choose the good.

An example of item 3 is also national defense, but this time while B must consume, B places a positive value on it. This is a nonoptional joint-impact good, but there is no technological incompatibility. Item 4 is illustrated by broadcast television. Person A consumes and B can consume if she wishes. It is a joint-impact good with no incompatibility. The issue in 3 and 4 is who pays how much when several use it. In case 4, if no B wishes to utilize the good, there is no conflict, in contrast to situation 3.

Various other terms and distinctions appear in the literature. Some focus on activities, some on resources or products, some on production, and some on consumption. Each has analytic utility, and the last word remains to be written.

A DETAILED EXAMPLE: NATIONAL DEFENSE

The above points can perhaps be summarized and further implications drawn in the context of an earlier example. Consider a certain geographical area

Table 3
Relationship of Incompatible-Use and Joint-Impact Goods

1. A consumes X_1, B cannot consume X_1	Incompatible-Use Goods	
2. A utilizes X_2, B must utilize X_2 (negative value)	Nonoptional	⎫
3. A utilizes X_3, B must utilize X_3 (positive value)	Nonoptional	⎬ Joint Impact Goods
4. A utilizes X_4, B can utilize X_4	Optional	⎭

where two groups of residents are considering how to protect themselves from outside enemies. One feels safe with a certain-sized army equipped with 100 nuclear bombs. The other group feels safe with only ten nuclear bombs and, further, feels unsafe with 100. This is a nonoptional joint-impact good, and it is not possible for both levels of this good to be simultaneously available. In contrast, with consumption of say, apples, one group could eat one apple per day and the other could eat two (though both cannot eat the same unit). Units of bombs do have a positive marginal cost, but units of users do not. Incidentally, it is also possible that there is a third group that prefers no army and does not fear the enemy. One person's good may be another's bad.

Defense happens also to be a good with relatively high exclusion costs. This creates the possibility of free riders and may prevent a private producer from receiving bids sufficient to produce the good even when people desire it. But it is important to understand the different consequences of high exclusion costs and high avoidance costs (see Burkhead and Miner 1971, pp. 29–31). With goods whose use is optional and different qualities simultaneously possible, the issue is who pays how much. But with nonoptional and preemptive goods, the issue can also be who gets to choose the good. These situations will be illustrated intuitively below and more technically in Chapter 11.

The different implications of exclusion and avoidance costs can be illustrated by making the unreal assumption that a magic meter exists to measure each person's marginal valuation. Now the high exclusion cost creates no problem for preference revelation. Each person can be charged the value of his or her marginal utility for the commonly available amount of the good. Is that the only source of interdependence?

The answer can be made clear if we consider again the case of incompatible-use goods. When consumers are price takers, each can adjust the quantity taken so that each person's marginal value equals the price. With a nonoptional joint-impact good, this situation is impossible. Whatever exists for one will be utilized by all, like it or not. If preferences differ, it is impossible for each person to equate marginal value to price. But, if we have a magic meter, it would be possible to charge different prices to each person so that each person's marginal value equals price for the commonly available supply (Lindahl equilibrium). Price could be negative. Between two or more people who have a positive value for the nonoptional product, it is a joint-impact good, but at the same time it can be an incompatible-use good between them and third parties with negative valuations. This point is illustrated if we assume that 100 nuclear bombs have zero or negative value to the pacifists and positive value to the insecure. It does not settle the problem for the pacifists to pay nothing. They want to be free of the overprotection or be compensated for it. Even when each person's marginal valuation is known, there must be a public decision on whose preferences will count when they conflict. Who has to pay whom to obtain or avoid an effect? The cost of production of nuclear bombs is given not only by the physical production function but also by the property-rights decision of how and whether to count the negative utility of those who do not want the product. B's lost utility is an input into nuclear bomb production, but whether it is a cost, and how much, depends on property rights. Cost is a social phenomenon whereby shares in output are determined.

It is frequently assumed that it is sufficient for human interaction if everything is owned. But that assumption is deceiving because what must also be considered is how every effect of human interdependence is accounted for. If we look only literally at units of commodities, we will miss the many ways people can affect each other, especially in the case of joint-impact goods. In the present case, it appears that everything is owned. Someone owns the factory to make nuclear bombs and the inputs for their manufacture and deployment. Buyers own their income. But this factor ownership does not describe the totality of the relationships among people. Tastes can conflict in ways other than who owns a certain input factor. In the present case, there is a conflict among those who want zero, ten, and 100 nuclear bombs. The key right is the question of whether A owns the right to fulfill his or her tastes when they conflict with B. Does A own the right to purchase ten nuclear bombs and expose B to the discomfort of underprotection or does B own the right to have 100 and expose A to the disutility of overprotection? This question exists even if A did not have any obligation to help pay for the nuclear bombs.

It might appear that joint-impact goods are the best of all possible worlds, since they can be enjoyed without being consumed. But, alas, when there are differences in taste, there is conflict, just as in incompatible goods. Incompatible goods require a right to determine who gets the particular unit. Joint-impact goods require a right to determine who gets to choose the commonly available units. (They also require a right to determine distribution of production costs among people with different positive marginal utilities, as discussed in Chapter 11). Markets reflect the balance of rights that are present but fail to reflect those that are not present. We can speak of the failure of a particular market (or administrative system) with its particular set of rights to reflect the tastes of a given person or group, but not of market failure in general. One group's market failure is another group's preferred world.

GAME-THEORETIC CONSIDERATIONS

Characteristics of goods take on importance only in relation to the kind and distribution of interests among people. Consider the case where the value of nuclear bombs beyond ten is zero to group A but equal to production cost up to 100 for B. If A buys ten first, B only has to pay for 90. If B acts alone to buy 100, A will not need to buy any. In this case, B will try to get A to help pay for at least the average cost of ten, perhaps threatening not to buy any if A does not help. If A guesses the extent of B's tastes, this may not be a credible strategy on B's part. The outcome is indeterminate except to say it depends on the relative bargaining strengths and skills of the parties. (For additional discussion see Chapter 11, especially Figure 6.) The level of output is very likely to depend on the agreement for cost sharing.

Bargaining in competitive markets (large numbers of buyers and sellers) is a misnomer (Morgenstern 1972). Consumers either buy or not. If enough do not buy a particular good at the initial offer price, either quantity supplied or price falls. There is no face-to-face negotiation or conversation between buyers and sellers. Haggling is a phenomenon associated only with small-numbers situations, large purchases, and imperfect markets. In that case, one person's behavior depends on the expected reaction of the other party. The result is indeterminate in the usual economic model. Where people act independently and impersonally, their price-quantity behavior is relatively consistent over time and not greatly affected by the marketing transaction itself (though some learning may take place). A consumer presents a demand schedule in the usual sense. But when people meet face to face in a strategic game, consistent behavior is a disadvantageous practice for the party using it. A person has no demand schedule, since bids vary with perception of the strategic situation at the moment. However, the directional result may be predicted by game theory and knowledge of the opportunity set, the taste for gambling, and the possibility of benevolence and malevolence. Just knowing that people prefer more to less is not sufficient behavioral information to predict the outcome of game-theoretic situations (Shubik 1984, chap. 19).

The perceived fairness of today's bargain influences willingness to bargain in the future. If A insists he has no demand for a joint-impact good and B later discovers that this was false, B may refuse to cooperate in the future. If both parties recognize this utility of maintaining credibility and trust, they may choose to reveal their demand and avoid strategic nonrevelation. Then again, they may become involved in an escalating series of mistrust and deception.

EFFECT OF ALTERNATIVE RIGHTS

The purpose of these classifications of interdependence is to provide a basis for studying how alternative institutions (rights) control interdependence and thus affect performance. Therefore, it is important for empirical analysis that the inherent character of a good not be confused with the particular rule chosen for it.

For example, in Table 1 flood control is considered a joint-impact good, not a public or private good. The form of ownership, type of transaction, boundary of firm, level of administration, and pricing rule are institutions that affect performance in the context of interdependence created by marginal cost being zero over some range combined with the degree of exclusion cost and avoidance cost. Institutional rules can alter the incidence or consequence of joint-impact features. It is possible to take an incompatible-use, low-exclusion-cost good with positive marginal cost and not charge the marginal user. But this does not make it a joint-impact good. Performance cannot be understood if institutional structure and inherent goods features are confused. If a person is not satisfied with the level of a joint-impact good, several alternatives might be pursued, each with different implications for cost sharing and who chooses.

First, accept grudgingly. Many goods have some degree of joint impact where the initiation of supply by one person enters into another's utility without added cost. In the great bulk of these, the law gives the right to choose to whoever acts. If A puts up a modern house in a traditional neighborhood, it is frequently his right to do so, and the neighbors enjoy the view without paying or must simply accept exposure to the disutility. They might try persuasion or even make some monetary offer, but in the bulk of cases this is simply not worth the effort (which might be considerable because of the free-rider problem discussed previously). Segregation is sometimes used to group people with similar tastes, but this creates other conflicts.

Second, buy more yourself (assuming you are not offended by unequal cost shares). Where the good has positive value and you regard the total supply as inadequate, you may simply pay producers to provide more. For example, A may have been spraying her yard for mosquitoes with only limited effect. She may decide next to pay a commercial firm to spray around the neighborhood.

Third, bargain. You can pay others to purchase more or less of the good. (This assumes that others have no obligation to purchase any. This assumption can be reversed and bargaining proceed from there.) For example, you might pay your neighbors to spray their own yards, paint their houses, mow their lawns, and so forth.

If a person wants more of a nonoptional joint-impact good where all persons have positive value for it, the problem is cost sharing and perhaps who chooses the quality and physical quantity. If A is providing some to himself and B, but B wants more, B can either produce or bargain with A to produce more. An example of such a bargain is the classic case of beekeepers and apple growers. Beekeepers may use a certain number of bees to produce honey, but apple growers may want more for pollination. For a given number of bees and honey, the MC of another use (for pollination) is zero. Bees are a nonoptional joint-impact input with positive value for both honey and apple producers. But it cannot be assumed that, as they begin to bargain and explore their interdependence, honey producers will be willing to expand if apple growers do not also offer to help pay for the present supply of bees. Does the apple grower have a right to receive free the joint product of the honey producer's bees and only pay for the marginal cost of more bees; or does the honey producer have the right to expect others to help pay for the bees' joint uses? In the small-number case, the situation is fraught with game strategy. Malevolence may develop, and the joint-impact good may not be produced despite its mutual benefit. This may be especially true if apple producers can't agree on the number and quality of bees to bargain for.

Where there are opposite tastes, the right for A to buy more or pay B to use more creates an exposure for C if the goods utilization cannot be avoided. The payment can be a matter of private contract, or a high demander may petition the government to offer a payment financed by taxes. Most governments offer monetary incentives to citizens to increase their purchase of certain goods (not all of which are joint-impact goods, however).

Even where everyone regards more physical units of the non-optional good as having positive value, there can be conflict over the physical quantity and quality of the good. The relevant rights are contained in such things as minimal or maximal consumption requirements.

Fourth, owners of a low exclusion cost JIG may sell it. Note that a good may be JIG among one set of users but incompatible between that group and a second group. If the owner in the first group can sell to someone in the second, others in the first group who had formerly not been excluded lose as the good is transformed by incompatible use. Government may therefore make the right nonexchangeable or set rules for decisions to sell by all joint owners.

Fifth, government may provide. Even when all benefit from the good, there is argument over cost sharing and who chooses the quantity and quality of the good. Rights pursuant to tax laws are important factors in who pays how much for joint-impact goods and thus in the distribution of welfare. As in the case of private bargaining, failure to agree may mean the mutually beneficial good is not produced.

Government provision causes everyone to purchase more. Whether others actually utilize more depends on the costs of avoiding the available supply. The total supply of nuclear bombs cannot be avoided. The total variety of television programs and channels can. The offer of publicly provided education or inoculation services can be avoided, but laws are frequently passed to require schooling and some vaccinations, though the source can be private. Some people will not notice or be able to utilize the good, but if taxes are used, they become unwilling riders in the sense that they have to pay for something they do not want. In the case of nonoptional goods, even if they pay nothing, they may be unwilling riders if they do not put a positive value on the commonly available supply. Even when a person pays no taxes, he or she is affected by the tax expenditures of others. Where joint-impact goods are present, it benefits a person to have similar tastes as his or her neighbors. One might expect people to make a certain investment in creating similar tastes in their fellows. But such investment runs into free-rider consequences. Exclusion and joint impact are often interrelated.

Sixth, regulate. In the case of nonoptional joint goods, a person negatively affected can turn to administrative transactions, which in effect give A the right to be free of a certain level of utilization by B or, in the case of positively valued goods, regulation may give A the right to expect B to maintain at least a certain level of utilization by B or, in the case of positively valued goods, regulation may give A the right to expect B to maintain at least a certain level of utilization on her own.[7] Regulation shifts factor ownership and the beneficiary pays nothing, but the person regulated has a cost.

The regulatory alternative directs the interdependence of joint-impactness in a particular way. An unwilling rider is a person who has to pay a tax for an unwanted governmental good or who by regulation has to provide privately and/or utilize a good at an unwanted level. A person exposed to regulation requiring a limit to private utilization may in parallel fashion be called an "unwilling abstainer" (prohibition of alcoholic beverages is both a literal and figurative example). For example, a zoning regulation may prohibit the use of flat modern roofs, which are offensive to traditional tastes. In general, land-use regulations are concerned with a variety of utilization patterns that are joint-impact goods and keep land use within certain bounds. If tastes differ, unwilling abstainers who cannot use their resources as they wish are the result.

Where you wish to increase the utilization of a certain good, you may seek a law requiring a minimum utilization. For example, the city may require all homeowners to clear their walks of snow. This requirement applies even to those who never leave the house except in a car. The supply of sidewalks has joint impact, and one person cannot leave it covered if another is going to be able to walk along it. A law may require all dog owners to get rabies shots for their dogs. Another law might require certain human inoculations. In the case of education, the law may require one to stay in school until a certain age is reached. But one person's right is another's exposure. If tastes differ, someone is an unwilling rider. This is true whether A has the right to expect that B will stay in school for a certain period or whether B has the right to expose A to the disutility of living in a world where her neighbors cannot read or write. The right to choose a privately or publicly provided joint-impact good is an important factor in the distribution of welfare.

Each of these six alternatives relates to a different composition of property rights and probably a different performance depending on the specifics. Rights in addition to competitive rules affect who gets to choose the kind and amount of joint-impact goods and the sharing of costs.

Those readers schooled in the market-failure approach will note that it focuses the issue on market versus administrative transactions in order to achieve consumer sovereignty and optimum output. The approach here focuses explicitly on who pays and raises the additional question of who gets to choose the product. It suggests that the key question is not how to achieve general consumer sovereignty, but which consumer is to be sovereign. Ownership of money and factors of production do not completely control this type of interdependence. In the situation of JIG, the rights in market pricing and tax incidence are critical as well as regulation of consumption and production.

The continuum of topics in Chapters 4 and 5 can now be summarized. Some goods have production (cost) functions such that there is not a marginal relationship linking input and output. This means that cost of output loses some of its meaning and there is no physical relationship to use as the bases for prices. There is something in common among goods marked by economies of scale, joint impact, overhead cost, and team production (input complementarity). The unit of measure and perspective differs, but all involve an interruption of the link between input and output, often referred to as "lumpy" or "indivisible."

1. Economies of scale: a particular *physical unit* of the *same output* can't be traced to a particular unit of *input*. (The source of this is fixed cost, team production, or complements.)

2. Joint-impact good: a particular *user* of the *same output* can't be traced to a particular unit of *input*.

3. Overhead cost: A particular *use* from among *multiple outputs* cannot be traced to a particular unit of *input*. (This is discussed in Chapter 11.)

All of these situations require a pricing rule (property right) to allocate the advantages of doing something together. Prices of outputs or inputs (including wages) cannot be derived from the production function. Cost is not simply a physical phenomenon, but is a matter of public choice of shares.

NOTES

1. The definition (but not the term) is that of Samuelson (1969, p. 108). He illustrates the need to distinguish the physical good from a person's sensing the good by noting that the definition applies to fireworks in the sky, rather than fireworks as registered on the retina of A's eyes versus fireworks observed by B. The latter definition would define joint-impact goods out of existence. Note that the good perceived by the different users can be quite different. This makes no difference for analysis as long as there is some expression of demand for the given physical commodity. The quantity unit is number of users for a given physical quantity and quality. Congestion must be accounted for, since the marginal cost of another user is not zero if the quality of the good changes with another user.

2. Joint-impact goods should not be confused with free goods, which may have a positive marginal cost of production but which are not scarce. Neither should they be confused with scarce goods that have positive marginal costs but that are provided free to the user as a matter of policy. Joint-impact goods are the opposite of incompatible-use goods where marginal cost is not zero. Note that a durable good can be joint-impact if used sequentially even though incompatible for simultaneous use. This means rights of stewardship are important to preserve the potential flow of benefits.

3. Mishan (1981, p. 431) defines an optional collective good as one "which a person may take all he wishes (up to what is available) at the going price. . . ." This is ambiguous. Mishan gives the following examples (p. 438): television transmission, the services of parks, bridges, light houses, street lights, museums, theatres, and galleries. He is probably speaking of the frequency of use but is never explicit. He does contrast variation in telephone service in the short run (number of calls) with long-run adjustments in the system. Mishan then defines a nonoptional collective good as one "which

bestows itself in some particular amount on each of the beneficiaries." His example (p. 439) of times during the year that clouds are seeded and the amount of rainfall precipitated indicate that this is a dimension of physical units. The reference to amounts is ambiguous because it does not distinguish the avoidance dimension from the preemption dimension. Other texts ignore the distinction altogether (Boadway and Bruce 1984, chap. 4).

4. When marginal cost is zero and when there is a sufficient plant to serve one person, all can be served. To create additional firms and plants in order to get competition (to control bargaining power) is to increase costs without increasing output (people served).

5. *Columbia Broadcasting System* v. *Teleprompter,* 476 F.2d 338, 349 (2d Cir. 1973). The United States Supreme Court earlier ruled that copyright did not apply to cable carriage of signals from nearby broadcast stations where the terrain made it difficult for some viewers to obtain a satisfactory signal. *Fortnightly Corp.* v. *United Artists Television Inc.,* 392 U.S. 390 (1968). Also see Posner (1972a). For a view arguing against copyright liability and program exclusivity see Chazen and Ross (1970).

6. Ibid.

7. Where this is a transferable right for A, when B wants to change the utilization, A can receive bids from B rather than having to pay B, as with the bargaining option.

Six

Transaction Costs

Human interaction is not free. Its costs are seldom distributed equally over the population, and choice of property rights affects how these costs fall on different groups. The existence of differential transaction costs creates opportunities for one person's choices to impact on others, and it is property rights that direct and control these choices. Three varieties of transaction costs can be distinguished: contractual, information, and policing. Policing costs are a part of what has already been discussed under the broader heading of exclusion costs. Contractual costs are the costs of reaching agreement with another party, discretely or continuously as the case may be. Lawyer fees, brokerage fees, and bargaining time are cases in point. Information costs are the costs of acquiring information about product (and input) price and quality now and in the future. Data costs, monitoring, control, and insurance are examples.

CONTRACTUAL COSTS

Ordinary production costs in producing time and space utility should not be confused with contractual costs. The ordinary production costs born by an actor because of the factor ownership of others is not a contractual cost. The latter are inherent in such things as the number and spatial distribution of owners and the character of the good.

There are some Pareto-better rules of contract that benefit most if not all parties (Tullock 1971, chap. 3). Over time, most parties stand to gain if a stable set of expectations is maintained. Much economic activity is forward looking, and, without stability and some degree of predictability, the planning horizon would shorten to the detriment of most people. There could also be much time wasted in specifying all contingencies in each written contract. Both parties can to some extent gain by leaving some features incorporated by inference in the common law of contract and standard forms.

There is always some effort involved in coming to an agreement with another person. In certain instances, the cost of negotiating the agreement can be more than the value of the right to the product one is trying to obtain. Two cases may be distinguished: (1) where large number of buyers (sellers) must act together; and (2) where input suppliers must act in timely sequence, simultaneously, and in critical proportions.

A buyer must pay contractual costs as well as the cost of the right to the resource use desired. Consider the case where a steel manufacturing plant owns certain air rights. The firm may find it profitable to utilize this resource for waste disposal (smoke). Use of the air for waste disposal is incompatible with use for clean breathing. If people who desire clean breathing air wish to acquire the rights to the air, they will have to make a trade with the steel firm. If the rights of waste disposal are very valuable to the firm (costs of changing its manufacturing process are high), it will probably mean that no one neighbor will be able to afford to purchase the right. If an effective bid is going to be made, it will have to be a group bid. The cost of organizing the group bid will be considerable when it is a large group. Because clean air is a good where exclusion is impossible, free-rider behavior is probable. An agreement or contract among potential consumers of clean air will be costly to obtain. It is conceivable that although the sum of each individual's value of clean air exceeds the value of waste disposal to the steel firm, nevertheless a bid will not be forthcoming and the smoke will continue.

Now, consider the opposite case where the initial property right was vested in common to all people of the air shed with the right to use freely for breathing, but any other uses require consent of all of the common owners. If the steel firm wants to acquire some of the air rights for waste disposal, it will be very costly to make a contractual agreement with the many owners. It is conceivable that the firm could afford to pay each of the owners more than what the clean air is worth to them, but when the cost of seeking everyone out is added in, the firm's bid may fall short. The situation is further aggravated by the possibility of strategic bargaining on the part of hold-outs even when most other common owners have agreed to sell. The last seller may demand an exorbitant price.

If the breathers do not own the air rights, contractual costs of organizing a bid will be high because of high exclusion costs. If better air is obtained somehow, it would be costly to police to keep nonbuyers from using it. If the steel firm does not own the right, contractual costs will be high because of the need to deal with many common owners. The existence of contractual costs on both sides of the transaction means that the location of initial right affects the eventual use of the resource even where market exchange is allowed. It also means that the distribution of income will be quite different.

Further implications of contractual costs can be seen in another example, the case of mosquitoes. It will be costly for anyone annoyed by bites to enter into a contract with his neighbors to buy spraying from a commercial spraying firm (unless there is a great sense of community or other learned behavior in which individuals do not calculate their individual advantage). For reasons already examined, the bid may fail even where there are more than enough people willing to pay the average per-person cost. It might appear in this case that it would be a universal blessing if these contractual costs could be reduced so that the bid would succeed. However, one person's contractual costs are another person's freedom from exposure to the impacts of the first person's purchases when resource use is incompatible. It may seem far-fetched in the case of mosquitoes, but for purposes of illustration, assume that there are some thick-skinned ecologists in the neighborhood who like to study mosquitoes and do not wish them killed. If the ecologists owned the mosquitoes, they could not be destroyed without the ecologists' permission. The existence of high contractual costs to organize a bid for mosquito control is the same as a property right for the ecologists. Change transactions technology and costs and you also change effective rights. If transaction costs decrease, spray will be purchased and the utility of the ecologists will decline.

Contract costs are also relevant in governmental bargaining and administrative transactions. Various procedural requirements, such as public hearings, create contractual costs to some, which are a benefit to others. The more agencies that must "sign off" on an action, the higher the cost of securing agreement.

Contract costs can be high in the case of large numbers of rights holders even where exclusion costs and therefore policing costs are low. This is why contract costs are treated here as a separate category and not just a part of the exclusion cost discussion of Chapter 3.

Hypothesis: Where tastes differ, the existence of transaction costs protects the utility of those interested in the status quo level of the good even without an explicit right thereto.

It frustrates those who want a new product. This means it is not always desirable to design institutions to minimize transaction costs. Various property rights affect the direction flow of contractual costs and their impact on performance. Among those to be discussed below are the doctrine of reasonable use, restrictive covenants, type of relief available for damages, and class-action suits.

Reasonable Use

There are legal frameworks for adapting to change without a specific contract. The reasonable-use doctrine can be illustrated with respect to water rights. Under riparian rights, no one party has an absolute right to control a particular volume of water, as is the case with appropriation rights. State courts have ruled that reasonable use includes some diversion and even some waste disposal. This doctrine has important consequences in the face of high transaction costs (Posner 1972b, p. 25). For example, any person desiring to obtain withdrawal or waste disposal rights would face high contractual costs in dealing with many common owners.

Hypothesis: In a situation of high transaction costs (in fact created by the law), a structure of reasonable use will result in a performance of changed used that would otherwise not occur, and the previous owners will receive no rents.

Complete ownership of water-quality aspects by common owners will not achieve this result in the face of high transaction costs, which prevent a disposal user from obtaining some of the stream capacity even where he or she will pay more than the sum that the individual owners might require for some of the stream's capacity. The bid may be eaten up by transaction costs. Their reasonable-use (or cognate) doctrine gives certain potential users the right to avoid high transaction costs (at the expense of third parties, who enjoyed the protection of these costs in preventing any waste-disposal use). It also affects income distribution when waste users up to some point do not have to pay for their new use.

With the appropriation doctrine, an individual who owns a given volume of water may use it (or sell) when others with priority have received their given volume. This structure of exchange rights allows for changed ownership and use. It also allows the first in use to collect rents from the bids of others.

The doctrine of reasonable use is in effect a variety of variable ownership. It means that uses can change somewhat without the need to get agreement among all owners. This gives flexibility in use without transaction costs. On the other hand, it creates uncertainty. For example, a user who requires a large fixed investment is never certain of the supply, since future new reasonable use by others may make the first use unreasonable. This is in fact a dilemma for irrigators under the reasonable-use doctrine.

Injunctive versus Damage Relief

People can make changes in factor uses without contracting. Entitlements are not self-protecting. It is not enough to know who owns a particular resource; the remedy that the law gives to the owner when his utility is affected by the acts of others must be investigated. The key structural variables are the right to injunction, compensation, and who bears prosecution costs.

The example of conflict over airport noise can illustrate other aspects of how rights affect the incidence of transaction costs. Jet airplanes flying low to approach a runway create disutility for nearby homeowners and lower the value of their property. The costs faced by the airlines depend on the character of rights (Baxter and Altree 1972; Posner 1972b, p. 26). If the air space is owned by the airlines, it will be costly for the large group of homeowners to organize a bid. But, even where the homeowners have some rights, the character of the right makes a difference. One alternative is for the homeowners to have the right to a civil injunction, which means that the airlines must deal with each individual homeowner and obtain permission to fly over. Thus a high transaction cost is put on the airline, which must deal with large numbers and face the possibility of exorbitant holdouts. Another alternative is for the homeowners to have the right to a court-determined compensation for the damages received. In effect, this amounts to the right of condemnation of an easement on the part of the airlines and represents a saving of contractual costs for the airlines and an attenuation of the rights of the homeowners. The homeowner is prohibited from holding out for more of the difference between the amount of damage to the value of his property and the cost of the next best noise-avoidance alternative that the airline has, such as engine modification. This alternative affects distribution of the surplus.

Some writers distinguish between "liability rules," where infringement is in effect allowed with compensation, and "property rules," with exclusive entitlements and no compensation (Polinsky 1980). If the right is protected by criminal law there is no compensation paid to the aggrieved party although there may be a fine paid to the state. Criminal law also differs in that the costs of the court proceedings are paid by the government and not the person aggrieved, and the burden of proof is more extensive than in civil proceedings.

Hypothesis: In a situation of high transaction cost, it makes a difference whether a resource owner has the right of freedom from trespass or nuisance with the power to enjoin as the remedy or only the right to receive damages (in effect to be subject to condemnation of an easement with only the power to receive a court-determined value for the easement).

The latter exposure to forced sale reduces the income of affected factor owners who usually get the average market value rather than what their unique bargaining position might achieve. This rule saves the buyer the cost of negotiating with many parties, some of whom can become strategic holdouts. (A similar example is provided by the Michigan Surplus Waters Act, which allows the condemnation of land by industrial firms that want to store water for low-flow augmentation to reduce pollution. Industry can buy land for water storage at the market price and not have to share any of its profits with the present landowners [Michigan Statutes Annotated 218. 301; Public Act 20 of 1964, later declared unconstitutional]. See Chapter 7 on producer surpluses.)

Owners who want to protect their unique-use value or bargaining power have a more valuable right if they are entitled to triple damages or if the violator is subject to criminal fines in addition to civil damage payments. This discourages a nonowner from using a resource owned by an unwilling seller, though the ultimate protection is the injunction backed by severe penalties for contempt of court. The character of remedies affects the impact of nominal factor ownership.

Covenants and Zoning

Contractual cost in achieving agreement on land use is cheapest when a single person owns a large parcel. A restrictive covenant may be made a part of the title, and each subparcel is sold subject to these covenants. People who do not agree with the covenants select themselves out and live elsewhere. This is the method of land-use control in Houston, which has no public zoning (Seigen 1970). The protection afforded by the covenants would not be very valuable if the agreement did not "run with the land" (if it were not binding on all subsequent purchasers). The right to expect the courts to enforce this initial agreement on all subsequent buyers is a valuable right for those whose tastes favor the status quo. While the covenant is a private contract, it requires a governmental action to enforce and to interpret it in such a way as to bind subsequent purchasers, although they did not sign the original contract.

While the covenant approach is sometimes portrayed as a nongovernmental approach, there is another aspect of public action involved. Under zoning, the transaction costs incurred to prosecute a violation are borne by government, but the cost of seeking court action against the violation of a contract like a covenant is borne by the individual. However, in Houston, where there is no zoning, the city aids the individual in bringing court action, thus paying much of the transaction costs.

Hypothesis: In a situation of high transaction costs, covenants result in fewer land-use changes than would zoning rights.

Some covenants are written to run forever, and others provide for renewal upon consent of some proportion of the present owners. The required proportion can again create a significant transaction cost for those who want the restrictions continued. Also, if someone wants to change the provisions while they are in force, there are great transaction costs involved in getting 100 percent of the common owners of the covenant rights. For example, a large amount of land was reclaimed from Lake Michigan in Chicago and converted into Grant Park. Office buildings were developed with views over the park to the lake. The views made the offices more valuable, and a large open space was made available to the public. A covenant requires that no building may be built in the open space without unanimous consent of all the peripheral owners. Such permission was obtained only once, to build an art museum. Those nonlandowners who enjoy the open space (even at the expense of worthy public buildings) benefit from the high contractual costs necessary to build in this area. Nondevelopment occurs even where all the landowners might otherwise find the gross bid of developers attractive but where the bid fails when transaction costs are netted out. Contractual costs to a developer are enhanced utility to the lover of open space (Dunham 1973).

Buyers of residential property cannot determine their bid price unless the future use of open land in the interdependent area is known (Henderson 1980). If there are many present and future developers and buyers, transaction costs may prohibit private contracts assuring future use. The desired assurances may only be possible through public zoning. With uncertainty and changing preferences, the costs of changing covenants versus zoning favor different people.

Key points to remember are that (1) in the face of high contractual costs, initial rights allocation is likely also to be the place of final resource use even if markets are allowed, and (2) contractual costs are a source of use right for third parties and influence whose preferences count in a dynamic setting.

Class-Action Suits

It has already been pointed out that the full implication of nominal ownership is determined by the type of remedy available to the person who is wronged. Further, the usefulness of the remedy is determined by the cost of court action where the wrong is of civil and not criminal nature. The right is empty if it costs more to assert it than it is worth. (In a sense, the transaction cost of seeking court protection is related to exclusion cost, as discussed in Chapter 3). High court costs prevent people with small claims from seeking redress even when there are many people in the same situation. Fraudulent manufacturers and merchants can take advantage of this and accumulate huge profits by damaging a large number of buyers to a small extent. The right to collective action becomes important. If a large number of small claims can be assembled, the probable benefit can exceed the cost of court action. These are called class actions, and U.S. courts have allowed such actions only selectively. For example, for some types of federal court action, it is not possible to aggregate individual claims for purposes of complying with the minimum jurisdictional amount of $10,000.[1] One purpose of the minimum is to keep petty disputes out of federal courts, but this is not a justification for refusing class actions where the sum of damages is great. The right to class action reduces transactional costs for consumers and exposes merchants to their claims, which increases risk and cost of doing business. Transaction cost for consumers means money in the bank for fraudulent businesses.

An alternative to the class action that accomplishes the same purpose is to permit the state to sue as parens patriae, where the violation of a right creates a small cost for a large number of people. Another right that bears on the distribution of transaction costs is the English and continental practice of requiring the losing party to a court action to pay for all costs of the proceeding. This requirement reduces transaction cost for a person who has a small claim and is relatively sure of winning if it is brought to trial. But if there is a chance of losing, the litigant is faced with a relatively large attorney's fee against the probability of a small-claim settlement. Small-claims courts that do not require the use of a lawyer are an attempt to reduce court costs. These are useful to settle disputes between local buyers and sellers and between neighbors, but they are not useful in action against large interstate manufacturers. The problems of presenting such a case require a lawyer, and there are considerable economies of scale.

Other Rules

Transaction costs enter into human interactions in small and subtle ways. They apply to administrative transactions as well as bargained. Michigan in 1974 passed a generic drug law that allows a pharmacist to fill a prescription order with the cheapest source of the generic drug instead of a more-costly trade-named drug of the same chemical content. This can be done only if the physician does not specifically order the trade-named drug. Drug manufacturers are third parties to this transaction. The profits of drug firms that can afford to advertise to persuade physicians to use their brand then depend on what transaction cost is imposed on the physician. Must he sign his name or initial a box beside a wording on the prescription blank indicating that the prescription should be filled with the branded drug named on the prescription form? Or must he write out his command or perhaps just write F.A.W. (fill as written)? Each of these imposes a different transaction cost on a busy physician and affects whether a branded or unbranded product is used. It is this type of subtle property-rights questions upon which fortunes are built. They are well understood by highly paid business lobbyists but escape the attention of the average customer and citizen.

Similar questions come up in socialist and public firms as well. In Michigan there is a conflict in the use of state park lands between pedestrians and users of motorized vehicles such as motorcycles and snowmobiles ("State Land May Open to Cycles," Detroit *Free Press,* September 30, 1974). The philosophy of reasonable, balanced use has been followed even though use by vehicles detracts from those who like tranquility. Both sides generally agree to the principle that cycles should be limited to certain areas. The issue is whether you put up a sign saying, "These areas are zoned for cycles" or a sign saying, "Cycles prohibited here." The cost of administration differs substantially. A zealous cycle rider has some motivation to remove a sign from a prohibited area and then, if arrested for cycling there, he will claim that he was ignorant of the prohibition. There is no such motivation to remove a sign that says this area is for cyclists (where it is understood that all nonsigned areas are for pedestrians only). Cost of administration is like a contractual cost for a private party, and it greatly affects who will actually use a given governmentally provided good.

Contractual cost is a cost of doing business (human interaction), as is transport cost or any other. While all costs have a physical dimension, it is public choice of property rights that determines their impact and consequences. Only a few of the rights that affect contractual costs have been explored here. Another aspect of contractual cost is simply the pain or joy of human contact and communication. In a competitive market, contact is impersonal. A shy person need not talk to a seller. She walks in, selects her purchase, pays, and walks out. On the other hand, if that person has a right to participate in a decision but this requires overt voice, this may be too painful for the introvert to use. Some meek consumers or organization members are taken advantage of and remain silent rather than speak up for their rights. An individual's use of exit or voice depends on his taste for face-to-face contact, among other things. A society that utilizes voice to exercise rights puts the meek at a disadvantage.

CONTRACTUAL COST AND FORM OF BUSINESS ORGANIZATION

Economic production is often affected by various input suppliers acting simultaneously, in sequence, or in critical proportions. Production is reduced if these combinations are not timely or balanced. This creates a kind of interdependence such that any given supplier can create costs by failure to be timely. This cost is possible even if other sources of supply are eventually obtainable, so the problem is not just one of ordinary monopoly power.

For example, in the production of steel it is advantageous to go from the foundry to the rolling mill without cooling the metal. A timely sequence is even more critical in agriculture. Soil preparation, planting, and harvest operations must be done either simultaneously or in sequence using fixed proportions of inputs. For example, if harvest labor is not available when the crop is maturing, all may be lost. The same is true for machine repair. This often requires great flexibility in moving a given laborer from one task to another.

This coordination may be accomplished by various institutional arrangements. In self-sufficiency, one person combines all functions. Specialized inputs can be arranged by custom, but this loses flexibility as optimal combinations change. Inputs can be assured by negotiated contract to the extent that combinations can be foreseen, regularized, and monitored. But where this is not possible, the cost of negotiating a contract for each new situation is prohibitive. Some labor contracts reflect this and provide only for broad definitions of required tasks and remuneration, leaving the details to the foreman and to the third party arbitration if disputes cannot be settled. In the case of nonlabor inputs, some firms turn to long-run contracts rather than more frequent spot-market negotiations. Likewise, a firm may integrate functions by internal hierarchical command of operating subunits rather than by market negotiation with external firms (Williamson 1975).

These various rights structures alter the consequences of contractual cost interdependence. A conflict is created between those who desire detailed advance job specification to prevent unanticipated labor functions that, if foreseen, would not have been agreed upon at the negotiated wage and those who benefit from flexibility in the use of labor. In part, the productivity of an owner-operated agricultural enterprise stems from its superior flexibility over hired labor with negotiated specialized work assignments. Otherwise the tractor driver waits while the specialized maintenance worker changes the flat tire.

The form of business organization affects the consequences of contractual cost and also information cost (to be discussed in the next section). The timely response of labor is part of Leibenstein's (1978) X-efficiency, and institutions affecting the cooperative attitude of labor can make a difference in two production functions, each utilizing the same nominal amount and skill quality of labor.

INFORMATION AND UNCERTAINTY COSTS

A person needs information to interact effectively in transactions with other parties. Property rights have a great deal to do with who has to bear the costs of acquiring information, how large the costs will be, and ultimately the costs of mistakes made. Interdependence is not created simply because information is costly but rather because of its differential impact on persons. The purely competitive model assumes perfect information and therefore does not raise any questions about how rights affect who bears information costs and the costs of uncertainty. Information cost depends on product homogeneity, spatial distribution of production, and technical complexity. This creates a role for specialized producers of information such as brokers and information services. Note that the use of the term *information cost* here is not the same as the role of information in a production function. The use here refers to information necessary for a transaction rather than physical production.

Consumer Information and Products Liability

For a market transaction, a consumer needs to know prices offered by various sellers, what the good will do, and prices and characteristics of alternatives.[2] This information is needed for the present and expected future state of affairs. Since it is not possible here to discuss all types of information, the focus will be product charactertistics.

To understand the role of information costs as they interact with alternative rules for product liability, first assume perfect information at no cost. For illustration, assume an unsafe good whose production and distribution cost is $80. The potential damage size is known and can be insured against for $20. The cost of the no-net-damage product package is thus $100 in total. Begin with the situation where the producer has no liability (caveat emptor). The buyer pays $80 for the product and $20 for insurance. Now, assume that a producer finds that a completely safe product can be made for $90. It is advertised as a safe product at the old going effective price of $100 (the total consumer price for the safe package). In the short run, the firm obtains a profit of $10, but if the industry is competitive, the long-run equilibrium price becomes $90.

Repeat the scenario if producers have strict liability (caveat venditor). First, assume that production cost of a completely safe product is $100. The buyer still pays $100. The placement of the liability makes no difference if the cost of insurance and extra cost of a safer product are equal, $20 in this case. If a safer product costs more than $100 to make, the producer will now buy the insurance instead of the consumer, but the cost to the consumer is the same $100, except for the possibility that producers can buy insurance cheaper than can many consumers. One important difference is that under consumer liability, the individual consumer has the option of discounting the risk and keeping $20 in his pocket instead of buying insurance. (For consumers as a group, of course, this will be lost later in damages.) But consumer liability does allow for individual differences in time preference and risk aversion (a type of gambling). Under producer liability, the insurance will be purchased and the cost passed on to all consumers regardless of their different preferences. What if cost of producing a safe product is $90? The end result is the same as before, with a new equilibrium price of $90.

Trade produces a symmetrical result, and a proposition of pure theory can be stated: if information cost is zero and contractual and policing costs are zero, the location of liability makes no difference for product quality or for total consumer prices. (This proposition is modified in Chapter 11.)

Consider contractual and policing costs first. Under consumer liability, the consumer takes her lumps, and no transaction occurs outside of the product sale itself. Under producer liability, the consumer must sue, and suing creates an additional cost to prove extent and cause of injury. Some injury will be absorbed because costs for relief exceed the cost of injury. Consumer liability would save transaction costs. Care must be taken not to make transaction-cost minimization an isolated objective. An isolated transaction-cost-minimization objective is like saying that no one should have property protection from bullies and thieves because it is costly for the world to have police. But, without these transaction costs, the weak would likely have no income.

The problem is made more complicated by the fact that potential damage is related not only to the product but also to its care by the user. With producer liability, consumers have less incentive to be careful. High costs would be involved if producers, to avoid risk, made contracts with all consumers. It is difficult to arrange the rules to achieve a given mix of consumer care and producer effort. There is a limit to what external rules can accomplish.

Now consider information cost. What if the consumer cannot determine probable loss, but information is cheap for producers? Start with an existing unsafe product costing and selling for $80. With consumer liability, some consumers find that they made a mistake and suffer a loss that they might have wished to insure for. With producer liability, the result is the same as in the case of perfect information—the product will sell for the old production cost plus insurance or the new safe-product cost, whichever is less. This will be more than the $80 above. Location of liability affects current price and mistakes.

Will producers supply the consumer with information to prevent or reduce mistakes? If consumers think the product is safe, advertising safety features at the higher price of $90 might get the innovator more customers in the short run before others can follow, but it has the disadvantage of creating consumer concerns where there were none before, and total demand for the product may fall. There is also the uncertainty of knowing whether consumers will believe the hazard exists or, if it exists, how to tell whether the higher-priced product has solved it. Thus, it may turn out that no product can be sold at $90. No innovator may be willing to bear this risk. Individual competitors in other industries have little incentive to point out the risk because advertising cost would be high relative to any increased sales they would receive.

It is conceivable that special private firms might supply the information for a price, but it would be hard to organize payment for such a high-exclusion-cost good. Some consumers may pressure for government to provide the information. (For a review of private and public consumer information organizations, see Thorelli and Thorelli 1974.)

The readers can ask themselves if they feel they have information to judge the probable damage from current products purchased. Further, are there not many products advertised at two levels of safety and at different prices? Calling attention to danger may reduce demand for that class of products in general. It appears that rules of competition are not completely determining in the face of information costs. The location of liability makes a difference for product price (which will affect resource use) and information mistakes.

If information is costly but cheaper for producers, then producer liability means that the producer will have an incentive to reduce damage to consumers. The knowledgeable consumer loses the opportunity to self-insure and buy the old cheaper, unsafe product, but this has little meaning in the face of high information cost. Where consumers differ in the ease with which they obtain information there is conflict. Government provision of information is an alternative to producer liability in preventing mistakes. It allows for self-insurance, but if consumers differ in information cost, there is still conflict. One person's opportunities create costs for others.

In order to be precise, the above discussion has been complex. Similar points can be made more intuitively and applied to any claimed product characteristic. Suppose a firm claims that its product relative to others in the industry will last longer, make the users healthier and sexier, and so on. How do property rights affect the accuracy of these claims? Will information be provided if the consumer cannot obtain it easily by experience? Where many repeat sales are common, the consumer can learn about product differences over a short time, but for large infrequent purchases, this is impossible. The producers of unique products have a similar problem of predicting costs, so cost-plus contracts are common in some construction and repair activities, research, and military hardware.

If a seller makes misleading claims that are difficult for the buyer to check, there is some incentive for competitors who lose business to provide information about each other's products. But, where the effect on any one competitor is small, it will not pay any one seller to go to the trouble to expose it even though the total sales diversion is considerable. The desire for the quiet life may cause even competitive firms to practice deception. Where everyone is doing it, each firm knows that if it stopped and could so inform the public, it could draw business away from competitors. But they must also know that other firms in the industry would notice the effect and be forced to follow suit, and the short-run profits would disappear and no one would enjoy the profits they did before when all practiced deception. In the small-number situation, there is little incentive to try for short-run profits by telling consumers that the industry has been cheating. If you are selling a product where you can get away with deception, it is more profitable if everyone continues than if one tries to benefit from more consumer information.

There is the further question of what constitutes deception. In the United States, producers have the right to practice "puffery" when making advertising claims (Preston 1975). Claims are made that are not literally true, but it is held that everyone expects and discounts this so that it is not interpreted as breach of contract if goods do not fulfill advertising claims. But, if the puff was of no effect, why spend money doing it? U.S. consumers are exposed to the right of advertisers to puff up their claims and incidentally pollute the visual environment in the process.

One way for a consumer to save information costs is to have the right to expect that only goods that meet certain standards may be sold. Thus, the consumer saves time otherwise spent examining the features of each brand. This concept is found in the U.S. common-law doctrine of merchantability (Williston 1948); thus, a product must do what a reasonable person would expect it to do. If not, the buyer may get a refund or there is negligence if the product harms the buyer. This is in contrast to rules of strict liability (Veljanovski 1981a). The court must determine what is reasonable, but the idea is that there is a customary expectation that is associated with each product. For example, a product sold as a car should provide safe transportation and not break down continuously. A buyer has the right to expect this performance without having to be an engineer and inspect each model. This right does not help in evaluating special features, but it does save information cost. This property right is also known as an implied warranty.

Some noncompetitive sellers try to escape this common-law right by attaching to their sales contract a small list of expressed warranty items and excluding all other protection not specified. (A 1975 federal warranty law defined what a warranty had to cover to be called a full warranty. All others must be labeled "limited warranty.") This practice is in use with auto dealers in the

United States who, through a national association, have agreed to have a common sales contract offered to buyers on a take it-or-leave-it basis; this is called a contract of adhesion (Lenhoff 1962). Thus, oligopoly and private collective action can deny a common-law property right that saves consumers' information costs. (Note that different kinds of rights interact. Performance related to a given property rule may differ depending on whether we are speaking of individual proprietors or corporations, competitors or monopolists, and so on.) Here is an example where an existing property right is changed not directly by legislature or court but indirectly by sanctioned private power.

Where common-law rights do not satisfy consumers, they may turn to administrative transactions. In the United States, the Federal Trade Commission has a program of policing the accuracy of representations made in advertising, labeling, and other sales material. The law does not allow the commission to award damages to a defrauded consumer. The rules of the commission tend to result from the initiative of competitors who feel harmed by the deceptive practices of others. In some cases, private property rights (common law and statute law) and rights involved in administrative transactions are interchangeable (Posner 1969).

Consumers can seek expended regulation, or they might seek some of the alternatives already noted, such as requirement that the loser pay costs of court proceedings, rights to class-action suits, or prohibitions of expressed warranties. The role of government in establishing and changing the rights of consumers is no less via the route of assigning private property rights than in direct regulation. The former may appear to be nongovernmental, since there is no bureaucracy involved, and the citizen must act on his or her own initiative in seeking court action. But, at base, there is no right in either case without public action. Some groups (A) can meet their needs mostly through private property in the courts (or lack thereof) and thus try to make it look as if those (B) who try to obtain rights involved in administrative action are using government and restricting freedom while they (A) are not.

Another administrative approach to the information problem is the certification and licensing of the provider, which is common in professions such as medicine. The premise is that the layman cannot determine product quality but that, if the state certifies the training, the product will be satisfactory. The inability of the consumer to judge the product is often artificially created by a professional mystique, and licensing procedures are used to restrict supply and enhance provider incomes. The ability of the public to participate in resource-use decisions that require technical information remains one of the dilemmas of modern institutional design. If the layman cannot judge the product, how can the regulator who certifies the provider be judged?

Not all conflicts involving information are between buyers and sellers. Some are between consumers who have different information needs. The merchantability concept or some administrative minimum standard for a good to be sold does save information cost for some buyers. But it tends to narrow the variability in product quality and price. (The producer could have the option of producing and advertising a substandard product, but this may turn off consumers.) Some people who are good at home repairs and have spare time will prefer lower-quality, cheaper goods, while others want a standard product that they can depend on. If information to tell the difference were cheap, everyone could have what they want.

Hypothesis: Where information is differentially costly, a right to expect a standardized quality product is valuable for some and an exposure to higher prices for others.

It cannot be both ways, and the public choice of rights determines whose tastes count.

Another example of regulated product quality is rental-housing codes, which for example, prohibit rental of basements without outside windows, require two entrances, and so on and in the process reduce the housing supply. Some may be able to evaluate the safety or comfort factors and relate quality differences to price differences. However, for others information is costly, and they may prefer a standardized product so that time does not have to be spent evaluating quality differences.

There is always a random element in product quality. It would be extremely costly to prevent all quality variability in a given manufacturer's product. Thus a few consumers will occasionally buy a "lemon." Who bears the costs of lemons? Under consumer liability and no standard of merchantability, the receiver of a lemon bears the whole loss. Under producer liability, the cost is borne equally by all consumers. This has a parallel in personal injury suffered at the hands of a criminal. The person mugged is sometimes selected at random. If the criminal is caught, he or she goes to jail, but the victim bears all of the damage. Some suggest that society at large should compensate these random losses. The problem is one of contributory negligence. There is a conflict between the careful person and the unthoughtful. The random occurrence has to be distinguished from the case where the victim was negligent. The transaction cost of making these distinctions can prevent an otherwise desirable performance from being obtained.

Various private institutions arise in response to information costs, such as guarantees, warrantees, brand-name reputations, chain stores, celebrity endorsements, and advertising (Akerlof 1970; Klein and Laffer 1981). These have differential impacts on competitors and customers and thus are matters for public ratification, rejection, or modification.

Sharing of Irreducible Uncertainty

Consumers are not the only ones who are uncertain about product characteristics. In some cases buyers of producer goods cannot fully determine product quality. Further, this uncertainty may be irreducible and equal for both buyer and seller. An important example is that of oil and gas in the ground. The institutional structure at issue is not one of product liability, since the seller cannot warrant product quality (amount of the resource and its cost of extraction). The structural alternatives involve the type of market and leasing arrangements offered by land owners to oil drillers.

Commonly found alternatives for bidding include bonus, royalty, and profit share. The bonus method requires the bidder to offer a given-sized payment to the owner before the resource quality is tested by drilling. In the royalty method, the bidder offers a monetary amount per physical unit after the oil is found (percentage of wellhead value), while in the profit share, it is expressed as a percentage of net revenues of the eventually discovered good. With the bonus method, the entire uncertainty is borne by the bidder. In the royalty and profit methods, the risk is shared, since the amount to be paid depends on the actual yield of oil. As the risk to the bidder increases, the offer price falls. If the parties differ as to risk aversion, some method of sharing risk will be preferred by both (Leland 1978; Reece 1978). If both parties are equally risk averse, the profit-sharing method would be attractive (the driller risks only the drilling costs and no further costs that are independent of to-be-discovered yields and revenues. But, this method is not widely found because of another kind of information cost—namely that of monitoring costs. The seller has a cost of determining the actual net revenues of the buyer and problems of joint-cost allocation. The seller finds it difficult to compare bids from seller with unknown differences in operating efficiency.

There are many other possible structural alternatives. For example, the bidding may be oral or sealed. With public oral bids, buyers with different costs of information can learn from observing the bids of others. These methods also differ in terms of the owner's ability to capture consumer surplus. Since this is to be discussed in the next chapter, it will only be touched on here. In the sealed bid there is an incentive for the person with a high and unique value for the resource to reveal it fully rather than make only a marginally greater bid than the next higher bidder. Other bidding methods also affect the ability of the owner to extract the entire unique willingness to pay. For example, in a Dutch auction, the owner's first offer to sell is set and then the price is incrementally lowered. The first bid is also the last. For further discussion of the effect of information cost and consumer-surplus situations in the context of alternative institutions see Milgrom and Weber (1982) and Engelbrecht-Wiggans (1983).

Information and Form of Business Organization

The above discussion involves relatively marginal alternatives in types of rights and their distribution among individuals. There is much discussion in economic literature over the choice of major varieties of economic systems (that is, capitalism and socialism) that involve whole sets of different rights (Pryor

1973, chaps. 2, 3; Wiles 1977). A full analysis of comparative systems is not possible here, but information cost is often asserted to be a major factor in choice of systems. The bundle of rights that is commonly associated with corporate capitalism includes the right of the owner (through a manager) to be a residual claimant on profit, to be the central party common to all contracts with input suppliers (including the right to alter the mix of suppliers), and to sell these rights. Alchian and Demsetz (1972) claim that this particular set of rights (as opposed to those usually found in small, independent, market-related individuals and firms or in socialist, not-for-profit, or cooperative firms) not only provides the proper incentive but also is most effective in reducing information costs (also see Grossman and Hart 1982; Williamson 1975).

Alchian and Demsetz note that modern industry is dominated by team production, where "two men jointly lift heavy cargo into trucks," for example. It is difficult to attribute a portion of the output to individual effort. There are gains to cooperative behavior, but the inputs must be coordinated, metered, disciplined, and rewarded in such a way as to prevent shirking. They deny anything like Veblen's concept of the "instinct of workmanship." It is asserted that labor has no learned standard of performance and will not continue to lift unless the wage can be correlated with effort. This correlation requires knowledge, and this information is costly. The essence of the argument then is that the large capitalist business firm can secure this information cheaper than can a firm operating under any other set of rights relationships. Because of profit incentive, the owner-manager will become a specialist in obtaining information of the relative productivities of team members and pay them accordingly.[3] This will be cheaper than having each input owner obtain enough information on the output of each other owner so as to agree intelligently on their relative contract prices.

Hypothesis: Where labor productivity information is costly, the outside stockholder firm will be more productive than the worker-owned, cooperative, or not-for-profit firm, where shirking will be rampant, since no one is rewarded for disciplining others.

This is a plausible argument and illustrates how the information-cost concept might be applied. This particular application, however, seems questionable. It is not obvious that all teams imply difficulty in obtaining knowledge of the contributions of its members. The hypothesis focuses only on market transactions to relate effort to output. It assumes that the only monitoring of a shirking team member is by a competitive outsider offering to take the shirker's place. For an outsider to obtain the information necessary for this to occur would be expensive. But some internal monitoring is possible. When two people are carrying a beam, no one knows better than those under it whether the other fellow is doing his share (even where the output is not divisible). The team members know this more easily than any foreman or central administrator. There are two incentive possibilities. In a worker-owned firm, one's fellow team members are in effect buying each other's services for a share of the output value. The other immediate team members can recommend that the shirker's share of revenues be decreased, or they can apply social pressure. Thus, the Alchian and Demsetz hypothesis could be modified to say that where learned standards of work pace and quality are absent, central administrative monitoring will obtain performance information cheaper if the only available alternative monitor is a competitive outsider offering to work for a lower wage (there is no incentive or possibility of inside-the-team monitoring and application of sanctions).

The best monitor in some cases will be oneself. Willing participation, internalized behavior, and status-grant transactions can be more productive than fear of a monitor. As Harvey Leibenstein (1983, p. 837) puts it, "The question is not whether managers are residual claimants and as such sufficiently motivated to do adequate monitoring, but whether the interaction between managers and other employees (as well as between peers within the two groups) generates optimal attitudes."

What are the incentives for everyone to work at the group norm? In the U.S. auto industry, workers contract for a wage and hours unrelated to output. In this case it is to every worker's interest to work as little as possible and still be employed. Reporting a shirker to the foreman puts no money in the "rat's" pocket and is likely to create malevolence. The ambiguity of the contractual output is advantageous for the bosses if they can speed up the assembly line and increase output for the same wage and if they can discipline the workers by threat of firing under manager supervision. If bargaining power between boss and worker favors the boss, this is a good system for bosses, since workers face a take-it-or-leave-it offer. The worker largely takes the pace dictated by the boss instead of some marginal increment he might prefer of the trade-off between wages and a slower assembly line. In the U.S. auto industry, this situation is reflected in high rates of absenteeism and low productivity.

The highly segmented, individualized production pattern of the United States is not the only way. The Volvo Company of Sweden is literally using a team approach for subassemblies. Groups of workers agree to be responsible for so many units a day. They may allocate the specific tasks among themselves as they wish in order to reduce monotony and regulate their pace so long as the quota is met; thus, each worker will want to share equally in work and wage. If the job can be done faster, the team gets more break time, rather than the boss getting more output and profit from the speedup. If some team member goofs off, the other team members know it and will realize that it comes out of their break time or means loss of wages when more units could be contracted for and produced. Social pressure can be applied. An individual may shirk and retain his income, but he will "earn" his colleagues' malevolence, which may affect total utility.[4] Some Japanese firms avoid central monitoring and reward workers according to seniority.

The role of specialization in information production is surely a worthy question in any specific instance, but it is too simplistic to assert that the highly centralized, capitalist form of business enterprise has grown primarily because it can provide input-output information the most cheaply in complex production situations. Stephen Marglin (1974) has offered an equally plausible explanation. He argues that specialization of labor and centralized management exist primarily to enable the bosses to control the workers and extract the surplus. When a worker has no identifiable product, he has no choice but to sell his labor to the few bosses that exist instead of the many final or intermediate goods consumers. Marglin argues that the technological efficiency of specialization is vastly overrated and that many workers are interchangeable in many jobs with short training periods. Even where specialization is physically efficient, it does not mean that one worker must do the same thing for a lifetime, even if it is advantageous for the boss to keep the worker ignorant of the larger production process.

Marglin makes an important distinction between physical efficiency(more output for the same input) and economic efficiency (more dollar profit for the same capitalist investment). He suggests that much of the historic increase in output came not only from greater output per man-hour but also from boss control of workers' hours when they would have preferred more leisure to more income. What Alchian and Demsetz (1972) in value-laden terms call shirking, Marglin (p.92) calls a preference for leisure, since he regards a backward-bending labor-supply curve as a natural phenomenon as long as the individual workers control the supply of labor.

Alchian and Demsetz gloss over just how management determines the marginal product of each input supplier in joint or team production. (They also gloss over the definition of output and ignore the impact of the production process on the human personality.) In many cases it is not a question of who (under what rights) will most cheaply obtain knowledge of individual contributions to output. The concept of marginal product is simply often without meaning. Of course, individuals in joint (team) production have to be rewarded somehow, and the manager is willing to supply this institutional function (for a price). It should be kept in mind that management is itself a team function in large-scale firms and output cannot be easily attributed to the decisions of the individual management team member.

To a large degree, where output is truly joint, property rights do not determine who can provide knowledge of marginal outputs the cheapest, but they do determine who gets to decide on the distribution of the benefits of the joint product. Thurow (1985) notes that some American firms program robots to eliminate worker control even where on-the-spot flexibility is more productive. It goes without saying that the capitalist system is an efficient system for the capitalist to obtain a significant share of the joint product and perhaps also for a higher rate of investment and hours worked than some workers might prefer. Of course, the same thing can happen in socialist systems, as witness the results of Soviet collective farms. Most observers agree that collective farms are not greater in technical efficiency than individual smaller farms, but the system of rights was effective in draining off capital and production surpluses for industrialization at the expense of the real income of the peasant (Volin 1970).

It may be useful at this point to note some potential differences between facilities used in common but owned by private entrepreneurs and those owned cooperatively by members. The group of users of a common facility owned privately are much less conscious of their "groupness" than members of a cooperative. They are much more like the consumers of automobiles produced in a common plant. The plant owner may see them as a group, but the consumers are not aware of each other. If they were, they might organize more effectively to solve common problems against the manufacturer. A consumer who is unhappy with the product of a private producer can exit and deny the owner his or her business. The member of a cooperative has this option plus that of voice.

Hypothesis: Buyers from consumer cooperatives can and do speak to fellow members more about the product and can let preferences be directly known to the manager.

A small complaint can be quickly communicated—that is, information cost on consumer preferences is less in the cooperative than in a stockholder-owned firm. People feel more at ease in communicating to a manager who is seen as their employee than to a corporate manager who is working for some invisible stockholder. This form of cooperative ownership creates a sense of community that may reduce free-rider behavior. Another factor is that during temporary shortages, the private owner is more likely to resort to price rationing (and earn rents) while the cooperative firm will use other means. These propositions relating business institutions to situations of high information cost should be amenable to empirical testing (see Chapter 12).

It should be emphasized that a person who formerly was not a factor owner may think that he will effectively participate when made a part of group ownership. However, depending on the rules of collective choice, the transaction costs may still prevent participation. This is true for corporate stockholders whether private or public (Schmid and Faas 1980).

Business organization is much more than a choice between capitalism and socialism. It is a system of many alternative internal incentive rules. For example, U.S. industrial chief executive officers have an average tenure of six years and their present and retirement income is directly related to current profits. Middle-level managers are responsible for independent profit centers and are promoted on the basis of quarterly profits. As a result many firms have investment payback objectives of less than three years (Thurow 1985, p. 149). But it is impossible to research and develop major new products and manufacturing and distribution systems in this time, and Japanese firms with longer planning horizons are driving the U.S. from many markets.

Part of the reason for the current business-incentive system is owing to information costs. Current returns are easy to monitor by supervisors and the stock market, while the present value of future innovation is uncertain. To meet the problem of foreign competition, Thurow suggests that managers' retirement pay be tied to performance of their companies after they retire and that there be more job security and promotion to top jobs from within to lessen the reliance on short-term performance. These internal incentive systems are partly a matter of learned and evolving corporate culture and partly related to public policies relating to taxation and mergers. Such cultural change, and especially the broader environment of attitude toward time preference and risk taking are a matter of institutional change not further discussed here.

Agriculture Tenancy

The form of the contract between an agricultural land owner and labor is influenced by information costs. Alternative structures are hired labor, share-tenancy, and fixed rent. A large literature is devoted to explaining the predominance of share-tenancy around the world. The logic of the marginal calculus suggests that the tenant might not provide labor to the point where marginal returns equal marginal cost if she only receives a share of those returns. This misallocation could be avoided by the landlord contractually specifying the required labor input. The transaction and information costs to enforce the labor requirement may, however, allow labor to reduce its input. But these costs also are present in other institutional alternatives.

Hired labor has opportunities for shirking without constant supervision, which is more difficult in the field than in the factory. A tenant paying fixed rent has no incentive for shirking and bears all of the costs of an uncertain harvest. Conversely, the landlord bears all of the costs of uncertainty with a hired-labor structure. If there was a perfect market in crop insurance, a fixed rental might be attractive, but lacking that, share-tenancy facilitates risk sharing. Eswaran and Kotwal (1985) view sharecropping as a partnership in which each partner provides some unmarketable factor, such as technical know-how, managerial ability, machinery, or credit. In summary, share-tenancy structure in the context of information and contractual costs results in a performance of superior labor and other inputs and broader risk sharing than would hired-labor or fixed-rent structures.

Uncertainty and Immobile Assets

If knowledge of present states is differentially costly, knowledge of future states is more so. Transactions take place in the present but in anticipation of the future. Cost of acquiring information on the future differs among the parties, and the consequences of being wrong may vary among the parties. Therefore, any rights that affect uncertainty also affect income distribution.

Consider the problems of making an investment today to produce a product to be sold in the future. If prices change, the value of these assets will change. This situation is particularly troublesome if the assets are for a single purpose and cannot be utilized for an alternative product or if there are costs associated with selling and moving to another use. For example, some machine tools needed for auto production can only be used in auto production. If consumers change their demand for the particular auto that the machine can produce before the value of the machine can be recovered, the investor will have made a costly mistake and resources will have been wasted. An immobile asset is one where capital losses occur because its present worth (future flow of the marginal value product, or salvage value if larger) is less than historic acquisition price minus capital recovered (depreciation). Such an asset may or may not remain fixed in its present use depending on the relationship of its marginal value product to opportunity cost, ie. salvage value (Johnson 1982; Johnson and Quance 1972). Oliver Williamson (1985, p. 32) says, "The special purpose technology requires greater investment in transaction-specific durable assets and is more efficient for servicing steady-state demands. When assets are transaction specific, competition prior to investment becomes monopoly afterwards."

Immobile assets create capital losses when investments do not fit demand whether or not the asset becomes fixed. Immobility is a measure of inflexibility and nonsubstitutibility at the margin. An asset may also become immobile when a new technology is created that makes an old process obsolete before its value is recovered.

Immobility also occurs with respect to human capital. Persons trained and comfortable in a particular occupation may suddenly find themselves unemployed as demand shifts or a new technology is created. Orthodox theory, with its focus on consumer sovereignty, largely ignores the power of some people to create large losses for others (Kanel 1974, p. 832). Thus, orthodoxy concludes that efficient market flexibility is a universal blessing.

John Kenneth Galbraith (1967) has referred to the "technological imperative for planning." The market will not produce information on future demand and prices sufficient to support the large immobile investments necessary for modern productivity. If we want to take advantage of certain technologies, we must be prepared to accept some planning that will ensure physical and human capital recovery in the main.

In most Western market economies, we have taken the attitude that if the costs of mistakes are borne by the investor, he will be more careful in acquiring knowledge. But some knowledge is impossible to obtain when large numbers of firms and buyers are acting independently. In the face of this, business firms resort to private planning. They try to manipulate consumer demand through advertising and other methods (including patent suppression). These methods can be used to maintain demand through the period of capital recovery and beyond to the advantage of the firm's profits. Labor resorts to featherbedding and other job-protection rules.

Galbraith (p. 33) has said that the "enemy of the market is not ideology but the engineer." He might have added that other enemies are the fickle consumer and the unpredictable inventor. Change creates problems when there are immobile assets. Different actions can offset this unpredictability, and these alternatives are controlled by property rights. Mention has already been made of advertising and purchase of patents to prevent new products and processes from destroying asset values. Prohibiting these would have a dramatic effect on the character of investments. It would be like making an investment in a country with an unstable government where expropriation is probable. No one would make long-term investments.

Another private planning device is diversification and conglomeration of firms. This device allows uncertainty to be spread over more products. If you produce only one product and demand changes because of fickle consumers or a discovery that your product causes cancer, the going concern may be destroyed. If the firm is diversified, it may be able to make up losses and stay solvent in other product lines. Yet there are other costs to consumers because of the market power of conglomerate firms. Antitrust laws in the United States have not been effective against conglomerates.

Oliver Williamson (1985) argues that ongoing private contracting will efficiently coordinate investments via vertical integration, performance bonding, and other hostagelike safeguards. For example, fruit farmers with immobile assets can collectively own a processing plant and thus in an uncertain environment, a price for the raw material need not be specified before sales of the finished product. But, the transaction-cost saving of this structure is threatened if there is no agreement on sharing of the net returns among the members where joint costs have to be allocated to different fruits (Staatz 1984). These private orderings work better among firms than between manufacturers and consumers.

Some public collective planning to reduce uncertainty may also be possible. For examples of modern planning in Europe, see Shonfield (1965) and Cohen (1969). Sometimes this takes the form of outright subsidies to firms that get caught in changing demand, such as the producers of military equipment, when government orders are reduced sharply. In World War II, U.S. farmers were promised guaranteed prices for three years after the war as an incentive to invest for greater wartime production. Another possibility is to have government guarantee a certain volume of business for a certain period. For example, U.S. oil producers hesitated to invest when they were not sure that the Arabs would continue their price-fixing cartel. The government might have contracted to cover the investment. (This has quite different distributive consequences than agreeing to a variable tariff that would keep prices for total output from dropping.) In effect, consumers as a group would be saying that they agree to buy a certain quantity at a certain price for a given period in exchange for the utilization of the lowest-cost technology.

In the context of high information costs, the distribution of the consequences of uncertainty and thus economic performance would be changed, thus creating a conflict among consumers. Some might prefer to encourage producers to use the best long-term technology, even if immobile, to achieve low per-unit costs and product prices in exchange for a guaranteed period of capital recovery. Other consumers might prefer the flexibility of not assuring their demand and be willing to pay higher unit costs associated with less-efficient investment in mobile capital goods. It is not clear that exposure to risk of changed demand is always to the benefit of consumers at a cost to producers. There are also intraconsumer conflicts.

Some consumers might be better off to agree to long-term purchases of certain goods rather than be manipulated by advertising and other price-maintenance schemes. It is not always best to let the losses of uncertainty fall willy-nilly, for the potential losers are going to take steps to protect themselves, steps that may not produce results favorable to some consumers. A particularly troublesome uncertainty is new knowledge of the safety of products. For example, we can regard exposure to change in demand based on new knowledge of the consequences of using a certain product as just one of the ordinary hazards of business. Take the case of cigarettes and cancer. We can deny the producers any property right in the value of their assets and say they should have known when they started that they had a bad product and now must bear the full cost of any change. Their reaction is intense lobbying to restrict the dissemination of knowledge, labeling, and so on. Producers will try to avoid the loss with all the power at their disposal. What would be their behavior if the cost of their equipment could be recovered from consumers and if perhaps low-cost loans could be made for conversion of the firm to other lines of production?

Hypothesis: In the situation of high information cost, the right to recover loss to assets from consumer-demand change produces a different set of investments and prices than the right to maintain demand by manipulating government and the consumer.

Losses owing to unpredictable shifts in demand have to be distinguished from cases where reasonable diligence would have prevented a business mistake. Practical administrative problems may make such a right impossible to implement. The objective might not be to prevent all losses but to prevent certain producer behavior to protect assets that may lower the welfare of some consumers. The theoretical point here is that information costs and immobile asset characteristics help suggest new situations where institutional alternatives can affect performance.

When asset immobility is combined with fewness, the consumer can exploit the producer more. Without specific assets, the producer would exit at prices below acquisition costs (Klein, Crawford, and Alchian 1978; Williamson 1981, p. 1548). Also, with immobile plants and machines, labor unions can bargain for higher wages even in declining industries. Safeguards and the advantage of continuing relations may or may not prevent it.

The producer with superior information or who is more risk averse may consider technologies that are more mobile but have higher average costs. But, this producer may be caught in a trap if others are more optimistic and invest in immobile assets with lower average costs. The producer with the mobile but higher-cost technology may be right for the long run but will go bankrupt in the meantime competing with lower-cost firms (who will eventually also be bankrupt when product prices fall). Collective action may be necessary to avoid this trap.

As a historical footnote, Marx (1894, p. 113) refers to loss of exchange value caused by improved technology as "moral depreciation" and expressed concern about the "overproduction of machinery and other fixed capital" and the subsequent convulsions created by falling prices. A Marxist or Veblenian might argue that the interests of the masses will be served only by the abolition of the profit system. However, it is a large assumption to say that all people want the same thing. Marx did see handcraft workers wanting a different set of goods and type of society than industrialized workers. Further, it is not clear that worker-owned firms, engineers, and planners necessarily care more for consumers than do capitalists. Is profit the culprit, or is it the rules that make one action profitable rather than another? Can different performances be ensured by changing from bargained to administrative or status transactions, or does performance depend on the detailed rules of each?

Uncertainty and Perishable Goods

Perishable goods create some of the same interdependencies in the face of uncertain demand (and supply) as do immobile assets. If an investment is made based on an expected output price, it can result in a loss if prices fall and the output cannot be stored to await price recovery. Various structures arise in agriculture to control this interdependence. Marketing orders and controls may require collective action to destroy part of an unexpectedly large harvest to avoid price collapse. Fresh-produce growers may collectively decide to limit fresh-market sales and divert more of the crop to a storable form to maintain fresh prices and share the risk of recovering the cost of preservation. The performance may differ from what would happen if the storage were done by non-farmer-owner processors.

Organized labor may take advantage of perishable-goods situations to strike for higher wages when the perishability enhances their bargaining power. In general, labor bargaining power is significantly greater in situations where demand for the labor input cannot be postponed to await for alternative supplies, such as in hospital, fire, and police services. Institutional structures often prohibit strikes in these perishable-goods situations where stockpiles and alternative sources are not possible. If employers had been certain of labor's future price, they may not have invested in certain perishable enterprises. On the other side, labor is the ultimate perishable flow good. If it is not used, it is lost forever. One might expect the development of worker-owned cooperatives to minimize these opportunistic work stoppages, but it has not happened in the United States.

Cost Discontinuities and Investment Coordination

A key problem in economic development arises from the fact that economies of scale in one industrial sector can affect returns to investment in another.[5] Information necessary for investment coordination may be lacking when there are substantial cost discontinuities. Reference was made in Chapter 4 to products with economies of scale. Not only do some products have economies of scale, but there are large, discontinuous changes in the cost function at certain threshold points. This problem is frequently illustrated in the context of the possibility for a country to substitute home production for imports (Chenery and Westphal 1969). Assume steel is imported and used in a fabricating industry. If steel can be produced domestically for less because of some innovation, fabricators will switch and buy domestic steel. The demand is there, and imports are replaced. Knowledge of this initial demand is provided by the market for all investors to see.

However, consider the situation where domestic steel could be produced for half the current import price if capacity could be doubled. But steel investors will not expand plants to this extent unless they are sure that profitable quantities can be sold at that price. Steel users will not expand to use this much steel unless they are sure they can actually get steel at half price.

The steel firm cannot make a big expansion and have excess capacity unused for several years while its lower prices possibly attract new buyers. Even if the future demand curve could be predicted, the optimum scaled plant may not be built because of the lag in the actual demand coming from expanded fabricating plants. The two kinds of plants are interdependent. The size of the one plant and its unit costs depend on the size of the other and vice versa. The decisions of one firm impact on the other. The two kinds of plants must be ready to go simultaneously. The problem for market coordination is caused by indivisibilities that prevent the externality from being accounted for.

This can be illustrated. If unfilled orders accumulate at current prices, the plant or some portion of it might be duplicated. But what if no further orders develop? If there are economies of scale and small increments to the plant may be added, the firm may take a small risk and expand and see if the extra production can be sold with the lower price. The demand curve in this case can be discovered by successive small expansions and market offers and sales. But if the cost function is discontinuous, the market alone contains no information on how much might be sold at sharply declining prices. This situation requires information on the accounts of a whole series of steel fabricators, which in turn requires detailed voiced communication and planning between firms (or the creation of a new firm that includes all related industries). Without this information in the face of indivisibilities, the steel firm underinvests because its new potential output cannot soon be sold at a price covering costs. It is not that it must capture a share of the profits created for other firms but that profits elsewhere do not immediately result in new demand, and the firm would go broke waiting. This problem is not solved alone by government ownership, since the underutilized, wasted plant remains regardless of who pays for the waste.

Information and contractual costs interact here. The information might be secured through negotiations among the different firms or by a firm investigating the purchase of related firms. The point is that this creates costs not incurred when the demand curve can be discovered by offering marginal quantities at marginally different prices. Other possibilities are for government planners to develop the necessary information and to facilitate the common timing of the related investments. Large, private, vertically integrated firms obtain the necessary information and coordination through internal communication, though as the size of the firm increases, there may be diseconomies of scale in information handling (Williamson 1981). Each of these alternatives implies a different set of property rights and performance to achieve lowest cost per unit of output.

Irreversibility, Time Lags, Option Demand, and Contingent Claims

In the above cases, uncertain knowledge of the future creates problems for producers and, indirectly, consumers. One problem involves the effects on producers when consumers reduce their demand, destroying the value of immobile assets. A situation of human interdependence also arises when there is little or no demand now but there might be in the future. Prediction of future demand is difficult for most goods. Leaving aside immobile assets, this is no special problem if supply can be developed quickly as needed. But in some cases, resource use is irreversible or, if reversible, the time lag in production response is costly.

First, consider resources whose use is irreversible. If something is used for one purpose today, it may be impossible to produce another kind of product tomorrow even if great demand develops. (Irreversibility is related to the distinction in the literature between flow and stock resources (Barlowe 1972, pp. 227–341.) If future values are predictable, their discounted present value may be greater than the value of a current use of the resource. But, if values are unpredictable, the option to consume a certain good may not exist in the future as bids for current irreversible use dominate (Weisbrod 1964). *Option demand* (existence value) refers to the desire to keep an alternative open in the future. Under certain circumstances, information contained in present profit-and-loss accounts may not reflect this demand.

For example, consider the alternative uses for the Grand Canyon of the Colorado River. It can be the site of hydroelectric dams and flat-water recreation or for wilderness uses. Assume that at the moment the bids from electricity users and speedboat users are greater than those from wilderness users. But someone may suspect that wilderness appreciation is growing and that at some future date these values (even discounted to the present) might be greater than for dam uses. If there are no substitutes for the natural resource, future high prices cannot call forth increased output. Will anyone put down money now to keep the option open? It is conceivable that there are people who have an option demand and would pay now for the satisfaction of knowing that the canyon will remain a wilderness site for their grandchildren's use (Krutilla 1967; Krutilla and Fisher 1975). Option demand (or value) is the amount that a risk-averse person would pay now to keep a future purchase open.

A term often used for a right to a future option is *contingent claim*, which is defined as a "a right to a variable amount of commodity, the amount to depend upon the state of nature which obtains" (Zeckhauser 1970). In this case, some may want the right to buy wilderness uses if tastes, skills, or technology develop for use of the outdoors in the future. An example of a market in contingent claims is insurance. People pay a premium that allows for a certain payment in the future if they die, are injured, and so forth. Comprehensive ex ante bargains would specify all contingencies and there would be no surprises (Fama 1980; Jensen 1983). But, fundamental uncertainty means that contingency categories cannot be specified and contracted for in advance.

High exclusion cost is another barrier to contingency markets. It would be difficult, though not impossible, to exclude people in the future from buying admission to the Grand Canyon Park on the basis of whether they or their parents had or had not paid to keep the option open. It would be costly to contact everyone in the country (even those who had never visited the park) to see if they were aware that unless they paid now the option would disappear. No one person would probably pay very much, so a great number of people would have to be contacted. Of course, if the government collected a general tax to preserve the canyon, some would be forced to pay who did not want the option. If A is to have the option, it may mean exposure of B to buy an unwanted option (or one less preferred to an alternative government expenditure, say, for health care). The problem of interdependence is raised not alone by the uncertainty of future prices or even the irreversibility of resource use but this in combination with high exclusion and contractual costs.

The irreversibility of stock-resource use led S. V. Ciriacy-Wantrup (1963, chap. 18) to advocate what he termed a "safe minimum standard" for natural-resource use. In the face of uncertain demand and uncertain technological improvements that create substitutes, a certain minimum of preservation would give some options for future use. Enforcement of this standard in the rate of use of certain resources would be like an insurance policy whose premium is paid by those who suffer higher current costs because of the reduced supplies of current goods. Whether those paying the premium are also the beneficiaries is another question.

Where this resource is already in public ownership, those who wish to retain the wilderness option will try to institute an administrative transaction that in effect will declare them the owners of the canyon. The owners then will wish to reject any bids from hydroelectric users. Such an action will be at the expense of electricity users, who will be forced to turn to more-expensive sources of supply. Also, people in the locality who had expected jobs from current resources development will be frustrated. Thus, local people often try to get a payment in lieu of the local taxes that would have been generated by development of the resource. Such payment is not as valuable to the local people as the right to sell out to electricity users, but it is better than nothing. The option demand for the wilderness lover from New York is at the expense of many in the state of Arizona, where the canyon is located.

The conflict among various members of the public could be settled by establishing factor ownership and markets if it were not for high exclusion costs. Those who fear that no substitutes for dwindling stock resources such as oil and coal will be found may wish to pay higher prices now to extend the time span of use. But, there is a conflict with those of different expectations and time preference. Those who are profligate in their use cannot be excluded from the extended-time availability made possible by those reducing their rate of use. Irreversibility plus high exclusion cost creates interdependence. Use taxes or rationing by government expands the opportunity set of the risk averse at the expense of those with a high time preference (preference for present consumption).

There is a certain similarity between the source of option demands or contingent claims in natural-resource uses and the problem of loss of immobile assets if demand declines, as discussed above. If the canyon is developed with a hydroelectric dam or if industrialization destroys a rare animal species, these processes are irreversible. Any future value that might develop after the irreversible use is begun will be lost to its owner. The product itself will be impossible to produce if there are no substitute inputs. If investment in material and human capital becomes obsolete before its value is recovered because of demand shifts or technological change, future value (which is reflected in present values) is lost. These are both potentially large losses. Society loses the potential productive life of these resources. Some other examples are suggestive. The machines used in agriculture are not useful for other types of production. As new technologies are developed rapidly, it often transpires that there was too much investment in old machines that have a useful physical life but no economic life. Losses in these immobile assets can be enormous and create losses to some farmers (Johnson and Quance 1972).

The same thing happens to human capital. People train themselves for a certain line of activity and build homes in a community only to find that demand changes and their experience is no longer needed and they have to move, losing both human and material capital. Many so-called depressed regions are in this predicament. Employers have no interest in renegotiating contracts since they may be bankrupt or are moving and do not need the goodwill of these particular workers. In a sense, government programs to aid depressed areas can be regarded as a type of national self-insurance policy premium where all areas pay into a common pool made available to the area that suffers the unpredictable loss because of demand shift or technological change. In countries like Sweden, the government does not guarantee income in such situations, but it does pay moving and retraining costs associated with fixed human capital. In 1974, French employers and the five major unions agreed to a plan providing for a joint employer-and-worker-financed plan that provides a year's salary to any worker who is unemployed because of changes in general economic conditions (*Time*, October 28, 1974, p. 94). The government granted an emergency fund and provides inspectors to make sure the layoffs are not caused by worker or employer ineptitude. Such distinctions may involve high information costs. The fact that France has a strong organization of employers (the Patronat) and only a few major unions makes the contractual cost of employer agreement reasonable.

The United States has formal government insurance programs where these markets have not developed privately, such as for crop insurance, unemployment and disability insurance, and social security. Informal insurance is provided through disaster relief. When government becomes an unsubsidized seller of contingent claims in lieu of private sellers, it is useful to ask if it is because of savings in contractual cost or because of better ability to predict (save information cost). It is usually not a question of who can get information the cheapest, since the future is seldom knowable to anyone, but that there are more opportunities for pooling the burdens of unpredictable loss.

Two varieties of future demand uncertainty can be distinguished. The discussion above applies to the situation where the total future demand is unpredictable. But in some cases the demand of a given individual is uncertain while the demand of all is predictable. There are goods for which an individual's demand canot be predicted because of the nature of the good. Zeckhauser terms these "probabilistic individual preference" goods. (They differ from the previous cases in that the problem is a change not in preference but in knowing when the preference applies; it is a matter of events rather than an evolution of preferences.) Examples are a person's demand for blood plasma or a fire engine.[6] The individual cannot predict his or her own demand for these services until certain events transpire and use is needed, though he or she may place a present value on the satisfaction of knowing they are there if needed (option demand). While the individual cannot predict need, the aggregate demand may be predictable. It is known approximately how much blood will be needed for a given city. In this case, private suppliers, such as in the case of blood plasma, will provide the good to people who did not know ahead of time that they would be consumers. Each user is charged enough at time of use to keep the service available.

The present value of future use of all individuals need not be collected now if the service can be paid for by the flow of fees over time. If this yearly flow is predictable, the necessary present investments can be made by private market firms (even if the particular individual customers are unknown at the time of the investment). But, when exclusion costs are high or joint-impact characteristics are present, there is additional interdependence. For example, people who normally drive to work might pay more than the usual bus fare when their car breaks down. Revenue from this source may be critical to the existence of the bus system. While a rider can be excluded from riding, it is costly to distinguish the desperate car user from the regular bus patron and price accordingly. A private firm could not collect, and the option demand of the occasional bus rider will not be met unless an administrative transaction is utilized. For example, a tax on all private cars might be collected to keep the bus system available to those who develop car breakdowns. The problem is exclusion cost and not simply the feature of probabilistic individual preference.

Another variety of uncertainty giving rise to contingent claims occurs when the interdependence of resource use and users is not clear. The extent of incompatibility in use may be uncertain. A new use is initiated with no apparent impact on existing uses. If incompatibility is later discovered, the initial user may be damaged. If we assume ownership in the initial uses, the probability of a criminal charge or civil suit for damages from an incompatible use may be sufficient to deter a would-be new user. But when the extent of the incompatibility is not known, this deterrent cannot function. The new user can become an unwitting thief. In some cases, the incompatibility is suspected, but the extent is unknown and thus the initial owner might prefer that an injunction be issued to prevent the new use, under which the proposed new user would be required to purchase a contingent claim to be exercised if incompatibility developed. (Recall the discussion of injunctive versus damage relief above.)

The situation may be illustrated with respect to the disposal of nuclear wastes. Builders of nuclear-powered electric generators believe that the waste can be disposed of in sealed containers. The only other resource needed is a bit of land to receive the container. Other resource owners fear additional incompatibility, however. They fear, for example, that underground water might be contaminated in the future. The nuclear firms prefer to face these claims for damages if and when they arise. This position is made even more attractive by federal law, which limits the total amount of liability. Water users would prefer prohibition or an injunction. The uncertainties of incompatibility and irreversibility combine to intensify conflict. The right to receive compensation to correct the damage can be more serious. The water users may fear that the party causing the damage will be unable to pay (compare the case of compulsory auto liability insurance noted below). The damage may be greater than the assets of the new user (unwitting thief). In this case, the initial owner would prefer that the potentially offending party be forced to buy an option to use from the initial owner or insurance from a third party. In many cases the immense but uncertain damage may be uninsurable. To require insurance is in effect to prohibit the new, potentially incompatible use. If the initial owner cannot obtain an injunction and insurance is not required, the current user is exposed to the possibility that use will be lost in the future without full compensation. In effect, the new user already owns a contingent claim and may destroy the old use at some unknown future date. The demand of unborn future generations will not be expressed in the market or by government. Only the living choose for the future generations.

To summarize, where total demand is not predictable, problems emerge in two contexts: (1) where assets are immobile and (2) where use is irreversible. In the first case, unused factors will be lost to producers, and in the second, future demand of some consumers will go unmet. Where higher future prices cannot signal increased output, people may want to purchase an option to buy (a contingent claim). Markets in options are found where transaction costs (exclusion) are not too high. Where they are relatively high, people may turn to government. But, when interests differ, one person's options for a good may mean others have to buy something they do not want.

The conflicts created by the unpredictability of aggregate demand apply to a great many goods where supply is not marginally expandable (cost discontinuity), use is irreversible, or assets are immobile. Further interdependencies are created by uncertainty with respect to the extent of incompatibility in resource use. The lack of certain information creates a unique set of opportunities for A to get in B's hair. Government assigns rights that control the direction of this interdependence whether by explicit action or silence.

In the subsections above, several situational variables have been identified where the differential response to information cost and uncertainty are especially relevant in determining the impact of alternative rules. These variables included the degree of asset mobility (fixity), cost discontinuities, and irreversibility in resource use. In the subsections to follow, these variables along with more general costs of consumer and producer information will be explored in the context of several sets of institutions relating to insurance, real estate, and labor markets.

Insurance

People are faced with low-probability events such as early death, fire, and accident. Risk averters may prefer to exchange a small cost now for reimbursement of an uncertain large loss later. This is the principle of insurance, with its concept of the common pool of insured people over which the risk of actual damage is spread. In some instances, however, people may discount certain rare and hard-to-predict events so heavily that few will buy insurance even where it is known that the damages over time are substantial to a certain class of people. One such example is that of people living or working in flood plains. Perception of potential flood losses is quite a different psychological matter than other classes of loss such as fire or accident (Kates 1962). The result is that when flood-damage insurance is offered, few people buy it, and thus the common pool over which the risk is spread is too small. If only a handful of people in a flood plain buy the insurance, each individual's premiums approach their average annual losses. Concerning the advantages of joint action with respect to insurance pools, people are interdependent. If you are the only risk averter in a group that ignores the risk of floods, you will not be able to buy insurance. One person's perception and choice impact on others. One person's total risk acceptance denies the rights of others to the benefits of risk spreading. People who do not like exposure to this kind of loss may seek a new right via a government transaction that makes insurance compulsory. The choice of whose interdependent interest is to count cannot be avoided.

Musgrave (1959, p. 13) uses the term *merit goods* to describe cases where one group's preferences are set aside and a good is provided for them at their expense whether they want it or not. People are saved from their own folly in the view of the persons who want the good. The term *merit goods* is value laden. The above situation is a conflict of interests where the securing of one person's interest is the exposure of others to things they do not want. It does not help to describe the case by labeling one of the interests as one of merit and thereby implicitly regarding the other as lacking merit, though such labeling may help to win uninformed public debate.

If my house is subject to flooding and I have no insurance, I may have denied you the opportunity to join a low-cost, risk-spreading pool, but I harm you in no other way. However, in the case of liability insurance, this may not be true. Some drivers may be willing to accept the risk of driving without insurance and exposing themselves to a costly judgment in court if they hurt another person. But they also expose the damaged person to the possibility that the damage cannot be collected even if the claim is approved by the court, since you cannot get large medical bills paid by a poor or even average-income person.[7] A few U.S. states and most countries of Europe have made auto liability insurance compulsory. Opponents regard such a law as a violation of freedom and note that it may prevent a poor man from having a car if he has to buy liability insurance. This argument is misleading.

The poor would be better off if any time they were in need they had only to steal. Many more people could drive cars if they could take a car at will. But property rights are well recognized with respect to the physical removal of cars. The question is whether one person has the right to be free of losses to the value of his car and person or whether persons with high-risk acceptance may be free of expenditures they do not want. One person's acceptance of the risk of income garnishment is the exposure of others to inability to collect for damages. In many states you cannot steal another person's car, but you can destroy its value. The consequences of physical interdependence are determined by property rights that specify which impacts are to be accounted for. The unpredictability of future events and different attitudes toward risk aversion create new varieties of interdependence that are subject one way or the other to property rights.

When the parties to transaction have asymmetrical information costs, the distributive consequences of a source of interdependence are shaped by alternative rights. For example, a seller of life or medical insurance must determine the health of a buyer in order to establish the correct rate. In some kinds of insurance, it is impossible for the seller to determine in advance the characteristics of the insured even when it is known that there are different classes of risk. The people who seek insurance may know which risk class they fall in, but it is costly for the seller to find it out. Such a situation is one of "adverse selection," since at a fixed price to all, the high-risk group gets a price break at the low-risk group's expense. If people are opportunistic and do not have internalized standards (such as in status transactions) that cause them to reveal otherwise undetectable information about themselves or their property, costs can be created for others if the latter cannot exit the firm.

Some types of insurance tend to decrease the care with which people act. Contributory negligence is always a problem to detect by an insurance firm. For this reason, insurance tends never to make a party who suffers a loss "whole." The person whose goods are damaged seldom is as well off after the loss as before. The habits of the nondetectable negligent create a cost for the careful person who cannot get full insurance coverage. It is difficult to design a system of rights that does not have differential effect on the careful and noncareful because of information cost. In insurance parlance this is called the problem of "moral hazard," but less prejudicially, Arrow (1970) calls it the "confounding of risks and decisions."

While the information necessary for initial classification of people into risk categories may be prohibitively costly, in the case of repeated accidents, the insurer builds up experience and can adjust rates accordingly (experience rating). The right of the high-risk insured to leave one firm and join another where his or her risk is unknown affects the costs faced by other buyers. The opportunities of the lower-risk person are expanded if exit is barred or if the insurance firms have the right to share their risk experience. This situation reduces the opportunities of high-risk persons and perhaps raises questions about the privacy of the records of all persons. Of course, if people were less opportunistic and had a sense of community, they would volunteer otherwise difficult-to-obtain information, and there would be no conflict.

Recording Real Property

Another area of significant information cost that deserves brief mention is that of information on property rights themselves. Exchange assumes that both parties know their respective existing rights. But it is often costly to establish ownership. This situation can be illustrated with respect to titles in real estate. Most U.S. states have a system of recording deeds. This system merely receives and stores chronological claims and does nothing to confirm them. The record must be searched for evidence of title and is not itself a confirmation of title. A few states, however, use the Torrens system of title registration, where a single certificate affirms rights. The predominant system creates uncertainty, reflected in the fact that Americans spent about $500 million to insure land titles in 1971. Most observers agree that the system is inefficient and could provide better information at less cost (Burke and Kittrie 1972). A low-cost title-information system is of interest to both buyers and sellers. However, as usual there are third parties involved. As Gene Wunderlich (1974, p. 90) notes, "There is property in information about real property." Private title companies assemble data from public records and provide an information service to buyers and sellers. The information base is sometimes duplicated by several firms or one firm will have a monopoly. Information tends to be a good with superordinary economies of scale. It has a high fixed cost to establish and a marginal cost less than average cost. There is a conflict between the rights of title companies and the interests of buyers and sellers to cheap, reliable title information.

Labor Markets

Information costs are an important source of interdependence in labor markets. Suppose that there are two groups of prospective employees. The first group may be high school graduates, and it is known that 95 percent can be expected to be prompt and attentive workers. The other group are dropouts, who are expected to be only 85 percent punctual. The employer knows that the probable costs of hiring and firing are lower for the first group. Even though 85 percent of the dropouts are just as productive as the graduates, they will not be hired until all the graduates are hired. This is known as statistical discrimination. The punctual dropouts will not be given a chance to prove their qualities because employers seek to reduce the probability of having to bear the transaction costs of hiring and firing. This situation occurs because it is costly to distinguish in advance the punctual from the tardy, so the dropouts are treated as an undifferentiated group.

If employers are to have the opportunity to avoid transaction costs of hiring and firing, the productive members of the dropout group will not have the opportunity of being considered for certain jobs. On the other hand, there might be a law prohibiting hiring in terms of group average characteristics; only after the characteristics of each individual became known could a person be dismissed. This right would create more opportunities for employees and create costs for employers. The same phenomenon of statistical discrimination occurs in auto insurance for teenagers. As a group, they have more accidents, so insurance companies charge all teenagers higher rates. Some teenagers are careful drivers but get charged the higher rates anyway because information to differentiate them from their wild-driving brothers and sisters is costly.

Information costs interacting with property rights can prevent a competitive market for labor. It can be observed that employers do not allow workers to bid for an existing job. For example, during a recession, unemployed workers generally are not allowed to offer to do the job of retained workers at a lower price. (The same issue arises in minimum-wage laws.) This right to be free of such competition is advanced by union bargaining but can also be found in nonunionized activities (Thurow 1975, p. 85). Some employers are willing to sacrifice any short-run cost minimization that might be available through wage competition for long-run profitability. Information and transaction costs are involved in this observed employee behavior (Akerlof 1984).

If one employee, A, fears that a fellow worker, B, is a competitor for her job, A will not transmit skills and information to B (Brown and Medoff 1978). On-the-job training may save an employer formal training and supervision costs if A has no fear that information she gives to B will be later used by B in bidding for A's job. If employers have the right to save training costs, then the unemployed or underemployed do not have the right to enter a particular job market by offering their services at a lower wage. Interdependent utilities also act to limit direct wage competition. Most production processes require a degree of teamwork. If a team member is added because of an offer to work for less, then the others may have their sense of fairness offended and lower team productivity. The controlling property rights may be contained in personnel manuals (Akerlof 1979; Solow 1980).

SUMMARY

One of the lessons of this discussion is that there are literally hundreds of everyday rules that affect the character of interdependence growing out of contractual and information costs. These interdependencies are not addressed by the rights competitive structure. Large numbers of buyers and sellers do not completely settle issues of who bears transaction costs. What it means to be an owner is not determined by the usual definition of factor ownership and income distribution.

It is costly to reach agreements with other people. If contractual costs are high enough, trade may be impossible, and the use stays with the original rights holder. Various laws attempt to reduce contract costs. Several were explored, including the doctrine of reasonable use and class-action suits. But care must be taken not to make contractual-cost reduction an isolated objective. One person's contractual cost is another's protection against change.

It is often costly to acquire information on how products will perform, who is not bearing the load, when you will need a product, or what future demand and supply will be. Property rights and different forms of organization can reduce the costs of information to given parties. In some cases, the only thing rights can do is distribute the costs of being wrong because nothing can be done to reduce uncertainty. Information costs also cannot be minimized in isolation. One person's information lack is another's source of income, and, if one person is to have more future options, another has less in the future or present.

Transaction costs are a cost of production like transportation, marketing, or any other. But, the key to rights-impact analysis is that these transaction costs are borne differentially by individuals. Just as rights affect the distribution of opportunities relative to incompatible use, they also affect opportunities growing out of transaction cost.

NOTES

1. *Zahn v. International Paper Co.*, 42 U.S.L.W. 4087 (U.S. Dec. 17, 1973). The United States Supreme Court ruled that each and every party to a suit between citizens of different states must have damages exceeding $10,000.

2. This section was stimulated by, but departs from McKean (1970a) and Posner (1972b). Also see "Symposium: Products Liability: Economic Analysis and the Law," *University of Chicago Law Review*, 38:3–141, 1970; Brown 1974; and Welch 1978.

3. In practice, this is difficult, as shown by the fact that when labor is categorized by its characteristics, there are still large differences in wages within each category (Thurow 1983, chap. 7).

4. A group of Detroit workers who worked in the Volvo plant said they preferred the impersonal supervision of the foreman to the social pressure of their team colleagues (Cook 1975).

5. One of the earliest uses of the term *externalities* arose in the context of this type of interdependence. Alfred Marshall was concerned with "how far the full economies of division of labor can be obtained by the concentration of large numbers of small businesses of a similar kind in the same locality." In the modern theory of economic development, it is seen as the issue of balanced versus unbalanced growth.

6. The option demand for the existence of a good or service (for example, a fire engine) differs from the option demand for damage reimbursement (such as fire insurance), which is discussed below.

7. The same issue is involved in damage deposits for housing rental (Schmid 1985b). Transaction costs are infinite where the damaging party has no payment capacity, even if court costs are low.

Seven

Surpluses, Demand and Supply Fluctuations, and Conclusions

People differ in their willingness to pay for the same kind of product. Resources differ in their productivity. These situational differences create surpluses and give rise to a variety of human interdependence that is ordered by property rights. Rights determine whether a surplus is captured by producers or consumers and whether the source of the surplus is a supply or demand phenomenon. In addition, price elasticity of supply and demand interact with fluctuations (peak loads) and shifts in supply and demand to create opportunities for different price structures and profit and loss controlled by property rights. With these two additional situations, the theoretical Part II of this volume is completed.

CONSUMER SURPLUS

Chapter 4 discussed consumer rights to be free of producers' attempts to practice price differentiation and capture all that consumers might be willing to pay. Additional points remain. Some types of option demands arise because of the inability to collect (or prohibition against collecting) consumer surplus. For example, some people do not ride the bus regularly, but they do when their car breaks down or the weather is too bad to walk. These people would probably pay more than the going flat charge for bus service. If these higher prices could be collected cheaply, the total might be enough to support the maintenance of a bus line that otherwise collecting only a flat rate would go out of business. Because it is difficult to separate out this class of buyers when they get on the bus, they may have to resort to some type of group action to express their demand that the bus line stay in business. This latter is termed an option demand, but it is a demand for the option to buy that arises because the full willingness to pay cannot be collected easily at the time of consumption.

Segmentation of the market by charging different prices for the same good to different classes of customers can be used by sellers to enhance profits. But, if profits are not wanted, it can be used to give a favored class of customer access to products at less than the average cost per unit or even the marginal cost. For example, some physicians reputedly charge patients according to the latter's income. The American Economic Association's membership fees are scaled to income, as are those for numerous other organizations. When utility service is maintained even though people cannot pay their bills, the costs are picked up by the paying customers. In short, price differentiation is a potentially powerful device to effect income transfer without openly taking income from one person and giving it to another. But in practice it has the same effect as a tax.[1] It should be noted that income-distribution effects can also occur from a failure to differentiate prices when there are differences in cost of service. An example is flat rates for sewerage even where new hookups are at a higher cost; another example is same-product prices to both users and nonusers of credit and delivery services. The widespread interdependence occasioned by consumer-surplus raises conflicts between producers and consumers and also among consumers. Atomistic competition does not control the capture of differential willingness to pay. Price differentiation is widely practiced in competitive industries such as airlines, hotels, and car rentals. Margins established by grocery stores vary widely among products.

PRODUCER SURPLUS

Producer surplus (or rent) is akin to consumer surplus (Mishan 1968). It arises from the fact of decreasing returns when different units of a factor of production are of different quality and productivity and are inelastic in supply. As production increases to the point where marginal revenues equal marginal costs, the superior intramarginal units of the factor earn a rent (a return larger than that needed to bring the factor into use). Producers owning nonmarginal resources would like all units of output from all units of the factor to sell at the same price so they could capture the producer surplus. Consumers, of course, would like to get the advantage of the differential productivity, though they might argue over which consumer gets it. A competitive market means that rents are captured by producers who own the superior inputs. Competition cannot prevent unequal income distribution. Government policy to effect the distribution of "unearned rent" has been an attractive subject for social reformers. John Stuart Mill proposed national ownership of all land rent appreciation. Henry George (1926, b. 8) proposed a tax on these rents and thought the resultant revenues might be sufficient to finance all government needs.

(For a discussion of the impact of site-value taxation, see Gaffney 1969.) The "single tax" would not cover present government budgets, but it is large enough to be the source of many private fortunes. In a communal society, the advantage of differential productivity in resources might be shared equally among all producers and consumers.

Ownership of producer surpluses is not only a matter of income distribution but also a factor affecting the ability of the public to guide resource use. One source of economic rent is location near centers of economic activity and transportation modes. Consider the attractiveness of a major highway intersection in the suburbs as a site for a shopping center. Assume that one quadrant of the intersection contains some unique natural features and backs up to an existing residential area. The local government may make a decision to zone the quadrant for low-density use and to zone another quadrant for commercial uses in order to control and direct certain externalities. This action has the effect of making a millionaire out of one of the owners of the designated land and denying great value appreciation to another. Owners are not likely to accept such an outcome and will try to manipulate the public investment and zoning decision either overtly or subtly. In fact, bribes and payoffs for rezoning are a major source of corruption in U.S. cities.

U.S. ideology has been that value increase is an independent natural force that some owners are smarter in anticipating than others and that their superior prowess should be rewarded with great profits. In other words, land-value appreciation is owned by the person who is lucky enough to own the right parcel at the right time. This ideology prevails even when the source of the value change is owing to the general growth of the community and public investments in transportation systems and when the particular location of the value is affected by public land-use-control decisions. The consequence of these ownership rights is not only that income distribution is affected but also that there is great pressure to change publicly made land-use plans.

Galbraith (1967, pp. 360–61) says, "Since the focus of market forces is the return to, and capital gains from land, this solution means that there must be public land acquisition wherever market influences are palpably adverse. Planning which under urban and metropolitan administration will never be strong, will not then have to contend in each decision with the resistances of the market. Those with a vested interest in bad land use are unlikely to welcome such a remedy. But, in the end, there will prove to be no other." It is curious why Galbraith suggests public land acquisition via the market rather than legislative declaration that appreciation gains are public or common property.

The conventional wisdom in economics has been that resource allocation and income distribution can and should be kept separate. But here is a case where the attempts by private parties to redirect and capture land-value change affect not only income distribution but also, simultaneously, resource use. Some writers advocate public ownership of land around cities, as exists in such countries as Sweden (Strong 1971). The performance of public ownership depends further on the structure of government. Corruption of public administrators is not uncommon. Another possibility is a special capital-gains tax on land-value change unrelated to real investment improvements in the land. Great Britain used such a device at one point and called it a betterment tax (Clawson and Hall 1973), and it is currently used in parts of Canada. The design of a tax to capture all rent is a high-information-cost good. A mistake could affect the supply of land development. This could be avoided by a tax to capture a part of the rent and such a tax requires less information to design. Still another rule alternative is to auction rezoning permission (Clawson 1960). All these alternatives imply public ownership of land-appreciation gains. If the property right in the land itself or the value changes thereof are held by the public, the great private gains that are possible in the manipulation of zoning decisions are removed and the public treasury is incidentally enriched (Schmid 1968; for the Italian case, see Magnani 1971).

It is possible to change the character of ownership of producer surpluses and remove the pressure for breaking public plans—but without changing to public ownership of the gains—by regarding value change as owned in common by landowners. (An experiment of this type is described in Strong 1975; also see Costonis 1974.) Thus, all the owners of land at the highway intersection (in the example above), or even in the whole metropolitan area, have a proportionate share in any rents that occur, and a particular owner of a parcel will not care whether his parcel is zoned commercial or low density. He gets the same share of the gain in either case. This same result is achieved when entire new towns are developed by a single owner. The single owner may find that total rents for the entire area are maximized when some parcels of unique natural beauty are left undeveloped to complement the parcels that are developed. If the naturally beautiful parcel is owned separately, however, its owner must develop it to get any of the rent gain.

There is no formal statute or deed that says the owner of land is also the owner of land value created by the community. It may not occur to us even to think in these terms. But this informal link is a valuable property right that shifts income as surely as any explicit tax and transfer. The tax, however, is open and explicit, and as such it draws continuing public debate and charges of the violation of freedom every time the tax bill and budget are passed. The property right in land-value appreciation is subtle and does not come up for periodic renewal. It is clear that those property rights that are built into custom and the common law and are protected by the courts are better to have than a right to an income transfer.

Not all the owners whose land value is increased by urban development actually benefit from the nominal market value, and in fact some may be harmed. In the United States, property taxes are usually assessed on market value. A farmer on the fringe of a growing city finds that taxes are increasing and a severe cash-flow problem is created when farm income does not increase. Those who sell for nonfarm use enjoy a surplus, but the intramarginal units that will not develop for some time (if at all) are burdened with a tax on the value of the marginal unit rather than the current income of the intramarginal unit. There is no way for all of those currently affected actually to sell at the nominal market price and avoid the squeeze occasioned by the tax. The market, which is often advertised as the paragon of freedom, is actually in this case coercive relative to the interests of the intramarginal owners. Many U.S. states have given relief to these owners by giving preferential assessment to farmland (Hansen and Schwartz 1975).

Technological change often creates rents for early adopters, even permanently where competition is weak. In agriculture, these rents are captured by land owners even when the technology was produced by public investment. Where inputs are complements, there is no separate marginal product and the division of rent is controlled by rights.

EMPLOYER SURPLUS

Differential productivity of factors and decreasing returns can occur even when the factors are identical. Assume that an employer can compute the marginal value product of labor (the addition to total revenue from hiring one more worker with other factors fixed). The employer will add workers as long as each adds more to revenue than to cost. With diseconomies of scale at the industry or firm level, the workers employed first add more to revenue than do the last employed. Yet in market competition, each worker is paid the same, namely the marginal value product of the last worker added.[2] This leaves a surplus for the employer.[3] This employer surplus does not disappear with competition. It is not the result of any overt restrictive or monopolistic practices by employers. It is inherent in the market rules when applied in situations of interdependence created by economies of scale. Employers get this surplus if they own the nonlabor factors with which labor is combined.

We need not go into the function played by these residuals in the combination of labor and nonlabor factors, since this is detailed in all principles books. The point here is that if the firms were owned by the workers, they would decide how to distribute the surplus among themselves (Shapley and Shubik 1967). An administrative or status-grant system could result in a different distribution of income than a market system (Wiles 1977, p. 70). McGregor (1977) describes a worker-owned plywood factory and the disputes between young and old workers as to distribution of profits.

FLUCTUATIONS IN DEMAND AND SUPPLY RELATED TO PRICE ELASTICITY

The time pattern of consumption for many goods is uneven. Examples are seasonal and time-of-day demands for energy and water (Sewell and Rousche 1974). Everybody jams the roads and transportation modes at the beginning and end of customary work periods, creating a variety of interdependencies among users at different times. Short-run supply is inelastic. If the transport system is expanded to meet the demand at peak-load periods, there will be unused capacity at other times. Someone must pay for this capacity. The implicit right involved in peak-load pricing schemes is a factor in income distribution and patterns of use and facility investment (Steiner 1957). A flat-rate charge means that people pay the same regardless of their time of use or consumer surplus. The persons who work have no options as to timing and would be willing to pay more than the shopper who can avoid peak-use periods. Does the shopper have the right to a lower price when some of the consumer surplus of the rush-hour users is collected? People differ with respect to the intensity of their demand for a given good at different time periods, and both are a source of consumer surplus. Property rights affect the distribution of these surpluses. For an empirical application to electric utilities, see Chapter 12. (In France, the state-owned trains have experimented with different fares at different times of the year. The 30 days of peak-period demand charge a 50-percent premium while 230 days are half rate (Levy-Lambert 1977, p. 303). The peak-load situation is an example of the general case of increasing cost to scale, which raises the interdependence and necessity for public choice to decide who is the marginal user who must pay the higher marginal cost.

The business cycle can also be seen in terms of a variable load factor (Clark 1923, chap. 18). Productive capacity is built for average demand levels and then lies idle during periods of declining demand. The right of a firm to lay off workers makes labor a variable cost, though for the whole society, it is an overhead cost that does not vary with output. Rights determine whose perspective of cost counts and motivates efforts to maintain uniform utilization. Rights affect how much is produced and who gets it.[4] It should be emphasized again that some of these categories of interdependence are mutually exclusive, while some goods can have several sources of interdependence, especially if the good has multiple uses and dimensions. For empirical work, the unit and goods dimension must be carefully specified.

The case of perfectly inelastic supply is the polar example of creating potential surpluses. For example, when drought occurs, there is an unexpected shortfall in supply of food. Nothing can be done that year to increase supply. Farmers who have nothing to sell are impoverished. Those in neighboring states where the drought did not occur find that prices have risen, and they have unexpected profits. Market bargaining is one way to ration the unusually scarce commodity. Price influences who will have the available supply. The relatively wealthy get the food, and the producers get high incomes. Other possibilities are administrative or status systems. Sir Henry Maine (1880, pp. 186–99) noted that in ancient economies, price was used to ration during periods of unusual scarcity only when one was dealing with strangers (also see Polanyi 1957). Charging all the market will bear was prohibited by custom when dealing within the community. Customary prices prevailed, and rationing was accomplished by status transactions. The administrative transactions of rationing can be designed to favor any chosen interest group. In contemporary society, people regard price increases to take advantage of temporary shortages as unfair, and firms caring for their reputations often avoid price rationing to clear markets (Kahneman, Knetsch, and Thaler 1986).

Surpluses can become producer losses when supply is shifted outward by technology in the face of inelastic demand. This was noted in the discussion of irreversibility in the previous chapter. In general, cost-saving technological change creates a surplus, which is captured by producers if output price does not change (Schumpeterian profit). If there is free entry, output price falls and producer surplus becomes consumer surplus.

SUMMARY OF SURPLUS INTERDEPENDENCE

These examples show the alternative property rights in surpluses that are possible, each with a different consequence for income distribution and economic performance (resource use). The existence of differences in intensity of taste for the same product (consumer surplus) and the differences in productivity of factors (producer and employer surplus) create a context of human interdependence where the particular property right chosen influences who gets what. Without an understanding of these people and resource characteristics and how they interact with property rights, we often regard present performance as the inevitable result of natural and somewhat mysterious forces that certainly benefit one person over another but that do not seem under human control. Those who benefit have a stake in maintaining the impression that it is natural that some property owners get rich and others do not.

Demand and supply characteristics create a situation of interdependence, the effects of which are distributed by alternative property-rights systems and rules. Surpluses and opportunities for income gain are distributed among different parties according to the rules of the game. The character of the product itself is also affected. In some cases, rules maintaining pure competition can prevent sellers from capturing consumer surpluses. But market competition does not prevent capture of producer or employer surplus. In conclusion, the right to collect rents or practice price differentiation is a public choice among the interests of competing groups.

CONCLUSION OF PART II: RIGHTS ALTERNATIVES
AND VARIETIES OF INTERDEPENDENCE

It has been the purpose of Part II to develop a set of concepts that are useful in empirical inquiry into how alternative property rights interact with different situations of human interdependence to influence who gets what. The applicability of the concepts will be further demonstrated in the following chapters, but several ideas can be emphasized at this point. The opportunities for one person to affect another have many different sources. The full range of sources of human interdependence must be appreciated if income distribution is to be understood.

Use rights to incompatible-use goods are an obvious source of welfare for a person. In an exchange economy, the ability of extract income from the exchange of things owned is governed by relative scarcity (supply and demand). Scarcity is a function of technology, the psychology of tastes, and power. A theory of power limited to how the rules of a competitive market control bargaining power leaves income distribution determined within the economic system. But if there are many sources of interdependence other than incompatible-use goods, the distribution of their ownership and pure competition in their exchange are insufficient to describe the full range of property rights that are sources of power and thus income and wealth. A similar point is made by Gunnar Myrdal (1974, pp. 732–33) and by Cambridge Capital Theory (Kaldor 1956; Pasinetti 1961). To restrict inquiry to factor ownership is to ignore many other rights that influence wealth distribution. Income distribution is influenced by public choice and is not given by preferences and the production function.

A person or group enhances its power to participate in resource use and to claim a portion of output in a number of ways. To illustrate this variety, a selection of power-giving rights discussed in Part II follows: right to use, exchange, and deny use of others in incompatible-use goods (Chapter 3); right of free entry to markets and to choose among many buyers and sellers (Chapter 3); right to be a free rider with respect to high-exclusion-cost goods (Chapter 3); right to practice price differentiation in the context of economies of scale (Chapter 4); right to have a joint-impact good financed by government taxes (Chapter 5); right to have injunctive relief (rather than receive damages) in the case of goods with high contractual costs (Chapter 6); right to utilize class-action suits in the case of goods with high contractual costs (Chapter 6); right to avoid product liability in the case of goods with high information costs (Chapter 6); and right to collect economic rents for goods with differential surpluses (Chapter 7).

Some people get their income and utility by owning such things as land or receiving a welfare check, while others get theirs by a monopoly license, tariffs, union shop rules, government provision of a service, protection from suit as a result of product failure because of prohibition of class actions, or peak-load pricing practices. All of these are determined by public action, which chooses among competing claims of individuals with different interests. Where there is an interdependence, there is an effective right to control it whether chosen consciously or by default. If one would inquire into why one person or country is poor and another is rich, one would want to know how alternative property rights interact with all sources of interdependence. There is more to economic policy than transfer payments and antitrust, monetary, and fiscal policy.

NOTES

1. J.M. Clark (1923, p. 428) suggests that "if more goods and services could be sold on similar principles, the rich would be quite as happy and the poor would have more of the necessities of life, without confiscating wealth or disturbing the system of scoring in our great competitive game wherein a man's success is measured by his money income."

2. A general discussion of scale economies was made previously in Chapter 4. The present point is included here because of its parallel with the other surplus situations. There is a long history of theoretical discussion of institutions controlling this situation. For example, Commons (1909) said, "Whenever the consumer . . . is in control, he favors the marginal producer, for through him he wields the club that threatens the other producers." He spoke of "the menace of competition" and said Marx was wrong in pointing to exploitation owing to noncontrol of the mode of production (factor ownership) when low wages were the result of the extension of the market. Thus, Commons was skeptical of socialist ownership and rather pointed toward collective bargaining.

3. Since with economies of scale average product exceeds marginal product, if all workers are paid the marginal product, a residual remains. Michael Harrington (1976, p. 125) suggests that this is part of what Marx meant by "surplus value." The point is also discussed by Thurow (1975, p. 216 and 1983, pp. 197–98) and Samuelson (1967, pp. 515–16).

4. Some writers such as Clark (1923) are concerned more with efficient utilization of factors of production than with equity issues. He states, "The question of justice between one consumer and another seems abstract, if not academic. It is the least important of all problems arising from the rhythms of business" (p. 173). If differential pricing cannot even out peak demand, Clark has no interest in the income-distribution effects and advocates uniform pricing.

III

Further Applications and
Development of Paradigm

Eight

Economic and Political Applications

In this chapter some of the concepts in Part II will be combined as needed and further developed in the context of several broad areas of public choice, including the form of business and political organization. Thus will be tested the utility of the concepts outlined above in producing insights and verifiable hypotheses as to the impact of alternative property institutions.

INTERNALIZATION AND CAPITALIZATION: THE RIGHT TO TRANSFER

It is important to distinguish use rights and exchange rights. In a self-sufficient economy, use rights are all that matters. Other than physical trespass, there is little that one person can do to another. Use rights remain the prime ingredient of some rather complex nonmarket organized economies.[1] In feudal Europe, people had a traditional right to utilize certain land for cultivation and had common access to certain pastureland. If a person could not make use of his entitlement, the land was simply absorbed by others. There was no way for a person to transfer rights explicitly to some specific other person. If one did not make use of it directly, there was no way to realize any personal value from the resource. One could not even make a gift of it to another specific person. One had use rights but not the right to exchange or grant.

In time exchange rights were added and markets developed for consumer goods, while land often remained subject to use rights. The transformation from use rights to markets in most resources was one of the most wrenching and misery-producing periods in history. Many words have been written trying to prove that this was all worth it and that the resulting market system went on to produce the best of all possible worlds (North and Thomas 1973). Many words have also been written criticizing this development and holding it responsible for many of our current human ills (Polanyi 1944). A discussion of any possible normative conclusions will be left to Chapter 11. Here some of the substantive performance implications of the right to transfer will be explored.

The right to transfer means that it becomes possible to gain assets by withholding what you own from others even when you cannot make use of it yourself. This is a proprietary scarcity. The right to withhold from others what they need but do not own is the potential substance for market income.[2] Coupled with the right to transfer, it is the engine by which it is possible for some people to accumulate great wealth and in effect have other people work for them. In a nontransfer economy, some people are more energetic and skilled than others and many have access to use rights in natural resources that are more productive than the resources of others. Differential access to resources means that some people will have more wealth than others, but the differences are limited (unless concentrated administrative control of labor is practiced). In an exchange economy, the differences can be and are extreme.

In a nontransfer economy with given use rights, the only cleverness that counts is against nature. But in an exchange economy, cleverness against other people redistributes assets even where total wealth remains unchanged. If one party can be fooled or kept in ignorance, the other may make a more advantageous bargain. In a modern market economy, a good deal of talent and energy goes into manipulation of paper asset values and tax avoidance that has little to do with production of wealth. Also, a lot of effort goes into creating scarcity to increase price. In a stable, nontransfer economy, no one can increase his other assets without increasing total wealth (except of course by plunder).

Internalization

A much-advertised advantage of the market is that both parties' satisfaction can be increased by exchanging what one has for that of another, which is preferred. Stated somewhat more abstractly, exchange allows the internalization of certain external effects. If A exercises her use rights in X in ignorance of the fact that B would be willing to give A a good that A would prefer in exchange for letting B utilize the good X, both have missed an opportunity to be better off.

The widely used concept of internalization can be confusing, since an external effect that is internalized does not disappear. Recall that externalities are an inevitable aspect of interdependence and can be shifted and transformed but never eliminated (Chapter 1). By definition, external effects are internalized when trade is allowed. But the interdependence externality does not go away. The nonowner substitutes the impact of the old externality (unavailable opportunity) for the cost of giving up the item exchanged. Market trade may enable A's interests translated into a bid to become an opportunity cost for B.[3] This is the definition of internalization. If A's bid is rejected because of inadequate purchasing power or high transaction costs, the former externality continues although it has been internalized. As long as A's pitiful bid is received, it has been internalized. In either case, market internalization does not cause interdependence externalities to go away, but it can change their form. When B's use of resources causes A to have reduced opportunities, rights allowing internalization can ameliorate this reduction.

In tracing the effects of alternative systems of rules, care must be taken to avoid an extreme partial-equilibrium analysis. (What follows is still partial equilibrium in the sense that feedback of institutional performance on attitudes and rule making is acknowledged here but is not the focus in the time frame chosen.) While it is true that with an even distribution of property rights between two parties, the right to trade can increase the satisfaction of both, we must inquire of the effects on third parties. For example, in most of the states of the eastern United States, utilization of water is controlled by use rights. These so-called riparian rights are not usable and not salable separate from the riparian lands. Thus, even though a riparian has no use for the water, he cannot sell it to a nonriparian who might put it to a valuable use. (In some societies, where labor is not exchangeable, the owner of land- and water-use rights could not obtain additional output by letting wage earners utilize a portion of the resources.) With a partial analysis, this situation appears inefficient, since resources cannot move to their most valuable use. The potential superior opportunity of a nonriparian is not internalized.

But we must examine how third parties are affected by others' potential choices. It can be observed that every time the riparian doctrine is challenged, it is defended by fishermen. Increased sales and diversions of water would affect the interests of fishermen. The fact that sale is prohibited (or that there are high transaction costs in obtaining consent from all of the owners in common on the stream) is to the benefit of fishermen. Water cannot now be made salable without affecting their interests. Prohibition of sale can prevent A and B from increasing their satisfaction and apparent value of output from the water. But the enhancement of their satisfaction is at the expense of C, who is not represented in that market. The use right of fisherman C is protected by the fact that A only has an incompatible-use right that cannot be sold. One person's limitation (rights attenuation) is another person's bread. The right to transfer is the right to create costs for the parties not represented in the market (that is, it is the right to create costs for others who are protected in no other way than by prevention of marketability). Where the uses of people are interdependent, the right to sell or otherwise transfer has external effects.

Any society must have some system for disaggregating scarcity. In a nontransfer economy, scarce resources are rationed or allocated when use rights are assigned or claimed by custom. In this context, changed users (and some-times uses) are difficult to create. For example, in certain communal tribal land tenures in Africa, each family has a traditional use right (Parsons, Penn, and Raup 1956, pp. 231–8). However, there is no provision by which the tribe could alienate part of the land to an outsider to make new uses. When the University of Nigeria was being built, it had difficulty obtaining land in the traditional tribal area. No one (either ordinary individual or chief) had the power to transfer land to someone else. This has important consequences. On the one hand, no tribal member can be dispossessed. There is never a destitute, landless poor. No matter how scarce the available resources, all have some share in its output. There is no need for a separate governmental welfare program or even private grants. On the other hand, quick reallocations of resources are difficult.

Use rights that cannot be sold provide great security to their holders if the rights conform to customary behavior. Where group norms change slowly, however, they provide little individual liberty to innovate. In addition, the liberty to try new things also creates exposure and insecurity. A mortgage on alienable land means the individual risks loss of the land. Where bargaining power and information availability are unequal, the move from use to ex-change rights often has resulted in a larger class of landless people (Parsons 1974). Where traditional use rights still exist in agriculture, it is a great chal-lenge to institutional design to create a system of rules that allows for mobility, creativity, and innovation and that draws forth extra energy without creating a very unequal income distribution.

The use rights of American Indians to the resources of their reservations is a good example. There is no way for a tribal member to leave the reservation and realize any benefit of past labor or birthright. This can be a significant barrier to labor mobility. But among Indians it means that it is harder for income distribution to be uneven, and no one can be completely denied access to resources or be subject to a bad bargain.

There are various other examples of nontransferable rights. For instance, some pension plans are only available if the worker continues to work for the company; again mobility is discouraged. In summary, internalization (addition of exchange rights to use rights) affects different parties in different ways.

Capitalization

There is one function that only the right to exchange seems capable of serving. This is the process of capitalization, which is a major part of what is meant by the capitalist system of organization. Capitalization is the process by which future values are converted into present values. Or, more concretely, it is the process by which A can enjoy present consumption that otherwise would have been used by B, who in turn uses the future output created by A. Invest-ment is possible in all economic systems whereby an action taken in the present has the possibility of increasing the flow of future output. In a system of nontransferable use rights, one must stick around if one is going to capture any of this future. But in a system of exchange rights, one can cash in one's claim, extract a present value of the future output, and leave for other activities. This basic situation can be explored in many contexts, and only a few will be noted here.[4]

Suppose that a person develops a new product or a cost-saving technology. Choice of rights affects the reward to the innovator. In a competitive market, the innovator earns a short-term profit until other firms enter the market and copy the product or process. While the short-run disequilibrium in supply and demand may produce sufficient incentive to innovate, these profits cannot be a source of large fortunes and great inequality in income. In other words, market competition distributes the benefits of innovation widely to consumers over time.

But where firms have market power and can prevent copying of new products and processes, the capital market plays a unique role in creating great rewards to innovators, instantaneous fortunes, and great income inequality. In the U.S. economy, large differences in rates of return persist over time (Thurow 1975, p. 143). If the right to a future above-average yearly rate of return can be sold in a stock market, the owner capitalizes the future flow into an instantaneous fortune. Buyers of stock seeking above-average return bid up the price of the stock of firms with high returns until the returns on the stock investment are again at the average. The buyer at this point earns only the average rate of return, but the purchasers have made the original innovator or stockholder wealthy without having to wait for the future output.

Some buyers of stock try to anticipate which stock will earn higher-than-average return on present prices. Lester Thurow (1975, pp. 142–54) argues that in fact great success is determined by luck (he calls it a "random walk") rather than superior intelligence. He notes that professional financial managers do not do better than the stock market average over time even though they can invest in market information.

To summarize, when noncompetitive industry is tied to a competitive stock market, it can result in greater income inequalities than are inherent in administrative or status-grant transactions. The rights of bargained exchange mean that successful innovators with market power and lucky betters in the casino that is called the stock market will achieve fortunes many times greater than that available to patient savings and reinvestment following the principles of compound interest.

This inequality-producing aspect of the stock market is often justified by arguing that the prospective high payoff to some in the stock market is functional in providing a source of new funds for creation of new capital goods. As people seek higher-than-average returns, they make available new capital to innovators. In fact, the issuance of new stock is seldom a major source of new investment. In 1972, of all private industrial and commercial investment (excluding residential structures) in the United States, 99 perrent was generated by retained earnings and depreciation allowances (U.S., Department of Commerce 1973, pp. 10, 38; Berle 1959, chap. 1). While this percentage varies with the business cycle, it suggests a plausible hypothesis that a prime effect of the stock market is to enhance inequality and not to obtain capital for new investment. Some insight into how rights affect savings and investment can be gained by examining some of the socialist economies of eastern Europe.

In Yugoslavia, workers in an industrial plant help decide how much of the surplus of their work will be paid in wages and how much will be reinvested in the firm. If money is reinvested, it should increase future surpluses and wages. But, if the worker should move to another firm, he would not be around to enjoy the future product that his reduction in current consumption helped create. The worker cannot sell his share to future output and take the money and invest in still another enterprise where he might expect future returns to be even higher. Some writers criticize this property system and argue that investment and production will be lower under such a system than it otherwise would be under the right to sell (Furubotn 1974).

But back to the main question of whose interests are to count. Some individual Yugoslav worker may think that there is money to be made in certain consumer goods, say, a pizza parlor. But others prefer to expand heavy industry and education. Productivity is always ambiguous. The real question is who gets to decide what outputs are the most important. There is no doubt that individual salability is related to mobility, but anyone who has seen a town that a major industry has moved from knows that certain costs were ignored by market choosers as they sought the least-cost (to them) location. Some person who has better opportunities elsewhere wants to sell out and take her capital, but this move may create costs for the person who has many immobile assets in the current location and few other opportunities. One person's right to sell can create costs for others. Whose interests are labeled as the most productive depends on your point of view.

Even setting aside the issue of the composition of output, the empirical evidence is not supportive of the theoretical prediction that the lack of rights to sell will lead to low investment decisions by workers' collectives. In fact, Yugoslav investment has been remarkably high. Some say this is because of higher-level regulation (administrative transactions), but not all of it can be so explained. Perhaps there are ideological substitutes for the individualized strivings that we have come to expect in the United States. It should be kept in mind that if every firm is making substantial reinvestments, a worker can move to another industry and not lose any benefits. Behavior under equality is different than under expectations of inequality.

In a highly mobile society, people may hesitate to tax themselves for public improvements that they may not be around to enjoy. They have in effect a use right but cannot sell their claim to a new immigrant when they leave.

However, if all or most communities are making similar investments, it does not matter. A person gets to use resources in the new community similar to the ones he or she paid for in the old community. Investment behavior is affected by the image people have of the broader system of which they are a part.

Some writers say that public ownership arises when some people do not want to bear the costs of their own actions as individuals (Alchian 1965). Everyone gets the same share of output regardless of his or her own personal failures. Some analysts predict that public ownership will lead to inefficient, low output. People cannot capture or bear the unique outputs they create. This argument was touched on earlier in Chapter 6 in the discussion on information costs related to the form of business enterprise. The same kind of question arises in public management.

It can be observed that some managers of government agencies do not aggressively pursue cost-saving opportunities. They appear to try to maximize their budget total, which gives them larger salaries and prestige. Any cost saving benefits the general taxpayer, but not directly the income of the manager. From the manager's point of view, the savings are common property, and no one is excluded. In a private, market-oriented firm, if the manager could cut costs, future earnings would increase and the present capitalized value of the firm would increase. This situation attacks stockholders and allows the manager to earn a higher salary or realize a gain on stock if he or she is also an owner.

This line of reasoning has led several authors to hypothesize that publicly owned electric utilities or airlines will have higher operating costs than private firms. Others observe that private corporations maximize sales and firm growth rather than profits, and in this sense they are similar to public firms. The above phenomenon has led William Niskanen (1971, chap. 18) to advocate that the bureaucratic director of a public agency should be awarded a share of any cost savings he or she creates. (It is assumed that the manager has the power to get orders carried out and that employees have no bargaining power. In reality the problem is more complex than just changing incentives of top management.) This share would be paid after leaving office. The problem with this idea is the difficulty of specifying product quality and quantity. The manager may be tempted to cut costs by cutting product quality (something that also happens in private business and even in socialist firms when they try to meet production quotas). Niskanen's plan requires a clear definition of what it is that the public agency is to produce. Of course, clarity is essential in any calculation of efficiency. Efficiency is meaningless unless we agree on the definition of relevant output and input—that is, whose tastes count.

No distinction has been made thus far as to the kind of good to which an exchange right applies. In some contexts, the right to one resource is a vehicle for access to other rights. For example, the right to land may be the point of access to political power. Thus, the right to exchange land may be the source of still further enlargement of political power while the right to exchange other goods has no such implication (see Penn 1961).

Lester Thurow (1985, p. 162) has also suggested that private manager's retirement benefits should depend on the success of the firm ten years after retirement. This would lengthen the planning horizon of the firm and deemphasize short-run profit maximization.

Capital, Credit, and Banking

Every economy has some system of rights by which someone is put in charge of organizing new productive opportunities, that is, put to work new potential and unused resources. In so-called capitalist countries, this is done by bankers. They are given the right to create money and to assign it to prospective entrepreneurs for a fee. The process allocates rights to command resources when a bank writes a number of dollars after a person's name. It is called a loan, but it is simply a creation of a property right in new resources. Typically, a person must already have accumulated significant resources in order to be eligible for a loan. The quality of the proposed use of new resources is not enough. In the words of David Bazelon, "Credit is status capitalized" (1959, p. 87). Note that banks create money without prior saving by individuals, though the new money if invested will result in savings.

Exchange (market) transactions are usually regarded as the distinguishing feature of capitalism, but with respect to creation of rights, the banking system essentially uses an administrative transaction. The banks cannot themselves use the new resources, so they are not exchanging one good for another. They are like a legislature distributing property rights to constituents. The fact that a fee (interest) is collected does not turn an administrative relationship between superior and inferior into one of bargained exchange between legal equals.

As an institution, capital is a system of rights allocating power. In precapitalist systems, investment required either individual decisions to save, trading profits, or collection of surpluses by those with power, usually the military. But, with fractional reserve banking, entrepreneurs can be given credit to command a share of current output to invest. Capital in the form of new debt money causes the economy to save. Part of the saving decision has become centralized in the hands of banks controlled by central banks independent of individual decisions. Surplus can be extracted involuntarily without the need for physical power under precapitalist tribute systems. Robert Heilbroner (1985, p. 40) emphasizes that capital is a social relationship of domination. The institutional means of this domination is credit created by banks. The future product is capitalized when an entrepreneur is given new credit created by a bank. This money commands a portion of current resources to create new commodities in the future which are retransformed into money again. This is part of the famed M-C-M sequence of Marx.

In socialist, centrally planned countries, the planning body allocates new opportunities and investment funds to government-owned industries according to a political decision. The criteria for who gets the funds are different than in capitalist banks, but the essential process of new-rights creation is the same.

Heilbroner (pp. 41–2) emphasizes that an essential part of capitalism is the process that results in peasants and workers being excluded from ownership of their tools and their own outputs. This dependency on the capitalist arises in part because of access to production credit.

There is a great deal of discussion in economics literature on monetary policy (interest rates and supply of money) but little on just who should own the rights to new potential resources. At present, the ownership of leveraged debt belongs to corporate stockholders, although the collateral for the debt is the whole going concern. When the banking system is seen in property-rights terms, new policy variables emerge for placing rights to new resources in the hands of various groups. This perspective has quite different implications from those of the usual redistributive welfare programs that attempt to transfer earnings after the initial rights to new opportunities have been vested. Also this view of credit-creation rights raises the question of why government pays interest on public debt created at times of unemployment when private borrowing is insufficient (for elaboration see Schmid 1982, 1984).

BOUNDARIES

There is a set of property-rights issues that can best be understood as boundary questions. They involve how a given person in his or her capacity as consumer or voter is grouped with other people. Everyone is aware of some of the issues in drawing the boundaries of political jurisdiction, whether that of nation, state, or some subdivision thereof. A similar type of issue is involved in grouping consumers, though the groupings are seldom only geographical. The question is one of defining the extent of the system over which performance is evaluated. Rights that determine subsystem identification are an inescapable choice in either the private or public sector.

Product Definition

There are a number of situations where the scale of product Y has some influence on the profitability of making product X. Such situations were discussed above in the context of obtaining demand information in the face of large cost discontinuities. The situation to be analyzed here is somewhat different. The amount of product X influences the profitability of Y because they are segments of a larger product sought by some consumers. An example is different links in a transport network, such as main lines and feeder lines. A problem of interdependence arises when all people do not have the same interest in each segment of the product.

Most transportation systems are composed of segments between points. Some people ride a long distance over many segments and others only use a portion. In the case of airlines in the United States, the segments may be provided by different firms. The existence of a feeder line may affect the number of customers and profitability of the main-line firm. This interdependence can be accounted for in several ways.

The main-line firm may offer the feeder firm a payment to help it stay in business. The external effect is internalized by market bargaining. Another possibility is expansion of the size of the firm to include both segments of its interconnected route. It is possible that the integrated firm will suffer losses on certain portions of its system, but the existence of the feeder routes may still contribute to overall profitability. If contractual costs or internal information costs are not too high, selection of either alternative will provide the entire route.

But there is an interdependence between customers that raises deeper questions than the existence of the total transport system or profit maximization. Some people ride the whole route and will pay for its total cost regardless of how the portions are priced. But some riders may only ride the feeder route and some only the main route. The feeder-route riders get a reduced-cost ride compared with the marginal cost of that portion of the route. The integrated firm may charge a flat price per mile regardless of the portion of the route used. Customers are treated as one large group, to the advantage of those riding the higher-cost feeder routes exclusively. The firm, in reaching its profit-maximizing pricing scheme, does not care about someone getting a reduced-cost ride. It might not profit the firm to try to charge more for the feeder route and lose customers on the whole system. The possibility of contracting or creating a single firm may make possible the maintenance of the whole system, but it does not speak to the question of different groups' different interests in portions of the system. Sometimes economists urge that, with nationalized or socialist firms, each separate product "stand on its own feet" (Munby 1962, p. 52).[5] Thus, each portion must cover its own marginal cost for that portion, and the profits of one portion are not allowed to cover losses on another portion, which must instead be dropped. This situation greatly harms some groups of riders and reduces profits to the socialist firm as a whole. As already noted, private firms would try to avoid this "mistake." The word *mistake* is put in quotes because, as often happens, one person's mistake is another person's benefit. The person who rides only the main line would have his fare reduced if he did not have to help pay for the feeder line. Something that is a mistake from the view of total profitability may be to some group's advantage. Again, the public must decide whose tastes count, as firms, whether private or socialist, decide on service boundaries and aggregation of groups of users. The public has to decide whether to allow the private firm to integrate and maximize profit for the system, to regulate competitors that might like to provide main-line service only, or if the service is nationalized, whether to make each segment pay its own way or not. (The latter issue came up during establishment of the ConRail reorganization of the northeast railroads in 1975.)

The problem raised by the airline case is repeated in other products. In retail stores, there are always some fast-moving, profitable items and some slower-moving goods, which nevertheless provide a variety that is very valuable to some customers and of no importance to others. When traditional stores offer a full line of goods and services, they attract competitors who undersell them by carrying only a few popular products. The full-line store finds it profitable to use profits on some high-volume items to subsidize a greater variety. The discount store upsets this practice by segmenting the market. A good example is that of bookstores. Certain high-volume paperbacks may help pay for slower-moving inventories of scholarly books. When buyers purchase some of both, the pricing practice does not matter, since what you spend on paperbacks makes the others less costly. But along comes a grocery store or drugstore that stocks a few profitable paperbacks at slightly reduced prices and draws off this trade from the full-line store. The result may be that the full-line store disappears.

This result harms some consumers, and they may try to change market rules. In some states in the United States, it is illegal for grocery stores to sell prescription drugs. Such prohibition is no doubt motivated by the wish of traditional druggists to avoid competition, but it does favorably affect their ability to stock a variety of slower-moving related items.

Some manufacturers realize that the availability of their full line in a store affects consumer satisfactions and the manufacturer's overall profits. For example, Creative Playthings, a U.S. manufacturer of children's toys, requires retailers to stock either all or none of its goods. Again, this situation can be interpreted in several ways. Laws in certain localities prohibit tie-in sales,[6] where the retail merchant must order not only the hot-selling selected goods but also a certain quantity of related goods. The manufacturer in effect takes advantage of a perhaps temporary shortage of one good that is in great demand and uses the occasion to unload some other good. Directly raising the price of the scarce good may be impractical. There is a conflict of interest over any pricing that captures consumer surplus (see Chapter 11). Tie-in sales are not just a nonstandard contract that efficiently substitutes for price.

But the full-line requirement can be of a different character. If some merchants can sell only a few high-volume items and undersell the full-line merchants, it may be that the full-line sellers disappear, and not only are the manufacturer's profits reduced but also some buyers lose the variety of choice they formerly enjoyed. Of course, the person with narrower tastes benefits. This conflict necessitates a public decision to determine whether or not a manufacturer has the right to offer only full-line contracts. The right of the manufacturer affects the rights of different consumers with different interests.

U.S. hospitals often do not charge for each individual department or set of services and equipment a price sufficient to cover their full costs.[7] For example, open-heart surgery or cobalt therapy units that have sophisticated equipment and personnel and are infrequently used are often priced at less than marginal cost. Thus, other more widely used services have to pay enough to cover these specialized services.

One result of this phenomenon has been the attempted entry of proprietary hospitals, which seek to supply only those services that are in themselves prof-itable. They attract customers by charging lower prices for those services than the existing nonprofit full-line hospitals. Property-right and institutional ques-tions therefore arise as to whether the law should allow this type of competi-tion or whether proprietary hospitals should be regulated in some fashion (for example, all hospitals must offer all services). A similar situation existed in the pricing of local and long-distance phoning before the breakup of American Telephone and Telegraph.

One's initial response is to suggest that each service should stand on its own feet. This, however, needs some examination if there is interdependence among the services so that the provision of service X affects the profitability of service Y or at least its quality and availability to consumers. Hospitals argue that to get good-quality doctors for their entire operation, they must provide special-ized equipment even if such equipment does not cover its own individual cost.[8] A further point is related to the earlier discussion of option demand in the face of information costs. In effect, hospitals make the appendectomy opera-tion user help pay for the existence of certain rare operations in case he might need them someday. The hospitals fill this option demand even where some users may not wish it. (This is one reason why consumer groups want to be represented on hospital governing boards and not leave all decisions to medical professionals.)

Groups of consumers with different interests cannot get what they want simultaneously. The pricing practices of firms, which in effect aggregate or sub-divide consumers, affect the cost to different groups as well as the quality and kind of service available. It is important to predict the consequences of differ-ent rules for different parties so that the concerned parties can choose the rules that best suit them.

A similar case involves the use of credit cards. Merchants honoring cards pay a substantial fee to the credit card company, such as American Express. Yet the person who pays cash is not given a discount equivalent to the cost of this service. There is no problem if everyone uses credit or the same frequency of credit. But those who consistently use cash subsidize the credit users.[9] They may then decide to use credit also, since its marginal cost to them is zero, even though they do not find the convenience of credit worth what the mer-chant has to pay American Express. Merchants may find that offering credit card sales increases their business and profits without differential pricing for each service offered. Do they have the right to do this even at the expense of people who do not want the service? The credit companies profit by such practices, which increase their business. Formerly, they only offered contracts to merchants that prohibited the merchant from offering cash customers a discount, but federal law has invalidated such contracts.[10]

The law, however, does not say that cash customers have a right to a discount but says only that they have the right to be free of the bargaining power of the credit card companies in preventing merchants from giving discounts if they want to. Few merchants will want to as long as total profits are enhanced by offering a full line of services at a flat price even if it is not in the best interests of some customers who are defined in a group that they would prefer not to be in.[11] Some competitor may try to develop a business out of catering to cash-only customers. But, given all of the other variables, it will be hard to convince customers that prices are lower by the amount of the credit charge. It will be hard to build a business on this basis. If cash customers are in the minority, economies of scale will keep merchants from catering to them exclusively. For purposes of unit cost, the cash-preferring minority wants to be included in the total group, but for pricing purposes, they would prefer to be in a separate group and not have to choose between different firms but rather between cash and credit payment to the same firm. Alas, groups conflict with each other and with the interests of the profit-maximizing firm.

The issue is how a given consumer gets thrown in with other consumers with different interests. If she is segmented out, she will be faced with different prices and available services than if she is mixed in with others. It is a boundary issue, though not geographical as in the case with political jurisdictions.

In summary, note with Alec Nove that "it is erroneous , even in elementary or abstract analysis, to present margins as if they had no context" (1969, p. 850; 1973). We have seen that the profitability of a feeder transport link is different if considered alone than if considered as a part of the profitability of the total system. The same was true for credit services, hospital equipment, and manufacturers' full-product line availability. Economists' conventional wisdom advises against cross-subsidization and insists that each portion of the product stand on its own feet (or, more colorfully put, "each tub should stand on its own bottom"). Nove was particularly concerned that if nationalized industries would heed this advice, it would reduce total profitability. The concern here is broader and arises from the fact that people have different preferences for closely related goods and services. Not all groups have the same interest in the pricing scheme and product mix offered by the profit-maximizing private or socialist firm. The issue is not profitability versus social goals but of a public-policy choice of the product relative to which profit is to be calculated.

Nove warns against the disease of "vulgarmarginalismus," which is loosely defined as being hell-bent to equate marginal cost and marginal revenue in ignorance of the context. The point of conflict in property-rights terms is who gets to choose the context. In effect, private merchants define their relevant product for purposes of calculating profit. This situation is acceptable to some

groups and harms others. Should the groups affected have the right to participate in the decision? The same issue arises in socialist firms and regulated
industries. Who gets to define what it is that the firm is producing? Typically
in the United States, the state public-utility regulating commissions have been
much more concerned with regulating the rate of return than with disputes
over quality of service.

Some of the normative rules put forward by economists will be examined in
more detail in Chapter 11. It is sufficient to note here that the economist's
rule of rules, that marginal cost should equal marginal revenue, has an institutional context. One is reminded of a theme from Chapter 1, where we noted
that costs do not exist in nature but are related to the system of property
rights. Note that the argument here is not contrary to the internal logic of
marginal cost and revenue equation but that there are many such points depending on the institutional rules. We are not talking about modifying the
market profit system with social values but about the basis for profit calculation. Of course, the market system can be replaced entirely with an administrative system. The argument here is not for one over the other but to point
out that substantial performance difference can be obtained in either system
depending on the rules defining the product and what segment is considered
marginal.

Political Boundaries

The ability of a person to have government act in accordance with his tastes
depends on the tastes of his fellow citizens. Who his fellow citizens are is
affected by where he lives and how political boundaries are drawn. Arguments
over political boundaries are as old as organized government. The drawing of
such boundaries can make a person a member of a majority or minority group
by throwing a person in different mixes of other people in a decision-making
unit. However obvious this fact is, it seems not to have challenged such slo-
gans as "Power to the People" and "The government is best which is closest
to the people" (see Breton 1974, p. 116). A series of cases will be examined
to see how property rights in political boundaries differentially affect people.
(For a general related discussion, see Dahl and Tufte 1973.)

It is instructive to observe the behavior of a political representative with
reference to the same issue when he represents different groupings of constituents. This issue was involved in a proposal to create a type of national park
on a peninsula in Lake Michigan. Most of the local people near the proposed
park opposed it, because they feared congestion and loss of private ownership
of individual cottage sites. The representative to the U.S. Congress from this
district reflected this dominant interest and opposed the park. Later, when he
became a U.S. senator elected by the people of Michigan, he supported the
park. The dominant interest in a statewide vote was the people of Detroit,
who wanted a public recreational area away from the busy city. It is also inter-

esting to note that the park was originally proposed by a senator from the neighboring state of Illinois, whose largest city was within easy driving distance of the park. The Michigan congressman and later senator was democratically elected, but he changed his mind when the boundary changed the character of the majority. It seems that "Power to the People" does not mean too much until we inquire which people. Likewise, democracy does not mean much unless we inquire into the rules for grouping people to vote. One-man/one vote does not speak to how that vote will be combined with others.

If the people in the vicinity of the park had the right to make the decision, they would have furthered their interests at the expense of lost opportunities for more distant people. The reverse is also true. The establishment of the federal park created costs for the local people for which they received no compensation. The interests of one group are an externality to the other.

For many years, it was a conventional wisdom in political science that the large number of local governments in the United States should be consolidated into a few super metropolitan governments. (For a critique, see Vincent Ostrom 1973, pp. 114–22.) The most often mentioned reason was to achieve economies of scale in the provision of services. An underlying reason may have been the intellectual appeal of a neat, centralized authority in contrast to the confusion of many local governments. More recently some scholars have pointed out that economies of scale in production do not necessarily require large political units that articulate demand for these services (Bish 1971; Tiebout and Houston 1962). They have pointed to the Los Angeles (Lakewood) plan where many politically independent units contract with suppliers who embody economies of scale but who can provide just the level and kind of service the local unit wishes instead of a common service for the whole area (Warren 1966). The supplier may be either a public or a private body or person. The decision units remain small and therefore are more likely to have homogeneous members than is the large metro government. This sounds like the best of all possible worlds, where each group gets what it wants at the lowest possible production cost. But the choice of one unit can have an impact on the opportunities of another unit, as was seen in the park issue above.

For many services, the purchases of one unit are of no interest to other people. But for unavoidable joint-impact goods, the right to make a choice according to one's interests creates costs for others. An example is provided by the different responses of different government units to the closing of a major commuter highway in East Lansing, Michigan. The university students of that community blocked the highway to protest the policy of the federal government in the conduct of the Vietnam War. The highway was the major route through the university community between a large central city and still more distant suburbs. The East Lansing political authorities were sympathetic to the protest and were in no hurry to reopen the highway forcibly. They were willing to bear a little inconvenience. The state police and the governor, who represented a broader constituency, had a different view and wanted the students removed immediately, by force if necessary. Where is the boundary of the controlling political authority? If it is local, external costs are created for commuters to the larger area, but if the decision boundary is larger, the interests of the local people are a minority that can be overwhelmed. Government represents the people, but which people?

There are a whole series of such issues. They include questions of city annexation, the drawing up of legislative districts (called gerrymandering when it goes against your interests), whether a city council should be elected at large or from wards (districts), and school consolidation (Blawie and Blawie 1973). The latter is now creating some anomalies. Some persons want to force the creation of large metropolitan districts so that schools can be racially integrated. However, the enlargement of districts means that in some central cities where blacks are nearing the majority of voters, they will become a minority again in the enlarged district.

One problem in the drawing of boundaries is that their significance for a given group changes with the type of question involved. One geographical area may include homogeneous tastes with respect to drainage or waste disposal but heterogeneous tastes with respect to police or schools. This is why the United States has so many special-purpose governments providing a single service. This confusion of overlapping governmental boundaries offends anyone with a sense of neatness and orderliness, but it allows a homogeneous group to further its unique interests (and create costs for others where interests conflict). It is perhaps a quirk of human nature that arguments over governmental boundaries are always couched in terms of abstract efficiency, prevention of waste and overlapping, or bringing government closer to the people rather than in terms of the real conflict of who is going to create costs for whom and why group A's preferences should count more than group B's. Some empirical evidence on the substantive consequences of boundary alternatives is noted in Chapter 12.

A person who finds herself in a decision group where her preferences are always losing out has several alternatives. She can try to change the preferences of the dominant group, use her vote and voice more effectively, try to change the boundary, or move (exit). The property rights involved in boundary definition determine which of these are real opportunities.

The exit option deserves further comment. In the discussion of joint-impact goods (Chapter 5), it was noted that for some goods it is impossible for two people to consume different kinds or amounts. For example, whatever quality of ambient air is available to A is necessarily available to and utilized by B. There is no escape if the person remains in the air shed. There is, of course, the option of exit from the area. By moving around, people may be able to form relatively homogeneous local political units to avoid conflict in preferences (Tiebout 1956). But such a solution is more complicated than might appear. One problem has already been noted above. Often, there are interdependencies among local governments. There may be no conflict within the unit, but there may be interdependencies between units. A second problem is immobility. It is costly to move (Scott 1964). When preferences differ, who bears the costs of moving?

Moreover, what is the responsibility of the departing group to those who remain? That people do move to form relatively homogeneous units is clear. Relatively rich whites have left the cities, and urban problems must be solved by those left behind. The issue is the right to exit when that creates costs for others. It is involved in the right of central cities to tax nonresidents who work in the city. It is involved when large factories leave a city for a new location. A parallel case is the right to join a group. Does a group have the right to be exclusive when new entrants create costs for prior members? This was the issue in a court case testing the right of Petaluma, California, to limit its size (Kirp 1976). The possibility to limit conflict by forming homogeneous units of local government is itself limited.

PREFERENCE AGGREGATION: CONTROL OF THE POLITICAL AGENDA AND VOTING RULES

Boundary control is only one way of grouping people and issues to aggregate preferences. Another has to do with the order in which items come up for vote in a legislative body. The rules committees of the U.S. Congress are very powerful because they decide which bills come to the floor for a vote and in what order. The formulation of winning coalitions of competing groups is affected by the order of consideration. This is formally demonstrated by what is called the "voter paradox" (Arrow 1963). Assume a decision unit made up of three people with a preference ordering for three different alternative ways for designing a certain program, as shown in the table below. Successive pairs must be voted on and a simple majority wins.

	Individual's Preference Ordering		
Individual	*1st*	*2nd*	*3nd*
A	X	Z	Y
B	Z	Y	X
C	Y	X	Z

Individual A prefers policy alternative X to Z and Z to Y and so on. Preferences are not single-peaked. If the vote is first taken on the proposition to choose between alternatives Y and Z, alternative Z will be supported by a majority of two individuals, B and A. But if the first choice is between another pair, a different winner emerges. When Z is paired with X, X will carry the majority. Few actual legislative votes take this exact form, but the general implication is clear. Control of the agenda is an important property right.[12] Coalitions of groups form around the basic idea that is first put forward. A common process is to add features to a legislative bill until the necessary majority is reached. The persons who can control this sequence have a great impact on what emerges since in many situations more than one set of coalitions is possible (Ingram 1969). The voter paradox leads to cyclic instability as coalitions can be reformed. Stability is a function of whether the losers think the outcome was fair (willing participation). Appeal to the widely accepted symbols of democracy do not settle the conflict between groups over the agenda.

Referendums are usually regarded as the purest form of democracy. Yet many examples can be cited where the wording of the proposition affected the outcome and produced a different result than might be expected from majority attitudes on the basic principle of the proposition. The group that can control the wording and get its proposal on the ballot first can exercise some impact on the result.

Referendums often contain a mix of features. For example, in 1974 Michigan voters had the opportunity to vote a bonus for Vietnam War veterans to be financed by a bond. Some may have supported the idea of veteran aid but objected to the form of financing. A second proposition proposed bonding for investments in public transportation equipment and facilities. The major portion was for bus transport but some was for airports and harbors. Some people may have voted against the proposition although they supported bus transport because they objected to aid for airports and harbors. The other modes of transport were probably added in the hope that this would build a winning coalition for the whole proposal. Or it may have been added by special-interest groups, which thought they could get a free ride out of a generally popular bus-transport proposal or by those who wanted the whole proposal defeated. The same problem of separating out the features one supports from those one does not is common in all representative political systems. Candidates represent a package of views on different issues. You may find that parts of the package you prefer are advocated by several different candidates for the same office but are embraced wholly by no one candidate. This situation is referred to by Bish (1971, p. 70) as the "blue plate menu problem." Voters are forced to choose among packages of issues where the packages presented to them are not directly under their control. They are free to choose, but the choices given to them are not of their liking. This is the now-familiar distinction between the freedom to choose within one's opportunity set and the freedom to choose the set.

The blue-plate-menu problem is not unique to public choice. It also occurs in the market. Many goods are made up of several features and not all combinations are feasible. Buyers are often forced to select among brands that represent different mixtures of these features. This indivisibility can also be inherent in goods. This is related to preemption in the case of joint-impact goods above. (Also as noted above in the section on product definition, buyers are often forced to buy a manufacturer's full line of products. This is why Albert Breton [1974, p. 50] refers to the blue plate menu problem as one of "full-line supply." It is the same issue as that of tie-in sales discussed above.) How often have you wished someone would combine the specific features of brand X and brand Y into the good that you really want? The fact that you buy brand X in the market is not confirmation that you approve of all features of the product any more than the fact that you voted for candidate X shows you approve of all of the positions taken by the candidate. Consumers and voters only have the exit choice of buy-or-do-not-buy or vote-or-do-not-vote, which hides much information about their preferences. The problem is that people do not agree on the packages of features that should be presented for choice. Thus, people agree on neither the property rights in the market nor the politics that controls who gets to put the packages together.

Breton (1974, pp. 115–16) argues that federal (as opposed to unitary) governments better reflect individual preferences since the representative from the smaller district must reflect the more homogeneous tastes of constituents. In small districts, though the opportunity for blue plate menus is reduced, the eventual conflict is only postponed or its location transferred. In a unitary system, the minority loses out to the majority at the time of a popular election. In a federal system, the loser is the one in a neighboring district who bears the cost of choices that are made within a district where she does not live but that have external effects. Care must be taken not to speak of preferences in the abstract. The point is not that one system or another better serves preferences but which group's preferences are better served. This is not to deny that there may be homogeneous preference in some cases.

In national decisions, preference aggregation is different with an electoral rule of plurality than with proportional representation (Commons 1907; Schumpeter 1942). These rules affect transactions and resulting winning coalitions and compromises between and among citizens, party leaders, and parties in the legislature. Breton and Galeotti (1985) hypothesize that proportional representation results in ideologically purer party platforms, which facilitates trust between citizens and representatives. Voters exchange votes for efforts by politicians to achieve the voters' interests. The information cost of a citizen is less when the party platform is narrow. If a party adds features to attract a plurality, it dilutes its position and makes it harder for its original supporters to monitor its performance and preserve its trust.

In proportional representation, there are more parties representing various views. These conflicting views are not compromised within the party. In parliamentary systems, the major compromises are made when the government is formed rather than on a day-to-day basis needed to form a winning coalition for a particular piece of legislation, such as in the U.S. Congress.

Hypothesis: The character of the winning coalition is different (different preferences count) depending on whether the compromise is made to achieve a plurality, to form a parliamentary government from various parties where none has a clear majority, or to achieve a majority vote among political representatives in a nonparliamentary, weak-party-discipline system.

The transaction and monitoring costs of any particular interest group and thus its ability to achieve its goals is affected by the rules for preference aggregation. However, groups may derive utility from seeing a politician wearing their label even if they do not affect legislative outcomes. Depending on the distribution of preference and the rules, a minority can influence outcomes by providing the margin of victory in forming a parliamentary government or on a particular legislative vote or by making a party modify its platform to achieve a plurality (Galeotti 1980). As always in economics, the margin is critical but the rules define the relevant margin.

Voting rules affect the aggregation of the preference of people with different intensities. The table above illustrated an outcome with binary voting, but other rules are possible. Point voting, for example, gives a certain number of points or votes to each person that may be distributed among various alternatives. If a person has an intense preference for a candidate in a multiseat contest, all of the person's points can be given to one candidate. This can lead to strategic voting when an individual tries to influence voting outcomes by not voting her true preferences.

Another alternative affecting communication of the intensity of preferences is vote trading (logrolling). A person attempts to get their preferred alternative by offering to support the other voters preferences where the person has only mild preferences. As Frey (1978, p. 76) notes, "Vote-trading always increases the utility of the voters participating. . . . The voter(s) *not* participating in the trade, on the other hand, suffer a utility loss." In the case of multiple vote trading it is possible for each voter to be worse off after trading (Bernholz 1974). While the individual trades are rational, the overall result may not be. The degree of unanimity needed for public choice is discussed in Chapter 11 in the context of welfare economics.

To conclude, it has been seen that rights relating to boundaries, agenda, and vote trading control many aspects of interdependence not addressed by the rules of pure competition in markets or simple democracy and majority voting in politics.

GROUP FORMATION AND GROWTH UNDER ALTERNATIVE INSTITUTIONS

In this section, some goods that combine several of the characteristics noted above will be examined in the context of alternative institutional frameworks. What are the conditions for group formation and growth? When will a group form under private contract alone? When will groups welcome new members, and when will they try to be exclusive?

Group Formation related to Information and Exclusion Costs and Size

Consider a good that is not divisible in the sense that the payment or effort by one person will obtain any usable quantity of the good. The total cost is such that it requires the contribution of many people to provide a usable amount of the good. (However, the physical amount of the good is variable.) Further, the costs of exclusion are relatively high. If the good is to exist for one person, it will be hard to exclude others. Examples are national defense, voting, and lobbying to secure government action, such as price support for farmers or a significant change in ambient air quality. (Note that some of these are also joint-impact goods and others are not, so this feature is not decisive in the discussion to follow.)

With low-exclusion-cost goods, a group of customers forms without anyone being particularly conscious of it. Anyone who does not in effect pay to belong to this group will not receive any of the good. Failure to buy (contribute to the good's cost) provides immediate feedback consequences. What is the case for a small group of people interested in a good as described above with high exclusion costs? Imagine a group of ten people, each willing to pay $100 for this good, which happens to have a total cost of $1,000. If no one offers to buy the good, it will become relatively obvious to all. The effect of one person's choice on others is easy to detect compared with the case of large groups, to be discussed next. It is imaginable that the ten potential consumers are scattered over the country and may not be known to each other (information cost). But let us suppose that this kind of information is not a problem or has been supplied by some private or public entrepreneur or leader. In this instance, the individual can perceive the effect of his not buying or the effect of any other individuals not buying. It is easy to see that his choice will make a difference. If he wants the good, he had better make a purchase or contribution, except if he hopes that some of the others might be induced to give even more and thus give him a free ride. The result may be strategic bargaining and game-theoretic considerations, already noted in the sections on exclusion cost and joint-impact goods. About all that can be said is that sometimes the good will be obtained through private market bargaining, and sometimes it will not (or at least not in the amount that in the absence of the temptation of strategic bargaining people might have been willing to purchase).

The key to understanding the small-group situation is that each person can perceive relatively easily the consequences of his acts. This is not the case for large groups. It is hard to perceive that your action will make a difference. Frohlich and Oppenheimer (1970) suggest that even with high exclusion costs, individuals calculate the probable contributions of all others and make their contribution when it could make a difference. But size does affect the ability to obtain the information necessary to make this calculation. If the group is large, the individual will find it costly to know how many people would give how much. But more fundamentally, how can a person estimate how much others are going to give and then decide on how much he will give when the people whose contributions he is trying to estimate are asking the same question? He is trying to estimate a whole series of interdependent decisions. This is not just a matter of high information cost; it is simply impossible information.

Even incompatible-use goods have information problems that are not solved simply by competitive markets. In order to make good decisions, a producer of an agricultural product needs to know not only demand but also the probable supply to be offered by the sum of other producers. But this information is impossible to obtain since everyone is simultaneously making interdependent decisions. If the current year's output is high relative to demand, prices are depressed and losses suffered. This is a signal to reduce output. But which and how many producers will get out? If everyone else reduces output, the individual can maintain or even expand output and take advantage of next year's higher prices. But if others are going to maintain output, A should get out of production. The inability of a firm to obtain the necessary information results in a cycle production pattern referred to as the "cobweb." Output alternately overshoots and undershoots an equilibrium price that will just cover costs of production.

In the small-group situation, experience is suggestive and gives useful feedback. For example, assume in practice that my failure to give usually suggests that it makes no difference. I fail to give, and the good comes anyway. This tells me something, and the next time perhaps I am tempted not to give again. Now the good ceases. But can I be sure why? Was my noncontribution decisive or would potential total donations still be short of total cost? Suppose I get information on the size of the shortfall. Can I assume that there are many people like me who will realize their mistake in not supporting something we really want and now make their contribution? This guessing game quickly becomes exhausting. It is difficult to imagine a prediction precise enough to identify the utility of my $10 contribution to a million-dollar project. The perfect-knowledge assumption of neoclasical economic theory misses a lot of real-world situations of interdependence.

It is probably a mistake to overintellectualize the decision-making process. Just because we can imagine some set of calculations consistent with observed behavior does not mean people actually think that way. Perhaps a bit of empathy would be more useful. When I contribute to the local public television station, I have no illusion that my contribution will be decisive. I have no estimate of the probable contributions of others, of total cost, or even of the number of people that watch public television in my area. I am not aware of any evidence that other viewers make these estimates. I am aware (after writing this book) that I have the opportunity of being a free rider, but I do not reflect on it long. I make a contribution because I agree with the purposes of public television and enjoy its programs, and it just seems like the right thing to do. I have learned a certain behavior. Scholarly people make contributions to scholarly and artistic enterprises in their communities, and it would pain me not to live up to my self-image as a scholar, even if no one in town knows I made the donation. I can imagine people making the decision on a variety of bases, and perhaps even some detailed calculations of advantage, but I would not care to make any interpretations of the sum of willingness to pay from observed voluntary contributions to goods with high exclusion costs and large numbers.

The high-exclusion-cost feature may imply a conscious calculation of advantage, but it also means that there is no quick and easy perception of the consequences of individual action. In this situation, some people are calculating and some are acting out of habit, sense of obligation, the fulfillment of some personality need, and so on. I suspect that some are not even aware of whether they are calculating free riders or whether they really do not value the good enough to make any contribution. (There is some reason to believe that not all choice follows a prior precise mental picture of what is desirable but that preferences are formed in the process of consumption. Preferences can be both a dependent and independent variable. Sometimes preferences guide consumption and other times they are derived from consumption (Shaffer 1969, 1980).

The role of the political entrepreneur cannot be ignored.[13] A person may incur certain organizational costs while offering a good to potential contributors in the hope of capturing a salary from future contributors. Such a person may seek legislation, such as the union-shop rule, to solve a free-rider problem; find a selective good to sell to finance the group activities that have high exclusion costs; or engage in propaganda and patriotic efforts to create a non-calculating sense of community to support contributions. People who have organizational leadership positions also gain some personal reward in terms of status.

Voting in the face of high exclusion costs for political outcomes can be conceptualized as an exchange of trust (Breton and Galeotti 1985; Coleman 1984; Salmon 1983). Trust is a substitute for policing cost. Politicians cannot contract with voters to vote the voter's preferences in exchange for votes. But if there is sufficient trust, both parties behave as the other expects.

The concept of product is again critical. Denton Morrison (1971) argues that there is a difference between a good conceived as a desired want and an action that is conceived as right and just. There is a difference between wanting a product and feeling it is deserved. When people contribute voluntarily to a reform movement, they perceive they are doing something more than the usual consumer purchase, which compares utility and cost. The person who contributes to the National Association for the Advancement of Colored People (NAACP) or a women's rights movement may perceive the product in a different emotional sense than the person who pays taxes for mosquito control. The former carries a heavy moral flavor of righting a wrong. Morrison speaks of products that have "reform utility." Albert Hirschman (1984a) similarly distinguishes instrumental and noninstrumental behavior. The latter makes a person "feel more like a real person" even if not instrumental in providing a physical good. Work toward an HEC good increases one's sense of belonging to the group, which may explain voting participation (Pizzorno 1983).

The knowledge that provision of high-exclusion-cost goods is improbable without heroic behavior can make such contributions more desirable to would-be heroes. Utility and knowledge are significant variables in predicting performance. Successful institutional design should stress morality, the heroic, and knowledge and should try to get the sympathy of the masses as well as provide side payments. (For a discussion of selective incentives versus ideological commitment, see Cell 1980.)

Albert Hirschman (1984b) has inquired into the characteristics of successful group action in providing high-exclusion-cost goods in developing countries. He emphasizes the accumulation of experience and trust. Past attempts at collective action, even if unsuccessful, increase the probability of future success.

The conclusion is that sometimes people make voluntary market contributions to these goods and sometimes they do not. People do make substantial contributions to churches, philanthropic organizations, and so on. But the same process of empathy tells me that not all of the present level of such goods that I now enjoy may always be provided for in that way. Some people would not get the level of these goods they are willing to pay for if private contract were the only alternative.

A commonly used institution in the United States is that of the tax referendum in a local government area. If a majority of the voters approve, all taxpayers must pay. The agenda is controlled by political officials who provide information on total cost and benefit and each taxpayer's share. There is no opportunity for strategic bargaining, and no voter needs to estimate the demand of others. The group forms, as in a market, without any conscious contract, and so transaction costs are low. The key ingredient is a preexisting organization and "contract" where most people agree that the whole procedure is legitimate. This system is widely used in the United States for public education and other local capital improvements and supplements goods provided through legislative representation at all levels of government.

Where groups are large and habits of giving and social bonds are weak, we turn to government finance; rules that help hold the group membership together, such as the union closed shop; or some mixture of goods with low and high exclusion costs, such as the American Farm Bureau or American Medical Association lobbying efforts or selling advertising to finance free broadcast television.

Or, we do without. Again, empathy tells us that there are goods and services of this type that people individually might pay small amounts for but that do not seem to be provided or are provided at low levels. Even casual observation dramatically contrasts the huge amounts of money raised for lobbying by small-member groups such as oil, sugar, milk, or tobacco producers and by special interests such as gun users and sportsmen with the small amounts of money spent by general consumer groups or voter groups such as Common Cause, which claim to speak for the interests of large numbers of people.

People who want national defense, environmental improvement, consumer protection, and so on have a special problem, because it is difficult for the individual to perceive that his or her action makes a difference. Mancur Olson (1965, p. 50) refers to such people as "latent groups," because without strong habit and social bond their interests can only be mobilized with the aid of selective incentives. (Compare Chamberlain 1974.) The problem is that these selective incentives are themselves a type of good that has high exclusion costs. Somehow, someone has to get an organization started, a referendum procedure instituted, and the union-shop law passed. Why then do some of these latent groups materialize and others do not?

There probably is no substitute for some minimum amount of internalized ideology (what B. F. Skinner would call learned, reinforced behavior) where people act without calculation of individual advantage. In many cases such an amount is sufficient. In other cases it is the base on which other selective incentives are built. In the formative period of many present organizations, there was a small group of dedicated (sometimes even called fanatical) people who devoted themselves to the cause. The processes that produce people like Eugene V. Debs, Mahatma Gandhi, or Martin Luther are very complex (Erikson 1958; Salert 1976). The role of the charismatic leader is often a factor in group formation, but more complex are the processes producing a widely held ideology that these leaders can take advantage of or that energize and nurture leaders. No latent group's success can be fully explained without consideration of its leaders. It helps if leaders and their apostles are emotionally committed. They act because they must act and not because of any calculation that worries about free riders. They have an ego and a vision that their acts will make a difference. The role of the heroic cannot be denied.

For the product or cause to gain wider acceptance, it helps if it can be described simply. In more-pejorative terms, it helps to have a slogan. You can get people to respond to a leader who proposes more money for national defense if the enemy can be dramatized in simple terms. Difficult as the civil rights movement was to organize, its objective can be described more easily than the many complex issues involved in something like consumer protection. It is hard to get an emotional reaction to complex goods; people's attention spans are exhausted before they are willing to reach into their pockets for a contribution or to vote.

Sometimes the difference is made by violence. The willingness of a few people to resort to violence cannot be ignored, and neither can the willingness of the rest of society to tolerate it in some instances and not in others (Graham and Gurr 1969). Social movements seem to require a certain environment of sympathy.

The role of the private entrepreneur in mixing goods with high exclusion costs and low exclusion costs is another factor. The rewards here probably are of the more material and calculated sort. The fact that the defense industry profits from national defense and that manufacturers do not profit from consumer-protection expenditures is a factor in explaining the amount spent on these two activities.

The large latent groups in the United States have an important ideological barrier against them that small groups do not have. There is an ideological preference for individual market organization, and this organization is sufficient for the interests of many small groups. But, at a certain point many large groups need governmental administrative transactions to sustain their interests. Competition between large and small has been most uneven because of the ideological commitment to the market, which is regarded as somehow natural and good while administrative actions are unnatural and therefore suspicious. When small groups compete with large groups, the prevailing ideology has the effect of a valuable property right that constrains the options of large groups.

The role of the family must be included in a discussion of the effects of group size, though it can only be touched on here. There is a class of goods where exclusion cost is low but information is needed to determine who is eligible to participate in their use. Group size and interpersonal relationships can affect the cost of this information. For example, in the winter of 1977 numerous migrant workers were unemployed because of a freeze in citrus-growing areas. Some taxpayers represented by government wished to provide aid to these people. On paper, it was easy to exclude ineligible people from the disaster relief, but it was expensive for government administration to determine eligibility. Many fraudulent claims were filed by people claiming to be fruit harvesters who had never been so employed. In some other societies, disaster relief would be provided by the extended family and the local community. People able to help would personally know those needing help; it would be cheap to determine need, and would-be free riders would be rejected.

A number of factors affecting provision of goods with high exclusion cost have now been noted, including group size, information cost, habits, political entrepreneurship, reform utility, transaction cost, ideology, and violence. Some of these are affected by changes in property rights and others are not. Some can be manipulated in the relative short run by a change in the legal rules while others are the result of a complex, long-term learning process embedded in informal cultural rules.

Group Growth: Exclusive and Nonexclusive Groups

We can observe some groups that welcome new members and others that do not. The reason for this is related to the combination of exclusion cost and joint-impact characteristics of goods. Inclusive groups welcome new members because they seek a joint-impact good where the marginal cost of another user is zero. Where it is costly to exclude users anyway, the more who contribute, the lower the cost to existing members. For example, environmental groups such as the Sierra Club want as many members as possible to help pay for their lobbying efforts. However, there is an ambivalence that derives from another aspect of nonoptional joint-impact goods. That is the fact that one member of the group cannot enjoy a different physical quantity or quality of the good. Thus, if current members have homogeneous tastes and agree on the level and kind of product sought, they do not want new members with different tastes. Therefore, some organizations, as they grow, welcome new members to lower the cost per member but become undemocratic, with policy making controlled by the old-guard establishment. This is why governments sometimes regulate the internal political rules of private organizations. Even where exclusion of users is costly, groups may try to exclude formal members who could affect policy.

Exclusive groups, on the other hand, do not want new members or new users because the marginal cost of another user is not zero. The cost of obtaining benefits for another person exceeds the revenues contributed by the new member. A producers' cartel does not want any new members because the market is fixed and would have to be shared with new entrants. Of course, if the existence of the unwanted new entrant cannot be prevented, it is better to have it a member than an outside competitor. The new member lowers the utility of old members but not as much as destruction of the cartel. Exclusive groups need 100 percent membership of the people who cannot be excluded from their product, if the product exists at all, and thus exclusive groups are hard to maintain.

Some lobbying groups are inclusive up to the point where another member raises costs more than revenues. For example, a group of churches seeking exemption from the property tax will welcome all churches as members of their lobbying organization. But they may not welcome more and more varieties of not-for-profit firms, because at some point the resistance of the rest of the taxpayers stiffens and the cost of obtaining the exemption exceeds the dues from new members. In other cases there may be economies of scale in lobbying. Larger groups may raise more resources to compete effectively with other groups, but they also raise the resistance of others. Pincus (1977) documents the history of U.S. tariffs, where at some point high tariffs achieved by special interests cause free-trade advocates to run for public office.

Other varieties of ambivalence also occur where the organization has multiple goods. Labor unions, for example, want more members to support their national lobbying activities but may erect high entry barriers to workers in some industries to avoid competition.

There are many consumer goods where exclusion is possible, but they are nevertheless owned by a group rather than an individual. The size of the group is related to the degree to which the good is a joint-impact good (Where there is no jointness, the good likely will be owned and used individually.) For instance, an individual golfer realizes that she cannot afford to have a course of her own. Another user does create extra cost, but there is a degree of jointness. The individual will seek other member-owners in a club up to the point where the congestion causes her total benefit to reduce faster than the average cost of membership declines because of the revenue from new members (Buchanan 1965; Rowley and Peacock 1975, p. 118).Certain goods then will be used in common with or without control on frequency of use by an individual. For some goods with a degree of jointness, the "club" is an alternative to government or individual ownership (Sandler and Tschirhart 1980). Group size will increase up to a point, and then new members will not be accepted. Persons can reduce conflicts by moving to the club or local community that provides their preferred mix of goods and prices (Tiebout 1956). The right of the club to exclusivity and the right of the community to control its size and homogeneity by zoning is thus instrumental.

Economies of scale create a type of jointness in that size affects the average return to each individual factor. Another firm "member" can be added without subtracting from the returns of previous members sharing equally in total output. A labor-controlled firm (or cooperative) will add new worker-members to maximize enterprise income per head of the existing labor force rather than add workers to the point where marginal cost (wage rate) equals marginal revenue, as would a capitalist firm (Wiles 1977, p. 70; see also the discussion of employer surplus in Chapter 7.)

To conclude, many public decision bodies are exclusive groups and do not welcome new members. Membership on bodies that decide rights issues between A and B is itself an incompatible-use good. Power has been defined here as participation. Membership on a rights-creation and -distribution body is equivalent to resource (factor) ownership in that it is the source of the opportunity to participate in decisions.

ECONOMY AND POLITY

Interrelationships of economy and polity are of concern to many institutional scholars. One view is to see votes and money as parallel ways to fulfill consumer demand. In the polity, parties compete for votes in the same way as firms compete for dollars, and similar equilibrium conditions apply. Downs (1957) uses the spatial-equilibrium model developed by Hotelling to predict that parties starting with different programs will maximize votes by moving toward the center (the median voter). Furthermore, it is argued that the result is Pareto-optimal (Riker and Ordeshook 1973, chaps. 11, 12). In this view parties (as firms) have no independent policy goals but must serve the median voter. Institutions seem to be of little significance except the usual ones of competition and free entry. This theory has concentrated on axiomatic propositions with little empirical testing.

Another view is that parties and the governments they form pursue independent objectives (Frey 1978, p. 155). They must give the voters enough to get elected, but there can be slack within which to pursue their own interests. And, this slack is not just the result of legal barriers to competition. It is hypothesized that voters have information costs and are myopic, forgetting performance during the early years of a president's administration but highly impressionable by income and inflation levels in election years. There is then no equilibrium of party programs and performance. Rather there is an evolutionary process as parties try to capture the sequence. Parties pursue some of their own ends during their early years in office and increase public spending and transfer payments close to elections, thus contributing to economic instability. Government, instead of just compensating for the usual business cycles, cause cycles of its own as the supply of government goods fluctuates. Empirical work by Frey (1978, p. 154) suggests that the U.S. and U.K. "governments pursue an expansionary policy before elections, when they are unsure about their re-elections." This model speaks of institutional variables for ideology and legal constraints, but the simple proxies used to represent them are questionable. A dilemma of empirical work using the usual econometric techniques is that available data are imperfect but the use of richer data turn the analysis into a qualitative story. The so-called institutional variables used to date in econometric studies are not instrumental in the sense that they clearly contrast performance being affected by institutional alternatives. The results are called explanatory and might even predict changes in public spending, but do not yet readily identify how one would change institutions to get a different performance.

SUMMARY OF PARADIGM APPLIED TO POLITICS

Voting and other forms of participation in public choice can be conceptualized in terms of transactions that are ordered by structural rules relating to situations of interdependence. First comes the right to participate. Then comes a host of other rules that condition that participation and influence eventual performance. For example, each voter may have the right to try to persuade other voters, much like goods producers use advertising to attract customers. In goods production, we saw that A's welfare is often a function of how many others share his tastes. Similarly, A's vote is worth more if many Bs have the same tastes. A is motivated to grant persuasive information to B, and vice versa.

In a sense, the time to participate and vote by a citizen is exchanged for some governmental rule (or product). This product may be a high-exclusion-cost good and thus invite free riders who will not bear the participation costs (applicable to lobbying activities discussed above as well as direct political participation of all kinds).

To summarize, different rules affecting A's participation in making property rights are highlighted by the paradigm (these are stated positively, but could be stated obversely):

1. Allow A the right to vote, hold office, and so on (a variety of factor ownership related to the incompatible-use characteristic of political participation). The right to exclude others depends on exclusion cost.

2. Put A in a unit where he or she is in a majority (boundary issue).

3. Arrange the decision rule (unanimity, majority, and so on) to affect a given person's veto power and decision cost (a variety of economy of scale).

4. Decrease A's transaction costs via ballot design, physical location, and registration requirement (information and contractual cost factors).

5. Allow the use of economic resources to persuade. A more subtle version is the impact of organization of economic activity on tastes and ideology (related in part to factor ownership and competitive rules).

6. Control the agenda to facilitate formation of coalitions including A.

7. Allow private contributions to political lobbying.

In short, the paradigm suggests there is much more to rules for making rules than is captured in vague concepts of democracy and the nominal right to vote.

SOCIAL TRAPS AND NONMARGINAL DECISION MAKING

It is one thing for a group or individual to fail to meet its preferences because it loses to a conflicting group; it is quite another to defeat itself. How is it that like-minded people fail to act in concert to obtain their objectives? Why do people who appear to prefer state of affairs X to state Y nevertheless act to bring about Y? The previous discussion of group formation had to do with provision of goods and services with money costs of production. Following the conceptualization of Olson, the large-group, high-exclusion-cost problem was conceived in terms of (1) one person or few presons never having a sufficiently large gain to be able to afford the total cost and (2) no one noticing when an individual exits the group. As stated, this is not directly applicable to situations where there is no money cost. (However, the following discussion may illuminate some of the elements underlying the Olson conception.) Here we note that people do not cease a behavior that all agree is leading everyone in the less preferred direction. It does not make sense to talk about one person paying another to do something that both agree leads to a superior situation. The problem is not simply to pay for the production costs of some common good, it is to cease self-defeating behavior. The subject is not the kind of product that governments usually provide with tax dollars, though it is the object of government policy. Perhaps some examples will make the topic clearer.

Depression: As total demand declines, each firm tries to solve its cash-flow problem by laying off employees. If all firms do this, total demand declines, creating still further layoffs. Most agree that the macroresult is undesirable, but no one firm will unilaterally keep its employees. Each firm says, "I will keep my employees if you do," but no agreement seems forthcoming.

Inflation has similar characteristics, but in a different direction (Maital 1982). A labor union pushes for higher wages only to discover others have done like-wise and the wage increase is defeated by inflation in consumer prices. No one union can practice unilateral restraint and survive. Firms are part of the same process. They try to solve their problem of increasing input costs by raising prices only to find that input costs have risen again. Of course, some gain from both inflation and depression.

Cold war: Each country tries to increase its security by buying more arma-ments. If each one does this, relative security does not improve. The cost of arms just goes up in an arms race. The only winner is the arms manufacturer. Most others agree that the macroresult is undesirable. Each country says, "I will reduce armaments if you do," but no agreement is forthcoming.

Price war: The case is essentially similar to that for the arms race. Each seller meets the competition and no one gains except consumers (see Chapter 4).

Population pressure: As population increases, resources per capita decrease. The decision to have children is probably governed by tradition and habit. To the extent that this is a calculated choice, each child is worth what the parents must give up to support it, and many decide to more than reproduce them-selves. Some agree that this macroresult is undesirable. Some may say, "I will not have another child if you do not," but no agreement is forthcoming.

Transportation deterioration: Decline in the quality of public transportation seems to snowball. When quality changes (or other options become more at-tractive), some former users will exit the system. Where there are economies of scale, each one who exits raises the costs of those who remain. As cost increases, others leave, quality further decreases, more leave, and so on in a familiar sequence. The riders try to solve their problem as best they can given their opportunity set. If each does this, public transport disappears.[14] Some people agree that the macroresult is undesirable. If the first bus rider to exit had been paid the difference between riding and his next best alternative, the whole spiral might have been avoided. Some might say, "I will contribute to prevent a few people from exiting if you will," but no agreement is forthcom-ing.

Agricultural surpluses: In a purely competitive industry such as agriculture, the early adopters of new cost-saving technologies increase their returns. As output increases, price falls and other producers must adopt the new techniques to survive. As they do so, the early adopters no longer earn profits. Most farmers understand this process that Willard Cochrane (1958) termed the agricultural "treadmill" but are powerless at the margin to extract themselves. When the treadmill is combined with immobile assets and fluctuating demand and supply, farmers produce too much, with low return and capital losses.

These are enough examples to illustrate the problem. They are some of the most vexing of our time and are not the bees-and-honey or even pollution case usually used to illustrate that there are a few, special problems where marginal decisions of each person in a market lead to situations that few want. Rather, they are representative of a wide range of problems.

What do these cases have in common? First, they all seem to have a group with a common interest—a group that may conflict with others but will not differ among themselves on the performance they prefer. Each individual tries to choose the best alternative open, but the result is not what each really wants. Seen this way, the following discussion cannot help but comment on the conventional wisdom, which asserts that welfare is best served when each person acts in his own self-interest without concern for others. This is Smith's fabled "invisible hand."

To a considerable extent, countries with market economies have built institutions based on mutual selfishness. Consumers, for example, may have a common purpose, but they do not see themselves as a group. Any standard economic-principles book can be consulted for the model that adds selfishness and lack of group consciousness to the rules for perfect competition and shows how the result is the lowest possible costs for everyone. Suffice it to say that in a market everyone looks for the best buy and makes marginal adjustments in inputs and outputs. For example, a firm is always on the lookout for cheaper production methods. But with competition, profit is short lived as others follow suit. The producers do not act as a unit, but each follows in turn.

In the case of consumers, if A finds that the price of a given product is too high, she exits to her immediate benefit. There is a micromotive leading to individual action (Schelling 1978). The consumer does not concern herself whether there are others who share her view. If others do share the same view, they individually will perform the same act. If enough exit, the producting firm will get the message and alter quality or price or go out of business, releasing the resources to someone who will try to please the consumers. The individual consumer increases welfare by acting alone, and if others join in, so much the better; the firm is reformed. The micromotive and the macroresult are consistent.

But this consistency is not always present. Take any one of the five examples noted above. In the case of a drop in aggregate demand, exit (that is, firing some employees) helps the firm's short-range balance sheet, but as other firms also make the same marginal calculation and adjustment, the macroresult is one that none desire; the micromotives result in a sum of behaviors that no one in any group wants. The lack of group consciousness prevents concerted action. It is not enough to act unilaterally and let the group form unconsciously. If everyone is not to fail to achieve her most desired position, it requires agreement on propositions like, "I will do X if you do X." If A suspects others may cheat, then A must cheat too or be greatly disadvantaged.

Why are conscious group agreements so hard to achieve? The answer is essentially an economic one. Exit is cheap (low transaction costs), while voice is expensive. It is cheap to buy or not, sell or not, hire or fire, and so on all by yourself. But it is expensive to voice your concern and communicate explicitly with another person. It is expensive to persuade, argue, cajole, negotiate. There is always the chance that what began as a benevolent or just selfish relationship will deteriorate into malevolence as voice proceeds. Of course, in the large-group case, voice to the individual seems unlikely to have any effect if it is thought about.

The term *social trap* has been applied to the following situation:[15] the micromotives are not consistent with what individuals who share a common preference want to obtain. In behavioral terms, it is when the micro and marginal reinforcers are not consistent with the macroperformance wanted. If each person makes the best marginal choice within his opportunity set, each will find that the goal he seeks evades him. This is not the usual individual-versus-group problem where the individual has objectives inconsistent with the welfare of a larger group. It is even more tragic; it is the individual versus himself. This author is loathe to use the adjective *social* because it is so often used in the global sense when the facts are one of interpersonal conflict. Yet it seems appropriate to call this a social trap in the limited sense that in some groups, the members fail to pursue their own interests. This is truly a trap with characteristics of a Greek tragedy. The trap is confounded if the microreinforcers are immediate while the macroresults are long run, but this is not the key distinction. Remember that the trap that causes one group to fail is often to another group's advantage (as in the case of cartels and consumers).

If the individual is to be successful, he or she must be aware of the group and have confidence in predicting the actions of others. Marginal choice within the available opportunity set is often not sufficient. It requires the nonmarginal choice of a different kind of opportunity set. In many market transactions, it is possible to further common interests without being conscious of each other. Not so in social-trap situations. It requires a consciousness of others for the individual to get out of the social trap. This consciousness need not be benevolent or self-sacrificing, though it probably helps. It does involve some measure of trust. If malevolence is present, the trap deepens.

Under what conditions does the social trap occur? What do the cases cited above have in common? The answer lies in the character of the production function and not simply the lengthy time between short-run benefits and long-run costs. The problem of the social trap is not lumpy inputs or outputs, although as we shall see below, these conditions often confound a solution.

The definition of social trap to follow differs somewhat from other literature on the topic. The problem of micromotives conflicting with desired macroresults is owing to the existence of competing lines of action whose production functions are such that the dominant activity has net benefits at the margin of effort while the dominated choice has less or none. The micromotive is supplied when there is some act under the individual's unilateral control that promises to produce some welfare improvement for that individual. The alternative line of action that would be consistent with the more-preferred, long-run result is marked by the fact that no matter how hard the individual tries, alone he or she can produce no net benefits or fewer than in the dominant activity. Higher net payoff from the mutually desired product cannot be achieved by any input change under the unilateral control of an individual. The altruistic, sacrificing person will achieve nothing for those loved unless the actions of others can be counted on, and thus love may not be enough. The preferred but dominated choice produces superior net benefits only when a certain threshold of inputs is reached, which requires trust that others will act in a consistent manner. Collard (1981, p. 37) suggests that a Kantian ethic is often needed to reach the necessary threshold. The Kantian would act only in a way that everyone could act and still achieve the desired result (regardless of concern over thresholds).

The social trap as here defined is related to the classical case of the "prisoner's dilemma" (Collard 1981, chap. 4). Mutually beneficial results for those caught in a prisoner's dilemma depend on mutual trust. If one person's trust is not reciprocated, that person is a sucker.

Where the social trap does not exist, it is possible for an individual to put in a little and get out a little. Reward is sufficient for some individual action. The shared objective of many individuals so acting takes care of itself without anyone's being conscious of those with similar objectives. But, in the social trap, no one can achieve any of the mutually preferred macronet benefits by any unilateral act. It takes the concerted inputs of many actors before there is any output with a net positive value.

Where a choice along a dominated payoff function competes with a choice along a dominant function, the dominant activity always wins unless there is an overriding habit, ethical code, or corrective institution offering reinforcements in a different direction. Choice of dominated alternatives is always more costly to organize because conscious joint action is required. The unseen hand and detached, impersonal selfishness work only when simple exit or effort is consistent with the individual's long-run preferred position. This is why people who want peace get caught in an arms race, and why all of the social-trap situations noted above occur.

So much for why social traps occur. Why do they persist? How can people get out? Is there an institutional corrective? The problem sounds like the usual problem of common property, as discussed in Chapter 3. The conventional answer to common property is to dissolve it in favor of individual property.

This is only possible if the trap were institutionally created in the first place rather than being inherent in the situation. The other conventional approach is to give up some democracy for authoritarian social control. It is conceivable that the right to choose along the dominant production function could be made a right held by some higher private firm or government. For example, the right to have arms could be sold by a world government (similarly for the right to have children and so on). Even assuming that those who do not pay could be excluded, there is the problem of who gets the receipts of the sale. Could the people ever agree on a superordinate authority? Not unless they are already committed to equality (Edney 1981, p. 16). If they do not agree on equality they will cheat or overthrow the authority. Keohane (1984) explores the possibilities of sustaining international cooperation without hegemony (a state powerful enough to enforce rules on other states) regarding money, trade, and oil.

The problem of exclusion cost cannot be ignored. Certainly in the case of the arms race, detection costs are substantial for the present parties and would plague any new superpower. In the case of public transportation, it is conceivable that a market could be organized to buy off existing patrons. Conceivably it would be possible to exclude future riders who did not help pay to retain current ridership, but in practice this would be costly to organize. Even where exclusion is possible, it may be costly to distinguish whom to exclude for what purpose. It is one thing to conceive of a group whose members share a common purpose, but it may be difficult to know who is in it unless they can be trusted to reveal themselves by voice. How do you tell who has better options than the public transit from those who are lying in order to get the payoff to remain as riders? When you have to rely on voice in order to decide whom to pay, you incur high transaction costs unless none are opportunistic. The problem is not just to decide whom to exclude from the bus, but whom to exclude from a subsidy to keep riding. The existence of conflicting groups is a barrier to organizing a group with a common purpose. The same sort of problem arises in the depression example. Suppose that some unit were given the right to sell the right to reduce employment. Even in times of drop in aggregate demand, those who share common purpose may want to let some firms who are having other types of problems exit and release resources. There might be substantial costs in determining whom to charge and whom to let go for nothing.

The problem of the social trap does not necessarily arise originally because of exclusion costs, but its solution is hampered by them. But though exclusion costs are formidable, the above discussion ignores a key problem. If a group's members cannot agree to pursue their shared and preferred goal, they surely can never agree to let some external unit own the right to control one of their present options. Perhaps this is too pessimistic. People do support government regulations, especially if there is some preexisting procedure and organization for voting and coercion of the minority.

An area of fruitful research would be to analyze successful solutions to social traps. For example, one variety of trap mentioned above is the price war, which while not unusual, is controlled. As noted in Chapter 4, a firm with economies of scale is tempted to use marginal cost pricing to attract new business and expand market share. But if everyone follows suit, any advantage is temporary and the new price may not be such as to pay late costs. Such businesses fear cutthroat competition, which spoils the market. In oligopolistic markets, the quick reaction of competition reminds the wayward firm of its folly and leads to corrective action. In addition, there seems to be a widely shared informal covenant that overcomes the temptation to choose the dominant production function, which in the long run is destructive to all firms. This covenant is frequently reinforced by exhortations at trade association meetings. There may also be certain accounting conventions that attribute a share of overhead to each unit sold so that managers are not reminded of strict marginal cost.

The role of group size is suggested above. In small groups people can see the difference they make and social pressure is practical. Experiments support the conclusion that small groups whose members can communicate are more likely to extricate themselves from traps—and to supply high-exclusion-cost goods (see Bonacich et al. 1976; van de Kragt, Orbell, and Dawes 1983). Research on actual case studies indicates that the upper limit may be about 150 people (Acheson 1975; Bullock and Baden 1977).

The emotive components of social traps also affect outcomes. Memory of past accommodations affects people's consideration of current alternatives. There are cumulative effects in the degree of trust. If trust deteriorates, communication ceases or becomes distorted, leading to further deterioration (Rotter 1980).

The social-trap situation can be summarized. Its essence is the divergence of micromotives and preferred performance arising out of competing options— one with a dominant production function and another with a dominated function.[16] The long-run, mutually preferred result is dominated by an alternative choice with higher payoffs to marginal, individual action. The preferred choice has a higher payoff only when the number of individuals choosing it reaches a certain threshold. In the social trap, the invisible hand becomes the invisible fist that pushes people away from their shared objective. The resolution of this trap must remain speculative. Even the most casual observer cannot miss seeing the persistence and intractability of many of these traps that everyone is caught up in (though everyone is not in the same one).

Though the resolution must be speculative, the alternatives can be briefly noted by references to the concepts discussed in earlier chapters. The role of group size cannot be ignored. Perhaps society might be organized into smaller groups. The other factor that emerges is the role of learned, shared behaviors and status transactions, where the individual does not calculate advantage apart from others in his group but rather has learned a standard operating procedure (ethical code) that is consistent with shared objectives and does not think to consider seriously the otherwise tempting dominant alternative with its rewards to individual, marginal effort. There are definite limits to externally applied property rights no matter how cleverly conceived and applied. The best way to avoid the social trap may lie in learning internalized habits of noncalculating behavior, trust, and honesty that are reinforced by cultural practices so that short-run rewards are ignored. Where work patterns and the mode of life create alienation, this learning will be very difficult.

NOTES

1. In a status system, people may not have the option of exchange but there may be a traditional serial movement of goods. In an administrative system, the administrator may command a goods movement although the producer or recipient may have no option of exchange.

2. Maurice Dobb (1947, p. 32) makes a related point when he notes that when the focus is on market exchangeables abstracted from physical reality, the proprietor of land contributes as much to output as labor does.

3. The right to participate in a use decision by making a bid is different from the right of a part-owner to veto a use and be the recipient rather than the sender of the bid.

4. See the empirical study of mutual savings and loan associations, where shares are nontransferable, in Chapter 12.

5. This subject is discussed by Samuelson (1969, p. 117) and Nove (1969); also see Shepherd (1968).

6. An example of a tie-in sale in the public sector is a university requirement for students to live in its dormitories, which reduces demand for private housing.

7. I owe this example to Jim Ward.

8. Mark Pauly and M. Redisch (1973) suggest that in not-for-profit hospitals managed from the point of view of the physicians, the resource mix is chosen to enhance physician income rather than firm net worth. Capital equipment is overused because it enhances physician income. Even if this is true, it does not speak to consumer differences in desire for different qualities and kinds of equipment.

9. If credit sales reduce robbery losses, the credit user should receive a discount for saving the credit firm money. Opportunity for reciprocal externality affects net consequences of the rule allowing product definition (grouping of services) to the parties.

10. The Fair Credit Billing Act, effective in 1975. (Also see "American Express Agrees to Allow Cash Discounts," *Consumer Reports*, June 1974, pp. 432–33).

11. American Express buys advertising urging people to become card holders and to utilize the card at named firms. Such advertising is paid for by a fee based on credit sales. If firms encouraged noncredit use by offering discounts, they would get the benefits of advertising without paying. O'Driscoll (1976) argues that prohibition of discounts prevents free riders. Like any rule that prevents free riders, it creates unwilling riders (customers who have the cost of credit included in prices but who would prefer discounts rather than credit and information services). For further discussion see Davis (1974), who says, "The definition of the alternatives is the supreme instrument of power" (p. 176).

12. Preferences are "single-peaked" when the alternatives can be measured with an agreed-upon, one-dimensional variable. For example, if the three alternatives in the

text are dollar levels of a budget and the proportions paid by each individual are pre-determined such that alternative X is $100, Y is $90, and Z is $80, then though individuals B and C have different preferences for budget size, they accept the dollar-dimensional relationships among X, Y, and Z, while A does not. Individual A prefers the two extreme budgets of X ($100) and Z ($80) to the available intermediate level Y ($90). This jumping over of the intermediate alternative suggested by the dollar dimension indicates that A rejects the scale, and thus preferences are "multiple-peaked." Multiple peaks might be expected when tax shares, choice among budget allocations to competing public projects, and choice or the quality of a nonoptional joint-impact good are at issue. Preferences would have been single-peaked if A had preferred X to Y and Y to Z. When preferences are single-peaked, majority voting will produce the same unambiguous result regardless of the agenda, and this result will be at the median of the preferred choices of all individuals. (See Black 1958; Musgrave and Musgrave 1974, pp. 83–90; Ochs 1974, chap. 3; Winfrey 1973, pp. 58–62.)

13. Acknowledged by Olson in the Appendix to the 1971 edition of his book. (Also see Breton and Breton 1965; Frohlich, Oppenheimer, and Young 1971; Gamson 1975; Wagner 1966).

14. It is common to argue that global welfare is increased when the number of alternatives to choose from increases. But in an interdependent world, this is deceptive. From the starting place of primary reliance on public transport, the introduction of more choice in the form of the automobile meant that the end result was only one form of transport. The original choice disappeared in the process. For other examples, see Dworkin (1982).

15. John Platt's (1973) use of the term is broader than that employed here and includes many intrapersonal conflicts that are the domain of psychologists. Cross and Guyer (1980) confusingly apply the term to cases of incompatible use where the reinforcers create conflict in preferences. Most cases they discuss arise primarily from the difference in short and long run.

16. The previous discussion of Chapter 8 focused on why, for example, a group that hates mosquitoes might not get organized to obtain mosquito spraying. It focused on the situation where no one has sufficient benefit to cover total cost. The current section is parallel but in slightly different terms. No one has sufficient inputs to achieve any net benefit. When this situation is tied to a competing action that presents micromotives working in the opposite direction, a different problem arises. The parallel to the mosquito case might be where the mosquito-hating group not only failed to buy spray but actually set about increasing the number of mosquitoes.

Nine

Restatement of Paradigm

VARIETIES OF INTERDEPENDENCIES

Many varieties of human interdependence in economic affairs have been explored. Different ways that the actions of A many affect the well-being of B have been noted. Property rights structure the allowable opportunities of A to affect B and vice versa. When interests conflict and one actor exercises his or her right, there is an impact on (cost to) B that is undesirable from B's view. Warren Samuels refers to these impacts as "coercion" and thus derives a definition of externalities that succinctly states the exposition developed above: "Externalities comprise the substance of coercion, namely, the injuries and benefits, the costs and gains, visited upon others through the exercise of choice by each economic actor and by the total number of economic actors" (1972, p. 104). When interests conflict, a change in rule can shift externalities from one part to another, but externalities cannot be eliminated.

The term *externality*, which is so common in the public-finance and public-choice literature, has been used sparingly here. The discussion has been instead of interdependence effects. These are seen to be ubiquitous and to have many sources. This view is in contrast to the usual one of externalities as rare and special events. If the narrow interpretation of *externality* can be avoided, it is a useful term that can be used synonymously with *interdependence effects* or even *interperson opportunity cost*. In this broader sense, it can be seen that there is no presumption that external effects should somehow be made internal via a change in property rights. It is true that when certain property rights are given, some interdependence costs can be reduced by trade for some, but not necessarily all, parties.

The varieties of interdependence effects given direction by application of a particular property right as discussed above can be aggregated into several categories that distinguish the way in which the external impact is generated. These distinctions exist in the literature, but the reader already familiar with them should be warned that their usage here is considerably broader. The distinctions will be briefly defined, and then the various kinds of interdependence outlined above will be summarized in these more aggregative terms. This additional conceptualization may further help form testable hypotheses on rule-performance connection.

The three overall varieties of interdependence or externalities are technological, pecuniary, and political. A technological externality or impact is one where somebody physically affects you or your good directly. A pecuniary externality is one where the good remains physically intact, but its value in exchange is affected. A political externality can be either technological or pecuniary, but the source is the working of government when it changes the rules of the game or makes administrative transactions. Different property rights control and direct each of these types of externalities.

Technological Externalities

An impact of A's choice on the opportunities of B is technological in the case of production whenever the output of a firm depends not only on the factors of production utilized by this firm but also on the output and factor utilization of another firm or group of firms (Scitovsky 1954). In the case of consumption, the effect is technological when the utility of a consumer depends not alone on goods he or she consumes but also on the consumption of others. Technological externalities are related to direct physical interdependence. The potential for technological externalities is rooted in nature and is illustrated by the elementary power of one person to strike another person or physically destroy or remove a good the other person was enjoying or planned to enjoy. The earliest laws and social conventions had to do with physical trespass. A person's use value was interfered with if others could come onto the land and graze it or destroy a growing crop. The common law of nuisance defined the freedom and exposures of parties to acts creating noise, smells, and health hazards (Beuscher 1957; Beuscher and Morrison 1955). Statutory laws of land-use zoning also attempted to segregate incompatible uses. These laws were concerned with ordering technological externalities via factor ownership.

In terms of the categories of interdependence of Part II, conflict over rights to goods where use and users are incompatible is the prime source of technological externality. The classic example in the literature is that of smoke damage. One industrial user uses the air claimed by other producers and consumers. Usually the literature identifies this type of impact as a rare event and regards most goods as involving no technological externality. In the paradigm developed here, this type of externality is seen as ubiquitous for all incompatible-use goods. If A uses the land for corn, it cannot be used by B for corn or anything else. This trespass is just as much a technological externality as is the smoke example. The error of the literature is partly ideological and partly owing to the fact that rights in land to grow crops are so long settled that they are taken for granted and people do not dwell on how A became an owner and B only a hungry wage laborer. Rights in the air became important much more recently, and the present law seems less settled and natural in our minds, so it seems plausible to regard the newer examples of interdependence as something special.

Some incompatible-use or -user goods also have relatively high exclusion costs. Where the cost of exclusion is high relative to the value of the good and while A may be the nominal owner, it will be difficult to prevent B's use (unless of course, B respects A's right in any case).

We have seen that not all goods are incompatible in use and users. Joint-impact goods have the characteristic that consumption by one person does not reduce the amount available to another. The good is used, but not consumed. If the good is nonoptional or preemptive, A cannot enjoy a different physical quantity or quality than is available for B's enjoyment (or disutility). If people have different tastes, A will suffer an impact from B's control over the choice of the nonoptional joint-impact good. Goods chosen by B that enter A's consumption function as a physical thing are a variety of technological externality.[1] Again, if tastes conflict, the externality can be shifted between parties but not eliminated.

Technological externalities are directed and controlled by the distribution of rights of factor ownership, criminal law defining theft, rights to sue for trespass or nuisance, government regulation, and rules that determine who chooses government or private purchase of nonoptional joint-impact goods. They may eventually affect exchange value, but the initial effect is a physical interdependence.

Pecuniary Externality

An impact of A's choice on the opportunities of B is pecuniary when the exchange value of a good is affected by A's market choices. The physical good remains intact, but its ability to command other goods in exchange is affected. There need be no physical contact between A and B, only a symbolic one that affects exchange value. (Technical externality also has effects on market value, but it is via a technical link rather than only a market phenomenon.) Where only use rights are allowed and exchange is prohibited, there can be no pecuniary externalities. Historically, as markets replace self-sufficient or nontrading economic systems, it was discovered that use rights and prohibition of physical damage were not sufficient to protect exchange values (Commons 1924). The law of trespass is not very helpful when your asset values are destroyed by changes in market values.

Pecuniary externalities are the signals that are used in the market to allocate resources. When consumers stop buying a product, losses are created that are a signal that resources should move to another use. Consumers do not physically affect the plant of a manufacturer, but these assets lose value. This type of externality is usually not protected by a property right, since the dominant interests wish to live in an economy of change. Sympathy for the manufacturer has never been strong because of ideology and the fact that he can shift his resources to other lines of production that are in greater demand. In that way, any pecuniary externality is short lived, and normal profits can be earned again. This was probably never completely true, and as John Kenneth Galbraith has pointed out, it is not true in much modern industry. There are immobile assets, which once committed to one line of production cannot be moved. Economic theory does not worry about pecuniary externalities because they are expected to be short lived. They are a signal to reallocate resources, and if that is done, normal profits are earned again. But the existence of immobile assets makes these pecuniary externalitites inescapable and permanent.

Technological change on the supply side is also a source of pecuniary externality. When someone invents a new cost-saving technique, other market competitors must adopt it or they will be ruined as the price drops. Again, if immobile assets are present, this cannot be done, and permanent losses occur to producers. Historically the feudal guilds were a property-rights system that protected against pecuniary externalities. A new technique could not be adopted unless the guild as a group approved it (Commons 1924, pp. 225–35). This prevented loss to producers but also slowed the rate of innovation and created lost opportunities for consumers. Modern union practices have some of the same features.

In the United States there is no explicit right to avoid pecuniary externalities associated with technological or demand change, but we do indirectly recognize them through various public subsidies to industry and agriculture, which are usually not regarded as compensation for rightful interest in exchange values but rather as humanitarian transfer payments (or payoffs to the politically powerful). Grants defined as one-way flows can be either a matter of right or of charity. You cannot tell a rightful payment from a gift without reference to the images in people's minds.

When A begins to buy more of a certain consumer's or producer's good, she will drive up the price for former user B if production costs increase to scale. B suffers a pecuniary externality. This market coercion is generally not protected by property rights. An exception was when the Russians wanted to buy American wheat in the fall of 1974. The sale was blocked by the president, who feared that it would sharply increase the price to American consumers. Consumers enjoyed the administrative transaction that prevented their suffering an external loss and farmers were denied a gainful pecuniary externality.

Under conditions of decreasing costs to scale, additional purchases by A lower the price to B. These pecuniary externalities mean that the real income of a person cannot be fully described in money terms without reference to how product prices are affected by the preferences and purchases of others. This is just as true for incompatible-use goods as for joint-impact goods.

Another source of pecuniary externality was discussed above in the context of information costs under conditions of cost discontinuity. Investment and expansion by one firm can reduce the cost of inputs it supplies to another firm. The second firm's profits thus increase related to the output of the first. This increase may cause the second firm to increase its orders and the profits of the supplier. Here is a whole series of pecuniary externalities. If the firms can expand marginally, the existence of these externalities is sufficient to coordinate their investment decisions. But in the face of cost discontinuities, some centrally planned action may be necessary to provide information on the possibilities of mutual advantage. This planning can be public or private.

The varieties of interdependence related to information costs are extremely complex, and only one further example will be noted here. Consider the cost of acquiring consumer information. In some cases it is much cheaper for the producer to obtain and provide the information than the consumer. If consumers do not have the right to expect this producer action, then the real value of their assets is less. They will have to spend more for the information. Transaction costs do not destroy someone's physical goods, but they can substantially reduce one's real buying power or prevent production of new goods.

Another category of interdependence has to do with products like electric utilities and airlines. Where marginal cost is declining, everyone wants to be declared the rightful owner of the privilege of paying the marginal rather than the average cost. The extreme case is that of joint-impact goods where marginal cost is zero. Firm owners (private or public) may find it profitable to practice price differentiation and charge different prices (taxes) to different groups. Their choice of which groups get the breaks produces pecuniary externalities. Any type of pricing practice or set of rules that causes one to be chosen over another will be greeted with conflicting opinions.

The capture of producer surplus is another type of pecuniary externality. If the market is used to ration resources in fixed inelastic supply, the owner of the intramarginal resource captures an economic rent that enhances her assets at the expense of buyers (see Chapter 7). If status or administrative transactions are used, price can be held to cost of production.

Depending on the distribution of rights, one party to an exchange may have many options and another may have few. For example, in a wage bargain, the employer may have many resources and can wait longer than can the worker. Thus there is great bargaining power on one side of the exchange, so that much can be obtained and little need be given up. Further, the employer may have many alternative workers to choose among, but the worker may have only one source of employment. Different rules can shift the predominance of power. With specialization and organization of unions, a strike is costly for not only the employer but also all his customers who have no alternative source of supply. A similar situation occurs when agricultural workers strike just as a perishable crop needs harvesting or when police and firemen withhold their services. It is a misnomer to call such a situation bargaining; while it has the trappings of the market, it is more akin to administration and command. When the rights are all on one side, the resulting transaction is a command even if the party is private. The dilemma of the wage bargain is one of the greatest problems of our time. We apparently are unable to conceive of an exchange system that is private and decentralized and that does not result in great losses of output owing to work stoppages and in substantial redistributions of income toward those workers who, because of the character of their product and or-ganizational success, have great bargaining power. Of course, it is a moral question to be settled politically as to what constitutes excessive skewing of bargaining power. Few with power ever admit to having more than they de-serve. It is easy to convince oneself that the origin of the power is superior effort, skill, and intelligence alone rather than being rooted in public decisions on property rights that distribute externalities.

When all of the varieties of interdependence (pecuniary and technological externality) are put together, their distribution constitutes part of the sub-stance of why one person is wealthy and another is poor. Remember that one person's external cost is the source of another's income. Externalities are not rare events but the very essence of everyday business and income distribution. A person with much property and a large opportunity set can derive very fa-vorable exchanges with someone who has little property. We are used to thinking of income distribution as simply annual incomes and bank accounts. But in-come distribution is dynamic. It depends on the property rights that one has that control who counts when human interdependencies arise. It depends on whose consent must be obtained when a person wants to act. It depends on who can extract a payment when another person needs something but does not own it. Income distribution is not simply a matter of natural scarcity but of the disaggregation of that scarcity into proprietary scarcity.

In summary, pecuniary externalities are controlled and directed not only by the rules of competition, such as laws resulting from the commerce clause of the U.S. Constitution preventing state and regional monopolies or rights of unions to organize whole industries and strike, but also by such things as sub-sidies to industries caught in rapid change in domestic or foreign demand, rights to develop vertically integrated firms or other types of central planning to coordinate investment, and rights to practice price differentiation. All of these influence the degree of continuity or change and the distribution of the costs and benefits thereof on conflicting interdependent parties.

Political Externalities

In the case of a technological externality, someone clobbers you physically, while with a pecuniary externality, someone acts to change the price (exchange value) of your assets. It is property rights that affect the opportunities and mutual interaction of different people. These rules can change, and when they do, they change the previous pattern of freedoms and exposures. This is defined here as a political externality, or interdependence. (The term is somewhat similar to what Buchanan and Tullock call costs imposed on the individual by collective action [1962, chaps. 6,7].) What public choice giveth it can take away. Thus government and public choice are the process by which a legitimate pecuniary or technological externality is distinguished from theft and war. An individual has rights because of public choice that allow him or her to create costs for others. When the public changes its mind, costs are shifted. A person who was allowed to affect another's assets physically or to alter their value by market choice now finds that instead of creating a cost for others, he is bearing the cost of the new freedom of others. Thus, political actions shift externalities and for a given individual create a cost where there was income or use before. If the courts require compensation for political externalities, it is called a "taking," but if no compensation is required, it is termed an "exercise of police power" (Samuels and Mercuro 1981).

Political externality takes many forms. It occurs, for example, when the law decides whether a broadcast television station owns copyrights when its signal is picked up by a cable firm. It occurs whenever new administrative transactions or regulations are made, such as rule for pesticide use or land-use zoning. It occurs whenever tax incidence changes. It occurs whenever a person must pay for some new public purchase or grant that he or she does not want.

Perhaps the failure to organize a political action is a source of externality as well as when successful action goes against you. Where exclusion costs are high and free riders exist, some people may want to provide themselves with a good but cannot organize it. If a person who pays for some governmental good that he does not want suffers a political externality, the person who suffers from mosquitoes but cannot organize collective action to provide control also suffers from a political externality because of the lack of government action.

No claim is made that the categories of interdependence are complete. One usually reaches diminishing returns in trying to force all things into exclusive categories. Still, these categories seem analytically useful in searching for alternative rights to control various interdependencies.

Much political philosophy constitutes choosing up sides in terms of these different kinds of externalities. If you are well endowed with property rights, you selectively oppose those technological externalities that you suffer. These are defined as theft. Those that are not theft either run to your advantage or you can trade for them cheaply. You favor maintenance of the pecuniary externalities that are the source of your income (probably taking care not to label them as such and pretending they are natural in origin). Since you prefer the status quo, you oppose political externalities as a general principle, but where it suits your purpose, you may favor some public expenditures and welcome tax exemptions. You publicly oppose government interference in the economy while using your economic power to encourage government to declare you the owner of newly valuable resources. You oppose any change in the status quo rights via direct redistribution or ownership or indirectly through regulation. Thus, in general you believe in selectively correcting new technological externalities, ignoring pecuniary externalities, and opposing political action to change them. It happens that much of this philosophy is implicitly supported by modern economic theory, which introduces another conception of externality that is termed "Pareto-relevant." The validity of this analysis is the topic of Chapter 11.

SUMMARY RESTATEMENT OF PARADIGM

This focus of this book is How do the rules of property structure human relationships and affect participation in decisions when interests conflict or when shared objectives are to be implemented? How do the results affect performance of the economy? In Chapter 1, a paradigm of structure, conduct, and performance was sketched. In Chapters 3–7, structure (rules) was seen to work its effect with respect to a number of categories of human interdependence. The chosen rules serve to order and direct this inherent interdependence with the effect that one interest or another is served. The paradigm is constructed in order to develop testable hypotheses about the performance resulting from a given rule when applied in a given situation. The impact of a particular institution is affected by the situation to which it is applied. Also the situational variables must be experimentally controlled in empirical studies if the impact of institutional variables on performance is to be separated out. The paradigm can now be summarized in terms of situation, structure, and performance variables.

Situation

In simplest terms, there are many ways for people to get in each other's hair. Since the inherent characters of the interdependencies differ, the impact of a particular variety of property right may differ. For example, protection against physical damage is sufficient to protect the interest of one party vis-à-vis another with respect to the use value of incompatible-use goods, but it may be insufficient to protect its exchange value in the market. For another example, the right to have sellers provide product-performance information is critical when information costs are high but of no importance when there is abundant, cheap, and perfect information. Understanding of the classes of interdependence is needed to hypothesize how alternative rules might affect performance.

Size and number of actors has not been treated as a separate source of interdependence (except in the context of economies of scale), but it interacts with the other sources. It is particularly relevant to the interdependence created by high exclusion cost (Chapter 3) and affects group formation (Chapter 8). Similarly the degree of specialization in production has not been emphasized, yet it is implicit, since a self-sufficient person has little occasion to interact and transact with others.

While the categories of human interdependence are critical for formulating hypotheses about rule-performance relationships, there is more to the human situation that might be termed the "scope of conflict" (Uslaner 1985, p. 117). An element of the situation is the distribution of interests among the population and the intensity with which they are held. It makes a difference whether preferences are single- or multiple-peaked or distributed randomly along a continuum or whether there is a majority preference for any particular rights alternative and the number of such alternatives. It is important to note not only the relationships among individual preferences but of those preferences to available resources and technology—that is, the learned degree of scarcity. There is both a social and technological dimension to the categories of human interdependence. This can change over time but is fixed for the period of impact analysis.

The character of the human personality is largely taken as a given and not categorized in detail. It was not made explicit whether the examples involve people with maximizing or satisfying characters or whether we are speaking of traditional or modern modes of thought or degree of time consciousness and length of planning horizons. These attributes of individuals were not listed and contrasted for each situational goods category but were noted where particularly relevant. Some attention was given to the degree to which certain behaviors are internalized, learned habits as opposed to calculating behavior responding to changes in perceived costs and benefits. Some of these psychological dimensions are made more explicit in the next chapter as they affect the performance of alternative rights.

To isolate empirically the impact of institutional choice, other variables that can affect performance must be held constant; thus the institutional analyst must utilize data from production economics. This area will be further examined in the review of empirical studies in Chapter 12.

To summarize, the situational variables include the classes of interdependencies given technology and psychology.

Structure (Property Rights)

The inherent situation creates interdependence, but it is the chosen structure of rights that gives order to this interdependence and determines the opportunity sets of the interdependent parties. Structure determines who has the opportunity to participate in resource-use decisions. It involves description of positions occupied by individuals, how the position is achieved, what authority (decision scope) the position entails, and which individuals are relevant and how they are weighted and aggregated. Several structures were noted in a number of contexts, and while they are partially overlapping, they can be summarized as follows:

Use versus exchange right: a basic distinction needs to be made between whether the rule is directed toward controlling use or exchange values. This distinction is related to whether we are working with interdependencies that produce technological or pecuniary externalities. Use rights are implemented by such things as the law of trespass and the common law of nuisance as well as direct governmental regulation. Conflict over exchange value is controlled by rules of competition and many other types of rights related to such things as transaction costs and pricing under economies of scale.

Type of transaction: The character of rules and sanctions differs among bargained, administrative, and status-grant transactions. The mix of these can be a major influence on performance.

Individual versus collective action: Rights differ with respect to not only the degree to which the individual can act without the permission of others but also the conditions for participation in shared decisions. This difference is illustrated by the distinction between sole proprietorship, partnership, and corporate organization.

1. *Sole proprietors:* When people are related as sole proprietors of various resources (including labor), each has a range of opportunities open that require no permission of the others. A may make certain resource uses, and if B wishes to escape the effects, B must persuade or bargain with A. Links to others involve market contract.

2. *Partnership:* When people are related as partners, no significant action can be taken without unanimous agreement. In U.S. law, each partner can bind the other partners with respect to third parties. But in practice, if there is not mutual consent, the partnership dissolves. In sole proprietorship, each person has a sphere of independent action with respect to different resources. In a partnership, each person participates in decisions with respect to the same resource. B need not bargain to avoid A's acts, but since in turn B cannot act without A's consent, there is a need for taste convergence or agreement so that, over a series of choices, each wins some and loses others. These trades of consent are face to face and personal (and thus information costs are reduced), while trades between sole proprietors are less so.

3. *Corporate bodies:* When people are related as members of a corporate body, decisions are taken without unanimous consent. The decision rule may vary, as can the basis for membership. For example, participation (or exclusion) can be based on one-person/one-vote (as in government and most private cooperatives), on proportion of resources contributed to the firm

(stock ownership), or of patronage (consumer cooperatives), or on the basis of an employment contract. The basis for participating in management decisions can differ from that used to divide the fruits of enterprise. For example, in consumer cooperatives, policy decisions are made on a one-person/one-vote rule, while net returns are divided on the basis of individual business done with the firm. In a vertically integrated firm or agency, subordinate divisions are nominally coordinated by administrative transactions, but ongoing bargaining is common.

Private and public ownership: This is another common distinction that belies its complexity. It is sometimes used to distinguish individual from collective action, yet there can be both private and public collectives and corporate bodies. Sometimes private ownership is applied to human relationships where, although some resources are corporately owned, there are major classes of owners. One such system of classification is management, capital owners, workers, and customers. Each group controls an aspect or set of resources. In capitalism, the capital owners are the residual claimant on net return, the central party to all contracts, and the exchanger of these rights. In a cooperative, two or more of these classes, such as capital owners and workers or customers, are combined. In a government, the various classes of participants are nominally combined, but conflicts are not necessarily eliminated. Both capitalist and public corporations can have a separate managerial class, even if the other classes are combined (workers own the means of production and are claimants on net return). If workers (citizens) have different interests, the rules for participation and representation affect whose interests count regardless of nominal public factor ownership. It is for this reason that this book emphasizes specific groups of people rather than the broad classes such as capitalist and worker. The exit option is associated with private groups, while citizenship is harder to shed. Public bodies monopolize the use of death and incarceration as legitimate sanctions controlling behavior and have the right to tax.

Regulation versus private property: We are used to thinking that government influence in the economy is primarily involved in regulatory prohibitions and requirements. This book makes it clear that opportunity sets of people also change as the courts apply and redefine the common law of torts, including that of trespass liability for negligence and nuisance. Private property is a misnomer in that it is publicly established and has meaning as it relates one person to another.

Collective action prohibited, allowed, or required: Sometimes collective action is prohibited, as with collusion in restraint of trade; sometimes it is allowed, as in the case of consumer class-action suits; and sometimes it is required, as in union membership, as a condition for employment. These three relationships to collective action have great effect on performance in high-exclusion-cost and free-rider situations.

Distribution of ownership: One dimension is the personal distribution of rights whatever their character. It is a factor regardless of the type of transaction and whether public or private. It is often described in terms of concentrated versus dispersed power and centralized versus decentralized decision making. In markets we speak of the size of the firm and its range of products, and with government we speak of agency jurisdictions and pluralism. Another element is often characterized as the issue of ownership versus control in corporate organizations. As new resources are created, public choice determines distribution of ownership (including that of bank credit).

Degree of market competition: This is related to the category above and had been the traditional focus of much economic theory. Antitrust rules are a common means for influencing the viability of the exit option as part of people's opportunity sets. Competition means more than many buyers and sellers. It means that calculation of advantage is encouraged. It can stimulate effort and innovation, but it also creates opportunism, stress, instability, and insecurity. To help another person may make him a more-effective competitor for your position. With respect to allocation of occupational position and exchange ratios, the alternative to competition is convention based on inheritance and tradition.

In the public-choice sphere, competition for office is mandated. For example, in the past on some American Indian reservations, the tribal government positions were occupied by traditional leaders. The 1968 Indian Bill of Rights Act mandated competitive elections.

Contract rules: There are a host of rules for what one party can do to get the agreement of another party to a transaction. One may control the use of a resource but cannot use the resource for bargaining. A critical subset of contract rules has to do with information responsibilities. In government, an important set of rules has to do with setting the agenda for choice. Pricing rules (for example, price differentiation) affect performance in both public and private firms. After a contract is made, it must be enforced if the parties fail to perform. A public choice is involved in deciding what type of contracts to enforce legally, what is enforceable upon unforeseen changes in conditions, what constitutes fraud (a lie), whether specific performance is mandated or simply damages are to be paid, and so on.

Contingent and noncontingent rights: Some rights are contingent on the occurrence of a specified future event and others are not. With high information cost it is impossible to specify all contingencies in an initial contract.

Rules affecting contractual costs: The rule of reasonable use, allowing the use of restrictive covenants, rules for class-action suit, and whether violation of factor ownership is subject to injunctive relief or only court-determined damages all affect relative wealth when transaction costs are significant.

Rules affecting information and uncertainty costs: The law of products liability, the form of business organization, and the rules of insurance and bankruptcy are a few of the rights that affect interdependencies created by information and uncertainty costs.

The consequences of information on costs are affected by contract rules specifying such things as the point in time in the production-distribution sequence when the terms of trade are determined, product quality, contingencies and settlement terms, and whether prices are reported for all to see.

Rules of taxation and public spending: For goods with high exclusion costs and joint-impact goods, rules controlling access to government affect what is available and who pays.

Boundary issues: These rules determine who is an intramarginal and who is a marginal user (e.g., price differentiation), affect realization of scale economies, and determine who is going to be part of a majority in a political subdivision.

Rules for making rules: These can include many of the above dimensions when applied to the public-choice process itself, such as the civil right to vote (related to incompatible use), decision rules (related to contractual cost and discussed below in Chapter 11 with respect to majority rule and public referendums), boundary rules, control of the agenda, and rules of collective action and group formation.

Aggregation rules: These prescribe how individuals are weighted in collective choices.

No claim is made that the above categories of rules are all inclusive. This is an area where further conceptual and theoretical work would be useful. But it seems sufficient to begin empirical work, and the list's length should indicate that there is more to alternative rules than those related to the degree of competition. It should also demonstrate that the content of people's opportunity sets and the distribution of power and wealth among parties are more complex than simply noting the relative size of people's bank accounts, stock shares, and landholdings. The list further indicates that the usual comparative systems of categories of property (state and capitalist corporate ownership, cooperatives, communes, and so on) are useful but limited. People interested in changing wealth distribution have tended to focus on a rather narrow set of policy options centering around direct subsidies, taxes, welfare payments, and price setting. Parts II and III above suggest a much wider set of institutional alternatives.

Government is influential in the economy in many ways other than in its taxing, spending, and regulatory powers. Public choice of the character of private property rights and detailed rules for their exchange influence performance no less than what is usually regarded as overt and direct government action (or interference, according to your viewpoint). The influence of government is ubiquitous and unavoidable.

This broader view has an implication for the interpretation of economic history. If we focus only on the enforcement of competition and direct government regulation and transfers, it is possible to get the impression that the government's role in the economy was minor until the last quarter of the nineteenth century and reached its peak with the myriad of new agencies created during the presidency of Franklin Roosevelt. But if we are sensitive to a broader set of institutional variables, the unavoidable, continuous role of public choice in ordering interdependence is illuminated in the common law of nuisance, contract, and early banking laws, to name only a few. Those doing applied work should note that situation is inherent and structure is chosen. The paradigm is mis-specified if the structure being examined is used to define the character of the goods situation.

Performance

The emphasis in this paradigm has been on substantive performance. The term *substantive* is meant to highlight the details of who gets what rather than imply judgment on the results in such global terms as *efficiency* or *freedom*. The reason for this distinction will be developed further in Chapter 11, but it can be summarized as an attempt to disaggregate these terms and inquire how rule alternatives affect whose interests and freedom are efficiently served.

Considerable scholarship has been invested in comparative systems analysis. Capitalist and socialist economies with varying degrees of centralization have been compared with respect to growth of GNP; fluctuations in production, employment, and inflation; and the relative importance of various industrial sectors.[2] This work is complementary to that in this book but has a more macroorientation. This book looks in greater detail at the personal distribution of wealth and opportunity among specific interest groups, which can also give a macropicture when aggregated. If analysis is to inform people of the impact of alternative rights on their welfare, it will have to include much more than prices and GNP and look into some disaggregations of such traditional groups as workers or consumers. Some additional performance categories are noted in the empirical work of Chapter 12.

While an attempt will be made to be descriptive and avoid normative conclusions, it must be acknowledged that any list of performance effects is a selection from an infinite number of effects and thus is conditioned by the values and experience of the observer. Some readers may wish to know of an effect that will not occur to the author to note, and all of us are constrained by the uneven availability of data. Further, people will differ in their interests along the chain from intermediate to final goods. Also, what is ignored as a minor effect on third parties may be some person's whole life.

Methodological Note

This is a book about public choice, yet its basic methodological perspective is on the individual chooser. It inquires about how rules affect individual choice and how these are aggregated. To tie individual to public choice, the concept of composite choice is needed. Care must be taken to avoid personalizing aggregate events as if a single entity had done the choosing. To say that the public has chosen is usually misleading if not purposefully mystical. Yet, for some purposes it is useful to speak not only of an individual as a decision unit, but also of firms, agencies, or even nations. These collectivities are a useful name for the composite of numerous individual choices. Sometimes this is a simple summation, such as a national vote for political office, and sometimes the result is a complex interaction whose final form may have been anticipated by no one. Not only is it sometimes useful to regard the decision unit as an aggregate, but performance may be in aggregative terms such as *price, output,* or *income distribution.*

The individual consumer or proprietor is not the same thing as a corporate enterprise, whether public or private. Robert A. Solo (1974, pp. 282–83) makes several observations of what he terms "organizational enterprise": (1) "Complexity of functions proliferates specialists whose positions are rendered quasi-autonomous by the particularity of their competencies"; (2) "The scale and diversity of an enterprise's activity goes beyond the individual's power of comprehension"; and (3) "Participants in decision-making will be character-ized by disparities in outlook and goals." For these reasons, when a corporate body takes a position and enters into a transaction with another body, the position represents a lot of prior internal bargaining resulting in corporate choice. This book speaks generally of parties to transactions without a sharp distinc-tion between situations where the individual is related to an individual, to a corporate group, or to a mixture of the two. This is done for economy in exposition, but in some situations application of the paradigm must develop a similar submodel to investigate how the choices of individuals within organi-zations result in a composite or organizational choice.

Before we turn to the task of empirical performance prediction, one further note on the stance of the individual calculus is in order. Some will be unne-cessarily put off by the words. This calculus does not postulate a greedy person. The individuals making up their minds as they interact with others on what group choices they wish to support can range anywhere along the greedy-al-truistic continuum. The person may have the tastes of a hermit or of one whose utility function is completely tied to the utilities of others. But the calculus still focuses on the individual as chooser rather than on some concept of the collective will as interpreted by commissar or philosopher king. The individu-al's concept of self is not constrained by what is called here the individual calculus. Nor does it deny collective influences on that self-concept.

NOTES

1. Person A can do many things to affect B's utility without making direct physical contact with B. For example, B may be pained by the knowledge that his neighbor is stone drunk every night. This may affect the use value that B obtains from his house. It may not affect the exchange value of the house unless other buyers have B's tastes.

In any case, the offending choice is a physical thing even if it is only a smirk or a smile as contrasted with a market choice. Therefore, it seems appropriate to include it as a technological externality. The choice that produces a technological externality is a tangible event even if the parties are not physically linked.

2. The usual groups identified are shareholders, workers, landowners, state, consumers, producers, and owner-managers. For a summary of this literature, see Pryor (1973) and Wiles (1977).

Ten

Psychology: Linkage of Structure and Performance

The purpose of this book is to provide a basis for empirical study of the relationship between alternative sets of rights and economic performance. The first ingredient is to understand the varieties of human interdependence, and the second is to understand how rights and rules structure and direct this interdependence. A third ingredient, the psychological attributes of individuals, has been only implicitly noted. The costs and benefits that affect behavior are the ones perceived by the parties to transactions and not necessarily those seen by lawmakers. The same cost may be perceived and acted upon differently by different people.

Sometimes, when predicting the effect of a rule change, it is sufficient to understand the variety of interdependence and how the new rule changes the directional flow or magnitude of costs and benefits to each party. The rule changes what it is advantageous to do. The analyst by empathy can imagine how the new flows and changed opportunities might affect behavior. In the case of a business firm, the analyst can examine the firm's accounts and get a good idea of how new costs and benefits will affect firm behavior. But in other instances, this elementary knowledge of the perceptions involved is not sufficient. The firm's objectives may be more complex than those reflected in its balance sheet and profit maximization, and persons within the firm may have conflicting objectives, including the appropriate time frame. A theory of advantage is not always a theory of behavior (Boulding 1958, p. 60).

Even when the effects of rules on the balance sheet are known, we cannot be sure how behavior will change. The firm may try to affect some other part of the balance sheet so that the old behavior can continue. For example, economic theory suggests that if a firm loses sales, it will reallocate resources among known production activities. However, depending on perceptions, it may resort to more advertising to create more demand or hire a better accountant to save taxes rather than adjust production. It may hire a lobbyist to influence public decisions on its property rights. We cannot presume that the costs created by the new rules are perceived with certainty or attributed to their correct source. Treating the firm as a whole responding only to its profit-and-loss statements avoids the necessity of inquiring into the perception and information processing of its human managers. For many purposes, this narrow perspective is sufficient, and in many cases it is not (Nelson and Winter 1974).

It is not possible to develop a full theory of behavior here that could be used in institutional analysis. It may be useful, however, to note several behavioral dimensions that property-rights analysts might keep in mind. Analysts are encouraged to make up their own minds as to how much of the following information is needed for prediction of performance in the given case and how much can be obtained by informal experience versus systematic inquiry. The answer depends on the questions asked and the length of run considered.

HABIT, NONCALCULATING CHOICE, AND ALTRUISM

The term *bounded rationality* captures much of the complexity of thinking. People have limited capacities for information processing. The mind is a scarce resource (Simon 1978). Experience suggests that action follows different degrees of reflection and calculation. Some action seems to follow stimulus immediately. In other cases, there is more conscious calculation of advantage and consideration of alternatives. Inertial behavior is common. People develop habits that continue until interrupted by sufficient events and learning (Leibenstein 1976).

Noncalculating behavior is particularly important in the context of interdependencies related to high exclusion costs. Some people may make a calculation and be tempted to become free riders. For others, contribution is based on habit, convention, or some sense of obligation and it may never occur to them to ride free. In game-theoretic situations, the personalities of the parties become potentially important. It may be necessary to know the parties' taste for gambling and risk. Some enjoy the game and derive extra satisfaction out of getting something for nothing and outwitting the other part. When one party's actions depend on the actions of others, the role of information and perception can become determinative of performance.

The predominant model in economics is that of constrained utility maximization. It is assumed that people have an orderly system of preferences constrained by a set of opportunities and resources that are selected to maximize utility. The concept of utility preferences is completely general and can include monetary and nonmonetized goods and services as well as the experiencing of human relationships. It can accommodate complete selfishness or heroic altruism. People have various capacities for trust and opportunism. Love is a variable, but it is a scarce resource. Can love then be incorporated into economics?

Suppose you have an altruist—that is, a person whose utility is a function or his or her own consumption plus the consumption of others. Such persons can increase their utility by reducing their own consumption and transferring resources to others in a grant transaction. One consequence of this is to prevent great losses to B of A's action to achieve a small gain when transaction costs are high. For example, suppose that A owns an empty lot along a busy street in a residential area. A can sell to a hamburger stand for $50,000. This, however, creates a loss in value of neighbors' (B) houses of $100,000. A's gain is less than B's loss, and there is an opportunity for trade. If we assume A has the right to build as he wishes, then B could pay A $50,000 to avoid the much larger loss of $100,000. This would occur if transaction costs do not overwhelm the cost advantage. If there are many B's and they face more than $50,000 in organizing and decision costs, A will go ahead. But high transaction costs are avoided by the altruist. The person who cares for his neighbors would never raise his income at their expense. Further, the $50,000 opportunity forgone by A may not be seen as a loss. It may leave no bitterness since it is not seen as a right of B limiting A but as A's self-limit. A is a willing participant and is not acting from fear of the police enforcing a zoning ordinance prohibiting nonresidential use.

The situation can be generalized by saying that where transaction costs are high (so that it is not possible to buy out others who have the opportunity to do harm), the existence of an altruist grantor can prevent an activity that will create more loss for A than gain for B. Further, the potential conflict owing to incompatible-use goods leaves no bitterness.

The consequences of having an altruist in the system can be further explored by assuming that neighbors A and B have no love for each other but are loved by a third party C, who has been making grants to both A and B. Again assume A has opportunity to gain by creating a nuisance for neighbors for whom he cares nothing. Still it is possible that C's love can make selfish A act as an altruist. If Party C makes grants to A based on A's income, the grant will be readjusted when A's income increases. If A knows this, he will not raise his income at B's expense as long as the grant from C is as large as the potential for A's gain. In other words, A can calculate the effect of his action taking into account his benefactor's changed grants. The incentive for egoist A to act as if he were altruistic is limited by the size of the linked grants received relative to alternatives. In a volatile exchange economy, the limited grant capacity of a few altruists will not go far, although the power of love is expansive if there is calculating behavior by the egoist. The head of a family can often prevent behavior by one sibling that is at the expense of another. Gary Becker (1974; 1976) refers to this as the "rotten-kid" theorem. The rotten kid is restrained from harming others he does not care for by the existence of linked grants. He also has incentive to increase the income of a sibling since when the brother's income rises, the head's grants decrease to the brother and increase to the altruistically acting rotten kid. The head of the household may be acting from love, but the effect is really that of an administrator handing out rewards and punishment by changes in grant flows. In the case of children, the head's grants are large relative to the opportunity of any child to better himself at the expense of other family members. In families, the information necessary for this to work is also cheap. But in the larger setting, if the rotten kid is not transformed into the loving kid by the love of the grantor, the initial love has limited influence if the only reaction is to calculate how to keep the grant coming.

The above process works on the assumption of individual calculation of advantage by both the grantor and linked grantees, though the original love of the grantor is not derived from calculation. Some writers deny the existence of grants and regard all transactions as exchange, and apparent grants are just to obtain grants from others, honor, or self-respect (Heath 1976). While this type of behavior can be observed, other behaviors are also present.

The grant is a sacrifice. People who make a sacrifice can get caught in its dynamics. A vivid example is when a nation sacrifices the lives of its youth for a cause. Even though the cause may come into question (as in the Vietnam War), the existence of past sacrifice means that to discredit the cause is to label that sacrifice as irrelevant. Thus new sacrifices may come to be thrown after old in a "sacrifice trap" (Boulding 1973). In the context of families, the head may continue to make grants to a child even when grown and with high income because the personality fulfillment of the giver is involved in the gift. Recalculation taking into account the income of the recipient and the price of giving is a question to be empirically determined, not assumed. Reinforcement of the past habits of the donor may prevent response to changes in recipient's income.

The presence of rationality is not sufficient for prediction. Rationality always refers to some set of preferences, but the outside observer cannot always know how these preferences are changing in the context of the transaction.[1] Any transaction can be a learning experience, but those involving love appear to be the most dynamic and seldom leave the parties' preferences unaffected. Love either grows or is rejected and resented and it deteriorates. The reaction to a grant can be more than a calculation of how to keep it coming. A grant can engender love in return or at least habitual behavior that is nondamaging to others. The outcome of situations of high-exclusion-cost and joint-impact goods as well as the social trap depend on the existence of and reaction to love, the degree of calculation, and the learning that takes place (and thus the stability of past habits).

Exploration of negotiational psychology is beyond the scope of this book, but the above illustration suggests some of its ingredients, which are further highlighted below as forbearance, malevolence and benevolence, interdependent utilities, willing participation, learning, and futurity.

FORBEARANCE

Property rights give structure to one's opportunity set. Still, a person does not exercise all of his or her options even when they are not forestalled by the anticipated actions of others. The analyst needs to know whether a particular person or group may forbear and not exercise some of its rights. The forbearance may be related to habit, information costs, or benevolence, among other things. (The distinction between habit and calculations should not be overdone. Calculation in a given situation may be a habit.) You can give a person new opportunities and not engender new behavior.

The role of alternative rights in creating a sense of community (and a lack of opportunism) is especially important in the context of high exclusion costs. Also, in many situations of high information costs, it is useful to ask not only how the rules affect who bears the costs but also why certain people take advantage of unequal information and others do not. Why do some people treat others without dignity as objects rather than subjects? This is one meaning of the Marxist interest in how the mode of production interacts with human personality.[2]

MALEVOLENCE AND BENEVOLENCE

This dimension has been made more explicit in the preceding chapters than some of the other psychological dimensions noted here. In the case of the free-rider situation, it was noted that an attitude of benevolence may forestall the temptation to ride free. In cases of game-theoretic behavior, the utilization of certain strategies may irritate the other party and turn him from a merely selfish person into a hateful person. In the case of economies of scale and cost discontinuities, there is possible gain from consciously coordinated investment by closely linked firms, but cooperation may be affected by malevolence.

INTERDEPENDENT UTILITIES

There are two senses in which people are interdependent. The first is where one person's consumption has a physical or price effect on another person's consumption. The second is an interdependence of knowledge. People's utility is affected by knowing about the consumption and utility of others. A is happy when she sees B is happy and is saddened when B is sad. In common parlance, this is loving or caring behavior. It is closely related to benevolence and forebearance, and plays an important role in the grants transaction. In Chapter 2 it was argued that there is an underlying covenant of self-restraint that supports any kind of rights and their exchange. At the point of bargained exchange, the parties require only mutual advantage. But the realization of this advantage may not reinforce the human integration necessary for rights to exist. Some degree of sacrifice and loving behavior seems necessary to keep intact the bonds that are supportive of peaceful rights utilized by willing participants. If there are no opportunities for grants transactions, the supportive structure for the exchange transaction may wither.

The marginal-value product of labor is not fixed but is affected by people's conception of fairness (Thurow 1983, chap. 7). People form ideas of appropriate wage differentials among jobs and when these are upset it affects productivity and labor unrest. Labor input measured in hours of a certain kind of trained person is inadequate. Because of high information and monitoring costs, labor negotiation is ongoing and never wholly a matter of initial factor ownership and formal contract (Williamson 1985, chaps. 9, 10). Rights are being created as well as exchanged during the continuous interaction of employer and employee. Where there is no ongoing organization and sense of community, these mutual expectations (rights) are more expensive to establish via court and legislature. Job security can affect worker motivation, cooperation, loyality, creativity, and monitoring costs (Parsons 1985). Institutions affecting workers' sense of fairness and security are related to the concept of X-efficiency, which is a measure of increased output that cannot be accounted for by changes in physical inputs (Leibenstein 1978).

Veblen (1899) emphasized a somewhat different dimension that he called "conspicuous consumption" (Seckler 1975). He noted that much consumption behavior is related to emulation; value is derived from others' admiration of your consumption; utility is relative to what others have (Duesenberry 1949). He argued that this doomed mankind to frustration, because no amount of economic growth puts every person at the top of the heap. In modern consumption theory, this type of interdependence is called the band-wagon and snob effects (Leibenstein 1950).

Interdependent utilities raise havoc with calculations of global efficiency. But more to the point here is how these utilities affect the reaction to a change in property rights. In some cases, a person's response to a new opportunity set may be affected not only by how the person sees the set changing his or her independent advantage but also how it affects those who are cared for (or subject to jealousy and hate).

WILLING PARTICIPATION

Behavior is modified and reinforced by rewards and punishments (costs and benefits). Rights can be altered to increase the costs or benefits to certain acts. But it makes a difference whether the new action is greatly begrudged. For example, costs can be heaped up, and at some point a person will change his behavior. But in some cases it leaves him bitter and rebellious. The new behavior may not yet be in equilibrium. The person still searches for ways to get around the rule and may find a new behavior pattern that is worse than the original one. Willing participation puts practical limits on majority rule. In the words of Alexander Bickel (1975), "If the minority believes with sufficient intensity that the majority is wrong, the majority may find it too costly to enforce its will." The impact of a rule change depends on its consonance with the prevailing ideology and thus how hard people try to avoid it.

John R. Commons coined the term *willing participation* to note the behavior that becomes internalized and its rationale legitimated in the mind of the actor. Willing participants are often better workers than someone who is fighting, kicking, and screaming all the way. In the field of industrial-accident reduction, knowledge of this psychological dimension led Commons (1950, pp. 10–11) away from the traditional approach via fines and criminal prosecution to the idea of workmen's compensation (Harter 1962, pp. 43–44). Workers were compensated for accidents regardless of fault, and this was made a cost to industry. If the employers could introduce better safety, they could individually save money on accident-insurance premiums and increase output from more-willing workers. Commons went further and helped employers form money-saving mutual insurance companies. Commons's success in creating new institutions was related to his going beyond looking for ways to increase the cost of certain actions to ways that fostered willing participation. He suggested the short-run positive reinforcement of safety behavior by firms through savings in insurance costs and increased productivity rather than the negative and more-distant reinforcers of fines and imprisonment.

The idea of willing participation is probably related to the modern behavioral findings that positive reinforcement seems to modify behavior more effectively and to be longer lasting than negative reinforcement (Skinner 1974). Actually, some of the most recent findings indicate that some mix of the two is the most effective. For some purposes the designer of new rules can largely ignore all this or rely on empathy. In other cases the analyst needs to know how particular people will react to a particular mix of costs and benefits and whether or not people will change their behavior but harbor deep resentment.

LEARNING

People learn in the process of choosing and transacting with each other. Much of economics sees people as having some preexisting set of preferences, which are then applied to choice situations in a framework of constrained utility maximization (for a critique, see Bogholt 1956; Dewey 1922.) But there is considerable evidence in the behavioral sciences that taste and personality develop in the context of being faced with interrupted behavior and the experience of choice. A new property institution redirects costs and benefits and can change people's perceptions. This implies a fundamental uncertainty (indeterminateness) rooted in the play of subjective imagination. Perceptions may be affected by a sense of participation in the creation of the rule even if the rule is not wholly of one's choosing. Where the new behavior that is sought from a rule change involves substantial learning, the analyst needs to take this into account. An alternative to the impact-analysis focus of this book is an analysis that would inquire into how interests are learned with the view to reducing conflict and thus the necessity to choose between A and B.

FUTURITY (EXPECTATIONS)

Many transactions in economics are forward looking. Present value is a function of expected future value. Thus, rules that affect information cost and the security of expectations are critical. The future is always uncertain and probabilistic and rationality is always bounded (high information cost). Different people perceive the future in different ways and may react to changed rules in different ways. How much knowledge of people's behavior with respect to future expectations do analysts need in predicting the effects of changed rules? Futurity is especially critical with respect to credit transactions.[3] Data on consumer optimism, buying, and savings plans are noted by monetary policy makers. During periods of rapid expansion, the central bank may act to raise interest rates to discourage borrowing. But if people's expectations are for further increases in rates, they may borrow more than ever to beat the next increase. In this case, the central bank could use some detailed information on people's expectations.

Economists are perhaps proudest of their knowledge of how to control depressions. Keynes suggested it is all a matter of government manipulating total spending, money supply, and interest rates. Yet there is evidence that these policies were not really successful during the Great Depression until the mobilization for World War II. External threat still plays a major role in creating a sense of community, and that sense plays a role in creating a psychology that reverses a spiral of decreasing expectations and provides a climate where new collective action is possible. Countercyclical policy is probably one area where prediction of performance could benefit from a more-formal study of psychological variables.

Knowledge of technology, endowments, preferences, and self-interest are not sufficient to explain institutional performance because of the role of expectations. There are many time frames within which actors may pursue their interests. The long term is not simply an aggregation of short-term maximizing decisions (Field 1970).

IMPLICATIONS FOR PROPERTY RESEARCH

Perhaps the meaning of the above considerations can be seen in an example. Consider the case again of the interdependence of apple and red cedar tree owners noted in Chapter 2. It is important for the analyst to understand that if the apple growers must buy out all the individual cedar tree owners, the orchardists are going to face very high decision and contractual costs but that apple production will continue to be reduced by the disease that comes from the cedar trees if property rights are vested in cedar tree owners. It is unlikely that cedar owners would be able to organize and buy out the apple owners. But the way in which the apple owners can exercise their rights introduces some complexity into the actual results. The orchardists must complain to the state entomologist, who must make a finding and actually order the destruction of the cedars. Thus another set of personalities is introduced into the decision. These bureaucrats have their own problems and sets of incentives. Experience suggests that they do not always act as the lawmakers or courts had expected. Yet it may be possible to predict the main thrust of such a changed rule of liability without doing a detailed study of the perceptions or contingencies for reinforcement of the bureaucrats and the forbearance, futurity, malevolence, or benevolence of the parties; and then again, it may not.

Any analysis of the link between rights and performance includes variables of human psychology. The paradigm developed here assumes no particular variety of personality. It is argued that the first steps in any analysis involve knowledge of interdependencies and how rules structure costs and benefits (that is, opportunity sets). Whether the psychological dimension can be added by the analyst's empathy and knowledge or people's profit-and-loss accounts or whether more systematic inquiry into the personalities involved is required depends on the particular applied problem area.

It is not argued that a change in opportunity set and advantage automatically leads to changed behavior. The persons involved may not perceive the change or may forbear. They may not take advantage of the change because of benevolence, or they may harm themselves if they can also harm others. It is argued that the directional impact of a changed opportunity set can be determined with informal estimates of these psychological variables in a significant number of cases. Obviously, if the investigator is working in an unfamiliar culture or with unfamiliar groups of people, more formal study of these variables will be needed.

The economic theory of rational behavior makes no judgment about a person's time preference, risk aversion, altruism, self-destruction, and so forth as long as the person maximizes, considers relative prices, and has transitive preferences stable over some time period. Yet preference conflicts are sources of interdependence and some rights decision is unavoidable as to whether people with certain preferences are to be allowed to pursue them. Drug addicts are rational in the narrow sense, but that does not justify making their preferences into opportunities or ignoring how preferences were learned. Impact analysts taking preferences and personality as givens must realize the limits. Given the preference function, any feasible change in the flow of costs and benefits may be insufficient to obtain desired behavior. The preference function itself may have to shift.

Institutional change, which has as its purpose the creation of new preferences, was dramatized by the largest social experiment undertaken anywhere in the world. This was the Communist Chinese approach to obtaining a radically different performance from their economy. The Chinese revolution was directed at much more than a change in formal property rights—that is, toward socialist ownership. It was designed to create a new person.[4] And if some seemed hopelessly trapped in the old ways, they were eliminated. The Chinese wanted a new kind of willing participant who internalized certain behavior and did not calculate individual advantage (or at least include different ingredients in the calculation than the capitalist individual). This has largely been abandoned since 1979 (Lardy 1983).

Development economists often speak of the degree of future orientation or planning horizons of people as a factor in investment and saving. Most governments take this as a given, and if private action is insufficient, the government does the investment. What could government do to provide a lifetime of experience that would change peoples' futurity (or some other aspect of their personality)?

It is tempting here to get into a discussion of the role of ideology in the evolution of property rights. This will be resisted because it takes us too far afield and has already been well explored by others (Solo 1974; Wolozin 1977). The manipulation of language and ideological symbols by one group to get a favorable response from another (even when it is not in their material interest to do so) is a major theme of both Pareto and Veblen (Samuels 1974b, chap. 5, pp. 124–27). Inclusion of certain symbols in the rule may trigger a response different from the individuals' best interest. This is a source of power itself controlled by other rules. The concern here is not to predict how future property rights might evolve, explain past changes, or suggest strategies to get rights changed. Institutional change is an important area of research, but it requires a somewhat different theory. It is possible that short-run choices of rights may interfere with long-run desired learning, but while waiting for man to learn a new ideology we may need to find some short-run instruments to get some improved performance. This book is about predicting the consequences for performance if a new rule were to be instituted. It is not yet clear how many psychological variables that are not evident to the reasonably well-informed institutional analyst must be included in rights-impact research.

NOTES

1. Commons (1934, pp. 90–93) refers to "negotiational psychology," in which preferences and rights are modified during human transactions.

2. A better term might be *mode of life*, as suggested by Harrington (1976, chap. 4).

3. The term *futurity* is from Commons (1934, chap. 9).

4. "Modelling economic motivation, moulding the socialist style of life, stimulating democratic initiative, cultivating the collective reason—all these forms of indirect management also imply developing the actual subject in society" (Wheelwright and McFarlane 1970, p. 148). For a related effort in Cuba, see Bernardo (1971).

IV

Possibilities of a
Normative Analysis

Eleven

Rules for Choice Among Alternative Institutions

Freedom for the pike is death for the minnow.

Isaiah Berlin

WHAT SHALL BE DONE ABOUT INTERDEPENDENCIES?

The focus shifts here from the positive analysis of the previous chapters to an exploration of the possibilities of a normative analysis.[1] The varieties of interdependence have been explored, and the prediction of substantive performance related to alternative property rules has been noted. What can the analyst now say about the best public choice of alternative property rights? Where people conflict, can the economist offer any prescription of what should be done? These are the questions of welfare economics that Schotter (1981, p. 6) defines as the study "that ranks the system of rules which dictate social behavior." This chapter will contain an argument that the answer to these questions is in the negative, although the economist can provide useful consumer and voter information.[2] But, regardless of the answer, its exploration should reveal more about predicting the substantive results of alternative institutions.

Like all scientists, economists are careful not to argue that the authority of science gives them the ability to tell others what they must do. One seldom sees an economist making a disciplinary argument for why A should have a right and B an exposure. Still, it is common to find arguments in the literature that purport to prove that private property and the market are the most efficient of all institutions and produce a maximum of social welfare (Alchian and Demsetz 1972). Some writers make a counter-argument that efficiency demands planning, government regulation, and socialist ownership (Galbraith 1967; Krutilla 1967). How do economists who eschew authoritative value judgments that favor A over B come to decide on which institutions are better? The route is through the doctrines of Pareto-better efficiency and consumer sovereignty, which are implemented by the competitive market (Buchanan and Tullock 1962, p. 92). What follows is an exposition and critique of this doctrine. It will be argued that competition and income distribution as traditionally defined do not speak to all of the varieties of interdependence discussed above. Because of this, many theoretical propositions about institutional choice are found wanting, leaving citizens to reach their own political compromises.

Pareto-Better Efficiency and Consumer Sovereignty

Initial income distribution is exogenously determined in most economic models. The determination of factor ownership is somehow made prior to economic analysis. There is some assumed political process that allocates ownership. The economist proceeds to ask how each property owner can maximize welfare without infringing on the property of others. The conventional answer uses the doctrine of Pareto-better efficiency as a guide to institutional choice. That institution is better that makes it possible, when starting from some given factor (or goods) ownership, for some person to be made better off without anyone else being made worse off. This maxim apparently enables the economist to keep out of the argument between A and B and still have some expert advice on the choice of institutions. If no one is going to be worse off, all ought to embrace the economist's suggestions.

The essence of the Paretian approach is the separation of income distribution and resource (factor) allocation. The distribution of ownership of factors is acknowledged to be a political question, but once it is settled, the economist asserts that his advice cannot be rejected by rational people who hold that persons with income should be able to use it as they wish. In other words, the consumer should be sovereign, and institutions should protect and further this sovereignty.

The institution that apparently fills the requirements is the market, which alone can ensure that only Pareto-better exchanges are made.[3] Starting with their original factor entitlements, each person voluntarily enters into trades to obtain factors and goods that have more utility to the individual than his or her original set. These are referred to as Pareto-better trades. Any opportunity of this sort that has not yet been consummated is referred to in the literature as a "Pareto-relevant externality" (Buchanan and Stubblebine 1962). If people have knowledge of them and they are not overwhelmed with transaction cost, the market will eliminate (internalize) all Pareto-relevant externalities when it is in equilibrium. People will then have made all of the mutually advantageous trades that are possible. Any further movement of factors and goods would be objected to by one of the parties and is termed Pareto-worse. A Pareto-worse goods movement would either involve theft or a new political distribution of property rights (income).[4] After voluntary market trade stops, only Pareto-irrelevant externalities are left.[5] These terms describe something about market trade and as such are positive. However, the terms also carry value-laden implications.

In order to understand the implications of the Paretian approach, the discussion must become more technical. The role of income specification in terms of goods or factors and the role of competition will be made explicit—but not in a detailed manner, since there are already numerous texts on the subject (Burkhead and Miner 1971; Ochs 1974, for example). The essence of the model can be seen by positing a two-person and two-good world in the context of an Edgeworth-Bowley box diagram as shown in Figure 2. This is a static model where the total amount of goods is given. It does not indicate effect of distribution on production. The horizontal axis shows the total amount of good

Figure 2
Conflict and Trade

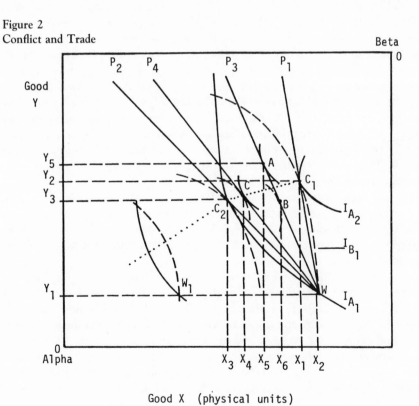

Good X (physical units)

X available and the vertical axis shows the amount of good Y. The amount held by A is measured from zero in the lower left-hand corner and the amount held by B from zero in the upper right. The original ownership of factors (or in this case of two goods) is assumed to be point W on the diagram. Thus, A has $0 X_2$ of good X and $0 Y_1$ of good Y, with the balance owned by B. There is some utility level of each person associated with this original position; this level is shown by the highest utility indifference curve of A and B that intersects this original goods endowment. What is the Pareto-optimal point, given this beginning? Can it be achieved through market bargaining?

As we move left along A's highest indifference curve I A_1, we find A as well off as before, but each such movement puts B on a higher indifference curve until reaching point C_2. Any point along this range makes B better off without making A worse off. A similar situation exists along B's highest indifference curve intersecting point W. Point C_1 makes A much better off with no worsening for B. The shaded area in the figure that is in the shape of a lens contains many points that are Pareto-superior to the starting place W and better than any point outside this area. Prices can be made explicit in the model by drawing a line from point W to point C_1 and also point C_2—thus illustrating the ratio in which good Y is traded for good X at those points. Given the original goods ownership (W) where A has much X and little Y and given the shape of the indifference curves, he would prefer price line P_1 to P_2, since Y is thereby cheaper and A can increase his welfare the most. B would prefer P_2. At price line P_1, B is no better off than at W, and there is no incentive for trade. B could buy X_1X_2 and sell Y_2Y_1 and stay on the same indifference curve I B_1. A would thereby be overjoyed to sell X_1X_2 and buy Y_2Y_1 and move to a higher level of utility. A would prefer an even lower price for Y, but, beyond that point B would refuse to trade and would just use the goods already owned. That is to say, any point outside of the lens is Pareto-inferior to any point inside.

The trading locus that A would prefer is Pareto-optimal once it is reached. Once point C_1 is reached, no departure can meet the Pareto-criterion. This is the point and implied price that would be reached if A is the strongest bargainer. It represents the best price ratio that A can achieve if he can dictate prices.

Person B would prefer price line P_2, in which case A stays on the same indifference curve that he started with (IA_1) and B improves her welfare. A can sell X_3X_2 and buy Y_1Y_3 and stay as well off as before. B will be pleased to buy that X_3X_2 from A and sell Y_1Y_3 and move to a higher indifference curve. B would like to reach point C_2, which is Pareto-superior to point W. Point C_2 once reached is Pareto-optimal, and no departures can meet the Pareto-test. We now have two Pareto-optimal points, and in fact there are an infinite number along the line between C_1 and C_2, which is called the contract curve (or conflict curve). This line defines the points of conflict between the parties given the original goods ownership. Any point off the line is inferior, and

Pareto-better trades can get to the line (ignoring transaction and information costs).

Where the parties will finish up along the line depends on their relative bargaining strength, and this depends on their total opportunity set. If one of the parties has much property and many other alternatives, while the other has little, the stronger party will make the best deal and force the price to the end of the conflict curve that is most advantageous. It is not enough then to know only the original goods ownership (or factor endowment). If competition is lacking, the relative wealth of the two parties may mean that one of the parties can afford to outwait the other and do without the particular product. The seller with a few alternatives may have to sell now or starve. This situation cannot be understood from knowledge of factor ownership alone. We need to know about all of the rights that each party has that give him or her bargaining power and also something of the personality of the people (Raiffa 1982). One may be a gambler and the other a risk averter. The parties may employ strategies to such an extent that they enrage the other person and prevent even Pareto-better trades from occurring. This is the formal model behind the earlier discussion of game-theoretic indeterminancy in Chapter 5 involving small numbers of bargainers.

This model clarifies a point made earlier. There are many Pareto-better solutions rather than a unique one even within the lens, and there are many outside it if rights change. While we cannot say which point along the conflict curve will be reached, we do know that if transaction costs do not interfere and if people do not get mad in the process, some point on the conflict curve will be reached. (This is not necessarily true under game-theoretic conditions). This is to say that one of the many Pareto-optimal points will be reached.

Pareto-optimality is just as consistent with monopoly rights as with pure competition. Bargaining power and skill influence outcomes. Most texts show that monopoly reduces welfare by restricting production. However, this theory is seldom explicated along with Pareto-better strictures. The abolition of existing monopoly advocated by most economists is not Pareto-better. This situation points to a selective application of the Pareto-criterion to policy.

The model also makes clear the role of the original rights distribution. If we started at point W_1 on Figure 2, we would reach a different set of points on the contract curve. They too would be Pareto-optimal. Pareto-optimality is only relative to a given starting place and does not instruct what that initial distribution must be. Alan Randall (1972, p. 25), states "Efficiency is an inadequate criterion because what is efficient changes as property rights, the distribution of wealth, and the distribution of income change. Just to demand efficiency leaves open the question of which of the infinite number of theoretically possible efficient solutions is preferable."

We have been examining transactions between two persons (or by extension among a few people). The situation changes significantly when there are large numbers of buyers and sellers. While the market has been referred to as a bargained exchange system with pure competition, there is literally no bargaining. No one person's actions can affect price. Everyone is a price taker. There are no explicit negotiations between buyers and sellers. As far as each person visualizes it, price is given and the only choice open is to adjust quantity taken. Each person adjusts purchases so that his or her marginal rate of substitution between goods is equal to the ratio of their prices. As all buyers do this, price may change, but it is not the result of explicit bargaining among the parties. Each person makes his or her buying and selling decisions independently. The conflict curve is not visible to anyone.

The relationships can be portrayed if we return to Figure 2; only now our two parties are not alone but are just two of many. Assume that in some previous time period the price ratio of the two goods was given by the line P_3. With the new indifference curves in the current time period as shown in the diagram, A is in a position to improve her welfare and move from her initial goods ownership at W through trade. She would like to move to point A, which is the intersection of the price line with her highest possible indifference curve. A wants to sell quantity X_5X_2 of good X and buy Y_1Y_5 of good Y. However, A's offers will not be fully accepted. There will be an excess of supply for X. B and all of the other like traders would prefer to move to point B, which is the intersection of same price line with his highest possible indifference curve. B only wants to buy X_2X_6 and sell Y_1Y_3. This is a disequilibrium. In the face of excess supply, the price of X will fall. It will fall because of the quantities independently offered and purchased and without any explicit negotiating. The price will eventually fall to price line P. The equilibrium is at point C. At this point, when the price line intersects the highest indifference curve of A, it is at the same quantity where the price line intersects the highest possible curve of B. The two parties have adjusted their own purchases and sales so that they reach the highest possible welfare given their preferences, original goods ownership, and prices. Point C happens to be on the conflict curve, which is Pareto-optimal.

Individual adjustments of quantities offered and taken in the competitive market indicate the preferences of the parties as constrained by their original goods ownership. The relative wealth and related bargaining power of the parties do not enter into the calculations. The rich man can put no pressure on a poor seller since the seller has many other possible buyers to turn to. Whether rich or poor, each person can only adjust his own actions to the given price. This situation is in contrast to the bilateral-monopoly or small-numbers case discussed previously, where the trades are influenced by the process of bargaining and the distribution of rights affecting bargaining power. This is the logic by which the competitive market is seen to implement the preferences of consumers made sovereign by the original distribution of income. It appears that performance is determined by competition and the original distribution of factor ownership.

Pure competition is like having an additional property right that prevents unequal wealth from being turned into bargaining power. It is like a law (for example, an antitrust law) that makes part of some people's total and large opportunity sets inoperative.

Space does not permit a complete general equilibrium model that incorporates such elements as production costs. For our purposes here, it is sufficient to note that total demand for the incompatible-use goods that we have been analyzing is obtained by summing horizontally the demand of individuals. This is shown in Figure 3. Person A is poor and buys less of the good at the given market price than does the rich B. Person A buys Q_1 and B buys Q_2, which sums to Q_3. In equilibrium, price equals marginal cost and the sum of the individuals' marginal values just equals the marginal cost of production. Supply equals demand, and no one can get more without someone getting less. The key point is that for incompatible-use goods in pure competition, each consumer is made sovereign by the ability to adjust quantity taken to the given price, with the only constraint being the original ownership of income. No one person can affect price, and thus power is limited by competitive rules.

The usual question raised about the Paretian model of pure competition is whether such competition actually exists in the real world. Economists are divided on the subject. Some say that the only approximation that exists is in some agricultural products and individual providers of some services. Others say that while competition is not pure, it is close enough for effective competition. Settling this argument is beyond the scope of this book. But regardless

Figure 3
Demand for Incompatible-Use Goods

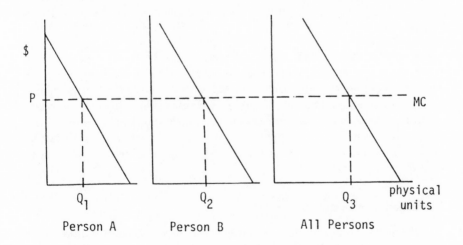

Note: The quantity on the horizontal axis is in physical units of the commodity.

of the degree of competition (number of buyers and sellers), there are many other ways for people to affect each other. Power is not just a matter of competitive rules.

In developing the following argument, several points will be examined. First, the character of the Paretian criterion itself will be criticized, and its implications for the debate over regulation or reliance on the market will be drawn. Then the traditional specification of income distribution in terms of goods or factors will be discussed.

The Paretian model labels certain changes in goods holdings as Pareto-better or -relevant and others as Pareto-worse or -irrelevant. It is easy to slip from Pareto-irrelevant to policy irrelevancy. Income distribution may fall off the research agenda. The terms may suggest that not only is distribution exogenously determined but also it is not a very important question. Note the following from Dean Worcester (1972, p. 58), who states that "making the better choice between two sets of property rights is a minor matter as compared to the need to establish some set of rights." Peter Steiner (1970, p. 40) suggests that we agree "some way, anyway" on social values and then use them to guide choice of institutions. It is one thing to be neutral between people as they struggle to be declared the owner of a resource and quite another to argue that it is a minor matter. The urgency to get on solid ground where one's nominally scientific craft can be practiced is often blinding.

What about the Pareto-criterion itself? Is it ethically neutral? (The position taken here is similar to that of Samuels [1972, pp. 68–93].) At first it sounds like a criterion that should have wide acceptance. It allows for improvements but protects from harm. Still, it implicitly gives stature to the status quo distribution of rights. To accept that only Pareto-better trades are legitimate is to accept the original distribution of rights as legitimate. The Pareto-criterion neither suspends judgment nor frees the analyst from choosing between A and B but rather accepts the choice between them already implicit in the existing distribution of rights and income. To accept the distribution of rights as a prior given and to employ the Pareto-criterion is to do the same thing. All statements of Pareto-optimality should be read as the conditions where welfare is maximized, given the original property endowments. One can be charitable to all writers who make Pareto-optimum-policy conclusions by adding the phrase "given the original property rights," even where it is inadvertently omitted. Of course, when the phrase is made explicit, the policy advice on alternative institutions loses its punch.

Regulation Versus the Market

Perhaps the subtle inferences from the hidden endorsements of existing rights distributions contained in Pareto-better conclusions can be illustrated with an example. With growing industrialization and use of chemicals, the ability of a manufacturer to affect downstream water quality was increased. Those harmed began to scream. Pigou (1946, pt. 2) looked at the situation and said pollution created a difference between marginal private cost to the manufacturer and marginal social cost. Pigou's conclusion led some to suggest government regulation, which would prohibit certain discharges or require that a certain stream-quality standard not be .violated or levy a tax on all waste discharge at rates that would maintain a certain stream quality (Kneese and Schultze 1975).

These solutions involve a direct role for government—that is, a movement of goods that not all parties agree to. It is not Pareto-better. Can the analyst then criticize these government actions? R. H. Coase (1960) argues that regulation is not usually desirable. J. A. Seagraves (1973, p. 620) argues that "governmentally levied stream charges would not necessarily encourage a market test regarding the optimum quality of the river. . . . and would imply a redistribution of property rights which is larger than necessary." The writer goes on to recommend a proposal that "would allow a downstream city to bargain with an upstream city so that the former might pay the latter to adopt higher standards than those dictated by their discharge rights." Nowhere does the writer say that the private market institution is superior only given original rights distribution or even why he presumed the upstream city has the right to use the waste disposal capacity of the stream. Perhaps this author agrees with the one who said that the distribution of rights is a minor matter, in which case it is of no importance whether the resource is owned by the upstream or downstream city or by the man in the moon.

The partial Pareto-logic can lead to an issue classification with heavy value implications. For example, in the case of pollution, it leads to the policy recommendation that a market be established for water-quality rights that have been vested in one party or the other. Some of the pollution then may be a Pareto-relevant externality that will be subject to a voluntary market bid by the downstream city in the case cited. If the bid is worth more than continued pollution by the upstream city, it will sell and pollution will cease or be reduced, and the result is Pareto-optimal. If the upstream city rejects the bid, the externality continues, and while internalized, it is termed Pareto-irrelevant, often with a strong implication that it is policy irrelevant as well. In that case, any government regulation to reduce pollution would have prevented Pareto-optimality and the most valuable use of the resource.

It is a heavy burden for a policy to bear the appellation "non-Pareto-optimal." The writer who would never want to be in the explicit position of arguing why A should own a resource and B should not nevertheless will label government regulation that protects A as "non-Pareto-better" and slip into an assumption that B owns the resource and the market solution is optimal. In effect, a writer who would never claim the capacity to define scientifically a social-welfare function that weighted conflicting interests nevertheless endorses the interests of the one over the other. Paul Samuelson (1969, p. 105) has warned against the analyst who "tacitly lapses into the cardinal sin of the narrow 'new welfare' economists: 'If you can't get (or even define!) the maximum of a social welfare function, settle for Pareto-optimality,' as if *that* were second-best or even 99th best."

Regulation is conceptually indistinguishable from any factor ownership. Does government regulate private water courses or does it grant the use of public streams to private parties under certain limits? If it is accepted that there is some role for public ownership, this ownership does not have to be complete. The government may only be interested in some aspects of a resource for public use and may wish to grant or charge for private use of other aspects. Neither a partial-use sale, nor tax, nor grant can be challenged on Pareto-efficiency grounds.

The Pareto-criterion can be used against the Pigouvian argument that the existence of externalities was a prima facie case for direct government action via regulation or punitive taxation. But we must be careful of overkill. In putting Pigou down, some have tried to put down all regulatory action. Some new regulation was never intended to improve the efficiency of existing rights but only to change these rights. Since Pareto-optimality just carries out given rights, it cannot be used to select these rights. Pareto-efficiency is derived from given rights, not instructive of them. The Pareto-criterion carries out the implications of an original distribution of rights. There are as many Pareto-optimal solutions as there are ways to define and distribute rights, as shown above. One must not avoid the necessity of making a moral choice between A and B by adopting the Pareto-criterion, which only confirms the one already made by implying it should continue.

It is a tautology to say that Pareto-optimal solutions depend on carrying out the original distribution of income and that this distribution should not be frustrated by regulation. If you agree with the original income rights, regulation that would change these rights is illogical. But people agree neither on the original rights distribution nor on whether it should be continued. If economists are silent as to the distribution between A and B, they must also be silent as to the regulation that implements A's rights as opposed to private ownership by B. If B owns, then regulation violates that ownership. But if A owns, regulation can be the vehicle of that ownership. The efficiency of regulation depends on who has the right and the performance objective one has in mind.

The above line of reasoning puts the ethical choice (value judgment) between conflicting parties back on the center stage of public choice. The Pareto-criterion does not avoid the necessity of this choice.

RIGHTS DISTRIBUTION AND RESOURCE ALLOCATION: THE COASE RULE

It seems intuitively obvious that the distribution of ownership of incompatible-use goods affects income distribution, but what can be said of resource allocation? There is a prominent line of reasoning that begins by asking the resource-allocation consequences of whether a resource is owned by A or B. The question is put in terms of a rule of liability for the effects of use by A on the welfare of B and can be illustrated by reference to the pollution example above. (This example was first developed by Kneese 1964, pp. 43–46.) Assume first that A owns the stream and can use it at will without any liability for damage to the fishing pleasure of B. A is a manufacturer and enjoys a profit of $10 because his riverside location saves him the cost of an alternative waste-disposal system. Pigou was wrong in implying that A would completely ignore his effect on B. Anytime B wants to make A an offer to stop polluting, A will listen (unless he is malevolent). Suppose B can only make an offer of $5. The offer will be rejected because it is not as valuable as the water's use for waste disposal, which will be continued. Now, suppose the property right is shifted to B, and A is now liable for any damage created. The direction of the bidding will now be reversed. B will be better off accepting any offer over her reservation price of $5, and A will be better off to offer any price up to $10. If they do not get mad at each other in the process, the resource will be sold to A and the pollution continued, as when A owned the resource originally.

This result has been worked out by Ronald Coase (1960) and deserves to be called the "Coase rule" (a devastating critique of which has been made by Samuels 1974a). The rule states that the distribution of ownership does not make any difference for resource allocation. Coase did note one important qualification having to do with transactions costs, which were explored in Chapter 6 of this book. Suppose that A is a large group instead of a single individual. Its total valuation is $10. But suppose the cost is $6 to get the group organized to make a bid if it does not already own. In that case, if it already owns, its reservation price is $10 and it would not sell to B for $5, but if it must buy, its bid to B is only $4 ($10 − $6 transaction cost) and the bid will be rejected. The use would differ depending on who originally owns. The Coase rule can then be stated as follows: "The ultimate result (which maximizes the value of production) is independent of the legal position if the pricing system is assumed to work without cost." Coase acknowledges that the market may be too costly to organize where a large number of people demand the same good. This problem will be explored in the next section. Writers following Coase's lead have noted that income distribution is different with the different property rules but ask us to keep our eye on the resource allocation. After all, is it not use that matters, and is not income distribution a minor side effect? The bastardized Coase rule is often shortened to conclude that property rights do not matter.[6]

This literature has come full circle. First, it argues against regulation because regulation gets in the way of Pareto-better trades. This argument puts the status quo income distribution on a pedestal. Then it implies that income distribution (factor ownership) is not very consequential since, in the process of making Pareto-better trades, resource allocation is unaffected. This implication knocks the status quo income distribution off its pedestal. You cannot have it both ways.

The Coase rule is itself a positive proposition (albeit extremely limited). But it must be kept in mind that regardless of the author's intent, models are used for policy implications. Many readers of this literature seem to remember two key messages: (1) regulation is bad and (2) there is no case for changing status quo rights since resource allocation is unaffected anyway. With cold logic, it seems that one might conclude that since rights do not matter, we might as well change them and equalize income distribution. But that would be a radical conclusion and the economic profession mainstream is not radical.

No one makes an explicit argument that rights do not matter for income distribution. But by emphasizing the consequences for resource allocation, attention is drawn away from income distribution. The Coase logic calls for another, more important research item. This is to look for ways to reduce transaction costs, since these are the costs that keep the theory from working perfectly. Transaction costs become the enemy of the people. The most obvious place where they are infinite is where goods are held in common and trade is prohibited. The Coasian analysis suggests that common property must go.[7] A new rule for institutional choice then becomes that all property should be private and individual except where transaction costs rule it out. Common-property rules exclude no one even though high exclusion costs do not exist inherently in the good. When people legally cannot be kept off, resource destruction may result. Also, where property is held in common, it may be used by a property holder when someone else would pay more to use it. This violates Pareto-optimality, but only if third-party interests are not possessing of rights. The fact that A cannot sell is sometimes the device by which C enjoys some use. Some people's use rights cannot be ignored when making Pareto-calculations of exchange rights.

Whether the reader thinks that income distribution is an important topic of research or whether we should accept existing rights that are direct and explicit and make them more valuable to existing owners by reducing transaction costs is up to his or her own value judgment. Before moving on, however, let us examine the Coase rule on its own ground of effect on resource allocation. Several complications need discussion. One involves the impact of rights on the marginal utility of money. This creates a difference between bid price and reservation price (compensating and equivalent variation [Krutilla and Fisher 1975; Mishan 1961, 1967]). This difference can be related to the Coase-rule discussion above. In the Bowley box of Figure 3, there are only two goods, and it is obvious that if you lose possession of one, both real income and the demand for the other good are affected, depending on the income elasticity of demand. If Coase had used the Bowley box, he would never have assumed that he could switch ownership from A to B and not affect resource use. If a change in original ownership of good X (e.g., from W to W_1) is not offset by new rights in Y, a change in X will affect the range of new Pareto-better points that can be reached on the contract curve.

The examples used by the Coasians implicitly or explicitly assume that the alternative rights distributions under consideration do not affect the marginal utility of money and thus do not feed back on the relevant demand curves. An assumption is made that whether A has the right or not, his real income is not affected, and therefore he buys the same mix of products with or without the right in question. The assumption is that income does not affect the demand curve; this restricts the theory to a set of minor and uninteresting cases. Many major debates over ownership are of the type that affect real income and would upset current consumption patterns. The point can be illustrated with the pollution case again. Suppose that the fisherman affected by pollution is poor. If he does not have the right to be free of the pollution, his bid price may be zero. He cannot offer the polluter anything to stop. But, if the fisherman is the owner of the steam, his real income is significantly different. He would never sell the stream for zero. His bid and reservation prices differ because the right affects his real income and thus his demand curve for the stream. Similar situations exist in many of the current major policy debates such as ownership of off-shore oil rights, copyright in photocopied material, and so on.

There is another possible effect of changing ownership between A and B. People do not have the same preferences; they use their incomes for different products. This affects demand for other goods and thus incomes of third parties (producer and consumers). For example, if a product has economies of scale, consumer A is affected if as a result of income redistribution between B and C the demand for the good declines and its per-unit production cost rises as less is produced (see Chapter 4). In public-investment analysis, it is common to note the indirect or secondary effects of an expansion in output on the income of input suppliers and subsequent processors of the output.

Another characteristic of Coasian examples is that they presume pure competition in the rest of the economy, but less than pure competition in the firms under consideration (or inexistence of rents). Recall the example of the polluting manufacturer earning a profit of $10. This noncompetitive return (or rent) allowed him to buy out the fisherman. What happens if the firm is in competitive equilibrium and earning no profit or rent while utilizing the stream for waste disposal? If the industrial firm owns the resource and the fisherman makes a $5 bid, the theory would suggest that the firm would accept the bid and go out of business, moving his resources somewhere else if earning the same or better competitive return as before (no rent or profit). But the mobile resource alone may not earn as much elsewhere as it did originally in combination with the second resource whose ownership is in question. In that case, A keeps it if it is owned but could not afford to buy. If the industrial firm does not own and the fisherman insists on using his property, the firm could not afford to buy out the fisherman, since the firm has no excess returns to pay for it. The firm moves. The theory produces its conclusion again that the right does not affect resource use. But it does so under an assumption that assets are perfectly mobile (as discussed in Chapter 6).

In the real world it seems highly unlikely that a competitive firm can pick up all of its assets and move to another location or line of production and earn the same returns as before. Industries understand this and oppose being denied ownership of streams because they will not be able to buy out other interests and still stay in business and thus will lose the value of their immobile plants. If the firm owns, it will sell only if bid exceeds value of immobile assets. If fishermen own, the firm cannot afford to buy. Resource allocation is affected by the distribution of rights where only competitive returns are being earned and some assets are immobile in contrast to the noncompetitive, perfectly mobile case (Posner 1972b, pp. 37–38). If the loss of waste-disposal rights were applied to all firms in an industry, it would shift the industry supply function to the left. Price would rise, production would drop, and some higher-cost firm would likely leave the industry (with accompanying loss of immobile assets). The effect on firm output depends on whether the increased waste-disposal costs change the output point where marginal cost equals marginal revenue (Davis and Whinston 1962).

The Coasian examples also make an assumption as to legal remedies available to owners and the ease of estimating damages. In Chapter 6 it was seen that the character of remedies for interference with an owner's use is an important detail of factor ownership. Assume B owns an apartment building with one side facing south. A is about to build a taller building that will cut off the sun to B's apartments. What is the effect on resource use of who owns the sun rights? Begin with the rights owned by B, who has a reservation price of $15,000. A's bid is only $10,000 and would be rejected by B. However, it is easy for A to interfere with B's use if the building is built anyway. B's effective right depends on the available remedies if A builds and blocks the sun. If B can get an injunction, then A will have no choice but to refrain from building. But if no injunction is issued, A can force sale of the sun rights. The consequence depends on the court-determined damage relative to B's reservation price. If B places some unique value on the sun that is not reflected in the market price of similar apartments, the court-determined damage is less than B's reservation price with a loss in the value of the resource. The use of the sun goes to A whenever A's bid price of $10,000 is equal to or less than what A expects to pay for damages. (If the damage award is more than $10,000, A has made a mistake but still uses the resource.)

Now, assume A owns. B will make a bid of up to $15,000, which exceeds A's reservation price of $10,000. Use of the sun rights shifts to B. In this situation, the location of ownership does affect who uses the resource for what. This is another exception to the Coase rule, which asserts the neutrality of resource ownership with respect to resource allocation (also see Schap 1986).

In producer-producer conflicts, the court-set damages reflecting market values are likely to approximate the owner's reservation price. But in conflicts with or between consumers over final-consumption goods, the objective damage award may depart from the subjective reservation price that would have prevailed if an injunction were available to the owner or if interdependence with the owner's use were further protected by criminal sanctions.[8] If the parties have differential ability to interfere with each other's use of a resource, any court award at less than the owner's reservation price (no injunction) means that a superior reservation price may be frustrated. These nitty-gritty details of what it means to be a factor owner cannot be ignored.

There is one further important contradiction to the Coase-rule implication that property-rights alternatives do not affect resource allocation. Firms and individuals who want to increase their income have two broad alternatives: (1) accept the rules of the game and utilize available opportunities, such as investment, or (2) utilize available resources to change the rules. In the latter case, wealth in one period of time can be used politically to change property rights and then enhance wealth in the next period. Resources can be given to political candidates and bureaucrats to influence public opinion.[9] When income is used to change rights and income in the next period, it will affect resource allocation. To those who have not read the Coasian literature, this will seem obvious, yet this literature persists.

The Coase rule applies only under certainty. While if transaction costs are zero, there might be a market for risk sharing, it is further necessary that risk attitudes be independent of wealth (Greenwood and Ingene 1978). If one party is more risk averse than the other, the original placement of the right can affect resource use.

On its own ground of impact on resource allocation, the Coase rule is severely limited in its application. For most of the interesting cases of public debate over rights, transaction costs are not zero, rights distribution would affect the marginal utility of money and risk aversion and thus cause a divergence between bid and reservation prices, exchange affects use rights of third parties, and many assets are immobile. Even if you only care about resource allocation, it is hardly true that the distribution of property rights does not matter.[10] And if you do care about income distribution, property-rights distribution matters even more.

The lack of data on the size of the above factors prevents resolution of debate. Those who like the policy implications of the Coase rule that existing property rights should be left alone deny that the above factors are empirically significant (Coase 1974b). Others believe they see enough examples of their significance to question this policy thrust (Goldberg 1974). The theory is relatively well developed, and it is time for more empirical work (Hoffman and Spitzer 1982).

INSTITUTIONAL CHOICE FOR JOINT-IMPACT GOODS

Joint-impact goods create an interdependence that raises some additional issues for property rights. When more than one person utilizes the joint good, the issue is who pays and who gets to choose the physical level of the good. This question arises even if the goods have low exclusion costs, but the problems are compounded when exclusion costs are high. Does the Paretian logic give any rules for appropriate property rights with these joint-impact goods? Is it adequate to describe income distribution in terms of money or factor ownership?

Suppose we are analyzing the demand for a good like broadcast television. (This case is parallel to what is often referred to as positive externality, such as the classic illustration of bees that produce honey and also pollinate fruit trees.) While many aspects of television present policy issues, quantity of the good is interpreted here as the number of available channels and the marginal cost of another channel is positive. The good is a high-exclusion-cost and joint-impact good with the characteristics that whatever number of channels are available to one viewer in the broadcast area are potentially available to all at no extra cost. Use of the good is avoidable, so the person who places negative utility on the good merely abstains and there is no interdependence with those who use it. There is preemptive conflict, however, if it is not possible for different individuals each to adjust their quantity purchased to a given price. If one person has three channels to choose from, then all have three (regardless of how many they actually use or the hours of use). For a joint-impact good the demand of individuals is summed vertically, as shown in Figure 4 (in contrast to horizontal summation for incompatible-use goods, shown in Figure 3). First, assume that in spite of high exclusion costs we have some magic meter to obtain individual demand curves and that these are as shown in the figure, which depicts what people will pay for a given quantity of channels.[11] At a quantity of three channels, the sum of individual marginal values just equals the marginal cost of producing the third channel. However, this Pareto-optimal equilibrium (Johnson 1971, app. C) is obtained by subtly introducing a new property right into the system.

A close examination of the demand curves for the individuals shows that at the Pareto-equilibrium, the parties are paying different prices. One person pays $5 and another $6. Since the quantity (number of channels) available cannot be adjusted to accommodate different preferences, the price has been adjusted as suggested by Lindahl (1958). This model contains an inexplicit value judgment. We might justify the fact that the rich take more of an incompatible-use good than do the poor in terms of their ownership of income (if we accept the legitimacy of the distribution of that income). But it takes an additional value judgment and right to insist that the rich (or persons with strong preferences for television) must pay more for the same good than another person.

Figure 4
Demand for Physical Units of Joint-Impact Goods

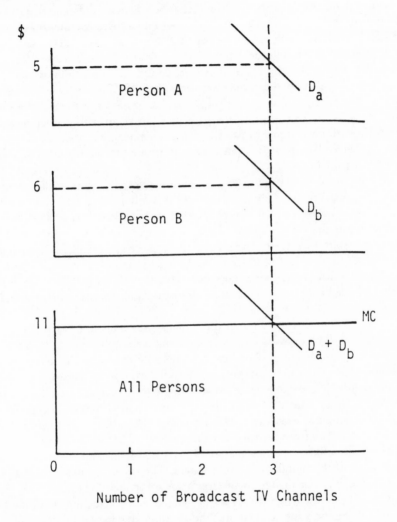

Number of Broadcast TV Channels

In settling conflicting interests, it is not sufficient to accept only the original distribution of money income even where demand is known.

More than one pricing scheme is possible. The marginal cost of another channel is $11. If the price were the same to all customers, a price of $5.50 would be sufficient to cover costs. This is not an equilibrium price, but whether it is a Pareto-optimal price depends on whose interests are backed up by a property right. At a price of $5.50, person A would prefer a lesser amount, but such a state cannot be achieved for two reasons. Person A cannot have a different quantity than that available to all consumers, because it is a preemptive good. Further, quantity of channels is not infinitely divisible. The consequence of moving from two to three channels is quite different than moving from two to three apples. Person A does not find a three-channel system worth $5.50 but will probably take it rather than stop watching.[12] Person B, on the other hand, would prefer to have a larger quantity at the price of $5.50. But it is not possible for the two parties to have different quantities available. At least, person B finds the three channels worth $5.50, even if more are preferred. Person B has a consumer surplus and does not have to pay as much for the three as she would be willing to pay. If we begin with a price of $5.50, person B will never agree to pay $6 for the same quantity. Such a move would not be Pareto-better for B, even if A were pleased to see his price drop from $5.50 to $5.

If there is no preexisting take-it-or-leave-it price, the parties might agree to the differential prices. However, even if they only have to pay what the marginal unit is worth to them, it is conceivable that some people may be offended by paying more for the same good than their neighbor (Tresch 1981, p. 118). Some may not want their consumer surplus captured by producers (see Chapter 7). A detached, objective observer might regard such an attitude as irrational, but it is hard to argue that it does not exist. If it does exist, some additional rule is needed that says whether this taste is to dominate over other conflicting tastes.

People with different values on the intramarginal units of incompatible goods do not like to be exposed to a discriminating monopolist and to be forced to pay more than their neighbors just because they have different elasticities of demand. Can it then be assumed that people are not concerned when other people with different marginal valuations for the commonly available joint-impact good are charged different prices? Samuelson (1969, p. 122) derisively calls this "interpersonal 'Robin-Hood' pricings." It is the same problem as differential pricing of goods with economies of scale discussed in chapter 4.

Economists like to postulate a set of exogenously generated preferences independent of the economic decision system. The system should make the prior tastes effective, not modify them (consumer sovereignty). However, the pricing policy discussed here needs to be related to the chapter on psychology above. Preferences are learned and the decision system can be an ingredient in this learning. Suppose I am a member of the group that values three channels at $6, while others value them at $5. I note that I pay more than my neighbor as a result. If the preferences before the multiple-level tax were unequal, are they likely to remain so after the tax? In the context of incompatible-use goods, I am aware that people who are poorer buy less of certain goods than I. But that does not cause me to question my own values, since my income is greater. But, if I become aware of different preferences for the same quantity of a good, I must begin to question my own values.[13] Why is this

Figure 5
Demand for Joint-Impact Goods with Bargaining

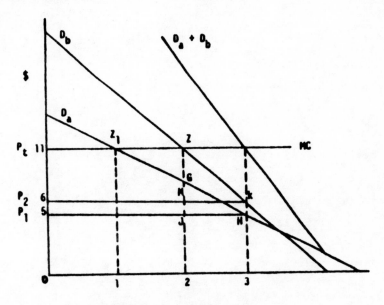

Number of Broadcast TV Channels

Note: The marginal cost of another channel is $11, while the marginal cost of another user is zero.

good so valuable to me? When the magic value-measuring meter is applied next time, I may have changed.

If the parties can bargain, they will negotiate over the amount of the good and the price (cost or tax share). This can be shown in Figure 5. Here, individual demand curves are added vertically as in Figure 4 but are shown on a single graph. A, acting alone, would buy a one-channel system at its marginal cost of P_t and B would aim to buy two at that price. If A discovers their

Figure 5
Demand for Joint-Impact Goods with Bargaining

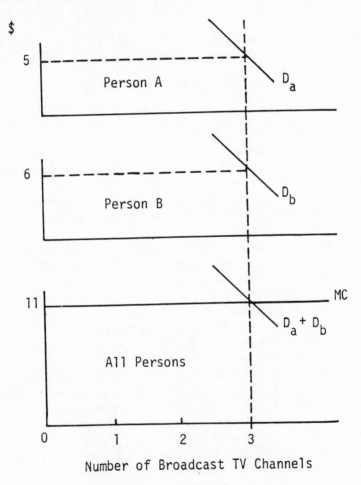

Note: The marginal cost of another channel is $11, while the marginal cost of another user is zero.

interdependence first and sees the effects of B's purchases, A will cut back and buy none hoping to enjoy a free ride. In the absence of bargaining, this move would be stable if B does not get mad. If bargaining can occur, the outcome becomes indeterminate in small-group situations as strategic bargaining is employed. (See Chapter 5.) There is no reason to think that the price rule of each person paying his or her marginal valuation will be the one chosen. Even if exclusion were possible (avoidance), it would not be demand revealing with preemptive goods. A high-demand person may pretend a low marginal value and then offer to pay a low price knowing that if she is allowed any use at a price, the physical quantity made available to her cannot be varied independently of others. Such a person cannot be distinguished from the person of genuine low demand.

Given B's purchase of two channels, A would buy more along the curve GH, and B in turn would buy more along ZK. It is possible for three channels to be purchased if A contributes the difference between the marginal cost schedule and B's demand schedule ZK. For all three channels, B pays P_2 and A pays P_1, which meets the pricing rule of everyone paying their marginal valuation, and output is optimal with the sum of these marginal values equaling marginal cost (production efficiency).

But several pricing schemes are possible. A could drive a hard bargain and insist that B pay P_t for two channels and P_2 for the third, while A paid only P_1 for the third (but of course can enjoy all channels because it is a nonexclusive joint good). B may not regard this scheme as fair even if both pay their marginal values. With the hard bargain at three channels, A enjoys a huge consumer surplus D_a, O, O_2, J, and H. Person B, on the other hand, has a smaller consumer surplus of D_b, Z, P_t plus triangle MZK. If B suspects this, he is going to try to get a better bargain or be mad if he cannot. If B drives a hard bargain he may insist that A pay P_1 for all three channels, or if really tough, he may require A to pay P_1 for the first and a price along ZX for the second and third (which again is P_1 for the marginal unit). In this case B pays nothing for one and pays P_2 for the marginal unit. A pays P_1 and B pays P_2 for the marginal unit, even though they pay various combinations of prices for the intramarginal units.

In each of these quite different total-cost shares, the price of the marginal unit to each party stays the same, and if we ignore real-income feedbacks, the quantity they want stays the same. As Buchanan notes, "Equilibrium may be consistent with almost an infinite number of sharing schemes for the costs over inframarginal units" (1968, p. 37).

The problem is actually much more complicated, as Buchanan (1968, chap. 3) has explained. You cannot get an individual's demand curve of the usual sort unless the average price does not vary with quantity—that is, average price must equal marginal price. Each demander is asked how much he or she wants at each average price. In other words, all intramarginal units cost the same as the marginal unit. But if the price of the intramarginal units is up for negotiation, there is no demand curve of the usual sort, and buyers are not sure how much they want at various marginal prices because of the income-feedback effect of the price of the intramarginal units. Buchanan (p. 44) suggests a convention that tax price per unit be uniform over various quantities for each person. He notes this is an arbitrary value judgment that distributes the gains of trade between the parties in a particular way. He suggests this needs to be a prior chosen constitutional rule, or what here is called a property right. To choose a tax share or market differential-pricing rule requires a moral choice in addition to that of money income distribution, reflected in the budget constraint. There is no reason based on Pareto-efficiency why one rule or another should be used for intramarginal prices. MC = 0 breaks the necessary connection between bearing costs and receiving benefits (prices).

Are we to have a constitutional rule that says the person with the highest marginal value is to pay more? When society made a choice on money income distribution, did it have in mind that the person with the higher demand would have to pay more? This is the issue raised by Paul Samuelson (1955). He developed a general equilibrium model where both cost share and amount of the joint-impact good are established simultaneously given a social-welfare function, which makes the trade-off between competing interests explicit. This elegant solution is elaborated in the literature and need not be detailed here (Burkhead and Miner 1971, pp. 66–74; Musgrave and Musgrave 1974, pp. 60–68). It highlights the fact that money income has no meaning for welfare until prices (tax share) of joint-impact goods have been set.

Samuelson and Buchanan make it clear that the marginal-pricing rule feeds back on the welfare of the parties.[14] Thus, we need a social-welfare function and public choice. (In the Samuelson model there are no prices, since the omniscient planner just delivers the net goods.) Money income distribution among parties does not speak to all of the ways they are interdependent. The problem is even more complicated in the case of nonoptional (high-avoidance-cost) joint-impact goods when one person places positive value on the good and another negative. What does the rule requiring the sum of marginal values to equal marginal cost mean in this case? Those harmed want to veto production of the good or be compensated.

The discussion of broadcast television above has been in terms of the optimum physical units of output (numbers of channels). Since exclusion costs were high, it was assumed that everyone could use whatever good was available. The implications for joint-impact, low-exclusion-cost goods should also be noted (which will also serve to reiterate the conclusion of the above discussion). Assume a scrambling device or cable delivery makes exclusion economic. If the marginal cost of another user is zero, what is the optimum number of users? Conventional welfare-economics theory using Pareto-better logic suggests that the optimal pricing rule is price equal to marginal cost (P = MC). The logic can be seen by reference to Figure 1 in Chapter 4. (This figure is developed in terms of decreasing cost goods, but the same logic applies to zero-marginal-cost goods.) Begin with a price on the average revenue curve (such as Pr) that exceeds MC. Additional users can be added who are willing to pay the additional cost of production, which in the case of pure joint-impact goods is zero. Apparently it is possible to improve the condition of all additional users who want the product without making any other user worse off. With joint-impact goods, even if exclusion is economic it is apparently the wrong thing to do. As already noted, exclusion will not reveal demand. And even if individual demands were known, their use is questionable. If the intramarginal consumers pay what they did before (for example, Pr), the fixed costs will be covered, but the market must be differentiated and some who add nothing to cost will be excluded.

Implementation of the P = MC rule, however, is difficult in a market. If the same price is charged all buyers, then the "correct" price of zero will not keep the private firm in business. A private firm might cover total cost by market receipts if it differentiated its market and charged different prices to different buyers (as discussed in Chapter 4 and above in the context of price bargaining among consumers, Figure 6). (See Rowley and Peacock 1975). This differentiation where feasible is often objected to by some buyers who regard it as unfair discrimination. We need a value judgment that decides whose interests are to count if we are to retain the private-market firm in this case. The market-failure literature suggests that the market be replaced by government provision via some taxation scheme that does not affect use at the margin (perhaps a poll tax). This solution implements the Pareto-better pricing rule of P = MC. However, inquiry must be made as to who pays the tax. The tax may be paid by those who do not want the good or who do not wish it at the price implied by the tax. Just as it required a value judgment on a market-pricing scheme, it requires a value judgment on a governmental pricing (taxing) scheme. One can speak of a Pareto-better pricing rule of P = MC only if one presumes a property right in how total costs will be financed.

Pricing Goods with Overhead Costs

Goods produced under economies of scale and joint-impact goods are parts of a continuum related to marginal cost decreasing and becoming finally zero. The production of this group of goods was conceptualized by J. M. Clark as being marked by the existence of "overhead costs." He also included certain aspects of horizontal and vertical integration (see Chapter 6 on cost discontinuities and investment coordination), peak-load situations (Chapter 7), and immobile assets (Chapter 6). Overhead costs refer to "costs that cannot be traced home and attributed to particular units of business," and thus "an increase or decrease in output does not involve proportionate increase or decrease in cost" (1923, p. 1). Conceptualized in this way, the policy problem for Clark was how to utilize underused productive capacity. If you could increase the output of a given product or a set of interrelated products without a proportionate increase in cost, this was a source of economic progress.

The same phenomenon can be looked at from the point of view of inputs or products. An input that cannot be traced to a particular unit or kind of output is an overhead cost. The products of these overhead (or joint) costs are either joint-impact goods or goods produced under decreasing cost. The pure joint-impact good is the polar case when another unit (user) can be obtained at no additional cost. Clark saw many governmentally produced goods, such as technological knowledge, as overhead inputs to industry, which could not be produced by a single firm because the inputs were not related to a particular firm's output (but contributed jointly to many firms' outputs). Each one of the users of a joint-impact good has joint costs with all the rest of the users. These joint costs cannot be mechanically traced to any one user. He saw that cost as a natural phenomenon had no meaning when overhead costs existed (p. 32). If the output is observed to change with added units of capital or labor attributed to that marginal unit, then none of the product will be available to cover overhead. The sum of marginal products would exceed total product.

Nevertheless, the overhead costs must be allocated and paid by someone. (For further discussion of joint-cost allocation, see Eckstein [1965, ch. 9] and Bain [1966a]). Clark argued that this allocation must be made with the objective of reducing idle capacity. And this could only be achieved by charging different prices to different users (that is, to attract a buyer to use the idle capacity required a lesser price than that charged to earlier purchasers). "The problem involves the allocation of certain general burdens where reasonable men may differ as to what is just apportionment. There is no natural system of prices in the old sense. Cost prices do not mean anything definite anymore. Efficiency requires discrimination and discrimination has no universally accepted standard to go by to keep it from degenerating into favoritism" (Clark 1923, p. 32). For price differentiation not to be seen as discrimination requires a widely shared value judgment. Clark argued that pricing under conditions of overhead costs was not something to be deduced by formula but was a cooperative choice, "a partnership between labor and the other parties in industry" in "amending the constitution of industry" (p. 482). Pricing policy during depressions, sharing of industrial knowledge, unemployment insurance, and a trade ethic for defining harmful price discrimination was up to public choice, which he hoped would be guided by the enlightened pursuit of reducing idle capacity of the whole economy.

Writing in 1923, Clark believed that the business cycle could be controlled by social-cost-keeping concerns replacing the more common individualistic canons of industry and labor. Yet it was the Keynesian policies of a more-centralized sort combined with the necessities for common action created by war that reversed the Great Depression and provided escape from the social trap. The attraction of mutual gain from fuller utilization of capacity has not yet been sufficient without other community-creating forces. Until we pay more attention to distributive conflicts involving decreasing cost and joint-impact goods, this community will be hard to achieve in peacetime. It is not possible for every consumer to be regarded as the marginal consumer and only to pay marginal cost. It is unacceptable for some labor to be paid less than customary in order to achieve increased employment in a depression. It is not possible for every firm, in response to a general decline in demand, to lay off employees and expect product demand to be constant. Labor is an overhead cost for the total economy and cannot be idled and stored until needed. Layoffs also destroy morale and team feeling and thus the marginal value product of labor (Thurow 1985). If we do not agree on the distribution of the gains and costs of full utilization of our resources, full production will not be achieved.

In summary, this discussion is not an argument for a particular pricing scheme. It is an argument that any pricing scheme has distributive consequences and that no statement can be made about the distribution of income unless property rights in the pricing scheme are made explicit. To understand wealth distribution, it is not enough to know who has money in their pockets if you do not know how the pricing policy will affect their real purchasing power and who gets to select the good. In short, there is a moral problem even if preferences are revealed and money income distribution is accepted. You cannot tell what a person is sovereign over until the price rule for goods with economies of scale and joint-impact goods is specified.

Policy and Theory

Some models are used to make actual empirical calculations and others are used to reach policy recommendations directly. The latter has been the historical use of the welfare model of pure competition. This model is used to argue, by abstract reasoning without any reference to empirical estimates, the supremacy of the market as a decision-making system. Most of the models employ utility-indifference curves that have no empirical content. If the assumptions hold, you get the best of all possible worlds regardless of whether half the world is unemployed or starving. The same uses are made of these "existence models" that have been examined here.[15] They are not meant to be used to make empirical estimates but to argue for certain policies. This fact is made clear by Burkhead and Miner: "Because of the inability to exclude, however, this analysis is essentially irrelevant as an approximation to any viable decentralized voluntary solution. At the same time, it does provide a normative guide for the evaluation of those political arrangements that endeavor to simulate a consumer-preference-directed solution to the provision of public goods" (1971, p. 95). This position ignores the problem of which consumers we are speaking of if interests in joint-impact goods conflict.

The ways in which these existence theorems are used in normative arguments are subtle. An example is provided by professional reaction to the model developed by Paul Samuelson noted above. His model of joint-impact-goods provision incorporates the pricing rule and goods ownership into choice of a social-welfare function. The model focuses public-choice issues on choosing directly between A's and B's total utility. The quantities of incompatible-use and joint-impact goods are derived from this choice. Resource allocation and income distribution are simultaneously determined in one overall moral choice between A and B. Richard Musgrave (1969) has objected to this abstraction. First, he notes a practical objection, that people cannot agree on a social-welfare function. He ignores the equally practical objection to any existence theorem that people cannot agree on money income distribution (factor ownership) either. Second, he argues there is no practical way to specify a social-welfare function in terms of utility. Money income can at least be seen. But no government can be very satisfied that real welfare is satisfactory by just agreeing on money-income distribution. Further, Musgrave's own models contain equally nonobservable variables.

These practical objections are beside the point. What is really troublesome are the policy implications of different but equally abstract and impractical models. Musgrave notes that if income-distribution policy cannot be settled independently of taxation and public-expenditure policy, there is no basis for distinguishing taxation for redistribution of income from taxation as a market-price surrogate for purchase of joint-impact goods (p. 133). Economists would not be able to say anything scientific about the global correctness of tax policy. It is this author's opinion that in fact income distribution and resource allocation are inseparable. Economists are going to be forced to the conclusion that has long been painfully obvious to the person in the street. Welfare (or real income) is not only affected by the resources one owns or money in the pocket but also by pricing policies (including tax policies) and the amounts of government goods provided (including joint-impact goods).

Whatever the motives of economic theorists, their theory shapes policy. For example, Tobin (1970) suggests that redistribution via public-expenditure practices is not proper. Thus only direct redistribution, such as the negative income tax, remains. There is something psychologically maddening about taking money out of people's pockets. Senator George McGovern, the unsuccessful Democratic candidate for president in 1972, found this out very dramatically when he suggested heavily redistributive taxes. If theory suggests this is the only way that income should be redistributed, then it constitutes support for the status quo, since such redistribution is unpopular.

Another implication has to do with our attitudes toward changing rights in the flow of government expenditures as opposed to factor ownership. The former can be changed drastically by any legislature, but court consent is required to change the latter. Some people have argued in terms of constitutional welfare rights, so that the courts would prevent wide fluctuations in welfare transfer payments. People whose well-being is tied to public spending and tax policy are disadvantaged compared with those whose income flow is protected by the courts. The fact that some economic theory suggests that only direct income distribution is efficient contributes to maintenance of this disadvantage.

PARETO-EFFICIENCY AND THE POLITICAL PROCESS

A political decision is Pareto-optimal only with a rule of unanimity. With less than unanimity, someone will pay for and potentially consume some governmental good that she does not want at the politically chosen price. Unanimity has its problems, too. First, it implies a preference for the status quo, which is a preference for the interests of A over B. Second, while unanimity can prevent some kinds of political externalities where someone has to pay for something he does not want, it increases decision costs. Whenever the individual wants to obtain a governmental good, he will have to obtain the consent of every other person. He has to balance off political externalities, decision costs, and doing without some good he wants. Thus most people will find it to their individual advantage to support a decision rule of less than unanimity, and the rule will vary by product (Buchanan and Tullock 1962, chap. 7). One might expect the rich, who can more easily find private substitutes for government goods, to favor a high degree of unanimity, which protects them from the poor, who might try to vote a tax and decide the kind and level of a jointly used good.

There are many ways of keeping the political system safe for those with money to buy what they want. Some of these were discussed above, such as the questions of agenda setting and the determination of voting boundaries. Perhaps the biggest question of all is what to do about two people with money who want different amounts or kinds of nonoptional or preemptive joint-impact goods.

There is another problem with the Pareto-rule that says resource and money-income ownership are inviolate. It is not popular in the Western democracies to deny explicitly the one-person/one-vote rule with respect to political choice, but this ethic is potentially in conflict with the Pareto-criterion. For the two rules to be consistent, voting power would have to equal the distribution of income. Where they are unequal and unanimity is not required, any majority voting on the government budget and taxes is unlikely to be Pareto-better. While even the rich may agree to some rule of less than unanimity, it is unlikely that all people will want the same rule. If we turn goods provision over to politics, the Pareto-criterion will not be met.

There is discussion about which kind of voting system best represents the median preference with given money income or which one best reflects intensity of preferences.[16] Still, few are willing to oppose the ethic of equality with respect to voting power, which is in conflict with protecting existing distribution of income (Habermas 1975; Wolfe 1977). We have seen some non-Pareto-better redistributions of income via extension of the voting franchise, though political choice is still reflective of income via campaign finance. Conservatives have long argued that joint-impact goods are a special case and that few real examples can be found. James Buchanan (1968, chap. 9) has developed a five-part categorization of goods in terms of jointness—he calls it "indivisibility."[17] He argues that only the case of pure indivisibility may be reason for government provision, and that of course is not necessarily best in the face of political externalities. Richard Musgrave (1969, p. 142) has opposed Samuelson's definition of joint-impact goods as all goods not on the knife edge of no jointness characteristics. This definition makes incompatible-use goods the rarer, special case, with most goods having some degree of jointness. This definition even makes Samuelson uncomfortable, and he admits, "If the experts remain nihilistic about algorithms to allocate public goods, and if all but a knife-edge of reality falls in that domain, nihilism about most of economics, rather than merely public finance, seems to be implied" (p. 109). Note that this is a nihilism over the high-priest function and not economics as a predictor of substantive performance.

Governance

It has been emphasized here that rights are antecedent to exchange and thus Pareto-better exchange cannot be a guide to choice of rights. This does not mean that rights are settled once and for all or in discrete moments of court or legislative action. People discover further interdependencies in the context of everyday business. They not only exchange what they own, they continue to explore and decide what each owns. Many reach localized accommodation as they go along (private ordering) without any recourse to court or legislature (Williamson 1985, p. 164). The common law is a formal ratification of many of these accommodations. Different forms of business organization may produce more or different decentralized accommodations.

The fact that these decentralized accommodations have lower transaction costs is relevant but not decisive for either welfare economics or prediction of institutional change. To find economizing behavior is not to settle the question of what to economize. One person's transaction cost is often another's opportunity. The choice among institutions is not alone one minimizing transaction costs if the total performance of who counts is thereby different.

SUMMARY: INTERDEPENDENCE AND POWER

Conventional theory draws attention to a very narrow set of institutional variables. It presumes that there are only two main sources of power: (1) the distribution of money income and factors of production and (2) the degree of competition as influenced by the number of buyers and sellers. By assuming that an ethical judgment had been made on income distribution via factor ownership, the welfare theorist felt free to advocate the competitive market as controlling all other sources of power. The institutional variables suggested by conventional theory are too limited for empirical research on substantive performance and for an adequate welfare economics.

The argument against the simple prescriptions flowing from consumer-sovereignty concepts can be stated as follows: you cannot tell what a person is sovereign over until you specify fully how property rights affect all of the ways for one person to affect another. Some of the points are summarized below.

First, the point of the argument is not to deny that competition or ownership of factors are relevant institutional variables. For incompatible-use goods, the degree of competition goes a long way in controlling the power that one person has over another even when one owns many factors and the other few. But this is far from the whole picture.

When incompatible-use goods are not produced under constant costs, the real income of a person is affected by the prices of goods, which are affected by the preferences and purchases of others. In other words, pecuniary externalities affect the real value of money income. The greater the variation in preferences, the less money income is a measure of real income. Further, there are many other ways that people are interdependent. Different rules affect the size and impact of information costs on different parties. The same point can be made with respect to all varieties of transaction costs. These costs affect how far a person's money income will go and what can be done with owned factors. The other varieties of interdependence discussed in Part II create additional sources of power of one person over another.

Second, with respect to joint-impact goods, there are additional institutional variables. In order to describe a person's opportunity set, we must know who gets to choose nonoptional joint-impact goods and how the costs of optional joint-impact goods will be shared. Government could charge people different prices (taxes) for the same good. But this surely requires an additional ethical judgment beyond specifying money income. The real utility of this income is unknown until the cost share (tax price) for joint-impact goods is settled.

Samuelson makes it clear that decisions on both money income and the pricing rule for joint-impact goods are necessary when policy is made on welfare distribution. Thus are destroyed any simple institutional prescriptions that assume the government has settled all problems of sources of power and interdependence between people when it approves of money-income distribution.

The discussion in this book has added several implications to those of the Samuelson model. In thinking about our ethical judgments concerning the relative welfare of different people, we must be concerned with not only money income and pricing rules for joint-impact goods but also a whole host of rules that control interdependence growing out of exclusion costs, transaction costs, scale economies, consumer and producer surpluses, and peak-load conditions.

Thus the world becomes more complicated, and a person can think his welfare is improved when he gets one variety of rule going in his favor only to find that welfare lost by another sort of rule going in the opposite direction. The narrow set of institutional variables suggested by conventional theory works to some group's advantage. While others are guarding the rights identified in the conventional models, their welfare can be reduced by changes in implicit rights in other areas.

These general points are examined further below in the context of a number of specific propositions on institutional choice that can be found in the literature. They purport to be prescriptions scientifically deduced from a simple normative judgment of the relative ownership of income, factors, or goods. But because of the inadequacy of ownership specified in this way to control all sources of interdependence, it turns out that these propositions make a hidden presumption of additional normative judgments that must be accepted before one can deduce a prescription for choice among alternative institutions.

A COLLECTION OF INSTITUTIONAL-CHOICE RULES: A SUMMARY AND CRITIQUE

In the following section, a summary and critique will be made of some of the suggestions in the literature that have been put forth to guide institutional choice under the guise of increasing something called social welfare. They are not mutually exclusive. The first several of these are a summary of the rules implied in the previous two sections of this chapter.

Prohibit all but Pareto-better change. The Pareto-criterion does not escape the need for a moral choice among the conflicting interests of people. It implements the choice already implicit in status quo property rights. To limit oneself to Pareto-better change only is to express preference for the current distribution of rights and income.

Pecuniary externalities should be ignored. This restatement of the rule above is subject to the same critique. As Armen Alchian (1965, p. 818) puts it, "Although private property rights protect private property from physical changes chosen by other people, no immunity is implied for the exchange value of one's property." Pecuniary externalities are those produced by the play of the market. If the value of your assets is destroyed by competition, that value is incidental to someone else's Pareto-better trade. One problem is that transactions often have third-party effects. Property rights determine whether these interests are to count and be included in the Pareto-better transaction. Some people's interests are protected by rules of theft against technological externalities. Other people's interests are protected by rules affecting market power, which in turn affects the value in exchange of one's assets. To argue only for protection from technological externality is to argue for the interests of one person over another (see Chapter 7).

The market will internalize all externalities that should be accounted for. This is another restatement of the Pareto rule. The market by definition will allow A to make a bid to B to avoid or secure some effect of B's actions. A's interest is internalized and becomes an opportunity cost to B (see Chapter 8). If A's bid fails, the consequences of the original distribution of rights are carried out. Another way to express this rule is to say that government regulation is bad. It is illogical to grant B a right and then take it away in a regulation. But public choice gave B the right in the first place, and this choice does not necessarily hold for all time. What the government gives it can take away. And when it wants to take away a part of what was given to B, rather than the entire right, it turns to regulation to give some rights to A. To argue against regulation is to argue for the supremacy of B over A. Regulation is not to reduce the freedom of all people. Freedom to choose within one's opportunity set must be distinguished from freedom to choose one's opportunity set. A's freedom is B's regulation.

The government must correct all externalities. Robert Haveman suggests that "when significant spillovers are found in the real world, collective action, usually through a government becomes necessary if efficient performance is to be secured" (1970, pp. 39–40). Another version of this is that the government must step in whenever there is a divergence between social cost and private cost. Harold Demsetz (1967, p. 345) says, "A primary function of property rights is that of guiding incentives to achieve a greater internalization of externalities." (See also Baumol 1965, p. 25.) But there is no way to remove all externalities; they can only be shifted. If A's acts are causing damage to B, a partial analysis may suggest that we do something about it. But if their interests conflict, the only thing to do is to choose between them. Either allow A to continue to affect B or give B the right that leaves A exposed to B's acts. It loads the argument to label A's interest as a social cost and B's as a private cost.

Goods with high exclusion costs must be provided by governments. The market will not reflect everyone's willingness to pay for these goods, as people are tempted to be free riders or conclude that their actions would not make any difference anyway. The fact that people do not buy a good in the market does not necessarily mean they do not want it. However, if the government taxes to provide the good, the free rider may be turned into the unwilling rider. While some may hide their tastes, others truly do not want the good but may be forced to buy it (see Chapter 3).

Joint-impact goods should be provided by government. Whether exclusion is relatively cheap or not, utilization of a joint-impact good by A does not reduce the potential availability to B by an equivalent amount. To prevent B's use even where possible is wasteful where marginal cost is zero.[18] Yet A and B may not agree on the quality and amount of the good that should be provided or on how they should share in its cost. A may want the good, and if it exists, B may not be able to escape being affected by it even when it has negative value to B or B wants a different quality. Where interests conflict, any rule for provision of joint-impact goods, whether private market or government, must choose between the interests of the parties (see Chapter 5).

The usual prescription for allocative efficiency of price-equal marginal cost (of another user) begs the question of who pays fixed cost. And the usual prescription for production efficiency that the sum of the individuals' marginal values equal the marginal cost (of another physical unit) cannot be implemented by public or private producers because of strategic nonrevelation of demand. Even if known, the rule presumes the rights of those with negative values to be compensated (negative price). If a negative value is allowed to influence quantity, then it is a right whose value is a willingness to sell rather than a willingness to pay. This is a matter to be decided by public choice, not assumed.

Distribute ownership to minimize transaction costs. Where parties conflict over the right to exclude the other from use of an incompatible-use good, Richard Posner (1972b, p. 18) offers the following economic principle: "The right should be assigned to the party whose use is the more valuable. . . . Transaction costs are minimized when the law . . . assigns the right to the party who would buy it from the other party if it were assigned to the other party instead and if transation costs were zero."[19] Thus, in effect, if A has the necessary income and preference to buy a resource from B, A should be declared the owner so that the cost of transactions might be saved for the economy! B, of course, now has nothing to sell and may go hungry, but Posner evidently judges this to be of no consequence, since transaction costs are minimized. The question of income distribution is only a zero-sum game anyway and of no interest to economists interested in maximizing total product. He is entitled to his value judgments as between the interests of A and B, but these should not be glorified by calling them an "economic principle." The so-called principle provides a method for allocating ownership to new resources at the margin but is silent on how ownership of previous goods (which supports present ability to bid) was determined. The government is not ethically neutral whether it declares A the owner of a new resource, auctions it to the highest bidder, or shifts rights from B to A, even if the Kaldor-Hicks potential-compensation test is met.

Some suggest that total wealth first be maximized and then redistributed according to some value judgment; thus some people would get their income via court-protected private-property rights while others would get theirs only by the grace of some legislative body. Such a situation represents a very unequal status and requires an additional value judgment.

The minimization of transaction costs can be applied to a number of cases of institutional choice. It was noted in Chapter 6 that collective (noncompetitive) modes of organizing work, including unions, facilitate trust and enable cost savings in training and supervision. But cost minimization has a context, and the resulting sticky wages and macroeffects are not to everyone's liking. Cost minimization by one set of parties often creates cost for others and it is rights that determine whose costs count.

Common property is inefficient. If goods are owned in common, trade is either prohibited or very costly, since the agreement of all is required. This situation can prevent some asserted Pareto-better trades. Such a rule expresses the value judgment that the rights of third parties whose interests are furthered by high transaction costs are not to count.

A variant of the above rule is that private ownership is most productive. As Alchian puts it, "Under public ownership the costs of any decision or choice are less fully thrust upon the selector than under private property. In other words, the cost benefit incentives system is changed toward lower costs" under private ownership (1965, p. 827).

This conclusion depends on how productivity (output) is defined and what the rules require either public or private decision makers to take into account (that is, what costs or inputs are relevant). There is no such thing as *the* cost. Costs that count are what they are because of rights and personality. Both are malleable. The private owner may make more profit, but there are as many profitable solutions as there are property-rights sets. The rules shape what actions are profitable. The public-choice question is, What is to be made profitable?

Option demands must be filled by government. [20] Where resource use is irreversible, present values may not reflect actual future demands, which if they develop will be frustrated by today's consumption. However, one person's options kept open are another's options foreclosed. If the Grand Canyon is kept wild for the grandchildren of current members of the Sierra Club, there will be higher prices for today's electric consumers. One person's options for children's future enjoyment is another's pain in the neck. To meet an option demand, like any other, is to choose between the competing interests of people (see Chapter 6).

Government investment planning is necessary with economies of scale and cost discontinuities. Where one firm uses inputs produced by the other, investment timing coordination can reduce both firms' unit costs and avoid unused capacity while the other firm reacts to price reductions. Such coordination is possible with a market firm by increasing the scale of the firm and sometimes by market contract. But decision costs may be significant in either private or public planning. If planning is done by vertical integration of ownership control, it may lead to restraint of trade, and if it is done by government, different groups will have an opportunity to shape the benefits of the coordination (see Chapter 6).

It is better to redistribute wealth in money than in kind. "General taxation, positive and negative, is the best way to moderate the inequalities of income and wealth generated by a competitive economy" (Tobin 1970, p. 276; also see Collard 1981, chap. 12). Henry Simons (1948, p. 38) states, "It is urgently necessary for us to quit confusing measures for regulating relative prices and wages with devices for diminishing inequality. One difference between competent economists and charlatans is that, at this point, the former sometimes discipline their sentimentality with a little reflection on the mechanics of an exchange economy." It can be easily shown that the recipient of a grant can reach a higher utility with the flexibility of money rather than the gift of a good. But the fact is that often the grantor's utility may be enhanced by changing the recipient's specific consumption. Consumption frequently has a degree of joint impact. What is efficient depends on whose interests count. Welfare recipients want money to spend as they wish, but some givers want to attach strings so the recipients' behavior will be changed.

Some writers say that redistribution is not a question that economic theory has any answers for. Yet they do feel free to pronounce that some techniques for redistribution are good and others are bad. If the prevailing public opinion is against direct grants via taxation because the receiver is seen as not earning them, then to restrict policy consideration to this method is in effect to argue for the status quo.

A free person should choose a unanimity rule. It follows that any government action by less than unanimity is a diminution of freedom created by force. This rule overlooks decision costs. There is a necessary trade-off between decision costs involved in getting unanimity for those things a person wants and the exposure to having the group choose something the person does not want (Buchanan and Tullock 1962). Depending on one's image of this trade-off, a free person may vote for a majority rule. No voting rule is going to please everyone, because everyone's trade-offs between reduction of external costs and decision costs, including political externalities, will differ.[21] Again, public rules will have to make a choice among people's competing interests. People may differ with respect to the voting rule they prefer.

A public referendum is the best reflection of public interest. One writer suggests that we should "pose issues of public policy in terms of whether society does in fact hold certain value judgments rather than in terms of the demonstrable inherent legitimacy of certain activities" (Steiner 1970, p. 39). But how shall we know these social value judgments? The same writer suggests that "survey data about public attitudes on issues exist and provide some sort of a base" (p. 45). Leaving aside all of the problems of who is to frame the questions for the survey, we still have the problem of what to do with conflicting attitudes. When pressed, most Western economists and political scientists fall back on democracy, and the purer the better after compromising with decision costs. But the concept of democracy does not settle the agenda-setting problem and the question of voting boundaries (see Chapter 8). Democracy is not merely to be in favor of the people. "Power to the People" is a demagogic slogan. The issue is always which people are to count when interests conflict.

The point is not to argue for or against the above propositions. Some of them fit the author's value judgments, and some fit better than many others. They are rejected as value-neutral rules of choice, and as such they are lies. They would be honest only if they were put forward as the explicit value judgments of the speaker.

ALTERNATIVE MEASURES OF PERFORMANCE

The lessons of the above point-by-point critique of rules for institutional choice can be summarized and extended by a critique of the conventional performance categories of freedom, efficiency, and economic growth. This critique serves to make the point of this chapter in a nontechnical way. It also illustrates why the conventional performance categories are not satisfactory for empirical studies such as those in Chapter 12 below.

Freedom

What is meant by the common assertion that the competitive market maximizes freedom?[22] Voluntary trade gives the appearance of freedom. If each party did not think he or she were better off, no trade would take place. Voluntary trade contrasts with government regulation, which has the outward appearance of force. But appearances often mask underlying factors of a different sort. The model outlined above inquires into a step previous to observed trades and asks how the parties obtained the rights to be traded. After it is decided that A has many rights and B has few, we can note B's efforts to rearrange his few goods into a better mix. If A agrees to trade, both are better off, but B's pile is still small relative to A's. Who says that this has to be? Why is it when A's interests conflict with B's in access to resources that A is more often the one found to have the right? Why is B mostly in the position of seldom creating a cost for A, while A has much that is a cost to B? Antecedent to the observed mutually beneficial trade is the prior mutual coercion that is given shape by the inescapable public choice of property rights. Where interests conflict in terms of this antecedent question of the rights of each party, increased freedom for A is more exposure for B. This is the significance of the quotation from Isaiah Berlin at the beginning of this chapter, "Freedom for the pike is death for the minnow."

The recipient of an order in an administrative transaction cannot voluntarily choose to abstain from the transaction. This situation nominally contrasts to a bargained, market transaction where parties are free to trade. However, where opportunities are unequal, the result is coercive. Robert B. Seidman asks, "Is it significantly different to say to a man, 'I will pay you a wage if you will work for me?' rather than 'You will get no wage unless you work for me?' Two hundred years ago Lord Chancellor Northington expressed it succinctly: 'Necessitous men are not, truly speaking, free men.' At law, to treat unequals notionally as equal is in fact to elevate the stronger to a position of domination" (1973, p. 556). (This is also a major theme of Ely 1914, pp. 555–618.) For a man of little property, the freedom not to agree to a wage offer is the freedom to starve.

There are some macrodescriptive uses of the term freedom. We may wish to contrast two countries with respect to the extent of participation in decision making. Some indexes of pluralism are possible without presuming a value judgment with respect to the conflicting participants. The issue is one of whose freedom rather than freedom in the abstract. The great moral choice in any society is whose freedom counts when interests conflict in the face of scarcity. Where people conflict, global freedom is without meaning and can only obfuscate the real conflict and the ethical question. When we look at human beings face to face as their personalities and preferences interact, it can be seen that the mutuality of the market is the second step built on the antecedent public decisions assigning the property rights that are then traded and rearranged. Freedom in the abstract is not a satisfactory performance variable.

Efficiency

Neoclassical theory has suggested that the market gives us not only freedom but also efficiency. A producer must search for the cheapest method to create his other product or be driven from the market. The theory of the firm and production economics is a set of calculations necessary to determine optimal input and output choices. But again, appearances are deceptive. The earlier discussion of costs and externalities (Chapter 1) is relevant. It is one step to minimize a set of costs and another to determine what effects to include in that calculation. Contrary to the suggestion of neoclassical theory, costs do not simply exist in nature but are selected by the public choice of property rights. Calabresi and Bobbitt (1978) refer to this as "tragic choices". It is property rights that determine what physical effects are to be accounted for by decision makers. It is property rights that exclude some people's misery from the cost-minimization calculations of business. Of course, to include it for A is to shift it to B.

A third step focuses on the rules for making rules, or what is sometimes referred to as the "constitutional level." This hierarchy of decision levels has been implicit in the discussion thus far. (A similar distinction is made by Ciriacy-Wantrup 1967, pp. 181–84; 1963, chap. 3.) The first level is that of specific combination of inputs and outputs by the private or public firm or individual. The property-rights rules of the second level are used by decision makers of the first level in making their optimal choices. Decision makers of the first level try to influence these property rights by participation at the third level according to political rules. Efficiency calculations are most meaningfully applied to decisions at the first level.

Economic efficiency is a concept from engineering and physics with values attached. It is simply an abstract expression of the ratio of values of selected input to selected output. It is property rights that do the selecting. It is the relative opportunity sets of individuals based on choices of antecedent rights and their choices from within those sets that determine the content of the input and output categories and influence their market value. In other words, choice in period two is a function of choice in period one. If effects X, Y, and

Z are included in one efficiency ratio but only X and Y in another, then the efficient use of resources will be different with each (in the second set, effect Z is priced at zero as seen by a decision maker). Efficiency is the derived result of the prior choice of the content of the input and output categories and not a guide to the choice of alternative sets of categories. In short, there are an infinite number of efficient solutions, each subsidiary to the choice of property rights, which define the content of input and output. Rights determine efficiency, not the other way around.

It is useful to speak of the efficiency with which a given institutional rule achieves a given performance objective. But for clarity, objectives need to be explicit. Efficiency and rationality are closely related. We often speak of someone being irrational when we presume some objective is being sought but do not see that the decision maker had other things in mind. A favorite academic critique of public policy involves the discovery of apparently inconsistent choices. For example, the United States had a policy of subsidizing irrigation development at the same time it was paying other farmers to reduce acreage planted because of surpluses. These choices are inconsistent in terms of overall food policy. Policies such as this emerge from the composite processes of the Congress as members search for laws that will achieve a winning coalition of votes (Ingram 1969). Such policies are hard to rationalize in any terms except that of political expendiency, but they may have utility in keeping the peace and preserving willing participation in the group. It may be necessary to buy support of westerners for an agricultural bill by paying them off in irrigation projects that reduce the overall effect of the bill. There may be other ways to make this trade, but then again there may not or they may be too costly to transact. Not all payments can be made directly in money but must be made in terms of policies that establish simultaneously partially conflicting rules and public spending.

One of the performance elements of political transactions is what Talcott Parsons (Parsons and Smelser 1965, p. 16) refers to as system maintenance. It is no good to maximize some material output if the country then erupts into civil war. System maintenance is hard to test empirically; it is difficult to be sure how any given trade-off contributed to maintenance of the community as a going concern. (This was discussed in Chapter 2.) This concern can be indiscriminately used to rationalize any decision a public body makes. Still, for all of its difficulties, it cannot be ignored.

Some people prefer a strong role for central planning to avoid inconsistent policies. Theoretically, central planning implies that one group's interests have been chosen along with consistent means thereto. However, most existing planned economies seem to have their share of contradictory policies also. Sometimes conflicts of interest are resolved by having clear winners and losers on each separate issue. A given group either loses consistently and its participation is coerced, or it wins some and loses some, so that overall it agrees to play the game. However, one can observe that agreement and acceptance are obtained where something is done to favor A, and at the same time the effect is lessened by simultaneously passing a partially conflicting policy on the same issue to favor B.

In sum, where there are conflicts of interest, it is not possible to ask only in general whether an institution is effective (efficient); one must also ask of its effectiveness for whose interests. Efficiency in the abstract is not a satisfactory performance variable.

Productivity and Economic Growth

These performance concepts are closely related to efficiency, which has already been discussed. It is common to say that property rights should be structured in such a way as to promote economic growth or maximize the net value of production. But there are problems in using economic growth as a performance variable because of its ambiguity.

How shall we know if institutions are enhancing productivity? A number of neoclassical writers have suggested a conception involving the divergence between private and social cost (Pigou 1946, chap. 9). The idea is that an individual may not account for the effects of all of his or her acts, and thus there is a difference between what he or she accounts for and the effects on society. The criteria for evaluation then focus on the costs and benefits of removing the difference between private and social costs.

Douglass North and Robert Thomas (1973, p. 4) have developed this theme and provide an example from the economic history of Spain. The earliest use of land was for sheepherding. The crown had granted the right of grazing to the shepherds' guild. As population increased, the products of a fixed-place agriculture became more valuable. Profit was possible in farming. However, anyone who improved and planted a field ran the risk of its being trampled by wandering herds. Evidently, the right was nontransferable, and there was no way for the farmers to acquire the secure use of the land, or the cost of organizing bids and communicating them to itinerant shepherds was too high. The conception of these writers is that the benefits captured by the shepherds did not consider all of the costs to society that seem to prefer less sheep and more agricultural products. Does this give us a basis for saying that such a common property-rights arrangement is detrimental to society and economic growth?

It is hard to argue against a consideration of all costs and an arrangement that maximizes net social benefit. But the language is better suited to the emotive than the analytical. If interests conflict in the face of scarcity, what does it mean to account for all costs?

When A's opportunity means a cost (forgone opportunity) for B and vice versa, then it is impossible to consider all costs simultaneously. What North and Thomas call "considering all costs" is a narrow theoretical concept defined as the ability of one party to make a bid for the rights of another. A potential bid of farmers frustrated by market prohibitions is labeled a social cost. But this lost opportunity for farmers is selectively perceived while other forgone opportunities are ignored. If land is made marketable, who gets to participate in the decision to sell? Some shepherds may have large fixed assets or great psychological commitment to herding as a way of life, while others may not. Thus, reservation prices (acceptable bids) will differ among individuals. Whose opportunity will be forgone? The right of participation will affect whether the farmer's bid will be accepted. Value of net output is not something independent of rights or something that can be used to deduce a correct rights system but is itself a partial function of rights.

The so-called social perspective is an attractive one, especially to consumers who apparently have let it be known in the market that they prefer more agricultural products and fewer sheep. Apparently the value of output would be higher and consumers would benefit if the land were owned by farmers—especially if the consumers do not care about any losses to fixed assets incurred by the shepherds or any costs to the mental health of the shepherd from being uprooted and changing jobs. One can imagine a Roquefort cheese lover who will not appreciate the reduced supply and higher price he has to pay for a staple of his diet. It is fine to say that rights should be a function of relative costs, but which costs are to be considered? Is the farmer also to pay the shepherd's and cheese lover's costs when acquiring the land? If so, it is possible that what first appeared to be a profitable output-expanding transfer is that no longer. It depends on what is included in output and what is considered as growth. Cost is not something given but something selected by public choice of property rights.

The above should not be interpreted to mean that nearly universal gains from the battle against nature are impossible. But no analyst can sit on high and guess that the gains exceed the costs and blithely call it social progress while leaving distribution issues to others. Some want to say that the first consideration is to maximize output and then let the political process or whatever available institution decide how to divide output. But it is the political process of establishing property rights that defines growth, efficiency, and maximum output in the first place. These terms derive their content from property-rights decisions. Those who are necessarily displaced when one type of growth is chosen over another must be asked if they prefer a share of the new product to the personal peace they enjoyed before (Morgenstern 1972, p. 1169). Only then are we sure everyone gains rather than just hiding our preference for one group's taste over another's. However, such a requirement preserves the status quo.

To conclude, the conventional performance variables of freedom, efficiency, and economic growth are misleading when employed for normative purposes and are unsatisfactory for empirical use. The concepts of social cost and economic growth turn out to be ambiguous. While it is useful for the analyst to search for common and widely held values, be careful of a partial analysis that ignores human interdependence in the face of conflicting interest. It is often argued that the test for an acceptable change in rights is whether any losses can be fully compensated by the gainers. But who gets to say what effects must be accounted for? This is part of the problem of public choice, not something to be presumed.

A BENEFIT-COST ANALYSIS OF ALTERNATIVE RIGHTS?

Some scholars argue that institutional alternatives should be and are chosen in terms of total (global) benefits and costs.[23] This argument is reflected in some of the examples used above, such as the Spanish sheepherding conflict, and its shortcomings can be further illustrated with another example. North and Thomas (1973) utilize a total benefit-cost analysis both to explain historical changes in rights and to justify them. They refer to piracy, which once preyed on the shipping of the Mediterranean. They note that shippers paid bribes to avoid a worse fate. These are not neutral words of description. This language assumes which acts are theft and thus makes a presumptive value judgment as between competing interests. By this logic, the subject of Russell's cowboy-and-Indian painting described in the Introduction would be labeled as theft by the Indian rather than a rent collection for use of the Indian's land.

An alternative is to regard the "pirates" as owners of the sea; then the bribes become market rents. North and Thomas (p. 4) see everything as a function of natural costs. The bribe was used as long as it was cheaper than building a navy to drive away the pirates. They see the navy as ensuring a right, while it can as well be seen as theft, which violates the previous rights of the pirates. They say, "Ultimately piracy disappeared because of the international enforcement of property rights by navies." They assume the subject of their analysis before they start by regarding the traders and shippers as the owners of the sea and pirates as thieves who couldn't compensate the shippers. They see the demise of the pirates as economic growth. Yet it can also be seen as a redistribution of rights at the expense of the former sea owners. Who considered the loss in food for the pirates' families as a cost? If the pirates own the sea, then the navy is the thief. Can we say at that point that the shippers were doing something useful while the pirates were not? On that ground, no one could own natural resources and collect rents from them. Any payment for use would be seen as a bribe or tribute to landlords.

Initially, bribes were cheaper than maintaining a navy. "However, with the expansion of trade it ultimately became evident that the complete elimination of piracy was the cheapest alternative" (p. 4). Cheapest for whom? For shippers or pirates? Pirates could be like any landlord. If landlords were eliminated, the distribution of wealth would be different. But that requires a value judgment and would not have the widespread appeal that efficiency in the abstract attracts.

The school of thought that argues that institutional alternatives should be and are chosen in terms of total benefits and costs and given relative prices relies on potential Pareto-improvement tests (Kaldor-Hicks) and has all of the problems noted above plus the fact that some people are actually left worse off (compensation not paid). The potential compensation test cannot be a guide to shifting rights without presuming who had rights before the shift. All propositions related to the analysis depend on an implicit assumption of who counts when interests conflict. The analysis attempts to choose alternative rights at one level while taking another level as given and unexamined. Efficiency calculations always depend on where you start, but they can never validate that starting place. Therefore, a benefit-cost analysis of alternative rights is always a partial analysis. Efficiency calculations always presume some set of rights and therefore cannot be a guide to rights, unless the prior rights are legitimated. Partial analysis has its place as long as its presumptions are clearly labeled. It can be used only when analyzing how rights affect a particular group interest.

Another example is provided by what is termed the theory of "induced institutional innovation" (Hayami and Ruttan, 1985). Institutions are seen as endogenous to the economic system and change results from exogenous change in factor prices influenced by technology and population. This theory predicts that efficient institutions will develop to make it possible for marginal cost to equal marginal revenue, which may have been thrown into disequilibrium by exogenous changes.

Hayami and Ruttan (pp. 99-103) illustrate their argument by reference to a rice-farming village in the Philippines between 1956 and 1976. The traditional property institution provided that people of the village who participated in the harvest and threshing received one-sixth of the rice. In 1958, a publicly built irrigation system was made available to the village, and in the late 1960s, high-yielding rice varieties were available accompanied by fertilizer, pesticides, and improved cultural practices. The effect of these new technologies was to raise farm income, and given the traditional rights, tenants and other laborers got some of this gain as well as the landlords. In Hayami and Ruttan's view, this created a disequilibrium and labor received more than its marginal product and more than its opportunity cost in other occupations (declining as a result of population growth).

Hayami and Ruttan argue that this situation induced institutional change, namely, a system where labor could get a share of the harvest only by giving uncompensated weeding labor. This in their view lowered the marginal cost of labor to its opportunity cost. The resulting performance gave all of the benefits of technological change to the landlords. Labor is still to be thankful, however, because if the old rights had prevailed and labor cost kept high, there would have been less employment. Thus the capture of the gains by the landlords achieved efficiency by restoring the equilibrium between marginal revenue and cost.

What would have been the substantive performance if landless labor had been given part ownership in the benefits of technology? It is only selective perception that regards a claim on net gain to the firm as changing the marginal cost of labor. A share of net return is not a marginal cost. Both landlord and labor will decide to work in the firm only if their marginal value product is greater than the wage they could earn elsewhere. Being owners need not change that calculation. A laborer who is also a stockholder does not change his or her own or the firm's calculations of resource allocation. Equilibria between marginal cost and marginal revenue is not unique to one ownership interest and thus cannot explain change in ownership. The particular equilibrium among many possible is rights dependent and cannot explain change in rights.

A test is provided by the same Philippine case. A law was passed giving former tenants the right to pay a fixed rent. As a result, these tenants assessed their opportunity costs (including value of leisure) and subleased the land at a rate that gave the hired labor only low nonfarm wages. This contracting achieved marginal equilibrium again with landless labor getting its nonfarm opportunity cost only. This equilibrium gave the original tenant a share of the productivity gains along with the landlord. If the original tenant can be made a part owner, why not all the landless labor in the village? There is no theoretical reason that they cannot be beneficiaries of public investments in irrigation and new plant varieties as well as landlords and original tenants.

Induced institutional innovation theory is a hidden presumption of desired income distribution. It tries to portray rights as derivative of only natural forces. Any human and cultural factors therefore only affect the speed by which presumptively efficient institutions are reached or sometimes result in bad institutions that do not fit nature. This ideology, masked as science, is part of the power struggle used by different groups to obtain institutions favorable to them. There is no way to have a welfare economics that does not require the taking of sides.

IS THERE A BETTER HOLE TO GO TO?

Society puts pressure on its scholars to provide authoritative answers to policy questions in the face of conflict. It is a measure of the insecurity of our civilization that these demands are made. An example of one such demand is contained in a letter dated October 12, 1966, sent to experts in the field of land-use policy by Milton Pearl, the director of the Public Land Law Review Commission.

To assist the Commission in achieving its objective, we are seeking the advice and counsel of persons like yourself, who are concerned with government, policy development, and public administration as they affect our political, social and economic well-being. Specifically, we solicit your assistance in helping us establish criteria that will serve all members of the Commission alike in reaching conclusions as to what constitutes "the *maximum benefit for the general public.*" Such criteria would put decision-making within the Commission on a plane *above relianace on divergent opinions* arrived at without reference to a common base.

The psychologist Erich Fromm (1941) describes points in history where people run from freedom and seek authoritative guidance. There always seems to be some dictator ready to answer our call. When people cannot take the responsibility for their destiny and live with the fear that they might later wish they had chosen another path, someone will come forward to announce that they have found the true way. Today's demands on scientific authority are not as dramatic as the German turn to Hitler or its equivalent in other countries suffering the economic crises of the late 1920s and 1930s. Still, economists, social scientists, and others are called upon for scientific answers to today's conflicts.

The title for this section is taken from a book by Joan Robinson, who writes, "The Keynesian revolution has destroyed the old soporific doctrines, and its own metaphysics is thin and easy to see through. We are left in the uncomfortable situation of having to think for ourselves" (1963, p. 95). She continues,

Perhaps all this seems negative and destructive. To some, perhaps, it even recommends the old doctrines, since it offers no "better 'ole" to go to. The contention of this essay is precisely that there is no "better 'ole." The moral problem is a conflict that can never be settled. Social life will always present mankind with a choice of evils. No metaphysical solution that can ever be formulated will seem satisfactory for long. The solutions offered by some economists were no less delusory than those of the theologians that they displaced (p. 146).

The message of this chapter is similar. The rules put forward by the new welfare economists are simply disguised value judgments and preferences for the interests of A over B. It would seem elementary logic to note that there cannot be a total benefit-cost calculus when interests conflict. Yet we seek it with the fervor of a sea captain searching for the lighthouse beacon.

When interests conflict, there must be a weighting of these interests. But who is the authority for that weighting? Whenever we speak of society, of the public, or the people wanting something, we implicitly have chosen one side or the other of the interests at conflict. We have made a selective value judgment without saying who gave us that right. If we say we have just observed some basic agreement and have derived our conclusion from it, we may be guilty of self-delusion. To attach the term *collective will* to some existing governmental decision or result that oozes out of a series of interacting individuals' decisions is only to glorify what exists, not to provide a test for it. The decisions of Congress can hardly be a guide to what Congress should do. The same is true of any decision. It is always a function of some set of rules that are selective of which conflicting interests to count. There is no way to break out—one is always chasing one's tail. You can use a vote to confirm the legitimacy of a market rule, and you can use a public-opinion poll to confirm the rightness of the voting rules, and so on ad infinitum, but you are still left with the need to choose between conflicting interests.

Peter Steiner (1970, p. 40) suggests that "we agree first (some way, any way) on collective values and then use them to make social choices." Any way, indeed! He suggests that we research the "revealed objectives of society instead of the derived ones" (p. 51). What he fails to see is that all revelations come through some institutional system and reveal as much of the institution as of some mystical public will. Change the rules, and you will get another revelation and another public will. Steiner was close to the truth when he noted, "Obviously the question 'What is the public interest?' has no simple answer. Indeed, asking the question invites the sort of smile reserved for small children and benign idiots" (p. 54). Indeed it is an illogical question altogether and not just a matter of acknowledging the complexity of the answer and promising that one day clever research will finally reveal the true rock of common value.

FROM GLOBAL EFFICIENCY TO INFORMED CONFLICT

There is no better hole to go to. There is not even any given hole. When interests conflict, to ask the question of what constitutes social welfare in total is to deny that conflict. There is no better hole because the question is inconsistent with the reality of human differences. (This is not to deny that at any given moment a given society has widely shared values. In this case, the rules affecting who chooses do not matter, since the choice is the same whoever chooses.) In the face of differences, the question assumes away the agony of moral choice of the question, Who is my brother? We stand naked in our differences without the clothing warmth of the high priests, economist or otherwise. People must and will choose their accommodation, or they fight, or they live in suspended hate and unwilling participation. If we insist on cloaking our choice in the metaphysics of social welfare, global efficiency, freedom for the people, or nearness to God, we can appreciate the chill that drives us. Perhaps the human animal can never stand complete self-consciousness and needs self-delusion and ceremonialism to get up in the morning. Still, they make our discourse more difficult.

It is not in the realm of science to abolish conflict. Differences there will always be. But we are capable of understanding conflict.[24] So much human conflict over proposed rule changes is simply uninformed.[25] People have little warranted knowledge of the range of real performance consequences of alternative rules. Such knowledge does not remove the conflict, but at least if one has such knowledge, one can make sure the conflict is over real differences in the type of world different people want to live in rather than over some mistaken notion of what kind of world a new rule would likely produce. The scientist can play the role of provider of consumer and voter information, which can be the background for people choosing (learning) their preferences both of goods (performance) and of institutions. This role does not short-circuit the process by which people make choices by telling them they have already really made the choice that will now be made known to them along with the derived deductions as applied to the case in question. Of course, provision of information is not value free, but it is of a different order than the value presumptions hidden in the choice rules discussed above. Information on impacts of alternative rights is itself subject to interdependence created by information costs. Those with access to cheap impact data can use it to influence public choice of rights.

To conclude, there is nothing in this chapter that should be interpreted as being against the calculation of specific efficiency when objectives of the individual chooser are made explicit. For the most part, the chapter is an argument against presumptive choices among conflicting interests contained in theories and calculations of global efficiency. Whenever there is conflict of interest, to speak of global efficiency is to make a value judgment weighting the interests of one party over another. The plea of this chapter is for the speaker to make explicit the weighting expressing his or her own value judgment or that of the client being served. Inquiry into which institution/right is better can be clarified by asking, Better for whom? Each must apply his or her own answer. This chapter is an argument against the high-priest role of economic analysis but not an argument for or against a different set of values than those presumed in neo-classical theory or any other. Much still can be done in predicting the substantive consequences of alternative property rights for the various parties.

It is to this task of providing warranted, empirical information of rules consequences that we now turn in Chapter 12. Our objective, however, is modest. There is no presumption that informed choice assures wisdom or peace.

NOTES

1. What is included in this section would be placed in most texts under the heading of "market failure." The term has been avoided so as not to prejudge the issues.

2. Since concepts are value imbedded, any analysis unwittingly has judgmental elements.

3. Only government action controlled by a unanimity rule would be Pareto-better.

4. Political alteration of rights is regarded as theft by some. Recall Pierre Joseph Proudhon's (1970) definition of property as theft.

5. The payment that is made is an externality, but Pareto-irrelevant. The Pareto-relevant have been internalized.

6. "Economists can also discount the idea that it is necessary to know who counts, or who is imposing upon whom or who has the property rights before one can usefully make efficient analyses of these troublesome joint products" (Seagraves 1973, p. 619).

7. Economists are nearly united in their opposition to common property. See, for example, Cheung (1970) and Demsetz (1967).

8. The symmetry could be restored if it were equally easy for B to interfere with A's use of the sun. But given their location, this is impossible. However, B could do

other things, such as blow up A's building. These opportunities are usually subject to injunction or criminal penalties, but if B could create a harm to A and the court would assess only a $10,000 damage and if A is aware of this possibility, A will not interfere with B's sun rights and B is the resource user whether A or B is the original owner. B creates and pays $10,000 damage to A to prevent the loss of a resource worth $15,000 or buys the resource outright for $10,000.

9. This point is extensively developed in Bartlett (1973). Bartlett asks what Pareto-optimality means when resources are used to influence demand as well as cater to it (also see Goldberg 1974, pp. 464-74).

10. There is nothing above that cannot be found in the literature. Even writers sympathetic to Coase will note in passing or in a footnote the many qualifications of the Coase rule. Yet the message that they wish us to remember seems to obscure these qualifications. For example: "To sum up, then: when negotiation is possible, the case for government intervention is one of justice not of economic efficiency" (Turvey 1963, pp. 309-13).

11. One such meter is "the demand revealing process," or the Clark tax (see Tideman 1977).

12. If A refuses to buy three channels for a price of $5.50, the producer may only provide two channels, which is not efficient.

13. If those who don't work get into the movies free, maybe those paying will decide not to work.

14. Nancy Ruggles (1968, p. 38) says, "Every pricing system results in some sort of income distribution. . . . In choosing a pricing system it thus becomes necessary to make specific assumptions about interpersonal comparisons of utility, and then to judge the pricing system in relation to these assumptions as well as in relation to the marginal conditions."

15. A term used by Breton (1974, p. 4) to indicate the definition of equilibrium conditions that are incapable of implementation by any known institution.

16. For a review of the literature, see Winfrey (1973, chap. 3), Ochs (1974, chap. 3), and Mueller (1976).

17. This has been sharply analyzed by Burkhead and Miner (1971, pp. 138-39).

18. Francis Bator (1962, p. 7) says, "The point is clear enough—public good and decreasing cost phenomena cause private decisions to go wrong." He hastens to add that inefficient markets may still do better than any alternative.

19. Posner suggests that since courts have used this right in the past in formulating the common law of nuisance, they should use it in the future. Since he criticizes a random assignment of property rights in the face of high transaction costs, it follows that he regards an equal initial distribution as inefficient.

20. Krutilla and Fisher argue that early discussions of wilderness-retention policy "could be based only on what some persons might regard as rather vague equity considerations." But they claim that "although we do not make any assumptions about the priority of rights, results (favoring nondestructive use) . . . are obtained solely from considerations of efficiency" (1975, p. 73). They do not make clear whose efficiency they are implementing.

21. John Rawls (1971) suggests that widespread agreement on constitutional rules could be obtained if people had to decide them before they knew their own position and payoffs in the ensuing economic game. The suggestion of Rawls is that people will favor equality. This seems doubtful, for people can and do differ in their concept of a

fair game, since some are risk-averse and others seek the thrill of gambling for an improbable but large payoff. For a critique, see Scott Gordon (1976).

22. See, for example, Hayek (1944), Friedman (1962), and Stigler (1975). Friedman says it is a loss of freedom for government to explicitly have an income distribution objective (equity). "Freedom is my god." This implicitly accepts current rights distribution and does not avoid equity choices. For a critique, see Samuels (1976).

23. This work has been collected in Eirik G. Furubotn and Svetozar Pejovich (1974). Also see Anderson and Hill (1974) and Posner (1972b). For a critique, see Ogus (1983), Veljanovski (1981b), and Kornhauser (1980, pp. 163-80).

24. "It is not the business of political philosophy and science to determine what the state in general should or must be. What they may do is to aid in creation of methods such that experimentation may go on less blindly, less at the mercy of accident, more intelligently" (Dewey 1922, p. 34). Also see Johnson (1986, chap. 9).

25. Kenneth Boulding (1973, p. 63) has formulated what he calls the law of political irony: "Political conflict rests to a very large extent on a universal ignorance of consequences, as the people who are benefited by any particular act or policy are rarely those who struggled for it, and the people who are injured are rarely those who opposed it. . . . Bad definition and the failure of perceptual discrimination are perhaps the most important source of bad politics."

V

Testing the Paradigm

Twelve

Empirical Institutional Studies

The institutional theory of this book is not intended to provide a global guide to labeling one set of rules as efficient or inefficient. The theory's primary use is in guiding empirical inquiry into the substantive consequences of alternative institutions. Comparisons are made among real alternatives and not with an abstract ideal. The purpose of the book is to provide a better basis for an empirical institutional analysis, perhaps best illustrated by a review of a sample of empirical studies. The review should demonstrate that (1) institutional analysis is a workable and useful field of inquiry, (2) the concepts of the book can be used to formulate hypotheses for testing, and (3) the short summaries illustrate less well the important role of acquiring knowledge of institutional detail and history. Before we proceed to this review, the conceptual elements from the preceding chapters will be summarized into methodological steps and the meaning of institutional research will be clarified.

There is a parallel between production-function estimation and a predictive institutional economics. In the same way that we explore the effect of alternative factor inputs on output of goods and services, we will explore the effect of alternative institutions on human behavior. The big question is, Do alternative institutions make a difference?

The basic model relates situation, structure, and performance. Situation refers to the inherent sources of interdependence. Structure identifies chosen institutional alternatives in terms of varieties of property rights and their distribution. The behavior and actions of people individually and aggregatively in firms and government agencies result in performance in terms of various intermediate products and finally the quality of human life. Policy analysis requires a total inquiry. But it is useful to distinguish between the study of institutions, which is concerned with the link between institutional alternatives and behavior, and production analysis, which studies the link between behavior with respect to resource combinations and goods and services. Such a distinction can be illustrated with an extract from an article by the author (1972, p. 894).

Consider zero population growth. It is one thing to analyze the result of ZPG on the economy in terms of income and productivity, but it is quite different to establish the connection between the alternative institutional rules that result in women having fewer babies. For example, what child-bearing behavior results from giving each woman the marketable right to bear two children? What difference does it make if the rights are initially sold to the highest bidder? . . .

Or, consider research on limiting fertilizer in agriculture. We need biological data on the relationship of fertilizer runoff and aquatic life. This can be combined with information on agricultural production and demand to indicate the effect on food prices and production location as a result of different levels of fertilizer use. This is not institutional research. One institutional alternative is a legal prohibition of fertilizer use. The question is whether this in fact will obtain the given behavior (or what other behavior it also will induce). Experience with liquor and pot prohibitions indicate that this institutional form does not always produce the implied behavior.

A maximization or simulation model utilizing a production function with different constraints on fertilizer use is quite different from simulating a behavioral reaction to alternative institutions which influence the amount of fertilizer actually used. Most of the current policy models are incomplete because they begin with an assumed conduct and inquire of performance.

People seem to find it both productive and irritating to associate with other people. It seems useful then for problem-solving research to first ask what is the good or resource at issue and then categorize the inherent cause of human interdependence that the good creates (situation). What is it about different goods that influences how one person can affect another for good or otherwise? Note again that these features exist prior to the analysis and are not determined by the rights being analyzed.

The next step is to specify the alternative institutions to be chosen as well as relevant institutional variables to be held constant. Again, the institutional or property-rights variables can be stated quite literally as rule X and rule Y, but it may be useful to categorize them in a more general manner in order to make comparisons among alternatives that are structurally similar even though differing in specific application. One such categorization (bargained, administrative, and status-grant alternatives) was distinguished. When a certain performance is desired, different mixes of those transactions can be made.

The major institutional alternatives are often phrased in terms of government regulation versus what is euphemistically called the free market, or government provision through taxation versus market bargaining and contracts.

Economists seem to gravitate toward grouping institutional alternatives in terms of market versus non-market decision systems. This probably is from habit and from argumentative strategy. Economic theory was born as people revolted against the kings, and the rules of feudalism were under pressure from a new merchant class intent on trade. Ever since, many economists have been preoccupied with rationales for the superiority of the market over government intervention (Arrow and Scitovsky 1969, p. 2). This is often an unfortunate dichotomy, since there are many ways to structure the opportunity sets in a market, and the difference in performance may be as great among alternative markets as between markets and nonmarkets. Certainly the dichotomy between capitalism and socialism, while useful in some respects, covers more differences within each than between in many instances.

In the review to follow, no one set of institutional categories will be slavishly followed. The choice is often dictated by the available studies or, for future research, by the availability of actual property-rights alternatives to be observed. Sometimes type of transaction will be contrasted, sometimes other ways to categorize rights systems will be used, and sometimes the alternative will be a different interpersonal distribution of rights within a given system.

The essence of the formulation is to relate the institutional variables to performance while considering the type of human interdependence involved in the situation. The utility of the theory is to specify carefully the institutional alternatives being tested and to know when to control for other background institutional variables. In practice, it is often necessary to control for other situational economic and technological variables that might affect the performance results observed. For example, in examining the effect of alternative forms of business organization on production costs, it is necessary to separate out the effect of economies of scale from the effect of the rules on managers' choices. There may be interaction and feedback between the two. Thus, the institutional economist often needs to combine knowledge of human behavior with knowledge of the physical production function.

The final step is the actual empirical test. Since the analyst seldom has the opportunity to set up an experiment assigning some people or states to one institution and some other people to another institution, success in this area of research depends on taking advantage of contrasts and changes as they occur. Formulation of causal tests in this context is called quasi-experimental design by statisticians. The emphasis in this review is not on statistical method, but some of the variety of designs will be noted. (The terminology used is loosely based on Campbell and Stanley 1963.) Since the emphasis is on model formulation and specification of the variables, no critique of methods will be made. The purpose is not to arrive at conclusions on the consequences of a given set of institutional alternatives, thus, the statistical method and weight of the supporting evidence in all available studies are not reviewed. Still, the author cannot entirely resist some casual empiricism in some cases where the available systematic studies seem most narrowly conceived and one-sided; nor can he resist a few comments to emphasize a theoretical point discussed earlier that might illuminate policy options.

Institutional research obtains knowledge from methodologies ranging from formal quantitative hypothesis testing to what McCloskey (1985) refers to as the "rhetorical methods" of history, case study, analogy, and introspection. The performance of alternative institutions is often sufficiently expressed in directional and qualitative terms (Simon 1978).

The cases reviewed below are loosely grouped into a number of commodity and problem areas. They are chosen to include a wide variety of situations to demonstrate the scope of possible institutional research and to test the generality of the theory.

NATURAL RESOURCES

The study of property rights in land has a long history. While landownership is no longer the major source of wealth in industrial economies, it is the basis for many current disputes over environmental policy. Land tenure remains an important issue in agricultural economies around the world (Cline 1970; Parsons, Penn, and Raup 1956). Several other natural-resource issues are explored below.

Air Pollution

Use of land for cattle ranching and citrus production is incompatible with use for airborne disposal of waste fluorides from the manufacture of superphosphates. This interdependence situation became known in Florida in 1955.[1] Apparently there was no legislation that specifically placed ownership of this dimension of land resource in the hands of farmers or phosphate manufacturers. Therefore the effective right accrued to whoever could physically appropriate the resource. Appropriation was done by the manufacturers to the detriment of the farmers.

What ultimate resource use might be expected under this set of property rules? The farmers could make market bids to the manufacturers to reduce the pollution. It seems reasonable to believe that the transaction costs of such a contract would be high relative to its value. Exclusion costs would be high, and free-rider behavior might be expected. (In the large-number case, it would be the unwitting free riders.) It would be costly for farmers to monitor the agreed upon waste-disposal level. Even if the farmers owned the resource, the transaction costs of making that ownership effective were high. The farmer would have to prove which particular plant caused the damage and prove that any observed reduction of farm production was in fact owing to the pollution. Court costs would be substantial. Information costs were formidable. In a situation of high exclusion and information costs, a market structure with factor ownership by industry could be expected to result in a performance of the resource being used by industry with few bids from farmers. In fact, it was observed that farmers made no bids. In turn, phosphate companies owned only 50 percent of the land affected by their operations in 1955. Court suits were filed.

In 1958, an air-pollution control district was funded by government. The exact character of the rights change is not clear, but "the companies were told to buy up those lands subject to pollution damages or face the prospect of having to get their emissions down to what was termed the 'minimum technologically feasible level' " (Crocker 1971, pp. 456–57). Apparently, the companies were not given the option simply to pay damages (see Chapter 6). This detail is critical to performance, as shall be noted below; it is not sufficiently descriptive just to say that ownership of the resource changed.

The companies now needed to acquire an input that they did not own. They had two major production options. They could install control equipment or purchase the land, whichever was cheaper, assuming they had a cushion of profit out of which to pay these new input costs. Apparently they chose a mixture of these inputs and increased the ownership of the land affected by their pollution from 50 to 80 percent and decreased the volume of fluoride emissions.

The relationship between exposure to fluoride and farmland productivity is a physiological one. Once people understand it, the relationship between land value and pollution should be constant over time, other things being equal, such as the volume of pollution. How is land value affected by ownership? If farmers own the marketable right to be free of damage, their money income is the same whether they receive their net income in the form of current damage payments reflecting the present value of future net income or normal unpolluted farm returns. The damage payment amounts to rental of a portion of the land's productive capacity. If an equation explaining land values is constructed with a pollution variable, the regression coefficient for the amount of pollution suffered by different parcels should be statistically nonsignificant.

If farmers do not own the right to be free of damage, they have a differentially productive asset depending on their exposure to pollution, just as if fertility differed. The regression coefficient for the pollution variable in this case should be significant and negative. An equation can be estimated for each year before and after the change in property right occasioned by the creation of the air-pollution control district.

Such a regression equation has been estimated by Thomas Crocker (1971) for citrus land. The dependent variable is land value. The equation includes a pollution variable as well as variables for tree quality, size, and land improvements. The regression coefficient for pollution is generally not significant prior to the change in property rights and is significant and negative after the change, contrary to the hypothesis above. Unfortunately, with correlation as the quasi-experimental design, all other possible explanations cannot be ruled out. The nonsignificance of the prerule pollution coefficient might be owing to lack of awareness of the causal effect between fluorides and citrus production. Damage is suffered, but no one is sure why. This awareness and the change in rules occurred together. While the potential causal effects of some variables are controlled in the regression, some remain unknown.

The postrule significant and negative coefficients need explanation. While the phosphate plants did acquire more land and did reduce emission, it is possible that some pollution remained uncompensated. Apparently the rule changed, but its administration was such that citrus growers did not have the effective right to be free of all damage. Perhaps what one observes is only a nominal rule change that should not be expected to produce a nonsignificant pollution coefficient. The size of the coefficients did decrease over time.

Crocker estimated another equation for pasture land. For the four years examined after the rule change, the coefficient for the pollution variable was significant and positive. Both the significance and the sign are contrary to the above hypotheses. This is where the form of the rule change may be critical. Somehow the ranchers were able to sell land to phosphate companies at more than agricultural rent. What right might explain this superior bargaining power? The phosphate firms, up to a point, find it cheaper to buy land than to reduce emissions. The capture of this saving is open to negotiation between phosphate firms and ranchers. If the firms had the right to use the air resource and had only to pay court-determined damages to the ranchers, the firms would capture all the cost saving. As noted in Chapter 6, this arrangement amounts to private condemnation. But, if the firms must negotiate to secure a willing seller, they will have to share the cost-saving difference between using air as a fluoride-disposal input and more-expensive techniques. In fact, since the phosphate plants have immobile assets limited in location to raw-material sites, the ranchers have great bargaining power. The strategic holdout has even greater power: land that was worth $150 per acre for ranching often sold for $250 to phosphate firms under the injunction rule. Alternatively, a court would base damages on the $150 value. This evidence suggests that the income-distribution consequences of the right to receive court-determined damages and the right to be free of damage along with the right to be a willing seller are quite different. The seller with a choice has the right to injunctive relief, as noted above in Chapter 6.

Why the different impact on citrus- and ranch-land values? Why could not citrus growers also extract premium payments from the phosphate firms? Why in fact did they continue to suffer damages after the rights changed? Crocker notes that some citrus growers did receive premium payments but offers no evidence explaining the difference between the regression results of the two types of land. In another connection, he notes that in general the pasture sites were closer to the phosphate plant locations than were citrus sites. Could it be that the citrus growers had higher transaction costs in proving that they were damaged by a particular plant? Other explanations may lie in the way that air-resource rights were administered. Is it possible that there is some reason for ranchers to be better organized and successful in getting their problems taken care of by government? Perhaps the air control district did not put as much pressure on plants to buy damaged citrus lands as it did for ranch land. Citrus land is considerably more expensive than ranch land, and phosphate firms may have found it cheaper to put in pollution-control equipment rather than buy land. But why did some damage persist? Perhaps the citrus growers faced high transaction costs in protecting their rights.

Another type of property right is possible. In 1964, the state abandoned the above rules and instituted emission standards. It can be hypothesized that since the land-disposal input is prohibited, the premium paid for ranch land would cease. In fact, in 1965 and 1966 the pollution regression coefficients were statistically insignificant for both citrus and ranch land. The agricultural users received less pollution but lost the right to bargain for land-sale value premiums with phosphate firms. The firms supposedly incurred greater costs as they used more expensive disposal resources.

There is one other performance difference that should be noted. It is possible to design rights to receive damage payments (fees) and rights to emission standards so that the agricultural landowners' wealth positions are similar with each type of rule. But emission standards also give rights to people who use the air resource but are not landowners.[2] One such group are tourists who pass through the area. If a phosphate owner reaches a market agreement with the landowner that results in use of the air for waste disposal, the interests of the tourists do not count. Those who want to pass through the area and to breathe clean air could also be given damages or injunctive relief, but the transaction costs would be high. The cost of court suit relative to individual benefit would prevent individual unilateral action.

Water Pollution

There are many aspects of institutions relating to water use that might be subject to empirical investigation. Only one will be noted here, namely, the consequences of achieving a given level of water quality via regulatory standards versus charges or user fees. Economists are nearly united in their preference for user fees. This preference is based largely on theoretical deduction of comparative efficiency rather than any systematic empirical observation of the performance of different institutions.

Theory of the firm calls attention to the least-cost combination of resource inputs in producing a given product. Many individual products involve production of wastes. These may be disposed of by using streams or by various treatment technologies. Most research in this area presumes some political process that decides on the level of water quality and the institutional question is simply one of asking if the rules permit the given quality level to be met at the lowest cost (Freeman, Haveman, and Kneese 1973, pp. 112–15). Usually some boundary is assumed, such as a river basin. This conventional formulation of the problem will be illustrated and discussed below.

Consider a basin where only two industries are located. Firm A, because of its particular product and available technology, produces 800 pounds of waste per day and is faced with a marginal cost of 3¢ for reducing waste to the stream by one pound. Firm B has a marginal cost for waste reduction of 15¢ and produces 1,600 pounds of waste per day. Initially 2,400 pounds of waste are released to the stream. Suppose that government decides that the performance goal is 1,600 pounds. This can be achieved by a regulatory standard that orders each firm to reduce its waste discharge by one-third. What is the cost of achieving this standard? Firm A now reduces its waste by 267 pounds at a marginal cost of 3¢ for a total firm cost of $8. Firm B reduces its waste by 533 pounds at a marginal cost of 15¢ for a total firm cost of $79. Total cost to meet the river basin performance objective and reduce waste by 800 pounds is $87.

This cost can be compared to that of the fee approach. Suppose that after some experimentation or experience from other areas, the government finds that a charge of 3.5¢ will result in the two firms adjusting their production processes so that a total of 1600 pounds of waste is discharged. (If the government knows the marginal cost schedule of waste removal for each firm, it can compute the charge that will reduce pounds discharged to any given level; if not, it can discover the appropriate charge by trial and error.) What is the cost of achieving the same water quality with the fee approach? Firm A, when faced with a fee of 3.5¢ per pound, will treat all of its waste at the cheaper cost of 3¢ and no waste will be discharged. Firm A's cost is .03 × 800 pounds equals $24. Firm B will find it cheaper to pay the discharge fee than to reduce its wastes. The cost to Firm B is 0.35 × 1,600 pounds equals $56. Total basin cost of achieving the performance objective is $80, which is cheaper than the $87 cost of achieving the same performance via a regulatory rule requiring a uniform percentage reduction for all firms. This difference would not always occur but does when treatment costs facing the firms differ widely. With the regulatory standard, a high-cost-of-treatment firm is forced to use expensive treatment technology rather than the cheaper assimilative capacity of the stream. The conventional analysis stops at this point and concludes that the institution of effluent charges is more efficient than regulation (Dick 1974, pp. 67–70).

The above analysis focuses on total costs, ignores their distribution, and thus leads to a policy recommendation with differential effects on different kinds of firms. Additional perspective can be gained by looking behind the economics of resource combinations to the implied property rights and opportunity sets (Burrows 1980). A regulatory standard implies that each firm owns some right to dispose of some quantity of waste in the stream. This is also implied in the doctrine of reasonable use. As the standard is increased, the amount owned by each firm diminishes and the amount owned by third-party environmentalists increases. If the application of the standard requires each polluter to reduce by a given percentage, the relative amount owned by each firm is constant and proportional to its preregulatory use.

An effluent charge changes this relationship. A charge assumes that the resource is totally owned by the government. If a charge is set to achieve a certain level of water quality, firms are thereby differentially treated. Recall that the charge means that the firms with higher treatment costs are allowed to substitute cheaper assimilative capacity of the stream for the higher-cost treatment. But where did they get the right to this stream capacity relative to the rights held under the prior rule of reasonable use? From the firms with lower-cost treatment. While total cost of treatment can be less with the charges approach, Firm A's cost increases greatly (from $8 with regulation to $24 with charges). This increase represents a redistribution of income between the firms as well as between the firms and third-party environmentalists. Thus, the manner in which environmentalist rights are expanded affects the relative welfare of each industrial firm. From this analysis, one might hypothesize that firms with low treatment cost would prefer the regulatory approach and high-cost firms the effluent charges approach. This hypothesis should be subject to empirical test. (This is quite a different hypothesis as to the demand for the two types of institutions from that offered by Buchanan and Tullock 1975, pp. 139–47.)

If transactions were costless, we might expect that resource combinations would be unaffected by the choice of institution. Under regulation, if Firm A owns a certain portion of the assimilative capacity of a stream, it will sell it to Firm B whenever Firm B's offer price exceeds A's cost of treatment. Firm B will be able to substitute the cheaper resource input obtained from A rather than utilize its own more costly treatment. But, in this case, A's welfare is enhanced because it is paid for the resource instead of suffering a redistribution.

In the eastern United States, where riparian water law is dominant, rights to assimilative capacity (or any use rights) are not transferable. Even if they were, it would be costly to exclude waste-disposal users who did not pay for the resource. It is one thing to police water quality below a firm's discharge point and determine if the reduction in quality compared with the quality above that point is within allowable limits. It is another to determine who is using the increased capacity made available when a former given user ceases and sells out. In short, there are high transaction costs for Firm B to seek out firms that might want to sell, and there would be high policing costs to keep other firms from using the resource. It can be hypothesized that regulation and charges are not likely to achieve the same resource use by industrial firms.

When the rights of third-party environmentalists are expanded, a conflict arises between two industrial firms in the sharing of the costs of redistribution. Thus, there is a conflict between achieving equal treatment between two firms and achieving lowest costs of attaining a given stream quality for both firms considered as a single firm—a conflict that would not occur if transaction costs were zero.

The above analysis is illustrated with reference to hypothetical cost data and can be extended to observation of the costs facing actual firms in a given river basin (Johnson 1967, p. 297). Such research is empirical, but whether it is empirical institutional research is another question. The research does not observe performance under two different institutions. We cannot be sure that firms will follow the orders of a regulatory body or that the quantities charged for are the quantities of waste actually discharged. While regulations and charges could be designed to obtain the same water-quality level, some interest groups may think that they could more effectively influence a regulatory body proceeding under historical regulatory procedures than a new body charged with leasing the public's water.

BUSINESS PERFORMANCE

Arguments over the form of business organization have an ancient history. Some of the alternatives include the degree of separation of ownership and control, stock versus mutual or cooperative firms, public versus privately owned firms, and capitalist versus worker-owned firms. Other organizational variables involve internal arrangements of individual and team work, supervisory relationships, worker participation in planning and management, partnerships (Leibowitz and Tollison 1980), and forms of productivity audit (Evan 1971). For a review of literature on how organizational structure affects the resolution of conflicts within multi-person managerial groups see Leibenstein (1979).

Manager versus Owner-Dominated Firms

Consequences of the separation of ownership and control constitute a classic issue at least since Adam Smith, who worried about the stewardship of the directors of joint stock companies (1937, bk. 5, chap. 1). The individual proprietor could easily see the relationship between effort and personal income. But in the large corporation, the welfare of the manager may not be closely related to the income of the stockholder. The dispersal of ownership is hypothesized to make it difficult for stockholders to select managers who best serve stockholders. Decision and information costs work against stockholders exercising their nominal rights to determine who manages the firm. (A contrary hypothesis is offered by Armen Alchian [1969].)

It is usually assumed that the stockholder has a singleness of purpose centering on dividends and profit rates, while the nominally hired manager is served by wages and other perquisites of position, including the easy life. Most studies of the consequences of the degree of owner domination focus on profit rates, testing the hypothesis that the interests of the manager are served at the expense of firm net return. While this focus seems reasonable, it should be remembered that stockholders have other interests as well. This fact was made clear in the United States during the Vietnam War, when various organizational holders of stock were forced by their members to ask if their stockholdings were in firms that made certain war materials. Fama (1980) argues that managers are disciplined by the market for their services and not directly by participating in profits. But, how do other firms get the information to know who to bid for?

Frederic Pryor (1973) defines a firm as under management control if no single individual or block controls more than 15 percent of the stock. Pryor estimates that 76 percent of major U.S. firms in 1963 were under management control. Various empirical estimates have been made on the consequences of the degree of managerial control, with conflicting conclusions. David Kamerschen (1968) used multiple regression analysis to test for the relationship between managerial control and profit rates. Variables held constant included several related to market power, growth rate, and size. Managerial control had no significant effect on profit rates. Another study using a similar technique for another data set found that managerial control had only a small influence on profits (Larner 1970). Still another study using a three-way analysis of variance found that manager domination led to a profit rate 5.5 percent less than owner-dominated firms (Monsen, Chiu, and Cooley 1968). Industry type was held constant.

John Shelton (1967) compared profit rates of identical restaurants in a large chain. Profits were higher where the restaurant was operated by the franchise owner rather than by a hired manager. Casual observation suggests that outstanding cuisine is found only in small, owner-operated restaurants as contrasted to chains or large establishments with much hired help, though a consistent quality can be found in some of the chains as contrasted to the uncertainty of the local greasy spoon.

A variety of the separation-of-ownership-and-control phenomenon is contained in the mutual firm that is nominally owned by the customers. In a mutual savings and loan association, each saver may own one share with voting rights. The management is little restrained by formal voting of the nominal owners in either mutuals or stock firms with dispersed ownership. There are some differences. In the mutual, the shareholding customer does not receive a dividend but obtains benefits in the form of services and prices not available to customers of nonmutuals. Shares are not marketable so that it is not possible to capitalize future earnings (see Chapter 8). It can be hypothesized that mutual shareholders have less incentive to use their time to influence managers to initiate cost savings that would create long-term net income since these future earnings are like high-exclusion-cost goods and cannot be captured in present values in the market. One must stay with the firm to reap the benefits of any future income gains.

A comparison of mutual and stock savings and loan associations has been made by Alfred Nicols (1967). Performance variables included growth in assets, market-share changes, expenses, gross operating income, allocations to reserves, and management nepotism. Some of these variables were tested in simple comparisons of averages between stock and mutual firms. Nicols also estimated a regression relating expenses to loan and savings activity. "When the California and Los Angeles stock data with respect to these variables are related to the regression coefficients, a mutual area with the same product mix would have had expenses of 62.6 percent . . . higher than what was actually achieved by the stock associations" (p. 342). Another major finding was a slower rate of growth of the mutuals.

If mutuals do not pay a residual profits dividend to shareholders, one might expect them to pay higher interest to their saver members. On the basis of a limited two-year observation of mutuals and stock firms in the same states, this was found not to be the case. The stock firms paid a higher ratio of interest to savings capital. If we hypothesize that capital mobility limits manager discretion in stock firms, it seems logical to expect that customer mobility would limit managers in mutual firms. How do mutuals maintain their customers?[3] This question raises a further question as to the relevant performance variables. Do the customers of mutual firms find some product there that they do not find in stock firms? This question remains to be explored.

Anyone with statistical training can compare the performance of alternative types of business organizations. But theory is necessary in order to know what independent variables to control for. Production and marketing theory suggests that we control for product mix, firm size, and market-power variables. Institutional theory suggests that we control for certain other human interdependence variables. Is the observed difference in mutual and stock firm performance because of the separation of ownership and control or because of the difference in marketability of rights to profit residuals or because of some other institutional factor? Is it possible that the effect observed is owing to degree of ownership dispersal rather than share marketability? This question remains to be answered.

Adequate institutional theory is critical if we wish to search for changes in one property-rights alternative to make it perform more like another. Is there some dominant feature of the mutual firm's structuring of opportunity sets that accounts for performance, or could a small change be made in one feature to change performance? Test of this cannot be conceived without an adequate institutional theory. Too often we are content with a plausible explanation for observed differences when the hypothesized cause itself has not been tested by separation from other potentially causal features. For example, it might be instructive to compare credit unions with mutual and stock savings and loan firms. This comparison is suggested by concepts of the role of status transactions and the sense of community. It was noted in Chapter 3 that learned behavior habits can substitute for the incentive otherwise supplied by exclusion from benefits. Credit union managers are exposed to national organizations and a history of cooperative ideology that may not be present for mutual managers. This fact might give some indication whether the observed mutual performance is inevitable or whether some factors might be changed to alter performance.

One of the problems in applying the results of empirical research is differences in scale. In experimental design, this is called a threat to external validity. The Nicols study suggests the performance of mutual firms in an economy dominated by the stock-corporation form of ownership. What would be the case if most firms were mutuals or cooperatives? Would they behave differently? Do we have any theory to guide further inquiry? One factor explored above was learned cultural habits. In a world dominated by mutual firms, these learned common expectations may be easier to create and may be sufficient to obtain cost-saving behavior. And, then again, this culture may be difficult to establish.

Since the purpose here is not to argue for any conclusions on the performance of institutional alternatives, the above is sufficient to demonstrate the type of hypothesis subject to test with a variety of quasi-experimental design methodologies. It is left to the reader to think whether all of the relevant variables have been controlled. From the list of types of human interdependencies in Part II, is there any reason to think that the ability of stockholders or customers to limit the discretion of managers might vary among different industries? What affects information costs and thereby the mobility of capital or customers as an incentive for managers to perform in the stockholders' or shareholders' interests? When these latter interests conflict, whose interests count under alternative property rights?

Private versus Public Ownership

The theoretical hypotheses for differences in private and public ownership have already been suggested. In a sense, the public firm is a version of the separation of management and control. The essence of the conventional hypotheses is that under public ownership, the costs and benefits of a decision are less fully borne by the decision maker than under private ownership. Or is it that the two systems may serve different owners rather than serve an undifferentiated set of owners more or less efficiently? This latter point will be pursued by raising questions about the performance variables used.

Ideal comparisons of public and private firm performance would utilize firms of the same size producing the same product in the same country. Alas, natural experiments of this type do not often present themselves for analysis. Few countries have major industries that are composed of both private and public firms. (Some time series analysis might be possible in the United Kingdom, where firms are alternately nationalized and privatized with political party victories.) A comparison of socialist and capitalist countries is not a good test of alternate ownership of firms because it is also involved with a different relationship among firms as well.[4] In the countries without strong central planning, public ownership is largely limited to utilities and transportation. As discussed in Chapter 4, these industries are marked by extraordinary economies of scale, and most countries prefer government regulation even if the ownership of the firms is private. Thus, the available comparisons are fewer than the amount desired to test the difference in private and public ownership, since both involve direct government regulation of price and often of service. There is also the case of mixed ownership (Seidman 1975). Nominal ownership via public members of a board of directors means little.

Airlines

Australia provides an opportunity to contrast the performances of a privately and a publicly owned interstate airline. The government regulates prices and routes and allocates needed capacity equally between them. They have nearly equal equipment and wage rates. Per-employee performance measures were tons of freight and mail carried, the number of paying passengers carried, and the revenue earned. A simple comparison by David Davies (1971) of the two companies over a number of years shows that the private company was more efficient with respect to these measures. A question might be raised as to the comparability of outputs, such as timeliness of service or labor relations.

Electric Utilities

The United States provides another example with its regulated privately and publicly (municipal) owned electric utilities. A commonly used experimental design is to formulate a regression including private or municipal ownership as a dummy variable and including variables that production theory would suggest might affect costs and outputs, such as size of firm. The results of various studies have been summarized by Louis DeAlessi as follows:

Municipal firms, relative to privately-owned regulated firms, in general will: charge lower prices; have greater capacity; spend more on plant construction; have higher operating costs; engage in less wealth maximizing price discrimination, including fewer peak-related tariffs; relate price discrimination less closely to the demand and supply conditions applicable to each group of users; favor business relative to residential users; offer a smaller variety of output; change prices less frequently and in response to larger changes in economic determinants; adopt cost-reducing innovations less readily; maintain managers in office longer; exhibit greater variation in rates of return. (1974, p.36)

The theory behind each of these results will not be reviewed here again except to note the theory related to rate structure. As noted in Chapter 7, different groups of customers have different demand elasticities, and separation of these groups is relatively cheap with respect to electric service. Business customers can be charged a different rate than residential when resale is relatively difficult. Massachusetts voters in 1976 turned down a referendum to prohibit industrial and residential rate differentiation. Price differentiation increases total revenue for any given level of output. As noted above, there is empirical evidence to support the belief that if public managers have less incentive to maximize profits, they will practice less price differentiation than private managers. (This hypothesis is complicated by regulation of total returns. Regulatory bodies have traditionally given more attention to controlling the overall rate of return than to allocation of charges among different users. This focus is now changing.) Is this difference owing to a simple lack of incentive to maximize returns, or is it in response to a different set of "owners," whose concept of fairness does not permit all the discrimination that is possible? The answer to this would require more elaborate tests.

The results summarized above were obtained to a large extent from regressions containing a dummy variable for private or public ownership, which is a very gross distinction that hides many variations in rules within each. In the earlier discussion of different kinds of transactions, the point was made that the market is not a single alternative. Many alternative rules and opportunity sets are possible within the market-bargained transaction. The same is true for administrative transactions. Much work remains to be done in specifying the institutional variable. Some progress has been made in this regard in a study of private and public electric utilities by Marc Roberts (1975). He focused on environmental practices as a performance variable. He found no consistent differences in these practices. Some private firms had clean stacks and protected the environment while some public firms did not and vice versa. His sample was comprised of three public and three private firms. Roberts suggested that performance is not determined by any simple private-public distinction but is a function of a complicated set of differences in history, fuel prices, external pressures, the strength of internal control mechanisms, and the balance of group perspectives within each organization (pp. 425-26). Alternative property rights apply not only to different groups of the public but also to different groups within the firm. These rights are not necessarily heavily circumscribed by public or private ownership.

Roberts does not regard the firm as a single profit-maximizing or utility-maximizing central computer. The following gives a flavor of the type of hypothesis he suggests: "In electric utilities, power plant operators value plant reliability. Hence, the forced outage rate of a system's facilities will be inversely related to the seniority and influence of the company's chief operating official and to the percentage of the organization's technical personnel who were operators at the time the plant was designed" (p. 426). This type of institutional data on administrative and status rights cannot easily be obtained for a large sample of firms. Roberts demonstrates the utility of the case-study approach, where a large number of subtle institutional variables can be obtained, but only for a few firms. A similar approach has been taken by David Granick

(1974) in a study of labor productivity as related to managerial performance in France, the United Kingdom, and the United States.

Fire Protection

In the United States fire protection is provided by municipal departments. One exception to this in Scottsdale, Arizona, presents an opportunity to test the performance of public and private firms. The city collects taxes and con-tracts with a private supplier for the service. Private contracting between in-dividual homeowners and firefighting companies was practiced in colonial America but has now disappeared. An analysis of this transformation from individual contract to municipally owned departments serving all might be instructive, particularly of the role of transaction costs. The primary impact of fire is damage to the individual property owner. If you do not buy the service, it is relatively cheap to exclude you from the service. However, if your neigh-bor does not buy protection, you may also be exposed to damage if the fire spreads. This could be accounted for by rules of liability, but most countries choose to have a tax-supported service equally available to all.

A comparison of the privately owned firefighting company of Scottsdale and municipally owned departments has been made by Roger Ahlbrandt (1973). He hypothesizes that the private company will provide lower-cost service. Pro-duction theory suggests that cost of service is related to size and wage rates. It might be possible to find several cities with public departments that are of the same size and wage level as Scottsdale, which would allow one to test the effect of ownership. A more sophisticated methodology was used by Ahl-brandt. He estimated a regression equation with data from 44 municipal de-partments with per-capita costs as the dependent variable. Independent vari-ables included population, area, assessed value, housing condition, wage index, equipment, and the fire-insurance rating index. (One additional variable was a dummy for paid, volunteer, or mixed departments. This might be interpreted as an institutional variable affecting some aspects of performance, but it is used by Ahlbrandt as a variable affecting factor costs.) The insurance-rating vari-able gives statistical control to output quality, since cost might be expected to vary with quality. This estimated cost function allows Ahlbrandt to plug in the appropriate variables for Scottsdale and derive what the cost would be if it were under municipal ownership. This cost can then be compared with the actual cost of the privately owned company. Such a comparison shows a 47-percent cost saving to the advantage of the privately owned company. In effect this figure represents a comparison of the cost for the average public firm with the cost for one private firm. It would be useful to note the variability in costs of public firms of the same size, and so on. Perhaps the skills of the managers are not held constant or the institutional alternatives affecting incentives are not fully specified by the public-private dichotomy.

The private company has made two key choices not typical of public departments. The private firm has made better use of new technologies developed by public research (U.S. Navy) and has built a new design of cost-saving trucks. It also has an arrangement with the city to utilize other city employees with additional pay to supplement the full-time firefighting employees. Firefighting is a service with peak loads, and employees are not utilized continuously. This cost saving, however, has not entirely escaped the notice of other city governments, but it has been resisted by firemen's unions. Failure to utilize police and other city employees as supplemental firefighters is a property right enhancing the employment of full-time firefighters.

There is some trade-off between cost saving and fire-damage risk. City employees who are called to aid full-time firefighters may create some time delay in service. Some citizens may prefer the trade-off available in Scottsdale to the one chosen by the typical city council and fire chief. One can imagine conflicting preferences in the same community. In any case, the research must exercise care in making cost comparisons. Difference in institutions sometimes means difference in product.

Education

It was hypothesized that private firms could teach disadvantaged children better than the usual public school teachers if payment was tied to learning gains (Gramlich and Koshel 1975). The performance variable was reading and math achievement. The experiment involved six different companies at 18 sites. The experimental design utilized matched groups of low-performing students. The companies used a variety of teaching methods. The results were equivocal. In areas where it is not clear what the best production methods are, an institutional evaluation of final performance is ambiguous. Do the results prove that private performance contracting does not work or that the educational production function is unknown regardless of institutional incentives? Most of the cases examined here involve formal legalistic rights, but the concepts can be applied to informal rights as well.

Human Blood Supply

One of the most precious goods in any society is human blood for transfusions. It can be transferred from producer to user under a variety of types of transactions. Various countries have different systems for provision of blood. Data on these systems have been assembled by Richard Titmuss (1971). No systematic experimental design is possible, but some evidence nevertheless emerges from international comparisons over time. Blood has some special characteristics as a product. It can be a carrier of a killing disease called serum hepatitis. However, the quality of blood is difficult to determine. Information costs are thus high. The most reliable determination of quality is the truthful reporting of medical history by the person producing the blood. Thus, the motivation of the individual from whose vein the blood is drawn is a critical factor in the health of the person who needs a transfusion. Japan represents countries who rely heavily on the market transaction to produce blood. Most of the blood is bought and sold. It is hypothesized that in market transactions, there is a minimum of feeling of community between the parties. The producer is motivated by the possibility of payment and not the needs of the buyer. Thus, it is possible that people who need money will sell blood and not reveal information about themselves that could determine its quality. The data reveal that Japan has one of the highest rates of posttransfusion hepatitis in the world.

An alternative relationship is that of the status-grant transaction, which Titmuss calls the gift relationship. Here the producer is not motivated by the exchange of goods but by an identification with the recipient. Where the welfare of the recipient is uppermost, there is no motivation to withhold information. In the United Kingdom, blood is given by voluntary donors. The hepatitis rate is very low.

The holder of status (who needs blood) has a property right in a status-grant society just as the owner of income and factors has a right in a bargained economy. It is no less a right for being a matter of custom and cultural practice. The empirical data suggest that a person who needs blood in a society utilizing status-grant transactions has a more valuable right than a person who owns income to buy blood in a bargained exchange economy.

The United States is in an intermediate position with a mixed system. In 1965–67 period, about 30 percent of the blood supply was purchased while 10 percent was from voluntary donors, with the balance some mix of payment and other inducements. Its hepatitis rate is also intermediate. (In passing it can be noted that one-half of the blood supply in the Soviet Union is purchased.) Studies of hospitals that switched from commercial to voluntary resources show dramatic drops in hepatitis rates (Sapolsky and Finkelstein 1977). But it should not be concluded that all volunteer blood is good and all paid blood is bad. There are other factors that interact with this type of transaction dichotomy to affect performance.

Again, questions can be raised about specification of the institutional variable. There are alternatives within the market system. A system of labeling might be instituted. Disease rates of different hospitals might be published so consumers can put pressure on hospitals to be more careful in choosing their source of supply. There are also alternatives within the status-grant system, such as group size and type of sanction applied.

The Titmuss data do suggest a relationship between the type of transaction and blood quality. But it is another matter to predict how quantity supplied would be affected if a country now using a mixed system permitted only grants. This requires more than casual observation of psychological variables.

It would appear that the historical experience of a people may be important in shaping behavior within a grant system. If a grant system were relied upon entirely in the United States, is the sense of community strong enough for supplies to be adequate, as it is in the United Kingdom? Has the United States had the same experiences, such as the common purpose created in the context of wartime survival under attack? The utilization of psychological variables at the level of national character is difficult, but small-scale experiments might be possible. For example, it might be instructive to determine if communities with volunteer fire departments produce a character of people with a greater sense of community. Or the direction of causation may run the other way: if people have a sense of community, volunteer fire departments are easier to organize. Or perhaps, the two feed back and reinforce each other. These are very difficult to untangle in a formal experiment, and judgments will have to be made from historical and case analysis.

Presence versus Absence of Direct Government Regulation

What the government can regulate is a question that must be asked even when a group does not like the results of market transactions. Just because the group has a reason to regulate does not mean that direct regulation can be made effective or that the group will want all of the associated consequences.

Inflation is a common feature of market economies and has characteristics of a social trap. One approach to controlling inflation is the rules of competition and monetary and fiscal policy. Another approach is price control, such as that imposed in the United States in August 1971.

The first phase of that price control lasted 90 days and was an absolute freeze (while the administrative agency was being established). Phase II lasted for 14 months, during which selected price increases were allowed by the administrative agency. The testing of its effect might appear to be a simple matter of checking the time-series record and comparing prices before and after the controls. But in order to determine the effect of the controls, we must establish what would have happened in their absence. However, there are no data to be observed where the same conditions occurred in the economy with and without price control. The only alternative is to project and estimate what prices would have been without price control. This has been done in a study by Edgar Feige and Douglas Pearce (1973), who constructed a simple time-series model that uses past rates of price change to predict future prices. More-sophisticated econometric models were used by others to provide statistical control for a number of other economic variables, but the general experimental design is the same. Feige and Pearce found that the actual observed price changes were less than the estimated price changes during Phase I for both the consumer and wholesale price indexes. In Phase II, the consumer index seemed unaffected by price controls and the wholesale index seems to have increased faster than was estimated. The analysts suggest that imposition of controls may actually have caused some otherwise forbearing sellers to raise prices in reaction to the controls.

When we leave aside the questions of experimental design, what can be concluded from tests where the institutional variable is a dichotomy between two very broad alternatives—presence or absence of controls in this case? Does the institutional variable need further specification? Previous discussion has suggested that public versus private ownership is too gross a distinction to capture all of the relevant property-right variables that structure the incentives and opportunity sets of the actors. Before we can draw conclusions on the effect of price controls, we would need to test for the effects of alternative systems of incentives for the government administrators. How is their performance monitored, and how are costs and benefits assessed to the bureaucrats? Perhaps it would be useful to compare the administrative structure and procedural rules used in the wartime price-control agency with that of the 1971 agency. There can be as much institutional variation within the broad category of price control as between price-control and so-called free markets.

To what extent must institutional models contain behavioral variables for those being regulated? To what extent are history and the current environment relevant in influencing how people will react to a change in the rules, such as imposition of price controls? A possible hypothesis has already been suggested that the controls may have caused some firms to raise prices that would otherwise have not. The same kind of problem arises in the administration of traditional monetary controls by the Federal Reserve Board. The board does not influence the rate of investment and borrowing by direct controls. In theory, it can affect these rates by influencing interest rates. But, in periods of inflationary psychology, a rising interest rate may be interpreted as a signal that rates will increase even more and that one should borrow now rather than being interpreted as a signal to postpone borrowing. Apparently neither economic models nor government policy has successfully incorporated these contextual psychological variables.

Consider the performance variables chosen for test. Feige and Pearce chose to restrict themselves to examination of the general price level. But inflation of the general price level is only a mild irritant if everyone's income moves together (Bazelon 1959, p. 107). Inflation is probably the most significant form of income redistribution at work in market economies. It may overshadow most overt changes in property ownership or redistribution via the tax system. Thus, an important performance variable is relative price change. Who are the groups whose real incomes are gaining at the expense of other groups? In this regard, the rules of access to the price controllers become critical.

Administrative transactions constitute one of the most direct ways that rights shape the content of opportunity sets. Prohibition of a certain action with appropriate fines as sanctions might appear to have an assured effect on performance. Yet the prohibition of liquor (1920 to 1933) did not eliminate drinking, and contemporary fines for speeding and drunk driving have not eliminated these practices. One response is to increase fines and surveillance.

For example, in 1955 after an increase in highway accidents and deaths, Connecticut implemented a crackdown on speeders. The number of driver's-license suspensions increased sharply. Analysis of accident rates using an extended time-series design with neighboring states as control groups suggests that the greater degree of enforcement did reduce accidents (Campbell and Ross 1968). In a sense, the increased fine (and probability thereof) can be conceptualized as a typical problem of estimating the price elasticity of demand for a product (fast driving). But the institutional question includes much more, such as the level of administration. The law may be passed by the state, the state police may make arrests, but the cases are heard by a local elected judge, who may be responsive to local demands that differ from those expressed at the state level (Broder 1981). Thus, boundary issues affect how a nominal right is actually applied. The results cannot be extended to other states unless the institutional variable is carefully specified.

Another institutional-specification problem arises from exclusion cost (quite literally, policing cost in this case). Just because a person does not have the right to drive fast does not mean that exclusion from that activity is cheap. The fine level is one thing, but police resources are another. In the case of drunk-driving prohibition, a complicating feature is the cost of obtaining information that proves a person was driving under the influence of alcohol if the driving was not actually witnessed by police. There are physical tests of blood and breath that can provide such evidence, but civil rights have often prevented their use (cf. contemporary drug testing). The effect of allowing breath tests for determining driving impairment potentially lowers information costs to law administrators. The impact on traffic fatalities was analyzed when these rights changed in the United Kingdom in 1967 (Ross, Campbell, and Glass 1970).

To summarize, institutional theory suggests that there is more to regulatory performance than the nominal prohibition and fine level. Interdependence created by exclusion and information costs, for example, is controlled by other types of rights.

Competition and Market Structure

The emphasis of this book has been to supplement the institutional variables suggested by the model of pure competition. However, there is no denying the importance of the degree of competition as a variable controlling the distribution of power. This has been an area of much empirical work and the subject of an entire subdiscipline of economics—industrial organization. Since this subject has been so thoroughly analyzed elsewhere, it is not necessary to repeat any case studies here. For some examples, see Bain (1966b); Philips (1971), Scherer (1970), Weiss (1971), and Mueller (1983).

PUBLIC SERVICES: POLICE

The point has been made that the simple dichotomy of privately and publicly owned firms ignores many possible alternative rules within each type. In this section, variation of property rights within the public sector will be examined.

There has been a strong reform tradition in political science favoring the political consolidation of various units of local government in the United States. This tradition borrows the economist's concept of economies of scale and argues that the larger political jurisdiction will be more efficient (see Chapter 4). It also is related to the notion of enlarging the size of the firm to internalize externalities. These issues have been combined here under the concept of boundary issues, as discussed in Chapter 8. What is the substantive result for different groups of people when they live in small political units as opposed to larger, consolidated units? One dimension of this has been tested with respect to police services by Elinor Ostrom and associates (1973). (Also see Mc-Dowell [1975] and Toma [1979].) The performance variable chosen is citizen satisfaction with the service received and opinion on the desirability of political consolidation. Data were obtained by personal interviews. A comparison was made of a number of matched communities—one a small independent suburb and another a community within a large central city. The two areas were matched on the basis of the usual socioeconomic characteristics, such as income, education, and racial mix. It was assumed that the two contiguous areas generally had the same set of preferences. The test was conducted in a number of cities, including Indianapolis, Indiana and Grand Rapids, Michigan. In general, the studies show that the people in the small, politically independent suburbs with their own police force were more satisfied with police performance than were the people in the neighboring area who received the services of the central city police. The people in the independent suburbs generally opposed consolidation.

The source of the difference in satisfaction appears to be the kind of technology and service provided. The independent, small police departments tend to provide a highly visible service with many patrols, while the central city police are organized into specialized bureaus with less visibility. Are the differences there because different group interests prefer one type of service over another, or is the city service the only type possible given a large department? The connection of the test above does not answer these questions. However, casual observation suggests that some large cities do put a great deal of discretion in management at the local precinct level, and there seems no technical-production reason why a large department cannot have many patrols if that is how they wish to use their resources. An alternate hypothesis is that the preferences of largely middle-class fringe areas of central cities are not met because the resources are used to meet the preferences of other groups. When crime rates are highest in the core area, an urban police department may choose to concentrate its forces there, at the expense of its fringe areas.

What is empirically observed may have little to do with size itself but with the fact that larger size usually means a more heterogeneous set of preferences. The drawing of a boundary affects whether a given group is in the minority or majority. The middle-class fringe areas of a central city may simply be outvoted by the residents and business interests of the core area. This speculation might be tested by comparing the police-service preferences of each of these groups. The property-rights issue may turn on who is responsible for the costs incurred in the high-crime areas. Should suburban tax dollars be used only for suburban service? The independent suburbs have been able to acquire this right subject only to some redistributive taxation and attempts to encourage regional planning. (See Hanf and Wandesforde-Smith 1972; Schmid and Faas 1980.)

PUBLIC-CHOICE RULES

Legislative Rules

There are rules for making rules that affect the outcome of public choice. What determines which group gets rights favorable to itself? One arena where this question can be asked is with reference to tariffs. A theory that pays no attention to situation might predict that there would be few tariffs, since the losses to consumers are larger than producer gains because the consumer pays the tariff and the increase in product price owing to smaller supply while producers receive only the benefit of higher prices. But in fact, producer pressure is more prevelant and successful than consumer interests.

Jonathan Pincus (1977) suggests that there is an asymmetry of response to tariff possibilities. There are many consumers relative to producers, and the gain to any consumer from opposing a tariff is small relative to the cost. As shown in Chapter 3, this would make no difference if exclusion costs were low and the small but numerous bids of consumers could be aggregated. So Pincus tests the proposition that the degree of exclusion and associated transaction costs affect which products have the most tariff protection. Exclusion cost is less for smaller groups of producers of intermediate goods than for larger groups of producers of final goods. This is supported by a regression model explaining the relative tariff rates passed in the United States in 1824.

Producers of different products have different costs of communication, discovery of group interdependence, and effectiveness of peer pressure related to the total number of proprietors and their dispersion. Pincus hypothesized that duties would vary positively with industrial concentration measured by market share and inversely with the geographic dispersion of sales by counties having the same kind of products, and this was confirmed by the evidence.

However, other measures of group size produce conflicting evidence. While industrial concentration was positively correlated with tariff rates, the number of establishments was also positively correlated, contrary to hypothesis. The Pincus model is not a test of the impact of alternative institutions combined with a given situation, but rather the effect of situational variation with a particular and largely unspecified institution. The intrinsic effect of high exclusion and transaction costs can be modified by structures. Casual observation suggests many examples where concentrated interests are more powerful than dispersed but individually small interests. Yet, the political rules place some limits on this. Further confirmation of the rules-situation interaction awaits the opportunity to compare tariffs for different products with different costs of exclusion in different countries with different public-choice rules.

Environmental legislation is an area where dispersed interests in high-exclusion-cost goods have won over concentrated interests. Kalt and Zupan (1984) studied the Congressional vote on surface-mining reclamation and inferred a substantial degree of institutional slack allowing political representatives to escape the concentrated mining interests and vote for what they conceived as a broad public interest.

Court Consolidation

Government settles conflicts among members of the public, and the rules of public choice influence whose tastes count. Just as factor ownership determines whose preference counts for incompatible-use goods, the rules of public choice determine whose preference counts in making the rules of factor ownership. One rule-making arena is that of the courts. Among the institutional rules affecting court decisions are those relating to judge selection and boundaries. Smaller jurisdictions are more likely to have people of homogenous tastes than larger jurisdictions. A group that is in the majority in a small jurisdiction may be an outvoted minority in a large jurisdiction. That is to say that a group's effective ownership and control depends on its boundaries.

There has been a movement in the United States to consolidate and enlarge local government units to achieve economies of scale (Warren 1966). The pricing issues created by economies of scale will not be explored here but rather the issues of changing product quality. A study of local courts in Georgia by Broder and Schmid (1983) recorded the satisfaction of residents with court decisions regarding drunk driving and other traffic violations. Prior to consolidation, the largest city in the county had its own court and the Spearman rank correlation between fine levels for different violations given by the court and preferred by the city inhabitants was higher when they had their own court than after consolidation. However, the satisfaction of county citizens outside of the city increased. In fact, a regression-discontinuity model showed that the fines given by the court for different violations were significantly different before and after consolidation. A change in the "ownership" of the court produced a different performance. The "efficiency" of achieving economies of scale is meaningless without the institutional context that determines the product quality that all must consume. The issue is always one of efficient for whom.

Civil Rights and Ballot Design

Some civil rights are a part of the rules for making rules. These rights determine who counts and participates in public choice of the rights that in turn determine who participates in resource-use decisions. The paradigm can be used to ask how a given right controls conflict growing out of a particular variety of interdependence. There are some striking parallels among the categories of human interdependence observed in participation in government and market decisions.

Chapter 6 illustrated the potential role of contractual costs in determining outcomes of market bargaining. The consumer's effective bid is reduced by the amount of the transaction costs, and this reduction often works to the advantage of other parties. Other areas that have been empirically studied are the determinants of campaign expenditures, political participation, advertising, and vote influence. (For a bibliography see Mueller 1976.) There are also costs associated with the exercise of voting rights. It takes time and energy to get to the voting place as well as to understand the available choices and their probable consequences (the same is true for consumer information in the market). Some very small differences in procedural detail can make a big difference in performance.

One factor affecting transaction cost is the design of the ballot. The party-column ballot, often referred to as the Indiana ballot, lists each office and the given party's nominees in a single column. A straight-ticket alternative is offered whereby a single mark gives the individual's vote to all of one party's nominees. This alternative saves time in the voting booth as well as time in acquiring candidate information. One can learn something about the general performance of the party and not bother to get information on specific candidates.

An alternative property right and opportunity set is contained in the so-called Massachusetts office-bloc ballot. The names of the candidates of all parties are listed after each office to be filled. There is no provision for voting a straight ticket with only one mark or lever. An opportunity to test the consequences of these alternatives was provided by Ohio in 1949 when the Indiana-type ballot was replaced with the Massachusetts-type ballot. The results have been analyzed by Donald Zauderer (1972). An extended time-series, quasi-experimental design was used. Observation of performance was made over the period from 1934 to 1964, with the change in institution occurring in 1949. The dependent variable chosen was what political scientists call the percentage of vote roll-off. This is the difference in the number of votes received by the office that received the greatest number of votes and the office receiving the least, expressed in percentage terms. There is differential interest and information available on different offices. The office of U.S. senator may receive many more votes from a given area than does a local official's, say city mayor or county sheriff. The percentage difference is the roll-off. If everyone's subjective evaluation of transaction costs and net benefits were the same, then a change in their absolute magnitude might be of little interest. However, if some groups fail to participate in the voting for some offices, the candidate is chosen by fewer people of a different group. The roll-off can be large enough so that the number of voters voting for some offices (A) but not for others (B) may be large enough to have determined the winners of those B offices.

Zauderer found that generally the ballot-design change, which increased transaction costs, resulted in a substantial increase in vote roll-off. When some wards and precincts were compared with differences in education and race, it was found that the increase in roll-off was progressively higher as one moved from upper to lower educational groupings, and within educational groupings the roll-off was higher in black districts than white. This implied that the Democratic party, which has proportionately more lower-educated voters, was placed at a competitive disadvantage by the change in voter rules.

Apparently it is not enough to be in favor of democracy; where transaction costs are differentially perceived, the particular rules for an election seem to make a difference. Just as there are many variations of rules within what most would define as a market system, there are many alternative rules within a democratic government system. The differences within may be as great as between systems.

In the earlier discussion of goods with high exclusion costs, it was noted that government taxes and spending can solve the free-rider problem at the expense of creating unwilling riders, who have to pay for something they do not want. Voting rules are important property rights affecting real wealth distribution. This fact is especially clear where one group can vote a tax that may be disproportionately paid by another. Several empirical studies have noted divergence in voting patterns on school tax referendums between property owners and renters who were otherwise similar (Peterson 1975; Sproule-Jones 1974; Wilson and Banfield 1965).

U.S. cities provide a wide variation in governance institutions that might affect whose preferences count. One cluster of representative structures might be termed Jacksonian democracy, including an elected mayor, election of council members by wards in partisan elections, and long ballots. Another cluster is the Wilsonian structure, including an appointed professional city manager, nonpartisan council elections at large, and short ballots (Maser 1985; Miller 1985).

It can be hypothesized that the above structures would affect demand articulation by those with higher transaction costs, such as the poor and uneducated, similar to that already noted in the case of ballot design. The voter registration and turnout rate is lower for poor blacks, which means that they are sometimes poorly represented even in cities where they have an absolute majority. With at-large elections, blacks can be outvoted by whites who turnout at a higher rate. With elections by wards, exclusively black wards can be expected to elect a black representative even with low turnout. Similarly, non-partisan elections mean that voters must obtain information on individuals rather than just party ideology. This is hypothesized to favor highly educated elites.

Empirical research supports these hypotheses. Cities with Wilsonian structures hire fewer black employees than Jacksonian cities (Stein 1984). Cities with at-large elections elect fewer black city council members with respect to their numbers than cities with wards (Engstrom and McDonald 1981). In general, cities with Wilsonian structures have lower correlations between socioeconomic variables and policies than Jacksonian cities and give more power to elites.

The above material is included to suggest the versatility of the paradigm and in no way exhausts the field. Access to government includes much more than voting rights. Some groups are more effective because they work through the courts or the bureaucracy (Viteritti 1973). One of the uses of the paradigm is to suggest alternatives to a group that finds its interests blocked in a particular avenue of power.

Some scholars reserve the term *public-choice theory* to refer to alternative forms of government and such issues as voting, constitutionality, social contract, decentralization, and bureaucracies (Mueller 1976; Tullock 1979). The term is used here to refer to the impact of rules for making rules as well as the resulting rules directing private transactions.

ECONOMIC DEVELOPMENT

All of the various institutional alternatives noted above with respect to natural resources, business organization, public services, and so on combine to have an impact on general patterns of economic development. In this section, several studies of developing countries will be examined along with a U.S.-Japanese comparison.

Africa

There is a great deal of discussion on the consequences of a highly centralized, planned, and directed economy versus what is misleadingly called the free-market economy (it will be made clear below why this is a misleading term). The histories of Kenya and the Gold Coast (now Ghana) during the period between 1900 and World War II provide a natural experiment to test the consequences of alternative institutions. Both were British colonies, but Kenya was marked by much direct intervention of the government in the economy that was absent in the Gold Coast. The following comparison has been made by Robert Seidman (1973).

Kenya was actively colonized by white settlers. The best land was kept for the whites, while the Africans were forced to live on reserves. On the other hand, in the Gold Coast whites were forbidden to own land. Factor ownership was thus restricted in both cases, but to the advantage of different groups. Institutions with respect to labor, however, were vastly different. It was in the interest of the white settlers to obtain African labor at low wages. Short of slavery, it is difficult to attract workers from their subsistence agriculture without higher-than-subsistence wages. Instead, the Kenyan colonial government instituted a poll or head tax. The only way for most to raise this cash was to work for the whites at whatever they wished to pay. The wage bargain was nominally voluntary, but in effect the white employers had greater bargaining power as the Africans had few alternatives. The rights of labor were even more restricted by passage of master-servant ordinances that prohibited an employee from leaving a job without the employer's permission and enforced certain work standards by criminal sanctions.

In the Gold Coast, there was no direct state intervention compelling the Africans to work for whites. There was already an indigenous export-oriented agriculture on small farms, primarily growing cocoa. Whites did not try to obtain ownership of the land and make the Africans work for them. The Africans were free to sell their cocoa in the market. However, bargaining power was very unequal. The crop was financed, purchased, stored, and shipped by a few European firms. Their fewness led to frequent price-fixing agreements, which went unopposed by the noninterventionist government. The government, of course, protected the buyers' property in docks, storehouses, and so on.

From the discussion in Chapter 8, we might hypothesize that large groups of producers will face high transaction costs in organizing any group activity. These differences in costs between the few buyers and the many sellers can create unequal bargaining power. The producer owns his farm and is free, but the freedom is limited to selling at the buyer's price or not selling at all. Producers did organize withholding strikes in 1930 and 1937 during periods of dramatically low prices but were not able to sustain an effective counter to the buyers' market power. This is consistent with experience in agriculture the world over. Farmers have not been able to organize for collective bargaining without the aid of government in reducing transaction costs and the free-rider problem.

The two countries differed greatly in other aspects. The government of Kenya intervened in the economy with transportation subsidies, credit programs, research, price support, and marketing boards. The Gold Coast had little of these. For example, there was no government credit program, and producers were continually in debt to the cocoa buyers. The fact that the government did nothing to clarify confused and conflicting land titles that made the use of land for bank credit difficult may also have contributed to the cocoa-buyers' power, but this is not explored by Seidman. The power of a particular group is a function of a large variety of rights that individually may appear of little consequence.

What is the result? The performance variable chosen was average per-capita income, which Seidman concludes was not substantially different in the two countries during this period. The profits of agricultural production went to Europeans and not native Africans (p. 569). Seidman's methodology is a simple cross-sectional comparison over a period of time. No statistical tests are possible. The performance variable may not be available for exactly the same years or in the same terms, and thus care is necessary in interpretation. The institutional variable is often multidimensional. One cannot be sure just which of the several property-rights differences may have caused the results, or even if one rule is working at cross-purposes with another. Also, just because we have a theory as to why a certain performance should follow from a given property right does not mean that when we observe the performance the explanation is proved. Performance may have been owing to an uncontrolled-for simultaneous event. This is the reality of much institutional research. It is not possible randomly to assign different countries to different institutions. The great bulk of evidence of institutional performance will be this type of historical case study.

The results of such studies as that of Seidman do indicate that there is more than one way to achieve a given performance. The Seidman study suggests the need to specify the institutional variable as carefully as possible. Those who hope to achieve a changed performance via changed factor ownership (land reform) must be aware of the total institutional framework, which can offset the effect of change in factor ownership. The market is not a single institutional alternative. There are alternatives within it that can make it perform in a variety of ways, including that identical to a given set of rules of an administered governmental system (and probably vice versa). These market alternatives are chosen by government; government is never neutral. The performance of the Gold Coast economy no less than the Kenyan economy was the result of government policy. The method can vary, but government choice is inevitable. The absence of government in doing nothing to help producers overcome their transaction costs or to prevent buyers from engaging in price fixing is no more or less coercive or interventionist than a head tax or subsidy. Both shape the real opportunity sets of the parties and thus the performance. Where interests conflict, there is no such thing as a neutral, noninterventionist government.

Asia

The adoption of new agricultural technologies is the source of great increase in output. The ability of different groups of farmers to utilize these technologies has a great deal to do with relative income distribution. How do alternative property rights and their distribution affect technological adoption? An opportunity to test the performance of alternative institutions is provided by a comparison of Pakistan and Bangladesh (formerly East and West Pakistan).

The characteristics of the technology under consideration should be noted first to determine what sorts of human interdependence its use involves. Tube wells for irrigation can be installed by an individual farmer, in contrast to a large dam-and-ditch distribution system. Still, the tube has economies of scale (see Chapter 4). Asian farms are very small, and it is not practical for each farmer to have a well. There are several institutional alternatives to accommodate the character of the technology. One is a market in water where a large farmer would put in a well and sell water to smaller neighbors. Another is for small farmers to organize a cooperative and in effect become joint owners of the well.

Carl Gotsch (1972) has explored the institutional conditions under which either of the above alternatives is possible. He contrasts the institutions of Pakistan and Bangladesh. This quasi-experiment allows for control of relevant engineering and economic factors. Irrigable areas, costs, and crop response are similar in the two areas, but institutions are quite different. Pakistan begins with a more-unequal size distribution of land ownership than Bangladesh. There are many more farms that are of sufficient size to install their own wells. Since there are no organizational problems for large farmers, it might be expected that the rate of technological adoption would be faster in Pakistan. It was. If one were interested only in the number of acres irrigated, a small number of large farmers would be preferred.

But what of the smaller farmers? Does being small in a society of unequal distribution have different results than being small when others are also small? In Pakistan, 70 percent of the tube wells were installed by farmers who had more than 25 acres, while the great majority of Pakistani farmers have less than 13 acres and only installed 4 percent of the wells. A market in water did not develop. Gotsch suggests several reasons. In addition to the economies of scale, there are geographic factors that create a monopoly. A small farmer is not likely to be able to buy water from a number of potential suppliers. Without something like public-utility regulation, the small farmer is faced with a monopoly price. The owner of the closest well also may not be in a position to offer credit. This might be solved by other market changes or by a government credit program, but it was not.

The role of malevolence cannot be ruled out. There is deep enmity between large and small farmers. The large farmer may not sell to a small farmer if it will make the small farmer better off, even though it also makes the large farmer better off.

If the market does not develop, what about the cooperative alternative? Gotsch offers several hypotheses as to why cooperatives did not materialize in Pakistan but did in Bangladesh. Rural politics in Pakistan is marked by extreme factionalism. Gotsch observes that individuals in the village do not form alliances even though they have a common goal. Contending political groups are dominated by the large landowners (patrons), and they recruit followers (clients) depending on their alternatives (Coyer 1973). Those who are tenants or need the goodwill of a particular moneylender have little choice. Others are recruited by any means available, including force. Gotsch concluded that class alignment is virtually impossible.

In Bangladesh, factionalism and dependence are less severe. There are fewer tenants, and people are more equal. It seems doubtful from the earlier discussion of the problems of organizing large groups that these qualities would be sufficient for success. Government assistance in organizing the cooperative can be hypothesized as a key factor in overcoming transaction costs.

The ultimate performance variable was the distribution of increased farm income. This follows directly from the adoption of the new technology. Only the large farmers in Pakistan adopted the tube wells, while many small farmers participated in Bangladesh. Possible cumulative effects should also be noted. New income from use of tube wells by small farmers may break their dependence on large farmer-moneylenders. Also, the experience with the production cooperative may also be utilized to organize for political action. Property rights operate at various interacting levels. One set of institutions (for example, tenancy and distribution in landownership) can affect the development of market and cooperative institutions, which in turn may affect the ability of different groups to obtain political power to change the rules of the game. Political and economic power are interdependent.

While this book has emphasized the impact of property rights on performance, it is not argued that property rights are always the decisive factor. Power is not the only variable. Differences in psychological variables may account for more difference in performance in this case example than differences in property rights. Of course, the two can be related and feed back upon each other.

Japan and the United States

Most of the studies noted in this chapter try to isolate the effect of specific institutional alternatives on a particular performance measure. They suggest that what we meant by economic development is controlled by a large number of rights as related to a large number of sources of interdependence. Since one might expect that there are many complements and substitutes among these institutions, the explanation of different rates of growth (however measured) among countries is a complex matter. Succinct specification of institutional structures is difficult, and attempts to explain growth by reference to such aggregates as capitalist and socialist or planned or unplanned are difficult, if not misleading. And the interaction of situation, structure, and performance often does not lend itself to neat econometric tests (or summary in a few pages).

There is a growing literature trying to identify the institutional and other sources of Japanese success and point out lessons for the United States (Johnson 1982; Solo 1984; Thurow 1985; Vogel 1981). It is not possible here to summarize or evaluate these studies, but some of the debate on industrial policy can be better understood in SSP terms.

One of the things that is different in Japan compared with the United States is institutions that can make a long-run commitment to develop and utilize a new technology or product. Japan's Ministry of International Trade and Industry is designed to commit capital to a new area and provide supporting infrastructure. This is addressed to the transaction costs stemming from cost discontinuities and investment coordination. The Japanese have had success in reducing the uncertainty of suppliers who can achieve economies of scale only by being assured of a market for their output, which in turn depends on achieving low prices. The Japanese firm will build large plants before the market develops, thus preempting competitors. American firms, on the other hand, have short planning horizons, partly because of the credit system and personal-incentive systems internal to the firm.

Interdependence stemming from interdependent utilities and its effect on labor productivity are addressed by different rights structures in the two countries (Aoki 1984; Cole 1979; Ouchi 1981, p. 25). The difference in incomes of workers and managers is less in Japan. Job security is higher in Japan so that workers can sacrifice current income to help the firm compete and be sure they will be employed if the firm succeeds. The effect of these and other institutional differences are controversial and depend on qualitative and directional evidence, but it does remind us that there is nothing automatic about institutional change. The property-rights structure makes a difference and there is no assurance that benign neglect of institutional design will maintain a country's economic position. The best argument that something better is possible is the fact that something better exits (even if its instrumentalities are uncertain).

CONCLUSIONS

This review indicates that empirical institutional analysis is both a workable and fertile field of study. Researchers need not restrict themselves to the traditional fields of research in production economics, monetary policy, or international trade in fear that institutional studies can only be polemical treatises of philosophy, history, and social criticism.

The review further indicates that the categories of human interdependence developed in Part II do provide a starting place in formulating useful hypotheses for relating institutional alternatives to performance. There is more to interdependence than is controlled by factor ownership and competition (or the right to vote). The key utility of this theory is in better specification of institutional variables. Research must move beyond the simple dichotomies of public versus private ownership, market versus nonmarket systems, capitalism versus socialism, or democracy versus oligarchy. Further theoretical development is needed in formulating models that can control for the relevant background institutional variables other than the main instrumental variables being tested. Such further work is especially critical where random assignment of the main institutional alternatives is not possible. With random assignment, other possible causal factors are controlled for (even when unknown) in the experimental design. But in quasi-experimental designs, the competing causal factors must be specifically accounted for. The researcher cannot know what to try to control for without adequate theory.

Adequate theory is not the only barrier to useful empirical research. Another problem is the lack of institutional variation. In many countries there is only one kind of institution or right applied to a particular commodity or governmental function. There are simply no institutional alternatives to observe. This explains in part why axiomatic and deductive reasoning is so popular. It is easier to logically prove that something is possible, impossible, or Pareto-better than it is to find two different institutions and accompanying performance to contrast.

Little reference has been made here to empirical research that does not identify instrumental variables that could be manipulated to change performance. For example, there is a large literature that has as its purpose to prove that both private and public decision makers are self-seeking, constrained rationalists and that this is consistent with observed outcomes. Knowledge of modes of information processing and decision making are certainly necessary in hypothesizing how legal change in opportunity sets will be utilized. But, one wonders if the repetition of this work has another purpose. The Pigouvian literature of market failure seemed to provide legitimacy for an enlarged government (more accurately, a shift in whom government serves). If it can be demonstrated that politicians and bureaucrats are self-seeking rather than serving the public interest (whatever that is), this provides a government-failure antidote to market failure. But if one wants to escape the whole notion of presumptuous failures and stick to substantive prediction of performance, this empirical typing seems less useful, even if one were convinced that self-seeking was meaningful without asking how people define themselves.

There is another point about instrumental variables. Explanation has several implications. One can find an association between two variables, but if the explanatory variable is not instrumental and cannot be changed, it may be intellectually satisfying but of little use to institutional design.

Morris Fiorina (1979, p. 49) critiques a study purporting to explain U.S. voter turnout over time by reference to information cost. First, Fiorina suggests that the dependent performance variable should be eligible electorate voting instead of percent voting among those of voting age. The authors utilized the proportion of households with radios and televisions as a proxy for information cost. They concluded that the availability of free information about candidates was positively correlated with voter turnout. Fiorina suggests that many other variables would show the same correlation. If his preferred dependent variable of eligible electorate voting were used, "This series shows a general decline since 1868 and will correlate *negatively* with *any* time series which captures technological advancement (radios, television, rifles, airplanes, even deodorant), the rational theory of voting behavior to the contrary not withstanding." For all of our econometric sophistication, model specification and interpretation remain troublesome.

Let us raise our sights and not let our explanation stop short. What good is it to know that radios are correlated with voter turnout? Perhaps government could manipulate the number of radios to achieve given performance, but this is not too useful. However, if researchers go on to ask how institutions and rights instrumentally interact with a given information cost (or differential information costs of different groups) we may be of more practical use.

In that regard, Robert Rabin (1979, p. 991) says that "documenting the proposition that law has an impact, without linking the findings to behavorial patterns and institutional change is a dead end." He illustrates with respect to the institution of a liability rule for charitable hospitals that were formerly exempt. A finding that such hospitals then increase room prices to cover liability insurance is not very surprising. More interesting would be such questions as, did the legal change cause changed safety practices in the hospital, cause cutbacks in service to different kinds of patients, or change the level of claims consciousness by patients. Hopefully, better theory will let us raise our sights.

The available empirical studies seem to suggest that prediction of performance can be made with knowledge of how rights affect opportunity sets in the context of a particular variety of interdependence combined with informal estimates of psychological variables. In other cases, the institutional analyst will require more formal estimates from behavioral scientists.

The cases examined primarily involve formal, legalistic institutions, but some cases suggest that the paradigm can apply to rights that are informal and embedded in the culture. In practice, one of the tough empirical problems is distinguishing the prevailing rule from the nominal.

The performance variables used in many of the studies seem quite narrow. They focus on some traditional items of interest to economists, such as profit rates, growth in income, and measures of certain costs. But many people who are not satisfied with the performance of current institutions have additional measures in mind. Institutional researchers have a major interest in development of the field of social indicators.

The time scope of the studies noted here is short. Observation is usually limited to a few years of comparison. But for some purposes, we want to know the performance of alternative institutions over many years of changing conditions. The test of many institutions is their ability to adapt over time rather than to achieve a given performance at any particular moment. Such adaptation is particularly relevant if some people are to avoid what they would consider a social trap. The point is made by S. V. Ciriacy-Wantrup (1967), who says that in institutional research, "Emphasis is on determining conditions for economic growth rather than on locating peaks, on avoiding dead-end streets rather than on computing the shortest distance, and on adaptability rather than optimum adjustment." For example, he suggests that we should look at 80 years of experience in California's irrigation districts and compare that state's performance with other states and nations that have different rules. This presents formidable methodological problems, however. In this length of time, many peripheral institutional and other changes occur, and it is difficult to control for them. Nevertheless, this is the reality of what we have to work with. There is a historical literature relating institutions to performance that is too vast to review here. (See, for example, Hurst 1956 and 1960.) Despite the statistical control problems, we shall have to learn what we can from it because it is all the evidence that is available in many instances; "the only alternative to seeking insights out of experience . . . is to rely upon the absolutes of ideology, dogma, or revelation" (Parsons 1974, p. 737).

Where institutional variation exists (or has existed), there is an opportunity to learn from it and to derive some predictions of how the duplication of the institution might perform in another time, state, or perhaps country. Theory helps to suggest what situational variables must be similar for the same results to be expected. In many cases of interest, however, policy makers ask the analyst to suggest the impact of a new institution (right) that has never been tried in a particular community or problem area. At such times, theory is especially necessary to utilize experience gained in observing the application of a given type of right to a given species of human interdependence to predict how a similar type of right would perform in the context of a similar sort of interdependence, even though the particular commodities differ. Thus, for example, experience with one high-exclusion-cost good is part of the ability to predict how a given right might affect performance with another-high exclusion-cost good. The only real test, of course, is to try it; all any scientific theory can do is to allow the process of experimentation to proceed less blindly.

NOTES

1. The following factual account is from Crocker (1971). The interpretation here departs somewhat from Crocker's.

2. Crocker (1971, p. 461) ignored this fact and made the erroneous assertion that "the subsequent imposition of emission standards was at least redundant and probably uneconomic."

3. Stock savings and loan firms are prohibited in some states. For example, in 1973 Michigan had no stock companies and had only recently passed a law allowing them. But this example is irrelevant to the above comparison, which is only made for each state where both forms exist.

4. There is a large literature comparing the performance of socialist and capitalist countries. This is well summarized in Pryor (1973, pp. 322-35). His general conclusion is that there is about as much variation in performance within each system as between. Also see Wiles (1977).

Bibliography

Acheson, J.M. 1975. "The Lobster Fiefs: Economic and Ecological Effects of Territoriality in the Maine Lobster Industry." *Human Ecology* 3: 183–207.

Ackerman, B.A. 1975. *Economic Foundations of Property Law*. Boston: Little, Brown.

Adams, John, ed. 1980. *Institutional Economics*. Boston: Martinus Nijhoff.

Ahlbrandt, Roger, Jr. 1973. *Municipal Fire Protection Services: Comparison of Alternative Organizational Forms*. Beverly Hills, Calif.: Sage.

Akerlof, George. 1984. "Gift Exchange and Efficiency-Wage Theory: Four Views." *American Economic Review* 74(2): 79–83.

———. 1979. "The Case against Conservative Macroeconomics: An Inaugural Lecture." *Economica* 45: 219–37.

———. 1970. "The Market for Lemons: Quality Uncertainty and the Market Mechanism." *Quarterly Journal of Economics* 84: 488–500.

Alchian, Armen A. 1969. "Corporate Management and Property Rights." In *Economic Policy and the Regulation of Corporate Securities*, edited by Henry Manne, pp. 337–60. Washington, D.C.: American Enterprise Institute.

———. 1965. "Some Economics of Property Rights." *Il Politico* 30: 816–29.

Alchian, Armen A., and Harold Demsetz. 1972. "Production, Information Costs, and Economic Organization." *American Economic Review* 62: 777–95.

Alves, Wayne, and Peter Rossi. 1978. "Who Should Get What? Fairness Judgments of the Distribution of Earnings." *American Journal of Sociology* 3: 541–64.

"American Express Agrees to Allow Cash Discounts." *Consumer Reports*, June 1974, pp. 432–33.

Anderson, Terry L., and P.J. Hill. 1974. "The Evolution of Property Rights: A Study of the American West." *Journal of Law and Economics* 17: 163–80.

Aoki, Masahiko, ed. 1984. *The Economic Analysis of the Japanese Firm in Comparative Perspective*. Amsterdam: North-Holland.

Arrow, Kenneth. 1974. *The Limits of Organization*. New York: W.W. Norton.

———. 1970. "The Organization of Economic Activity: Issues Pertinent to the Choice of Market versus Nonmarket Allocation." In *Public Expenditures and Policy Analysis*, edited by R.H. Haveman and Julius Margolis, pp. 59–73. Chicago: Markham.

———. 1963. *Social Choice and Individual Values*. 2d ed. New York: Wiley.

Arrow, Kenneth, and Tibor Scitovsky, eds. 1969. *Readings in Welfare Economics*. Homewood, Ill.: Richard D. Irwin.

Atiyah, P.S. 1980. *Accidents, Compensation, and the Law*. 3d ed. London: Weidenfeld and Nicholson.

———. 1981. "The Theoretical Basis of Contract Law: An English Perspective." *International Review of Law and Economics* 1: 183–205.

Atkinson, A.B., and J.E. Stiglitz. 1980. *Lectures On Public Economics*. New York: McGraw-Hill.

Axelrod, Robert. 1984. *The Evolution of Cooperation*. New York: Basic Books.

Ayres, C.E. 1962. *The Theory of Economic Progress*. 2d ed. New York: Schocken Books.

Backhaus, Juergen. 1985. "Public Policy toward Corporate Structures: Two Chicago Approaches." *Journal of Economic Issues* 11: 365–73.

Badelt, Christoph. 1985. "The Economics of Volunteer Groups: A Neoinstitutionalist Approach." Unpublished.

Bain, Joe S. 1966a. *Northern California Water Industry*. Baltimore, Md.: Johns Hopkins University Press.

———. 1966b. *Industrial Differences in Industrial Structure*. New Haven, Conn.: Yale University Press.

Baldassarre, Antonio. (curatore). 1985. *I Limiti Della Democrazia*. Roma-Bari: Gius Laterza and Figli.

Banfield, Edward. 1958. *The Moral Basis of a Backward Society*. New York: Free Press.

Baran, Paul A. 1957. *The Political Economy of Growth*. New York: Monthly Review Press.

Barlowe, Raleigh. 1972. *Land Resource Economics*. Englewood Cliffs, N.J.: Prentice-Hall.

Bartlett, Randall. 1973. *Economic Foundation of Political Power*. New York: Free Press.

Bator, Francis, M. 1962. *The Question of Government Spending*. New York: Crowell-Collier.

Baumol, William. 1982. "Applied Fairness Theory and Rationing Policy." *American Economic Review* 72: 639–51.

———. 1979. "Quasi Optimality: The Price We Must Pay for a Price System." *Journal of Political Economy* 87(3): 578–99.

———. 1965. *Welfare Economics and the Theory of the State*. 2d ed. Cambridge, Mass.: Harvard University Press.

Baumol, William, and J. A. Ordover. 1977. "On the Optimality of Public-Goods Pricing with Exclusion Devices." *Kyklos* 30(1): 5–21.

Baxter, William F., and Lillian R. Altree. 1972. "Legal Aspects of Airport Noise." *Journal of Law and Economics* 15: 1–113.

Bazelon, David T. 1959. *The Paper Economy*. New York: Random House.

Becker, Arthur P., ed. 1969. *Land and Building Taxes: Their Effect on Economic Development*. Madison: University of Wisconsin Press.

Becker, Gary S. 1976. "Altruism, Egoism, and Genetic Fitness." *Journal of Political Economy* 84: 817–26.

————. 1974. "A Theory of Social Interactions." *Journal of Political Economy* 82: 1063–93.

Becker, Lawrence C. 1977. *Property Rights: Philosophic Foundations.* London: Routledge & Kegan Paul.

Benham, Alexandra, and Lee Benham. 1975. "Regulating through the Professions: A Perspective on Information Control." *Journal of Law and Economics* 18: 421–47.

Berle, Adolf A., Jr. 1959. *Power without Property.* New York: Harcourt, Brace and World.

Bernardo, Roberto. 1971. *The Theory of Moral Incentives in Cuba.* University: University of Alabama Press.

Bernholz, Peter. 1974. "Logrolling, Arrow Paradox, and Decision Rules." *Kyklos* 27: 49–61.

Besen, Stanley M. 1974. "The Economics of the Cable Television 'Consensus'." *Journal of Law and Economics* 17: 43–52.

Bessen, Jean-Francois. 1978. *Economic Publique, L'echange Sans Marche.* Paris: Presses Universitaires de France.

Bettelheim, Charles. 1975. *Economic Calculation and Forms of Property.* New York: Monthly Review Press.

Beuscher, Jacob H. 1957. *Materials on Land Use Controls.* Madison, Wis.: College Typing.

Beuscher, Jacob H., and Jerry W. Morrison. 1955. "Judicial Zoning through Recent Nuisance Cases." *Wisconsin Law Review* 1955: 440–57.

Bickel, Alexander M. 1975. *The Morality of Consent.* New Haven, Conn.: Yale University Press.

Bish, Robert. 1971. *The Public Economy of Metropolitan Areas.* Chicago: Markham.

Bittlingmayer, George. 1982. "Decreasing Cost and Competition: A New Look at the Addyston Pipe Case." *Journal of Law and Economics* 25: 201–29.

Black, Duncan. 1958. *The Theory of Committees and Elections.* New York: Cambridge University Press.

Blawie, James L., and Marilyn J. Blawie. 1973. "The Other Cease Fires: Wind Down of the Domestic Wars; Cause for Concern about the Relationship between Crime, Contract, and Local Government Structures." *Journal of Urban Law* 50: 545–629.

Boadway, Robin, and Neil Bruce. 1984. *Welfare Economics.* Oxford, U.K.: Basil Blackwell.

Bogholt, Carl M. 1956. "The Value Judgment and Land Tenure Research." In *Land Tenure Research Workshop,* edited by Walter Chryst and Marshall Harris, pp. 131–7. Chicago: Farm Foundation.

Bonacich, Phillip. 1976. "Cooperation and Group Size in the N-Person Prisoners Dilemma." *Journal of Conflict Resolution* 20: 687–745.

Boulding, Kenneth. 1973. *The Economy of Love and Fear.* Belmont, Calif.: Wadsworth.

————. 1970. "The Network of Interdependence." Unpublished paper read at Public Choice Society Meeting, February 19.

————. 1968. "The Legitimation of the Market." *Nebraska Journal of Economics and Business* 7: 3–14.

————. 1958. *The Skills of the Economist.* Cleveland, Ohio: Howard Allen.

Boulding, Kenneth, and Tapan Mukerjee, eds. 1972. *Economic Imperialism: A Book of Readings.* Ann Arbor: University of Michigan Press.

Bowles, Roger. 1982. *Law and Economy*. Oxford, U.K.: Martin Robertson.

Braverman, Avishay, and Joseph Stiglitz. 1982. "Sharecropping and the Interlinking of Agrarian Markers." *American Economic Review* 72: 695–715.

Breton, Albert. 1974. *The Economy Theory of Representative Government*. Chicago: Aldine.

———. 1965. "A Theory of Government Grants." *Canadian Journal of Economic and Political Science* (May): 175–87.

Breton, Albert, and Raymond Breton. 1965. "An Economic Theory of Social Movements." *American Economic Review* 59: 198–205.

Breton, Albert, and Gianluigi Galeotti. 1985. "Is Proportional Representation Always the Best Rule?" *Public Finance* 40: 1–16.

Breton, Albert, and Anthony Scott. 1978. *The Economic Constitution of Federal States*. Toronto: University of Toronto Press.

Breton, Albert, and Ronald Wintrobe. 1982. *The Logic of Bureaucratic Conduct: An Economic Analysis of Competition, Exchange, and Efficiency in Private and Public Organizations*. New York: Cambridge University Press.

Broder, Josef. 1981. "Citizen Participation in Michigan District Courts." *Law and Economics*, edited by Warren Samuels and A. Allan Schmid, pp. 166–78. Boston: Martinus Nijhoff.

Broder, Josef, and A. A. Schmid. 1983. "Public Choice in Local Judicial Systems." *Public Choice* 40: 7–19.

Bromley, Daniel W. 1985. "Resources and Economic Development: An Institutionalist Perspective." *Journal of Economic Issues* 19: 779–96.

———. 1982. "Land and Water Problems: An Institutional Perspective." *American Journal of Agricultural Economics* 64: 834–44.

Bronfenbrenner, Martin. 1985. "Early American Leaders: Institutional and Critical Traditions." *American Economic Review* 75(6): 13–27.

Bronstein, Daniel A., and Donald E. Erickson. 1973. "Zoning Amendments in Michigan." *Journal of Urban Law* 50: 729–49.

Brown, Charles and James Medoff. 1978. "Trade Unions in the Production Process." *Journal of Political Economy* 86: 355–78.

Brown, John P. 1974. "Product Liability: The Case of an Asset with Random Life." *American Economic Review* 64: 149–61.

Brun, Andre. 1979. "Review of Property, Power, and Public Choice." *Journal of Economic Issues* 13(3): 747–49.

Buchanan, James M. 1975. *The Limits of Liberty*. Chicago: University of Chicago Press.

———. 1972. "Politics, Property, and the Law: An Alternative Interpretation of Miller, et. al. v. Schoene." *Journal of Law and Economics* 15: 439–52.

———. 1968. *The Demand and Supply of Public Goods*. Chicago: Rand McNally.

———. 1965. "An Economic Theory of Clubs." *Economica* 32: 1-14.

Buchanan, James M., and Warren J. Samuels. 1975. "On Some Fundamental Issues in Political Economy: An Exchange of Correspondence." *Journal of Economic Issues* 9: 15–38.

Buchanan, James M., and William C. Stubblebine. 1962. "Externality." *Economica* N.S. 29: 371–84.

Buchanan, James M., and Gordon Tullock. 1975. "Polluters' Profits and Political Response: Direct Controls versus Taxes." *American Economic Review* 65: 139–47.

———. 1962. *The Calculus of Consent*. Ann Arbor: University of Michigan Press.

Bullock, Kari and John Baden. 1977. "Communes and the Logic of the Commons." In *Managing the Commons*, edited by Garrett Hardin and John Baden, pp. 182–99. San Francisco: Freeman.

Burke, D. Barlow, and N. Kittrie. 1972. *The Real Estate Process and Its Costs.* Washington, D.C.: American University Press.

Burkhead, Jesse, and Jerry Miner. 1971. *Public Expenditure.* Chicago: Aldine.

Burrows, Paul. 1980. *The Economic Theory of Pollution Control.* Cambridge: Massachusetts Institute of Technology Press.

———, ed. 1981. *The Economic Approach to Law.* London: Butterworths.

Calabresi, Guido and Philip Bobbitt. 1978. *Tragic Choices.* New York: W.W. Norton.

Campbell, Donald T., and H.L. Ross. 1968. "The Connecticut Crackdown on Speeding: Time Series Data in Quasi-Experimental Analysis." *Law and Society Review* 2: 33–53.

Campbell, Donald T., and Julian T. Stanley. 1963. *Experimental and Quasi-Experimental Designs for Research.* Chicago: Rand McNally.

Carter, Michael R. 1985. "A Wisconsin Institutionalist Perspective on Microeconomic Theory of Institutions: The Insufficiency of Pareto Efficiency." *Journal of Economic Issues* 19: 797–813.

Caves, Richard E., and Marc J. Roberts, eds. 1975. *Regulating the Product, Quality, and Variety.* Cambridge, Mass.: Ballinger.

Cell, Charles P. 1980. "Selective Incentives vs. Ideological Commitment: The Motivation for Membership in Wise Farm Organizations." *American Journal of Agricultural Economics* 62: 517–24.

Chamberlain, John. 1974. "Provision of Collective Goods as a Function of Group Size." *American Political Science Review* 68: 707–16.

Chazen, Leonard, and Leonard Ross. 1970. "Federal Regulation of Cable Television: The Visible Hand." *Harvard Law Review* 83: 1820–41.

Chenery, Hollis P., and Larry Westphal. 1969. "Economies of Scale and Investment over Time." In *Public Economics*, edited by Henri Guitton and Julius Margolis, pp. 359–87. New York: St. Martins Press.

Cheung, Steve. 1978. *The Myth of Social Cost.* London: Institute of Economic Affairs.

———. 1970. "The Structure of a Contract and the Theory of a Non-Exclusive Resource." *Journal of Law and Economics* 13: 49–70.

Ciriacy-Wantrup, S.V. 1967. "Water Policy and Economic Optimizing: Some Conceptual Problems in Water Research." *American Economic Review* 57: 179–89.

———. 1963. *Resource Conservation.* Berkeley: University of California Press.

Ciriacy-Wantrup, S.V., and Richard Bishop. 1975. "Common Property as a Concept in Natural Resources Policy." *Natural Resources Journal* 15: 713–27.

Clark, John Maurice. 1923. *Studies in the Economics of Overhead Costs.* Chicago: University of Chicago Press.

Clawson, Marion. 1960. "Suburban Development Districts." *Journal of the American Institute of Planners* 26: 69–83.

Clawson, Marion, and Peter Hall. 1973. *Planning and Urban Growth: A Comparison.* Baltimore, Md.: Johns Hopkins University Press.

Cline, William R. 1970. *Economic Consequences of a Land Reform in Brazil.* Amsterdam: North-Holland.

Coase, Ronald. 1974a. "The Choice of the Institutional Framework: A Comment." *Journal of Law and Economics* 17: 494–95.

———. 1974b. "The Lighthouse in Economics." *Journal of Law and Economics* 17: 357–76.

———. 1960. "The Problem of Social Cost." *Journal of Law and Economics* 3: 1–44.

———. 1946. "The Marginal Cost Controversy." *Economica* 13: 169–82.

Cochrane, Willard W. 1958. *Farm Prices, Myth, and Reality.* Minneapolis: University of Minnesota Press.

Cohen, Stephan. 1969. *Modern Capitalist Planning: The French Model.* Cambridge, Mass.: Harvard University Press.

Colander, David, ed. 1984. *Neoclassical Political Economy.* Cambridge, Mass.: Ballinger.

Cole, Robert E. 1979. *Work, Mobility, and Participation: A Comparative Study of American and Japanese Industry.* Berkeley: University of California Press.

Collard, David. 1981. *Altruism and Economy.* Oxford: Martin Robertson.

Commons, John R. 1950. *The Economics of Collective Action.* New York: Macmillan.

———. 1934. *Institutional Economics.* New York: Macmillan.

———. 1924. *Legal Foundations of Capitalism.* New York: Macmillan.

———. 1909. "American Shoemakers, 1648–1895." *Quarterly Journal of Economics* 25: 39–84.

———. 1907. *Proportional Representation.* 2d ed. New York: Macmillan.

Convery, Frank, and A. Allan Schmid. 1983. *Policy Aspects of Land Use Planning in Ireland.* Dublin: Economic and Social Research Institute.

Cook, David T. 1975. "Drawbacks Found in Assembly Alternative." *Christian Science Monitor,* October 30.

Cook, Virginia G. 1976. *Corporate Farming and the Family Farm.* Lexington, Ky.: Council of State Governments.

Cosciani, Cesare. 1977. *Scienza Della Finanzi.* Torino: Unione Typografico-Editrice Torinese.

Costonis, John J. 1974. *Space Adrift.* Urbana: University of Illinois Press.

Coyer, Brian. 1973. "Patterns of Social Dominance and Political Interactions in Agrarian Societies." Paper read at International Studies Association Midwest meeting, April.

Crain, William M., and Robert B. Ekelund, Jr. 1976. "Chadwick and Demsetz on Competition and Regulation." *Journal of Law and Economics* 19: 149–62.

Crocker, Thomas D. 1971. "Externalities, Property Rights, and Transactions Costs: An Empirical Study." *Journal of Law and Economics* 14: 451–64.

Cross, John G., and Melvin J. Guyer. 1980. *Social Traps.* Ann Arbor: University of Michigan Press.

Dahl, Robert A., and Edward R. Tufte. 1973. *Size and Democracy.* Stanford, Calif.: Stanford University Press.

Dahlman, Carl. 1979. "Problem of Externality." *Journal of Law and Economics* 22: 141–162.

Davies, David G. 1977. "Property Rights and Economic Efficiency: The Australian Airlines Revisited." *Journal of Law and Economics* 20: 233–6.

———. 1971. "The Efficiency of Public versus Private Firms: The Case of Australia's Two Airlines." *Journal of Law and Economics* 14: 149–65.

Davis, J. Clarence, III. 1974. "How Does the Agenda Get Set?" In *The Governance of*

Common Property Resources, edited by Edwin T. Haefele, pp. 149–77. Baltimore, Md.: Johns Hopkins University Press.

Davis, Otto A., and Andrew Whinston. 1962. "Externalities, Welfare, and the Theory of Games." *Journal of Political Economy* 70: 241–62.

DeAlessi, Louis. 1980. "The Economics of Property Rights: A Survey of the Literature." *Research In Law and Economics* 2: 1–47.

———. 1974. "An Economics Analysis of Government Ownership and Regulation: Theory and the Evidence from the Electric Power Industry." *Public Choice* 19: 1–42.

Demsetz, Harold. 1967. "Toward a Theory of Property Rights." *American Economic Review* 57: 347–73.

DeVany, Arthur S. 1975. "Capacity Utilization under Alternative Regulatory Restraints: An Analysis of Taxi Markets." *Journal of Political Economy* 83: 83–94.

Dewey, Alice G. 1962. *Peasant Marketing in Java.* New York: Free Press.

Dewey, John. 1922. *Human Nature and Conduct.* New York: Modern Library.

Dick, Daniel. 1974. *Pollution, Congestion, and Nuisance.* Lexington, Mass.: Heath-Lexington.

Dobb, Maurice. 1963. *Studies in the Development of Capitalism.* Rev. ed. New York: International.

Doeringer, Peter B., and Michael J. Piore. 1971. *Internal Labor Markets and Manpower Analysis.* Lexington, Mass.: D.C. Heath.

Dorner, Peter. 1971. *Land Reform in Latin America.* Land Economics Monographs, no. 3. Madison: University of Wisconsin, Land Tenure Center.

———, ed. 1970. *Cooperative and Commune.* Madison: University of Wisconsin Press.

Downs, Anthony. 1957. *An Economic Theory of Democracy.* New York: Harper & Row.

———. 1967. *Inside Bureaucracy.* Boston: Little, Brown.

Duesenberry, James. 1949. *Income, Saving, and the Theory of Consumer Behavior.* Cambridge, Mass.: Harvard University Press.

Dunham, Allison. 1973. "Separation of Ownership from Decisions about Usefulness." In *Perspectives of Property,* edited by Gene Wunderlich and W.L. Gibson, Jr., pp. 9-16. University Park: Pennsylvania State University Press.

Dunlop, John T. 1977. "Policy Decisions and Research in Economics and Industrial Relations." *Industrial and Labor Relations Review* 30: 276–77.

Dworkin, Gerald. 1982. "More Is Better than Less: The Case of Choice." *Midwest Studies In Philosophy.*

Eckstein, Otto. 1965. *Water Resource Development: The Economies of Project Evaluation.* Cambridge, Mass.: Harvard University Press.

Edney, J.J. 1981. "Paradoxes on the Commons: Scarcity and the Problem of Equality." *Journal of Community Psychology* 9: 3–34.

Ely, Richard T. 1914. *Property and Contract.* New York: Macmillan.

Engelbrecht-Wiggans, Richard. 1980. "Auctions and Bidding Models: A Survey." *Management Science* 26: 119–42.

Engstrom, R., and M. McDonald. 1981. "The Election of Blacks to City Councils: Clarifying the Impact of Electoral Arrangements on the Seats/Population Relationship." *American Political Science Review* 75: 344–54.

Epstein, Richard A. 1985. *Takings, Private Property, and the Power of Eminent Domain.* Cambridge, Mass.: Harvard University Press.

————. 1973. "Toward a Theory of Strict Liability." *Journal of Legal Studies* 2: 151–77.

Erikson, Erik. 1958. *Young Man Luther*. New York: W.W. Norton.

Eswaran, Mukesh, and Ashok Kotwal. 1985. "A Theory of Contractual Structure in Agriculture." *American Economic Review* 75: 352–67.

————. 1976. *European Broadcasting Union Review*. 27: 43–45.

Evan, William M., ed. 1971. *Organizational Experiments: Laboratory and Field Research*. New York: Harper & Row.

Fama, E.F. 1980. "Agency Problems and the Theory of the Firm." *Journal of Public Economics* 88: 288–307.

Fama, E.F., and M.C. Jensen. 1983. "Separation of Ownership and Control." *Journal of Law and Economics*. 26: 301–26.

Favero, Philip. 1977. "The Processes of Collective Action: Small Electric Companies in Michigan." Ph.D. thesis, Michigan State University, East Lansing.

Feige, Edgar L., and Douglas K. Pearce. 1973. "The Wage-Price Control Experiment: Did It Work?" *Challenge* 16: 40–44.

Feldman, Allan M. 1980. *Welfare Economics and Social Choice Theory*. Boston: Martinus Nijhoff.

Field, Alexander J. 1981. "The Problem with Neoclassical Institutional Economics." *Explorations In Economic History* 18: 174–98.

————. 1970. "On the Explanation of Rules Using Rational Choice Models." *Journal of Economic Issues* 13: 49–72.

Fiorina, Morris P. 1979. "Comment on Public Choice in Practice." In *Collective Decision Making*, edited by Clifford Russell. Baltimore, Md.: Johns Hopkins University Press.

Fischel, William A. 1985. *The Economics of Zoning Laws: A Property Rights Approach to American Land Use Control*. Baltimore, Md.: Johns Hopkins University Press.

Fleming, R.W. 1975. "The Significance of the Wagner Act." In *Labor and the New Deal*, edited by Milton Derber and Edwin Young, pp. 121–57. Madison: University of Wisconsin Press.

Forte, Francesco. 1984. "Democracy as a Public Good." *Economia Della Scelta Pubbliche* 3: 143–54.

Freeman, A. Myrick, II, Robert H. Haveman, and Allen V. Kneese. 1973. *The Economics of Environmental Policy*. New York: John Wiley & Sons.

Freidman, Lawrence M. 1965. *Contract Law in America*. Madison: University of Wisconsin Press.

Frey, Bruno. 1978. *Modern Political Economy*. New York: John Wiley & Sons.

Friedman, Milton, 1975. *There's No Such Thing as a Free Lunch*. LaSalle, Ill.: Open Court.

————. 1962. *Capitalism and Freedom*. Chicago: University of Chicago Press.

Frohlich, Norman, and Joe A. Oppenheimer. 1970. "I Get by with a Little Help from My Friends." *World Politics* 23: 104–20.

Frohlich, Norman, Joe A. Oppenheimer, and Oran R. Young. 1971. *Political Leadership and Collective Goods*. Princeton, N.J.: Princeton University Press.

Fromm, Erich. 1941. *Escape from Freedom*. New York: Avon Books.

Frydman, Roman. 1982. "Toward an Understanding of Market Processes, Individual Expectations, Learning, and Convergence to Rational Expectations Equilibrium." *American Economic Review* 72: 652–68.

Furubotn, Eirik. 1974. "Bank Credit and the Labor-Managed Firm: The Yugoslav Case."

In *The Economics of Property Rights,* edited by Eirik Furubotn and Svetozar Pejovich, pp. 257–76. Cambridge, Mass.: Ballinger.

Furubotn, Eirik, and Svetozar Pejovich. 1972. "Property Rights and Economic Theory: A Survey of Recent Literature." *Journal of Economic Literature* 10: 1137–62.

————, eds. 1974. *The Economics of Property Rights.* Cambridge, Mass.: Ballinger.

Gaffney, Mason. 1965. "Property Taxes and the Frequency of Urban Renewal." In *Proceedings of the Fifty-Seventh Annual Conference on Taxation,* edited by Walter J. Kress, pp. 272–85. Harrisburg, Pa.: National Tax Association.

Galbraith, J.K. 1967. *The New Industrial State.* Boston: Houghton Mifflin.

Galeotti, Gianluigi. 1980. "Public Choice and Problems of Preference Aggregation." In *Public Choice and Public Finance,* edited by K.W. Roskamp, pp. 77–96. Paris: Cujas.

Gamson, William A. 1975. *The Strategy of Social Protest.* Homewood, Ill.: Dorsey Press.

George, Henry. 1926. *Progress and Poverty.* Garden City, N.Y.: Garden City.

Gerschenkron, Alexander. 1969. "History of Economic Doctrines and Economic History." *American Economic Review* 59: 1–17.

Glaeser, Martin G. 1957. *Public Utilities in American Capitalism.* New York: Macmillan.

Glass, G.V., G.C. Tiso, and T.O. Maguire. 1970. "Analysis of Data on the 1900 Revision of German Divorce Laws as a Time Series Quasi-Experiment." *Law and Society Review* 6: 539–62.

Goldberg, Victor P. 1974. "Institutional Change and the Quasi-Invisible Hand." *Journal of Law and Economics* 17: 494–95.

Goodrich, Carter. 1968. "State in, State out: A Pattern of Development Policy." *Journal of Economic Issues* 2: 365–83.

Gordon, Scott. 1976. "The New Contractarians." *Journal of Political Economy* 84: 573–90.

Gordon, Wendell. 1980. *Institutional Economics.* Austin: University of Texas Press.

Gotsch, Carl H. 1972. "Technical Change and the Distribution of Income in Rural Areas." *American Journal of Agricultural Economics* 34: 326–41.

Graham, Hugh D., and Ted R. Gurr. 1969. *The History of Violence in America.* New York: Bantam Books.

Gramlich, E.M., and P.P. Koshel. 1975. "Is Real-World Experimentation Possible? The Case of Educational Performance Contracting." *Policy Analysis* 1: 511–30.

Granick, David. 1974. "Why Managers Perform Differently in Different Countries." *Challenge* 17: 27–34.

————. 1972. *Managerial Comparisons of Four Developed Countries.* Cambridge: Massachusetts Institute of Technology Press.

Greenwood, P.H., and C.A. Ingene. 1978. "Uncertain Externalities, Liability Rules, and Resource Allocation." *Agricultural Economics Research* 68: 300–10.

Gregory, Christopher. 1982. *Gifts and Commodities.* New York: Cambridge University Press.

Grossman, Sanford J., and Oliver D. Hart. 1982. "Corporate Financial Structure and Managerial Incentives." In *The Economics of Information,* edited by John J. McCall, pp. 107–40. Chicago: University of Chicago Press.

Habermas, Jurgen. 1975. *Legitimation Crisis.* Boston: Beacon Press.

Haefele, Edwin T., ed. 1974. *The Governance of Common Property Resources.* Baltimore, Md.: Johns Hopkins University Press.

Hagman, Donald G. 1975. "A New Deal: Trading Windfalls for Wipeouts." In *No Land Is an Island*. San Francisco: Institute for Contemporary Studies.

Hamilton, W.H. 1932. "Property according to Locke." *Yale Law Journal* 4: 964–80.

Hanf, Kenneth, and Geoffrey Wandesforde-Smith. 1972. *Institutional Design and Environmental Management: The Tahoe Regional Planning Agency*. Research Report no. 24. Davis: University of California, Institute of Governmental Affairs.

Hansen, David E., and S.J. Schwartz. 1975. "Landowner Behavior at the Rural-Urban Fringe in Response to Preferential Property Taxation." *Land Economics* 51: 341–54.

Harrington, Michael. 1976. *The Twilight of Capitalism*. New York: Simon and Schuster.

Harter, Lafayette G. 1962. *John R. Commons: His Assault on Laissez-Faire*. Corvallis: Oregon State University.

Haveman, Robert. 1970. *The Economics of the Public Sector*. New York: John Wiley & Sons.

Hayami, Yujiro, and Vernon W. Ruttan. 1985. *Agricultural Development*. Baltimore, Md.: Johns Hopkins University Press.

Hayek, Friedrich. 1944. *The Road to Serfdom*. Chicago: University of Chicago Press.

Head, John G. 1974. *Public Goods and Public Welfare*. Durham: Duke University Press.

Heath, Anthony. 1976. *Rational Choice and Social Exchange*. Cambridge, U.K.: Cambridge University Press.

Heckathorn, Douglas D., and Steven M. Maser. 1987. "Bargaining and Constitutional Contracts." *American Journal of Political Science* 31: 142–68.

Heilbroner, Robert L. 1985. *The Nature and Logic of Capitalism*. New York: W.W. Norton.

———. 1962. *The Making of Economic Society*. Englewood Cliffs, N.J.: Prentice-Hall.

Henderson, J. Vernon. 1980. "Community Development: The Effects of Growth and Uncertainty." *American Economic Review* 70: 894–910.

Hirsch, Werner A. 1979. *Law and Economics*. New York: Academic Press.

Hirschman, Albert O. 1984a. "Against Parsimony: Three Easy Ways of Complicating Some Categories of Economic Discourse." *American Economic Review* 72(2): 89–96.

———. 1984b. *Getting along Collectively: Grassroots Experience in Latin America*. New York: Pergamon Press.

———. 1970. *Exit, Voice, and Loyalty*. Cambridge, Mass.: Harvard University Press.

Hoffman, Elizabeth, and Mathew Spitzer. 1982. "The Coase Theorem: Some Experimental Tests." *Journal of Law and Economics* 25: 73–98.

Hohfeld, W.N. 1913. "Some Fundamental Legal Conceptions as Applied in Judicial Reasoning." *Yale Law Journal* 23: 16–59.

Holler, M.J., ed. 1983. *Coalitions and Collective Action*. Vienna: Physica-Verlag.

Horvat, Branko. 1982. *The Political Economy of Socialism*. New York: M.E. Sharpe.

Hoskins, W.G., and L. Dudley Stamp. 1963. *The Common Lands of England and Wales*. London: Collins.

Hostetler, John A. 1975. *Hutterite Society*. Baltimore, Md.: Johns Hopkins University Press.

Hurst, J. Willard. 1960. *Law and Social Process in United States History*. Ann Arbor: University of Michigan, School of Law.

———. 1956. *Law and the Conditions of Freedom in the Nineteenth Century United States*. Madison: University of Wisconsin Press.

Hyde, Lewis. 1983. *The Gift, Imagination, and the Erotic Life of Property,* New York: Vintage Books.

Illich, Ivan. 1976. *Medical Nemesis.* New York: Random House.

———. 1973. *Tools for Conviviality.* New York: Harper & Row.

Ingram, Helen M. 1969. *Patterns of Politics in Water Resource Development.* Santa Fe: University of New Mexico, Division of Government Research.

Intriligator, Michael D., ed. 1971. *Frontiers of Quantitative Economics.* Amsterdam: North-Holland.

Jensen, Michael. 1983. "Organization Theory and Methodology." *Accounting Review* 50: 319–39.

Jessua, Claude. 1968. *Couts Sociaux et Couts Prives.* Paris: Presses Universitaires de France.

Johnson, Chalmers. 1982. *MITI and the Japanese Miracle.* Stanford, Calif.: Stanford University Press.

Johnson, David B., ed. 1977. *Blood Policy: Issues and Alternatives.* Washington: American Enterprise Institute.

Johnson, Edwin L. 1967. "A Study in the Economics of Water Quality Management." *Water Resources Research* 3: 297.

Johnson, Glenn L. 1986. *Research Methodology for Economists: Philosophy and Practice.* New York: Macmillan.

———. 1982. "An Opportunity Cost View of Fixed Asset Theory and the Overproduction Trap: Comment." *American Journal of Agricultural Economics* 64: 773–75.

Johnson, Glenn L., and C. Leroy Quance, eds. 1972. *The Over Production Trap in U.S. Agriculture.* Baltimore, Md.: Johns Hopkins University Press.

Johnson, Harry G. 1971. *The Two Sector Model of General Equilibrium.* London: George Allen & Unwin.

Jones, Stephen R.G. 1984. *The Economics of Conformism.* Oxford, U.K.: Basil Blackwell.

Junker, Louis. 1967. "Capital Accumulation, Savings-Centered Theory, and Economic Development." *Journal of Economic Issues* 1: 25–43.

Kahneman, Daniel, Jack Knetsch, and Richard Thaler. 1986. "Fairness as a Constraint on Profit Seeking: Entitlements in the Market." *American Economic Review* 76: 728–41.

Kaldor, Nicholas. 1972. "The Irrelevance of Equilibrium Economics." *Economic Journal* 82: 1237–55.

———. 1956. "Alternative Theories of Distribution." *Review of Economic Studies* 23: 83–100.

Kalt, Joseph P., and Mark A. Zupan. 1984. "Capture and Ideology in the Economic Theory of Politics." *American Economic Review* 74: 279–300.

Kamerschen, David R. 1968. "The Influence of Ownership and Control on Profit Rates." *American Economic Review* 58: 432–47.

Kanel, Don. 1985. "Institutional Economics: Perspectives on Economy and Society." *Journal of Economic Issues* 19: 815–28.

———. 1974. "Property and Economic Power as Issues in Institutional Economics." *Journal of Economic Issues* 8: 827–40.

Kanovsky, Eliahu. 1966. *The Economy of the Israeli Kibbutz.* Cambridge, Mass.: Harvard University Press.

Kant, Immanuel. 1959. *Foundations of the Metaphysics of Morals,* translated by Lewis W. Beck. New York: Bobbs-Merrill.

Kapp, K. William. 1968. "In Defense of Institutional Economics." *Swedish Journal of Economics* 70: 1–18.

Kates, Robert. 1962. *Hazard and Choice Perception in Flood Plain Management.* Chicago: University of Chicago, Department of Geography.

Kelso, Louis O., and Patricia Hetter. 1973. "Corporate Social Responsibility without Corporate Suicide." *Challenge* 16: 52–57.

————. 1967. *Two-Factor Theory: The Economics of Reality.* New York: Random House.

Keohane, Robert. 1984. *After Hegemony: Cooperation and Discord in the World Political Economy.* Princeton, N.J.: Princeton University Press.

Khandwalla, P. N. 1977. *The Design of Organization.* New York: Harcourt, Brace, Jovanovich.

Kirp, David. 1976. "Growth Management, Zoning, Public Policy, and the Courts." *Policy Analysis* 2: 431–58.

Kiser, Larry L., and Elinor Ostrom. 1982. "The Three Worlds of Action: A Meta-theoretical Synthesis of Institutional Approaches." In *Strategies of Political Inquiry,* edited by Elinor Ostrom, pp. 179–222. Beverly Hills, Calif.: Sage.

Klein, Benjamin, R.G. Crawford, and A.A. Alchian. 1978. "Vertical Integration, Appropriable Rents, and the Competition Contracting Process." *Journal of Law and Economics* 21(2): 297–326.

Klein, B., and Keith Laffer. 1981. "The Role of Market Forces in Assuring Contractual Performance." *Journal of Political Economy* 89: 615–40.

Kneese, Allen V. 1964. *The Economics of Regional Water Quality Management.* Baltimore, Md.: Johns Hopkins University Press.

Kneese, Allen V., and Charles L. Schultze. 1975. *Pollution, Prices, and Public Policy.* Washington: Brookings Institution.

Knetsch, Jack. 1983. *Property Rights and Compensation.* London: Butterworths.

Knight, Frank. 1966. *Risk, Uncertainty, and Profit.* Boston and New York: Houghton Mifflin.

Kornai, Janos. 1971. *Anti-Equilibrium.* Amsterdam: North-Holland.

Kornhauser, Lewis A. 1980. "A Guide to the Perplexed Claims of Efficiency in the Law." *Hofstra Law Review* 8(3): 591–639.

Krutilla, John V. 1967. "Conservation Reconsidered." *American Economic Review* 57: 777–86.

Krutilla, John V., and Anthony C. Fisher. 1975. *The Economics of Natural Environments.* Baltimore, Md.: Johns Hopkins University Press.

Kuperberg, Mark, and Charles Beitz, eds. 1983. *Law, Economics, and Philosophy.* Totowa, N.J.: Rowman and Allanheld.

Lancaster, Kevin J. 1979. *Variety, Equity, and Efficiency.* New York: Columbia University Press.

————. 1966. "A New Approach to Consumer Theory." *Journal of Political Economy* 74: 132–57.

Landa, Janet. 1976. "An Exchange Economy with Legally Binding Contract: A Public Choice Approach." *Journal of Economic Issues* 10: 905–22.

Lang, Mahlon. 1980. "Economic Efficiency and Policy Comparison." *American Journal of Agricultural Economics* 62: 772–77.

Langlois, Richard N., ed. 1986. *Economics as a Process.* New York: Cambridge University Press.

Lardy, Nicholas R. 1983. *Agriculture in China's Modern Economic Development.* New York: Cambridge University Press.

Larner, Robert J. 1970. *Management Control and the Large Corporation.* New York: Dunnellen.

Lee, Richard B., and Irven DeVore, eds. 1968. *Man the Hunter.* Chicago: Aldine.

Leibenstein, Harvey. 1983. "Property Rights and X-Efficiency: Comment." *American Economic Review* 83: 831–42.

———. 1979. "A Branch of Economics Is Missing: Micro-Micro Theory," *Journal of Economic Literature* 17: 477–502.

———. 1978. *General X-Efficiency and Economic Development.* New York: Oxford University Press.

———. 1976. *Beyond Economic Man.* Cambridge, Mass.: Harvard University Press.

———. 1950. "Bandwagon, Snob, and Veblen Effects in the Theory of Consumer Demand." *Quarterly Journal of Economics* 64: 193–207.

Leibowitz, Arleen, and Robert Tollison. 1980. "Free Riding, Shirking, and Team Production in Legal Partnerships." *Economic Inquiry* 18: 380–94.

Leland, Hayne E. 1978. "Optimal Risk Sharing and the Leasing of Natural Resources." *Quarterly Journal of Economics* 92: 413–37.

Lenhoff, A. 1962. "Contracts of Adhesion and the Freedom of Contract: A Comparative Study in the Light of American and Foreign Law." *Tulane Law Review* 36: 481.

Lerner, Abba. 1944. *The Economics of Control.* New York: Macmillan.

Levy, Julian H. 1966. "Focal Leverage Points in Problems Relating to Real Property." *Columbia Law Review* 66: 275–85.

Levy-Lambert, H. 1977. "Investment and Pricing Policy in the French Public Sector." *American Economic Review* 67: 302–13.

Lindahl, Erik. 1958. "Just Taxation: A Positive Solution." In *Classics in the Theory of Public Finance,* edited by Richard Musgrave and A.T. Peacock, pp. 168–76. London: Macmillan.

Lindblom, Charles E. 1977. *Politics and Markets.* New York: Basic Books.

———. 1965. *The Intelligence of Democracy: Decision Making through Mutual Adjustment.* New York: Free Press.

Lineberry, R., and E. Fowler. 1982. "Reformism and Public Policy in American Cities." In *Classics of Urban Politics and Public Administration,* edited by William Murin. Oak Park, Ill.: Moore.

Little, I.M.D. 1957. *A Critique of Welfare Economics.* 2d ed. London: Oxford University Press.

Locke, John. 1690. *An Essay Concerning the True Original Extent and End of Civil Government.* New York: Hafner.

Macaulay, Jacqueline, and Leonard Berkowitz, eds. 1970. *Altruism and Helping Behavior.* New York: Academic Press.

Macaulay, Stewart. 1963. "Non-Contractual Relations in Business." *American Sociological Review* 28: 55–66.

MacKaay, Ejan. 1982. *Economics of Information and Law.* Boston: Kluwer-Nijhoff.

Macpherson, C.B. 1978. *The Meaning of Property, in Property: Mainstream Critical Positions.* Toronto: University of Toronto Press.

Magnani, Italo. 1971. *La Teoria Pura Dell'Equilibrio Della Citta E Gli Effetti Delle Imposte.* Milan: Franco Anglei.

Maine, Henry S. 1880. *Villge Communities in the East and West.* 3d ed. New York: Henry Holt.

Maital, Shlomo. 1982. *Minds, Markets, and Money.* New York: Basic Books.

Manne, Henry G. 1975. *The Economics of Legal Relationships: Readings in the Economics of Property Rights.* St. Paul, Minn.: West.

Marglin, Stephen A. 1974. "What Do Bosses Do? The Origins and Functions of Hierarchy in Capitalist Production." *The Review of Radical Political Economics* 6: 60–112.

Margolis, Howard. 1982. *Selfishness, Altruism, and Rationality.* Cambridge, U.K.: Cambridge University Press.

Marx, Karl. 1894. *Capital.* 1967 rev. ed., vol. 3. New York: International.

Maser, Steven M. 1985. "Demographic Factors affecting Constitutional Decisions." *Public Choice* 47: 121–62.

Mashaw, Jerry L. 1985. *Due Process in the Administrative State.* New Haven, Conn.: Yale University Press.

McCloskey, Daniel. 1985. *The Rhetoric of Economics.* Madison: University of Wisconsin Press.

McDowell, George R. 1985. "Political Economy of Extension Program Design," *American Journal of Agricultural Economics* 67: 717–25.

———. 1975. "Whose Preferences Count? A Study of the Effects of Community Size and Characteristics on the Distribution of the Benefits of Schooling." Ph.D. dissertation, Michigan State University, East Lansing.

McGregor, Andrew. 1977. "Rent Extraction and the Survival of the American Agricultural Production Cooperation." *American Journal of Agricultural Economics* 59: 478–88.

McKean, Roland, 1970a. "Products Liability: Implications of Some Changing Property Rights." *Quarterly Journal of Economics* 84: 611–26.

———. 1970b. "Products Liability: Trends and Implications." *University of Chicago Law Review* 38: 3–63.

McWilliams, Carey. 1945. *Small Farm and Big Farm.* Public Affairs Pamphlet no. 100. New York: Public Affairs Committee.

Meade, James, M. 1964. *Efficiency, Equality, and the Ownership of Property.* London: George Allen & Unwin.

Mercuro, Nicholas, and Timothy P. Ryan. 1984. *Law, Economics, and Public Policy.* Greenwich, Conn.: JAI Press.

Meyers, Frederic. 1964. *Ownership of Jobs: A Comparative Study.* Los Angeles: University of California, Institute of Industrial Relations.

Michigan Statutes Annotated. 1964. 281.301. Public Act 20.

Milgrom, Paul R. and Robert J. Weber. 1982. "A Theory of Auctions and Competitive Bidding." *Econometrica* 50: 1089–1122.

Miller, Gary J. 1985. "Progressive Reform as Induced Institutional Preferences." *Public Choice* 47: 163–81.

Miller, Gary J., and Joe A. Oppenheimer. 1982. "Universalism in Experimental Committees." *American Political Science Review* 76: 561–74.

Mirowski, Philip. 1981. "Is There a Mathematical Neoinstitutional Economics?" *Journal of Economic Issues* 15(3): 593–613.

Mishan, E.J. 1981. *Introduction to Normative Economics.* New York: Oxford University Press.

———. 1969. "The Relationship between Joint Products, Collective Goods, and External Effects." *Journal of Political Economy* 72: 239–48.

———. 1968. "What Is Producer's Surplus?" *American Economic Review* 58: 1269–82.

———. 1967. "Pareto Optimality and the Law." *Oxford Economic Papers* n.s. 19: 255.

———. 1961. "Welfare Criteria for External Effects." *American Economic Review* 51: 594–613.

Mitchell, C. Clyde. 1955. "Needed: A More Realistic Approach to Farm Policy." In *Contemporary Readings in Agricultural Economics,* edited by Harold Halcrow, pp. 230–34. New York: Prentice-Hall.

Monsen, Joseph R., John S. Chiu, and David E. Cooley. 1968. "The Effect of Separation of Ownership and Control on the Performance of the Large Firm." *Quarterly Journal of Economics* 82: 435–51.

Montias, John M. 1976. *The Structure of Economic Systems.* New Haven, Conn.: Yale University Press.

Moore, T.G. 1970. "The Effectiveness of Regulation of Electric Utility Prices." *Southern Economic Journal* 36: 465–75.

Morgenstern, Oskar. 1972. "Thirteen Critical Points in Contemporary Economic Theory: An Interpretation." *Journal of Economic Literature* 10: 1171–74.

Morrison, Denton E. 1971. "Some Notes toward a Theory of Relative Deprivation, Social Movements, and Social Change." *American Behavioral Scientist* 14: 675–90.

Morrison, Denton, E., and Harriet Tillock. 1979. "Group Size and Contributions to Collective Action," *Research in Social Movements, Conflicts, and Change,* vol 2, edited by Louis Kreisberg, pp. 131–58. Greenwich, Conn.: JAI Press.

Mueller, Dennis C. 1976. "Public Choice: A Survey." *Journal of Economic Literature* 14: 393–433.

Mueller, Willard F. 1983. "The Anti-Antitrust Movement." In *Industrial Organization, Antitrust, and Public Policy,* edited by John V. Craven, pp. 19–40. Boston: Kluwer Nijhoff.

Munby, D.L. 1962. *Cahiers de L'Institut de Science Economique Applique,* no. 130 (October): 52.

Musgrave, Richard. 1969. "Provision for Public Goods." In *Public Economics,* edited by Julius Margolis and Henri Guitton, pp. 124–44. New York: St. Martin's Press.

———. 1959. *The Theory of Public Finance.* New York: McGraw-Hill.

Musgrave, Richard, and Peggy Musgrave. 1974. *Public Finance in Theory and Practice.* New York: McGraw-Hill.

Myrdal, Gunnar. 1974. "What Is Development?" *Journal of Economic Issues* 8: 729–36.

———. 1957. *Economic Theory and Underdeveloped Regions.* London: Duckworth.

Nelson, R.R., and S.G. Winter. 1974. "Neoclassical vs. Evolutionary Theories of Economic Growth: Critique." *Economic Journal* 84: 886–905.

Nicols, Alfred. 1967. "Stock versus Mutual Savings and Loan Associations: Some Evidence of Differences in Behavior." *American Economic Review* 57: 337–46.

Niskanen, William A. 1971. *Bureaucracy and Representative Government.* Chicago: Aldine.

Nitzan, Shmuel, and Jacob Paroush. 1985. *Collective Decision Making: An Economic Outlook.* Cambridge, U.K.: Cambridge University Press.

Norgaard, Richard. 1985. "Coevolutionary Development Potential." *Land Economics* 60(2): 160–73.

North, Douglas C. 1981. *Structure and Change in Economic History.* New York: W.W. Norton.

North, Douglass C., and Robert P. Thomas. 1973. *The Rise of the Western World.* New York: Cambridge University Press.

Nove, Alec. 1973. *Efficiency Criteria for Nationalized Industries.* London: George Allen & Unwin.

———. 1969. "Internal Economies." *Economic Journal* 79: 847–60.

Ochs, Jack. 1974. *Public Finance.* New York: Harper & Row.

O'Driscoll, Gerald P. 1976. "The American Express Case: Public Good or Monopoly?" *Journal of Law and Economics* 19: 163–78.

Ogus, A.I. 1983. "Social Costs in a Private Law Setting." *International Review of Law and Economics* 3: 27–44.

Ogus, A.I., and C.G. Veljanovski, eds. 1984. *Readings in the Economics of Law and Regulation.* Oxford, U.K.: Clarendon Press, Oxford University Press.

Olson, Mancur. 1982. *The Rise and Decline of Nations.* New Haven: Yale University Press.

———. 1965. *The Logic of Collective Action.* Cambridge, Mass.: Harvard University Press.

Ostrom, Elinor. 1986. "A Method of Institutional Analysis." In *Guidance Control and Evaluation in the Public Sector,* edited by Franz-Xaver Kaufman, pp. 459–75. Berlin: Walter de Gruyter.

Ostrom, Elinor, et al. 1973. *Community Organization and the Provision of Police Services.* Beverly Hills, Calif.: Sage.

Ostrom, Vincent. 1973. *The Intellectual Crisis in American Public Administration.* University: University of Alabama.

Ouchi, William G. 1981. *Theory Z: How American Business Can Meet the Japanese Challenge.* New York: Addison-Wesley.

Parsons, Kenneth H. 1985. "John R. Commons: His Relevance to Contemporary Economics." *Journal of Economic Issues* 19: 755–78.

———. 1974. "The Institutional Basis of an Agricultural Market Economy." *Journal of Economic Issues* 8: 737–57.

———. 1942. "John R. Commons' Point of View." *Journal of Land and Public Utility Economics* 18: 245–66.

Parsons, Talcott, and Neil J. Smelser. 1965. *Economy and Society.* New York: Free Press.

Parsons, Kenneth H., Raymond J. Penn, and Philip Raup, eds. 1956. *Land Tenure.* Madison: University of Wisconsin Press.

Pasinetti, Luigi L. 1961. "Rate of Profit and Income Distribution in Relation to the Rate of Economic Growth." *Review of Economic Studies* 29: 267–79.

Pauly, Mark. 1968. "The Economics of Moral Hazard: Comment." *American Economic Review* 58: 531–37.

Pauly, Mark, and M. Redisch. 1973. "The Not-for-Profit Hospital as a Physician's Cooperative." *American Economic Review* 63: 57–99.

Penn, Raymond J. 1961. "Public Interest in Private Property (Land)." *Land Economics* 37: 99–104.

Perlman, Selig. 1928. *Theory of the Labor Movement.* New York: Macmillan.

Perroux, Francois. 1969. *L'Economie du XXe Siecle.* Paris: Presses Universitare de France.

Perry, Elizabeth, and Christine Wong, eds. 1985. *The Political Economy of Reform in Post-Mao China.* Cambridge, Mass.: Harvard University Press.

Peterson, George E. 1975. "Voter Demand for Public School Expenditures." In *Public Needs and Private Behavior in Metropolitan Areas,* edited by John E. Jackson, pp. 99–119. Cambridge, Mass.: Ballinger Publishing Co.

Pfaff, Martin, ed. 1976. *Grants and Exchange.* Amsterdam: North-Holland.

Phelps, Edmund, ed. 1975. *Altruism, Morality, and Economic Theory.* New York: Russell Sage Foundation.

Philips, Louis. 1971. *Effects of Industrial Concentration: A Cross Section Analysis of the Common Market.* Amsterdam: North-Holland.

Pigou, A. C. 1946. *The Economics of Welfare.* 4th ed. London: Macmillan.

Pincus, Jonathon. 1977. *Pressure Groups and Politics in Antebellum Tariffs.* New York: Columbia University Press.

Pizzorno, Alesandro. 1983. "Sulla Razionalita della Scelta Democratia," *State e Mercato* 7: 3–46.

Platt, John. 1973. "Social Traps." *American Psychologist* 86: 641–51.

Polanyi, Karl. 1957. *Trade and Market in the Early Empires.* Glencoe, Ill.: Free Press.

———. 1944. *The Great Transformation.* Boston: Beacon Press.

Polinsky, A.M. 1983. *An Introduction to Law and Economics.* Boston: Little, Brown.

———. 1980. "On the Choice between Property Rules and Liability Rules." *Economic Inquiry* 18: 233–46.

Posner, Richard A. 1979. "Some Uses and Abuses of Economics in Law." *University of Chicago Law Review* 46: 281–306.

———. 1972a. "The Appropriate Scope of Regulation in the Cable Television Industry." *Bell Journal of Economics and Management Science* 3: 98–129.

———. 1972b. *Economic Analysis of Law.* Boston: Little, Brown.

———. 1969. "The Federal Trade Commission." *University of Chicago Law Review* 37: 47–66.

Preston, Ivan L. 1975. *The Great American Blow-up: Puffery in Advertising and Selling.* Madison: University of Wisconsin Press.

Proudhon, Pierre Joseph. 1970. *What Is Property?,* translated by Benjamin Tucker. New York: Dover.

Pryor, Frederic C. 1973. *Property and Industrial Organization in Communist and Capitalist Nations.* Bloomington: Indiana University Press.

Rabin, Robert L. 1979. "Impact Analysis and Tort Law: A Comment." *Law and Society Review* 13(4): 987–96.

Raiffa, Howard. 1982. *The Art and Science of Negotiation.* Cambridge, Mass.: Harvard University Press.

Randall, Alan. 1972. "Welfare, Efficiency, and the Distribution of Rights." In *Perspectives of Property,* edited by Gene Wunderlich and W.L. Gibson, Jr., pp. 25–31. University Park: Pennsylvania State University Press.

Raup, Phillip. 1975a. "Nature and Extent of the Expansion of Corporations in American Agriculture." Staff paper P 75–8. St. Paul: University of Minnesota, Department of Agricultural and Applied Economics.

———. 1975b. "French Experience with Group Farming: The GAEC." Staff Paper P 75–22. St. Paul: University of Minnesota, Department of Agricultural and Applied Economics.

Rawls, John. 1971. *A Theory of Justice*. Cambridge, Mass.: Harvard University Press.

Reece, Douglas K. 1978. "An Analysis of Alternative Bidding Systems for Leasing Offshore Oil." *Bell Journal of Economics* 9: 659–69.

Regan, Donald H. 1972. "The Problem of Social Cost Revisited." *Journal of Law and Economics* 15(2): 427–37.

Reisman, David. 1982. *State and Welfare: Tawney, Galbraith, and Adam Smith*. London: Macmillan.

Rich, Richard C. 1980. "A Political Economy Approach to the Study of Neighborhood Organizations." *American Journal of Political Science* 24: 559–92.

Riker, W.J., and Peter Ordeshook. 1973. *An Introduction to Positive Political Theory*. Englewood Cliffs, N.J.: Prentice-Hall.

Rinaldi, Alfonso. 1979. *Interventi Pubblici E Struttura Produttiva*. Milano: Dott. A Guiffre Editore.

Roberts, Marc J. 1975. "Evolutionary and Institutional View of the Behavior of Public and Private Companies." *American Economic Review* 65: 415–27.

Robinson, Joan. 1963. *Economic Philosophy*. Chicago: Aldine.

Ross, H.L. 1973. "Law, Science, and Accidents: The British Road Safety Act of 1967." *Journal of Legal Studies* 2: 1–75.

Ross, H.L., D.T. Campbell, and G. V. Glass. 1970. "Determining the Social Effects of a Legal Reform: The British Breathalyzer Crackdown of 1967." *American Behavioral Scientist* 13: 493–509.

Rothschild, K.W. 1971. *Power in Economics*. Harmondsworth, U.K.: Penguin Books.

Rotter, J.B. 1980. "Interpersonal Trust, Trustworthiness, and Gullibility." *American Psychologist* 26: 442–52.

Rowley, C.K., and A.T. Peacock. 1975. *Welfare Economics: A Liberal Restatement*. New York: John Wiley & Sons.

Ruggles, Nancy. 1968. "Recent Developments in the Theory of Marginal Cost Pricing." In *Public Enterprise*, edited by Ralph Turvey, pp. 11–43. Harmondsworth, U.K.: Penguin Books.

Runge, Carlisle F. 1984. "Institutions and the Free Rider: The Assurance Problem in Collective Action." *Journal of Politics* 46: 154–81.

Sabetti, Philip. 1977. "The Structure and Performance of Urban Service Systems in Italy." In *Comparing Urban Service Delivery Systems*, edited by Vincent Ostrom and Frances P. Bish, pp. 113–45. Beverly Hills, Calif.: Sage.

Sacks, Stephen R. 1983. *Self Management and Efficiency: Large Corporations in Yugoslavia*. London: George Allen & Unwin.

Salert, Barbara. 1976. *Revolutions and Revolutionaries: Four Theories*. New York: Elsevier.

Salmon, Pierre. 1983. "Savons-nous enfin quelque chose de la bureaucratic?" *Analyses de la Societe d'Etudes et de Documentation Economiques Industrielles et Sociales*. 32: 9–15.

Samuels, Warren J. 1984. "A Critique of Rent-Seeking Theory." In *Neoclassical Political Economy*, edited by David Collander. Cambridge, Mass.: Ballinger.

———. 1974a. "The Coase Theorem and the Study of Law and Economics." *Natural Resources Journal* 14: 1–33.

———. 1974b. *Pareto on Policy*. Amsterdam: Elsevier.

———. 1972 (1981). "Welfare Economics, Power, and Property." In *Law and Eco-*

nomics, edited by Samuels and Schmid, pp. 9–75. Boston: Martinus Nijhoff.

Samuels, Warren J. 1971. "Interrelations between Legal and Economic Processes." *Journal of Law and Economics* 5: 435–50.

———, ed. 1976. *The Chicago School of Political Economy.* East Lansing: Michigan State University, Graduate School of Business Administration.

Samuels, Warren J., and Nicholas Mercuro. 1981. "The Role of the Compensation Principle in Society." In *Law and Economics,* edited by Warren J. Samuels and A. Allan Schmid, pp. 210–47. Boston: Martinus Nijhoff.

Samuels, Warren J., and A. A. Schmid. 1981. *Law and Economics: An Institutional Perspective.* Boston: Martinus Nijhoff.

Samuelson, Paul. 1969. "Pure Theory of Public Expenditure and Taxation." In *Public Economics,* edited by Julius Margolis and Henri Guiton, pp. 98–123. New York: St. Martin's Press.

———. 1967. *Economics.* 7th ed. New York: McGraw-Hill.

———. 1958. "Aspects of Public Expenditure Theories." *Review of Economics and Statistics* 40: 335–36.

———. 1955. "Diagrammatic Exposition of a Theory of Public Expenditures." *Review of Economics and Statistics* 37: 350–56.

Sandler, Todd, and J.T. Tschirhart. 1980. "The Economic Theory of Clubs: An Evolutionary Survey." *Journal of Economic Literature* 43: 1481–1521.

Sapolsky, Harvey M., and Stan N. Finkelstein. 1977. "Blood Policy Revisited: A New Look at the Gift Relationship." *Public Interest* (Winter): 15–27.

Savas, E.S. 1977. *The Organization and Efficiency of Solid Waste Collection.* Lexington, Mass.: Lexington Books.

Sax, Joseph. 1972. "Michigan's Environmental Protection Act of 1970." *Michigan Law Review* 70: 1003–106.

Schap, David. 1986. "The Nonequivalence of Property Rules and Liability Rules." *International Journal of Law and Economics* 6: 125–32.

Schelling, Thomas C. 1984. "Self-Command in Practice, in Policy, and in a Theory of Rational Choice." *American Economic Review* 74(2): 1–11.

———. 1978. *Micromotives and Macrobehavior.* New York: W.W. Norton.

Scherer, Frederic M. 1970. *Industrial Market Structure and Economic Performance.* Chicago: Rand McNally.

Schmid, A. Allan. 1985a. *A Conceptual Framework for Organizing Observations on Intellectual Property.* Washington: U.S. Congress, Office of Technology Assessment.

———. 1985b. "Neo-Institutional Economic Theory: Issues of Landlord and Tenant Law." In *Contract and Organization,* edited by Terence C. Daintith and Gunther Teubner, pp. 132–41. Berlin: Walter DeGruyter.

———. 1984. "Broadening Capital Ownership: The Credit System as a Locus of Power." In *American Economic Policy,* edited by Gar Alperovitz and Roger Skurski, pp. 117–37. Notre Dame, Ind.: University of Notre Dame Press.

———. 1982. "Symbolic Barriers to Full Employment." *Journal of Economics Issues* 16: 281–94.

———. 1981. "Innovations Institutionelles et Resources Naturelles." *Economie Rurale* 143: 33–40.

———. 1972. "Analytical Institutional Economics: Challenging Problems in the Economics of Resources for a New Environment." *American Journal of Agricultural Economics* 54: 893–901.

―――. 1968. *Converting Land from Rural to Urban Uses.* Baltimore, Md.: Johns Hopkins University Press.

Schmid, A. Allan. 1960. *Evolution of Michigan Water Laws: Response to Economic Development.* Circular Bulletin no. 227. East Lansing: Michigan State University, Agricultural Experiment Station.

Schmid, A. Allan, and Ronald C. Faas. 1980. "Medical Cost Containment: An Empirical Application of Neo-Institutional Economic Theory." In *Law and Economics,* edited by Warren Samuels and A. Allan Schmid, pp. 179–87. Boston: Martinus Nijhoff.

―――. 1975. "A Research Approach to Institutional Alternatives in the Administration of Agrarian Development Programmes." *Agricultural Administration* 2: 285–305.

Schmitz, Andrew, and David Seckler. 1970. "Mechanized Agriculture and Social Welfare." *American Journal of Agricultural Economics* 52: 569–77.

Schotter, Andrew. 1981. *The Economic Theory of Social Institutions.* New York: Cambridge University Press.

Schultz, T.W. 1968. "Institutions and the Rising Economic Value of Man." *American Journal of Agricultural Economics* 50: 1113–22.

Schumpeter, Joseph A. 1942. *Capitalism, Socialism, and Democracy.* New York: Harper & Row.

Scitovsky, Tibor. 1976. *The Joyless Economy.* New York: Oxford University Press.

―――. 1954. "Two Concepts of External Economies." *Journal of Political Economy* 62: 143–51.

Scott, Anthony. 1964. "The Economic Goals of Federal Finance." *Public Finance* 19: 241–88.

Seagraves, J.A. 1973. "On Appraising Environmental Institutions." *American Journal of Agricultural Economics* 55: 617–21.

Seckler, David. 1975. *Thorstein Veblen and the Institutionalists.* Boulder: Colorado Associated Press.

Segall, Marshall H. 1976. *Human Behavior and Public Policy.* New York: Pergamon Press.

Segall, Marshall H., D.T. Campbell, and M.J. Herkovits. 1966. *The Influence of Culture on Visual Perception.* Indianapolis: Bobbs-Merrill.

Seidman, Harold. 1975. "Government-Sponsored Enterprise in the United States." In *The New Political Economy: The Public Use of the Private Sector,* edited by Bruce L.R. Smith, pp. 83–108. New York: John Wiley & Sons.

Seidman, Robert B. 1973. "Contract Law, the Free Market, and State Intervention: A Jurisprudential Perspective." *Journal of Economic Issues* 8: 553–76.

Seigen, Bernard H. 1970. "Non-Zoning in Houston." *Journal of Law and Economics* 13: 71–148.

Sen, Amartya. 1982. *Choice, Welfare, and Measurement.* Oxford, U.K.: Basil Blackwell.

―――. 1970. *Collective Choice and Social Welfare.* London: Oliver and Boyd.

Sewell, W.R. Derrick, and Leonard Rousche. 1974. "Peak Load Pricing and Urban Water Management: Victoria, B.C., a Case Study." *Natural Resources Journal* 14: 383–400.

Shaffer, James. 1980. "Food System Organization and Performance." *American Journal of Agricultural Economics* 62: 310–18.

―――. 1969. "On Institutional Obsolescence and Innovation." *American Journal of Agricultural Economics* 51: 245–67.

Shapley, L.S., and Martin Shubik. 1967. "Ownership and the Production Function." *Quarterly Journal of Economics* 81: 88–111.

Sharkey, W.W. 1982. *The Theory of Natural Monopoly*. Cambridge, U.K.: Cambridge University Press.

Shelton, John P. 1967. "Allocative Efficiency versus 'X-Efficiency': A Comment." *American Economic Review* 57: 1252–58.

Shepherd, William G. 1968. "Cross-Subsidization in Coal." In *Public Enterprise*, edited by Ralph Turvey, pp. 316–50. Harmondsworth, U.K.: Penguin Books.

Shonfield, Andrew. 1965. *Modern Capitalism*. New York: Oxford University Press.

Shubik, Martin. 1984. *A Game-Theoretic Approach to Political Economy*. Cambridge: Massachusetts Institute of Technology Press.

Simon, Herbert, A. 1978. "Rationality as a Process and as a Product of Thought." *American Economic Review* 68: 1–15.

Simons, Henry. 1948. *Economic Policy in a Free Society*. Chicago: University of Chicago Press.

Skinner, B.F. 1974. *About Behaviorism*. New York: Alfred A. Knopf.

Smith, Adam. 1937. *The Wealth of Nations*. New York: Modern Library.

Solo, Robert A. 1984. "Lessons from Elsewhere." In *American Economic Policy*, edited by Gar Alperovitz and Roger Skurski, pp. 43–55. Notre Dame, Ind.: University of Notre Dame Press.

―――. 1974. *The Political Authority and the Market System*. Cincinnati, Ohio: South-Western.

―――. 1967. *Economic Organizations and Social Systems*. Indianapolis, Ind.: Bobbs-Merrill.

Solow, Robert M. 1980. "On Theories of Unemployment." *American Economic Review* 70: 1–11.

Sosnick, Stephen H. 1968. "Toward a Concrete Concept of Effective Competition." *American Journal of Agricultural Economics* 50: 827–53.

Sproule-Jones, Mark. 1982. "Public Choice Theory and Natural Resources: A Methodological Explication and Critique." *American Political Science Review* 76: 790–804.

―――. 1974. "A Description and Explanation of Citizen Participation in a Canadian Municipality." *Public Choice* 17: 73–83.

Staaf, Robert, and Francis Tannian, eds. 1973. *Externalities*. New York: Dunnellen.

Staatz, John M. 1984. "A Theoretical Perspective on the Behavior of Farmers' Cooperatives." Ph.D. thesis, Michigan State University, East Lansing.

Stein, Lana. 1984. "Implementation of Affirmative Action at the Local Level." Ph.D. dissertation, Michigan State University, East Lansing.

Steiner, Peter. 1970. "The Public Sector and the Public Interest." In *Public Expenditures and Policy Analysis*, eidted by Robert Haveman and Julius Margolis, pp. 21–58. Chicago: Markham.

―――. 1957. "Peak Loads and Efficient Pricing." *Quarterly Journal of Economics* 71: 555–610.

Stigler, George J. 1975. *The Citizen and the State: Essays on Regulation*. Chicago: University of Chicago Press.

————. 1970. "Director's Law of Public Income Redistribution." *Journal of Law and Economics* 13: 1–10.

Stigler, George J., and C. Friedland. 1962. "What Can Regulators Regulate? The Case of Electricity." *Journal of Law and Economics* 5: 1–16.

Strong, Ann Louise. 1975. *Private Property and the Public Interest: The Brandywine Experience*. Baltimore, Md.: Johns Hopkins University Press.

————. 1971. *Planned Urban Environments: Sweden, Finland, Israel, the Netherlands, France*. Baltimore, Md.: Johns Hopkins University Press.

Sudgen, Robert. 1981. *The Political Economy of Public Choice*. Oxford, U.K.: Martin Robertson.

Swisher, Carl. 1954. *American Constitutional Development*. Boston: Houghton Mifflin.

Taylor, John F.A. 1966. *The Masks of Society*. New York: Appleton-Century-Crofts.

Thorelli, Jans B., and Sarah V. Thorelli. 1974. *Consumer Information Handbook: Europe and North America*. New York: Praeger.

Thurow, Lester C. 1985. *The Zero-Sum Solution*. New York: Simon and Schuster.

————. 1983. *Dangerous Currents: The State of Economics*. New York: Random House.

————. 1975. *Generating Inequality*. New York: Basic Books.

Tideman, T. Nicolaus. 1977. "Introduction to the Demand Revealing Process." *Public Choice* 29(2): 1–13.

Tiebout, Charles M. 1956. "A Pure Theory of Local Expenditures." *Journal of Political Economy* 64: 416–24.

Tiebout, Charles M., and D.B. Houston. 1962. "Metropolitan Finance Reconsidered: Budget Functions and Multi-Level Governments." *Review of Economics and Statistics* 44: 412–17.

Titmuss, Richard M. 1971. *The Gift Relationship: From Human Blood to Social Policy*. London: George Allen & Unwin.

Tobin, James. 1970. "On Limiting the Domain of Inequality." *Journal of Law and Economics* 13: 263–77.

Toma, Mark. 1979. "The Impact of Institutional Structures on City-County Consolidation Outcomes." *Public Choice* 34: 117–22.

Tool, Marc. 1970. *The Discretionary Economy: A Normative Theory of Political Economy*. Santa Monica, Calif.: Goodyear.

Trebing, Harry. 1976. "The Chicago School vs. Public Utility Regulation," *Journal of Economic Issues* 10: 97–126.

Tresch, R.W. 1981. *Public Finance*. Plano, Tex.: Business Publications.

Tribe, Keith. 1981. *Genealogies of Capitalism*. London: Macmillan.

Tullock, Gordon. 1979. "Public Choice in Practice." In *Collective Decision Making*, edited by Clifford S. Russel. Baltimore, Md.: Johns Hopkins University Press.

————. 1971. *Logic of the Law*. New York: Basic Books.

————. 1970. *Public Means, Private Wants*. New York: Basic Books.

Turvey, Ralph. 1963. "On Divergences between Social Cost and Private Cost." *Economica* n.s. 30: 309–13.

Ullman-Margalit, Edna. 1977. *The Emergence of Norms*. New York: Oxford University Press.

Umbeck, John. 1981. *A Theory of Property Rights with Application to the California Gold Rush*. Ames: Iowa State University Press.

Unger, Roberto M. 1986. *The Critical Legal Studies Movement*. Cambridge, Mass.: Harvard University Press.

U.S., Department of Commerce. 1973. *Survey of Current Business* 53 (7). Washington, D.C.: Government Printing Office.

Usalner, Eric M. 1985. "Energy, Issue Agendas, and Policy Typologies." In *Public Policy and the Natural Environment,* edited by H.M. Ingram and R.K. Godwin, pp. 101–22. Greenwich, Conn.: JAI Press.

van den Doel, Hans. 1979. *Democracy and Welfare Economics.* Cambridge, U.K.: Cambridge University Press.

van de Kragt, A.J.C., John M. Orbell, and Robyn M. Dawes. 1983. "The Minimal Set as a Solution to Public Goods Problems." *American Political Science Review* 77: 112–22.

Vanecko, James J. 1969. "Community Mobilization and Institutional Change." *Social Science Quarterly* 50: 609–30.

Varian, Hal R. 1975. "Distributive Justice, Welfare Economics, and the Theory of Fairness." *Philosophy and Public Affairs* 4: 223–47.

Veblen, Thorstein. 1904. *The Theory of Business Enterprise.* New York: Charles Scribner's Sons.

———. 1899. *Theory of the Leisure Class.* New York: Macmillan.

Veljanovski, C.G. 1982. *The New Law-and-Economics: A Research Review.* Oxford, U.K.: Centre for Legal Studies.

———. 1981a. "The Economic Theory of International Liability: Toward a Corrective Justice Approach" In *The Economic Approach to Law,* edited by Paul Burrows and C.G. Veljanovski. London: Butterworth.

———. 1981b. "Wealth Maximization, Law and Ethics: On the Limits of Economic Efficiency." *International Review of Law and Economics* 1: 5–28.

Vernon, Raymond. 1971. *Sovereignty at Bay.* New York: Basic Books.

Viteritti, Joseph P. 1973. *Policy, Politics, and Pluralism in New York City: A Comparative Case Study.* Beverly Hills, Calif: Sage.

Vogel, Ezra F. 1981. *Japan as Number One: Lessons for America.* New York: Harper & Row.

Volin, Lazor. 1970. *A Century of Russian Agriculture.* Cambridge, Mass.: Harvard University Press.

Wagner, Richard. 1966. "Pressure Groups and Political Entrepreneurs: A Review Article." *Papers on Non-Market Decision Making* 1: 161–70. This journal is now called *Public Choice.*

Wandschneider, Philip. 1986. "Neoclassical and Institutionalist Explanations of Changes in Northwest Water Institutions." *Journal of Economic Issues* 20: 87–107.

Warren, Robert. 1966. *Government in Metropolitan Regions: A Reappraisal of Fractionated Political Organization.* Davis: University of California, Institute of Governmental Affairs.

Webb, Walter P. 1931. *The Great Plains.* New York: Grosset and Dunlap.

Weinberg, Louise. 1975. "The Photocopying Revolution and the Copyright Crisis." *Public Interest* (Winter): 99–118.

Weisbrod, Burton A. 1964. "Collective Consumption Services of Individual Consumption Goods." *Quarterly Journal of Economics* 78: 471–77.

Weiss, Leonard. 1971. "Quantitative Studies of Industrial Organization." In *Frontiers of Quantitative Economics,* edited by M.D. Intriligator, pp. 362–403. Amsterdam: North-Holland.

Welch, William. 1978. "The Product Liability System and Certain No-Fault Proposals." Ph.D. thesis, Michigan State University, East Lansing.

Wheelwright, E.L., and Bruce McFarlane. 1970. *The Chinese Road to Socialism.* New York: Monthly Review Press.

Whinston, Andrew. 1962. "Price Coordination in Decentralized Systems." Ph.D. thesis, Carnegie Institute of Technology, Pittsburgh.

Wilber, Charles K. with Robert S. Harrison. 1978. "The Methodological Basis of Institutional Economics: Pattern, Model, Storytelling and Holism." *Journal of Economic Issues* 11: 61–89.

Wiles, P.J.D. 1977. *Economic Institutions Compared.* New York: Halsted.

Williamson, Oliver E. 1985. *The Economic Institutions of Capitalism.* New York: Free Press.

——. 1981. "The Modern Corporation." *Journal of Economic Literature* 19: 1537–68.

——. 1975. *Markets and Hierarchies: Analysis and Antitrust Implications.* New York: Free Press.

——. 1966. "Peak Load Pricing." *American Economic Review* 56: 810–27.

Williston, Samuel. 1948. *The Law Governing Sales of Goods at Common Law and under the Uniform Sales Act.* Rev. ed. New York: Baker, Voorhis.

Wilson, James Q., and Edward C. Banfield. 1965. "Voting Behavior on Municipal Public Expenditures: A Study in Rationality and Self-Interest." In *The Public Economy of Urban Communities,* edited by Julius Margolis, pp. 74–91. Baltimore, Md.: Johns Hopkins University Press.

Winfrey, John C. 1973. *Public Finance.* New York: Harper & Row.

Wiseman, Jack. 1983. "Beyond Positive Economics: Dream and Reality." In *Beyond Positive Economics?,* edited by Jack Wiseman, pp. 13–27. London: Macmillan.

Wolfe, Alan. 1977. *The Limits of Legitimacy: Political Contradictions of Contemporary Capitalism.* New York: Free Press.

Wolozin, Harold. 1977. "Institutionalism and the Image of Man." In *Economics In Institutional Perspective,* edited by Rolf Steppacher, Brigitte Zogg-Walz, and Hermann Hatzfeldt, pp. 29–46. Lexington, Mass.: D.C. Heath.

Worcester, Dean A., Jr. 1972. "A Note on the Postwar Literature on Externalities." *Journal of Economic Literature* 10: 57–58.

Wunderlich, Gene. 1974. "Property Rights and Information." *Annals of American Academy of Political and Social Science* 412: 80–96.

Zahn v. International Paper Company 1973. 42 USLW 4087, December.

Zajac, Edward E. 1978. *Fairness or Efficiency: An Introduction to Public Utility Pricing.* Cambridge, Mass.: Ballinger.

Zauderer, Donald G. 1972. "Consequences of Ballot Reform: The Ohio Experience." *National Civic Review* 61: 505–7.

Zeckhauser, Richard. 1970. "Uncertainty and the Need for Collective Action." In *Public Expenditures and Policy Analysis,* edited by Robert Haveman and Julius Margolis, pp. 96–116. Chicago: Markham.

Author Index

Subject Index

About the Author

A. ALLAN SCHMID is professor of agricultural economics and resource development at Michigan State University in East Lansing. Dr. Schmid was a visiting scholar at Resources for the Future in Washington, D.C.; visiting professor at the Economic and Social Research Institute, Dublin, Ireland; University of Bath, United Kingdom; and University of Perugia, Italy; budget analyst for the civil works program of the U.S. Army Corps of Engineers; and consultant to the U.S. Congress, Office of Technology Assessment.

Dr. Schmid has published in the area of institutional economics in such journals as the *American Economic Review*, *Journal of Economic Issues*, *Public Choice*, *American Journal of Agricultural Economics*, and *Journal of the American Institute of Planners*, and he is the author of *Converting Land from Rural to Urban Use* and *Law and Economics* (with Warren Samuels). He has earned a B.S. degree from the University of Nebraska and M.S. and Ph.D. degrees from the University of Wisconsin, Madison.